SINGLEHANDED SAILING

SINGLEHANDED SAILING

The Experiences and Techniques of the Lone Voyagers

Written and Illustrated by
RICHARD HENDERSON

International Marine Publishing Company
Camden, Maine

OTHER BOOKS BY RICHARD HENDERSON

First Sail for Skipper
Hand, Reef and Steer
Dangerous Voyages of Captain William Andrews (ed.)
Sail and Power (with B.S. Dunbar)
The Racing-Cruiser
The Cruiser's Compendium
Sea Sense
Singlehanded Sailing
Better Sailing
East to the Azores
Choice Yacht Designs
Philip L. Rhodes and His Yacht Designs
John Alden's Yacht Designs

© 1976 by International Marine Publishing Company
Library of Congress Catalog Card No. 75-37369
International Standard Book Number 0-87742-062-9
Printed in the U.S.A.
Fifth Printing, 1982

Published by International Marine Publishing Company
21 Elm Street, Camden, Maine 04843
(207) 236-4342

This book is dedicated to
Dr. Roger P. Batchelor

Contents

Preface

"Men should tell what they know", wrote the British author-sailor Weston Martyr. Singlehanded sailors do not always tell what they know, at least not all of what they know, but when they do speak, we who sail with crew should listen, for we can learn a great deal. Although it has been argued that a singlehander knows only how to handle his own craft, and he has no one to point out his errors, the fact remains that it is far more difficult to manage a boat alone, and a loner learns of necessity how to avoid mistakes. By and large, I think it is safe to say that the majority of veteran singlehanders are among the greatest seamen.

The purpose of this book is partly to familiarize the average yachtsman with the history, personalities, and motivations of the great singlehanders, some of whom are not at all well known even to those who follow the literature of the sea. My main purpose, however, is to present and try to analyze the techniques, methods, and relevant experiences of the solo seamen, so that all sailors can profit. Not all the experiences are examples of what to do, for even the greatest sailors are fallible, and occasionally we may learn what not to do, but the important thing is that we are inspired and taught. The reader may never have any serious intention of embarking on a solo voyage, yet many yachtsmen handle their boats alone when day-sailing, sailing overnight, or standing watch. And what veteran sailor has not found himself handling a boat shorthanded at times? Very often there will be children, an inexperienced wife, or greenhorns aboard, so that the skipper will virtually be managing alone.

For the most part, I fear the experiences related between these covers have to do with hard times: gales, capsizings, collisions, hallucinations, groundings, dismastings, and so forth. The difficulties are what concern us, because we should know how they can be handled. As the old adage advises, "Be ready for the worst, and the best will take care of itself."

Nevertheless, it should be pointed out that blue-water sailing alone need not be hazardous or awkward. A great many voyages have been made without any really unpleasant incidents, and the good times normally far outweigh the bad. There will be plenty of days when the sun is warm on one's back, when fair weather cumuli cast fleeting shadows on rolling blue seas, and the lacelike wake will seem to gurgle and hiss with joy. For a sailor who is well prepared, there is probably little risk, but the sea is never completely predictable, and there is always some small element of danger. That is primarily what makes a passage alone or shorthanded a challenge and a true adventure.

RICHARD HENDERSON
GIBSON ISLAND, MARYLAND

Acknowledgements

I'll not attempt to list everyone from whom I've gleaned bits of information used in this book, for I've lost track over the years, and some informants might be inadvertently left out; but a few standouts, who have been most helpful in one way or another, come quickly to mind. My very special thanks go to Roger C. Taylor of the International Marine Publishing Co., William W. Robinson and Rosemary Curley of *Yachting* magazine, J. D. Sleightholme of *Yachting Monthly*, Philip L. Budlong of the Mystic Seaport Marine Historical Association, Neal T. Walker of The Slocum Society, Dr. Susie Scholz, D. H. Clarke, Frank Casper, John Letcher, Francis C. Stokes, John Guzzwell, John Rock, Richard C. Newick, Edward Karkow, Irving Groupp, John Moon, James Tazelaar, Pete Hodgins, Sarah S. Henderson, Dennis Guinee, and Patty M. Maddocks.

SINGLEHANDED SAILING

1 / A SHORT HISTORY

No one will ever know who made the first extended passage single-handed. It was probably made inadvertently by a castaway or a fisherman who was blown far offshore by a storm. Deliberate singlehanded voyages, though, could have been made in ancient times. It seems quite possible that the early Polynesians, who were such proficient oceanic voyagers, could have produced a few singlehanders. Then there are the tales about Sinbad-type sailors, dating from the Old Kingdom of Egypt (around 2000 B.C.), who, according to records on papyrus scrolls, passed through the gate to the unknown ocean beyond the Red Sea. On the other side of the globe, there is the legend of the Taoist mystic Hsii Shih, who, by himself (he implied), discovered the "Blessed Islands" in about 200 B.C. It wasn't until the second half of the nineteenth century that authentic solo passages of great distances were recorded with any accuracy.

Early Voyages and Influential Pioneers

Several remarkable solo voyages in the early 1800's have been reported, but they have never been authenticated. The first and most improbable of these is the voyage supposedly made by a Captain Cleveland of Salem, Massachusetts, who is said to have sailed a 15-foot boat almost around the world at the turn of the century. It was reported that he crossed the South Atlantic, rounded the Cape of Good Hope, crossed the Indian and then the Pacific Oceans, and eventually reached the west coast of the United States via Alaska. A more probable voyage is one made by J. M. Crenston, who reportedly sailed the 40-foot cutter, *Tocca*, from New Bedford to San Francisco, a distance of 13,000 miles, which he covered in 226 days. No one seems to know whether or not Crenston passed through the Strait of

Magellan. It is conceivable, though not likely, that he was the first single-hander to round Cape Horn. There is also some evidence that Bernard Gilboy made an early passage lasting approximately six weeks from British Columbia to Hawaii.

Much later, in 1882-1883, Gilboy made an authenticated Pacific crossing in the tiny double-ender, *Pacific*. His log was rediscovered not many years ago and published under the title *A Voyage of Pleasure*. An amazing aspect of this voyage, which lasted for nearly half a year and covered about 7,000 miles, is that Gilboy never stopped and went ashore, although he passed near numerous islands. He had many misadventures, which included a capsizing and consequent loss of mast, compass, rudder, and stores (the experience will be described in detail in Chapter 8). Eventually, Gilboy abandoned his voyage when he allowed himself to be picked up by a large schooner a mere 160 miles from Australia, his destination.

Alfred Johnson, a hand-line Banks fisherman, is given credit for the first solo Atlantic crossing. His boat was a 20-foot, decked-over dory named the *Centennial*, in honor of America's 100th anniversary, for the year was 1876, and Johnson hoped to display his boat after her passage in the Philadelphia Centennial Exposition. He sailed from Gloucester on June 15th and landed in Abercastle, Wales, fifty-nine days later. Johnson spoke many vessels during his crossing and kept track of his whereabouts by getting positions from their navigators. One captain of a passing vessel became so concerned about Johnson's welfare that he offered to take the singlehander aboard, boat and all, and then drop him off near Ireland without a word being said, but Johnson firmly declined. Although the singlehander made light of his hardships, he had some rough experiences, including a capsizing during a gale on the second of August. Even though the *Centennial* carried some ballast and her gaff-rigged mast was supposedly fitted with a tabernacle so that it could be lowered in heavy weather, she was caught off guard by a breaking sea and rolled completely upside down. Fortunately, Johnson was attached to the *Centennial* by a long safety line, but it took him twenty minutes to right the boat. Of course, everything on board was soaked including his bread and other stores, but worse than that, his water was spoiled and his stove lost. Several days later, however, he got some basic supplies from a passing ship and struggled on until reaching the Welsh coast on August 12th.

Johnson inspired others to cruise alone, but probably not nearly as much as did two British singlehanders of that era, R. T. McMullen and, particularly, John McGregor, even though these mariners made no extremely long passages offshore. McMullen was admired for his uncompromising seamanship and his ability to singlehand large, heavy vessels with complicated rigs, such as his 20-ton *Orion*. His exploits were made known through his book,

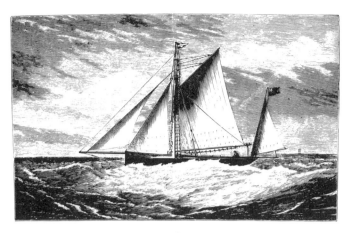

R. T. McMullen singlehanding the cumbersome Orion *in 1877. (From* Down Channel *by R. T. McMullen)*

The 21-foot canoe yawl Rob Roy *sailed by John MacGregor, who did so much to popularize singlehanded cruising in coastal waters. (From* The Voyage Alone in the Yawl Rob Roy *by John MacGregor)*

E. E. Middleton caught in a bad cross sea in his canoe yawl Kate *during her singlehanded voyage around Britain in the late 1860's. (From* The Cruise of the Kate *by E. E. Middleton)*

Down Channel, first published in 1869. McGregor started a craze for cruising in canoes. In 1867, he received notoriety by solo-sailing the 21-foot, decked-over but cabinless yawl, *Rob Roy*, from London to Paris and return, across a wide part of the English Channel, to attend a regatta and "Boat Exhibition." He inspired a great many people to cruise, including sailor-authors E. F. Knight and E. E. Middleton. McGregor's book, *The Voyage Alone in the Yawl Rob Roy*, which is enhanced by charming engravings showing details of his yawl and her accommodations (see Figure 1-1), especially captured the imaginations of would-be solo sailors.

Seagoing Cockleshells and Early Solo Ocean Racing

In an era noted for cockleshell voyages, the most dedicated single-hander in minute craft was undoubtedly the Yankee from Beverly, Massachusetts, William Albert Andrews. Although he has often been written off as a stunter and a crackpot, Andrews was certainly a true pioneer and a seaman. *Rudder* magazine (in June, 1891) even called him "a man of extraordinary intelligence" and said that he "has more of the practical side to his character than most people would suppose who have followed his career." Of course, it must be admitted that Andrews took some dangerous chances, and he eventually lost his life at sea. He might also be criticized for inspiring emulation. But be this as it may, he is an important figure, historically at least, for he survived six extended voyages in tiny boats, held the record for the smallest boat to cross the Atlantic for about three quarters of a century, and was a participant in the first transatlantic race for singlehanders.

FIGURE 1-1: JOHN MacGREGOR'S YAWL, "ROB ROY"

Watch on deck

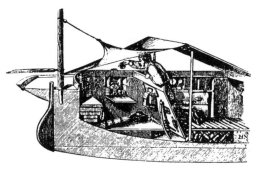

Cooking in rain

FIGURE 1-2: WILLIAM ANDREWS' "DARK SECRET"

MESSAGE BUOY

A former soldier, who served for over four years in the Union Army during the Civil War, and a piano maker by trade, Andrews had limited nautical experience before his first voyage in 1878. That year he made a transatlantic crossing with his more experienced brother, Asa Walter, in a 19-foot dory, the *Nautilus*. Brother Walter was ill during much of the forty-five day crossing and died not long after returning to the United States. After that, William took to singlehanding.

His first solo voyage, in 1888, was an attempted Atlantic crossing, and one of his purposes was to set a record for the smallest boat to make such a passage. A lot of preparation and unconventional thinking went into the planning of this venture. Some of Andrews' equipment included torpedoes to scare off whales and swordfish, a unique waterproof suit, rubber envelopes for messages, and a contraption for shooting them aboard passing ships. He also had at least one message buoy (see Figure 1-2) which consisted of a cork ring buoy supporting a flag with the words, *"Pick This Up"* and a Mason jar holding the message. Andrews had a lateen-rigged boat built with such unusual features as watertight bulkheads, a hollow keel that was said to hold forty gallons of water, and a 200-pound iron shoe that could be dropped off by the untwisting of a single screw. According to a detailed report in the New York *World*, the boat was only 12 feet, 9 inches long, and she was named the *Dark Secret* at the insistence of a sponsor who was promoting a theatrical production of the same name. The voyage itself was a flop, for Andrews had more than his share of headwinds, while his boat leaked badly and was a disappointing performer. He spent sixty-two miserable days at sea and had not quite reached the mid-Atlantic (longitude 39° 50′W) when he decided to accept being rescued by the westbound Norwegian barque, *Nor.*

Undaunted by the failure of the *Dark Secret* venture, Andrews set about preparing for another transatlantic crossing. This time he decided to challenge another singlehander to a race across the ocean, for a prize of $5,000 and a silver cup. Andrews showed such confidence in his ability as a small boat seaman that he boldly announced his intentions, after completing the race, to ship his boat to Japan from which point he would attempt a Pacific crossing via Hawaii. The race challenge was accepted by Josiah W. Lawlor, the son of the famous boatbuilder and designer, Dennison J. Lawlor. Lawlor was an experienced sailor and had recently sailed across the Atlantic in an unusual water-ballasted lifeboat called the *Neversink.*

The two competitors built 15-foot boats, both of which were called dories, but that term was very loosely used by the newspapers in those days. *Rudder* magazine (June, 1891) described Andrews' boat, named the *Mermaid,* as a "sort of dory-shaped craft," while a sketch of her appearing in *Le Yacht* showed a boat bearing little resemblance to a dory. Lawlor's boat, the *Sea Serpent,* was described in detail to me by a subsequent owner, John Moon, a singlehander and former yachting reporter. She was a double-ender, not unlike a Colin Archer sailing lifeboat. I submitted a drawing to Mr. Moon of what I imagined the *Sea Serpent* looked like based on his description, and his reply was: "If you had seen her, you could not be much nearer the mark. The only differences are trifling." I've tried to correct those differences in Figure 1-3. The *Mermaid* carried a sloop rig with a "bat's wing" mainsail, a sort of cross between a gaff and sliding gunter rig; while *The Sea Serpent* was sloop-rigged with a bowsprit and a sprit-rigged mainsail, which was divided by a diagonal seam, "lobster boat fashion", running from clew to throat. The two halves of the mainsail were laced together, but they could be easily unlaced to reduce area and convert to a leg-of-mutton rig.

The race began from Crescent Beach, near Boston, on June 21, 1891, before a large crowd, but due to a light, unfavorable breeze, each competitor had to turn back and restart, Lawlor a day later and Andrews two days later. They were bound for Mullion Cove, Land's End, England, where the *Nautilus* had landed many years before. The competitors announced their intended tracks before starting, and Andrews' was to be far south of his rival's, but, according to their reported positions, Lawlor's track was actually the farther south for most of the race (see Figure 1-3). *The Sea Serpent* was evidently the better sailor, and she had more favorable winds, for she gradually pulled far ahead of the *Mermaid.* Lawlor's boat was the more seaworthy, too, at least in the important matter of stability and the ability to self-right, because she had a ballasted keel, whereas the *Mermaid*

FIGURE 1-3: THE FIRST SOLO TRANSATLANTIC RACE

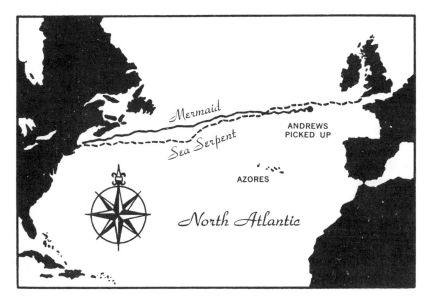

Approximate tracks of the MERMAID and SEA SERPENT in 1891

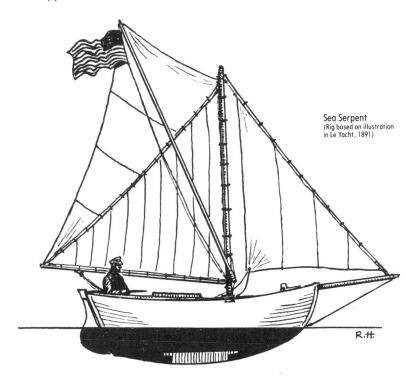

Sea Serpent
(Rig based on illustration
in Le Yacht, 1891)

was a centerboarder with no external ballast. Lawlor did capsize on two occasions when the *Sea Serpent* broached to, but he had a relatively easy time righting the boat. In contrast, Andrews said that he capsized seven times, and on one occasion it took him a half hour to right the *Mermaid*. That incident was reported by Andrews' hometown paper, *The Beverly Citizen*, which described a great sea during a gale rolling the *Mermaid* bottom side up, in which position she remained for some time with Andrews trapped under the vessel's deck. After some moments of struggling, the singlehander escaped through his sliding hatch and swam from under the overturned hull where he could grab hold of the shallow keel. About thirty minutes later the boat righted, but a great many supplies were lost. The storm raged on, and two days later, on August 20th, the cold, wet, and hungry singlehander was rescued by the steamer, *Ebrus*, bound for Antwerp. He had raced to within about 600 miles of the English coast.

Si Lawlor had reached England at Coverack near the Lizard on August 5th, after having sailed about 2,800 miles in forty-four days. Compared with Andrews he had an easy time of it, but he had not been without his share of adventures. Aside from the two capsizings already mentioned, he was supposedly attacked by a shark. Several reports stated that on the night of July 24th, Lawlor was awakened from a nap by a jostling of his boat and a crunching noise. Leaning over the side, he spotted a large shark gnawing on the boat's stem. With great resourcefulness, Lawlor reached for an exploding yacht salute, wrapped it in paper, and after lighting the fuse, threw it at the shark's head. The greedy brute snatched the salute and it exploded in his mouth. Lawlor was no longer bothered by that particular shark at least.

Andrews must have felt rather humiliated by his defeat, for he made a wager with Lawlor that he would cross the Atlantic the next year in thirty days. Lawlor also decided to make the passage again in an attempt to break his own record. Both men built new boats for the competition. I know little of Lawlor's craft except that she was called the *Christopher Columbus*, but the details of Andrews' boat are well known. She was a folding boat built of cedar and canvas, resembling a sneakbox. Her dimensions (as published in Andrews' log) were 14 feet, 6 inches length on deck; 5 feet, 5 inches beam; and 3 feet depth. She had 350 pounds of ballast on her keel, and she could be folded up into a package about six inches thick. She was flush decked and had a sliding hatch that could cover the cockpit in heavy weather. Her rig was similar to the *Mermaid*'s with the bat's wing mainsail, except that the new boat had a short bowsprit. Andrews christened her the *Sapolio* after the product of a soap manufacturer, who had decided to sponsor the voyage.

The original plan was to sail the shortest course from Newfoundland to

The Tinkerbelle, *skippered by Robert Manry, who finally wrested from William Andrews the record for the smallest boat to make an eastbound Atlantic crossing. William Verity later crossed in that direction in a 12-foot boat. (Keystone Press Agency Ltd.)*

Ireland, but Andrews heard of a celebration in honor of Columbus' discovery of America to be held in Palos, Spain, and so he decided to make Palos his destination. Lawlor set out much earlier than Andrews and was not heard from again. He was evidently lost at sea. The *Sapolio*, however, set sail on July 20, 1892, from Atlantic City and made a successful crossing to Spain by way of the Azores. She was the smallest boat to have crossed the Atlantic, a record that held until Robert Manry's voyage in the 13½-foot *Tinkerbelle* (Chapters 2 and 8) and John Riding's in the 12-foot *Sjo Ag*, both during the summer of 1965, although historian Jean Merrien has reported that Harry Young sailed a 13-foot, 9-inch undecked sloop from New York to the Azores in 1939. It took Andrews 31 days to sight the Azores, but he didn't actually land at Angra until six days later, on August 26. Three days after that, he set sail for Spain and reached the village of Burgau, Portugal, on September 20, having had a frightening encounter with finback whales not far from Cape St. Vincent (see Chapter 7). His crossing had taken 61 days, counting the three he spent ashore in the Azores. About a week later he reached his eventual destination at Palos and received a hero's welcome (see Chapter 2). Although Andrews had fulfilled his dream of a solo crossing in the smallest boat, he was not long satisfied, for in 1898 he made another attempt to sail alone from America to Europe in a 13-foot boat called the *Phantom Ship*. He made the mistake of sailing too late in the season, on August 24, and experienced extremely heavy weather. His boat leaked like a sieve, and most of his food spoiled. After enduring 27 days of hardships, the singlehander asked to be taken, boat and all, aboard a passing ship.

Yet, on his return home he began making plans for a voyage in an even smaller boat. Since he still had the *Phantom Ship*, he decided it would be economical to take her apart and rebuild her into a new boat. The result was another folding craft only 12 feet long with a depth of 22 inches and a beam of 5 feet, which he named the *Doree*. He cast off bound for the Azores on June 17, 1899, but again the voyage did not succeed. Three weeks after his departure, he was picked up by the steamer, *Holbein*, and headlines in the *World* screamed, "Andrews was Half Crazy — Privation Had Unhinged the Mind of the Daring Sailor Who Tried to Cross the Ocean in a Dory." The singlehander was reported to be incoherent and semi-delirious when rescued, but he had an explanation for his state. He told a reporter for *The Strand Magazine* that he was dazed and nearly asphyxiated from leaking carbonic acid gas, which had escaped from his bottles of Sarasota water. Whether this was true or whether he was suffering from hallucinations, I do not know, but he found after speaking a passing ship that he had completely lost track of four days of time.

The seventh and final voyage of Andrews was made in what was reported as a 20-foot dory called the *Flying Dutchman*, the original name for the older *Sapolio* before she had been sponsored (one report said the new boat was named the *Dark Secret*). This was to be a honeymoon cruise, for Andrews had taken a new wife. The two set sail from Atlantic City bound for Spain in the summer of 1901. After about one week at sea, the honeymooners spoke the steamer *Durango*, and that was the last ever heard of William Andrews or his bride. Apparently, they sailed into heavy weather and oblivion.

My correspondent, D. H. Clarke, an English authority on small boat voyages, maintains that Andrews' last voyage was actually the third transatlantic race for singlehanders, the second having been between Lawlor and Andrews in 1892, the year of the *Sapolio's* crossing. Andrews' challenger in 1901 was the amazing Howard Blackburn, who singlehanded the 25-foot sloop *Great Republic* from Gloucester to Lisbon that year. Blackburn did challenge "any man" to a solo race, and he made a very fast crossing in 39 days, but the challenge had been dropped a considerable time before he sailed, because there had been no takers. Furthermore, he specified that the race be sailed singlehanded (Andrews had his bride, of course), and Blackburn was returning to the United States on a ship at the time of Andrews' departure in the *Flying Dutchman*. Thus, not many people would consider it a race. A better case could be made for a race in 1899 between Andrews and Blackburn, for that year the latter crossed in the 30-foot downeast sloop *Great Western*, and he got under way on the same day (though in a different location) as Andrews in his *Doree*. It was said that each singlehander hoped to be the first across.

Howard Blackburn is perhaps the most remarkable of all singlehanders, because he had no fingers. He lost them as a young man while a fisherman aboard the Gloucester schooner *Grace L. Fears*, which was working on Burgeo Bank about sixty-five miles off Newfoundland in mid-winter, 1883. His story is one of incredible courage and endurance.

While tending trawls from a dory, Blackburn and his companion, Tom Welch, became separated from their schooner on account of a sudden wind shift and a blinding snow storm. They lay to an improvised drag for nearly two days, all the while chipping ice from the boat and bailing nearly constantly to keep her from swamping. They never could reach the mother vessel, and Welch died of exposure during the second night. After the storm abated, Blackburn decided to try for the shores of Newfoundland. He had lost his mittens while rigging the drogue, and his fingers were frozen stiff, but the tough fisherman had formed his hands into cupped sockets that could receive the oar handles so that he could row in a crude fashion. Three days later, having had no food or water and with seriously frostbitten hands and feet, he reached help in Newfoundland, where he was taken in by a destitute family and nursed back to health. Miraculously, he survived, but at the cost of losing many toes, all of his fingers, and half of each thumb.

It is difficult to conceive how Blackburn could have later solo-sailed two boats across the Atlantic when he had no fingers. Joseph Garland, who wrote a biography of Blackburn, *Lone Voyager*, tells us that the singlehander held lines by pinching them between his hands and half-thumbs. To haul on a line, he would take a turn around his waist, lean back, clamp the line with one hand over the cockpit coaming (or elsewhere), take in slack and then repeat the process. One might say that he was "swigging" the line with his body. Of course, there were many other tasks, such as taking sights and lighting his running lights or stove, that were extremely difficult to perform without fingers, but somehow he managed.

After his Atlantic crossings, Blackburn made a remarkable inland voyage in his 25-foot *Great Republic*. He took her from Gloucester down to New York, up the Hudson River, through the Erie Canal, across the Great Lakes

Blackburn at the helm of his trim little Great Republic *just before the start of his celebrated Atlantic crossing in 1901. (Courtesy of Sandy Bay Historical Society, from* Lone Voyager *by Joseph E. Garland)*

to Chicago, and down the Mississippi River to Columbus, Kentucky, where the boat was shipped by rail to Mobile, Alabama. Then he sailed her along the Gulf coast and down around the tip of Florida. The *Great Republic* cruise came to an end when she went hard aground at Coconut Grove. The boat was saved, but Blackburn sold her, and she is still in existence, having recently been bought and preserved by the Gloucester Historical Commission. The really remarkable aspect of her inland cruise was that her draft was almost the same as the depth of some of the waterways on which she traveled. She was towed through the Erie Canal by mule power and through the Chicago Drainage Canal, which was nearly 100 miles long and little more than three feet deep, by manpower. Blackburn and a helper took turns walking along the canal's bank with the tow line over their shoulders while, as Blackburn wrote, "hundreds of snakes would run across the path and sometimes crawl over our feet, many of them six and seven feet long."

Another offshore solo voyage was made by Blackburn not long after his return from Florida in 1903. This time he attempted to cross the Atlantic in a 17-foot dory he named the *America*. The voyage was extremely rough

The beginning of Blackburn's unsuccessful attempt to cross the Atlantic in the 17-foot dory America *in June 1903. (Courtesy of Philip Kuuse, from* Lone Voyager *by Joseph E. Garland)*

The remarkable Howard Blackburn, blue-water singlehander without fingers. (From Lone Voyager, *by Joseph E. Garland, courtesy of the author)*

with gales and heavy seas. After about two weeks at sea, off Cape Sable, Nova Scotia, the *America* capsized. Blackburn was trapped below under his sliding hatch, which was jammed shut, but the dory soon righted herself. The compass, lantern, food, and other supplies were lost, so Blackburn headed into Clark's Harbor near Cape Sable when the blow subsided. Some days later, he set off again, once more ran into a storm, and again capsized. This time he was on deck and was thrown overboard, but he managed to grab the main boom, haul himself to the side of the dory, and right her by putting his weight all on one side. In addition to his problems with the capsizing, Blackburn was sick with an infected knee, so he wisely gave in to the Atlantic and headed back to Nova Scotia.

This voyage might also be considered an attempted transatlantic single-handed race, for Blackburn was competing against a German-American, Ludwig Eisenbraun, who left to cross "the pond" shortly before Blackburn in the 19½-foot "dory" *Columbia*. Eisenbraun was also turned back by the heavy weather, but started off again much later in the season, after Blackburn had abandoned the project, and eventually reached Gibraltar via Halifax and Madeira.

The Circumnavigators

The first authenticated solo circumnavigation is that made by the ex-captain of square-rigged ships, Joshua Slocum, who sailed the 37-foot *Spray* around the world in 1895-1898. According to Slocum the *Spray* "had served as an oysterman" and was "about a hundred years old" when he first acquired her. He completely rebuilt the boat himself and modified her by adding a deeper keel and raising her bulwarks. The circumnavigation started from Gloucester in an easterly direction, but at Gibraltar Slocum decided on an east to west rounding after receiving a warning about pirates along his intended route through the Mediterranean and Red Seas. From Gibraltar, the *Spray* recrossed the Atlantic, passed around the tip of South America via the Strait of Magellan, proceeded across the Pacific, through the Torres Strait north of Australia, rounded the Cape of Good Hope, and completed her voyage at Newport, Rhode Island.

Among Slocum's many adventures, the highlights were: being chased by pirates in a Felucca off the African coast, being buried by a freak wave off Patagonia, fighting hostile Indians and williwaws in the desolate Strait of Magellan, and sailing through the frightening "Milky Way" breakers near

The famous Spray, *with Joshua Slocum at her helm, proudly displays her ensign at Hyannis Port, Mass. in 1907. (Courtesy of* Yachting *magazine)*

Captain and Mrs. Joshua Slocum on board the Spray. *(Courtesy of* Yachting *magazine)*

Cape Horn at night in a gale. Captain Josh became famous for his clever (but apparently unoriginal) method of repelling his barefooted Indian boarders by "at-tacking" them, i.e., sprinkling the decks with tacks. His book about the voyage, *Sailing Alone Around the World,* was a best seller and is now considered a literary classic. It has one shortcoming, however, in that it lacks technical details. Sailor readers often have to guess exactly how Slocum managed such matters as self-steering and navigation without a decent chronometer (see Chapter 5). Nevertheless, the book is exciting, has great charm, and has inspired a host of adventurers to follow in the wake of the *Spray.* In 1909, Slocum and his beloved boat were lost at sea making a winter cruise to the West Indies. The purpose of the voyage, he said, was "just to save buying a winter overcoat."

Another circumnavigation made completely singlehanded did not occur until over a quarter of a century after Slocum's return, when Harry Pidgeon performed the feat in his 34-foot yawl, the *Islander*. Pidgeon was a landsman until relatively late in life, but he had manual skills and a yearning to visit the South Seas; he built himself a hard-chine yawl, an enlargement of the "Sea Bird" class (see Chapter 3) and studied navigation in the public library. After making a trial cruise with an unsatisfactory crew, Pidgeon decided to sail alone. He set off for the South Sea islands in 1921 from California with little thought of rounding the world, but after reaching his destination and spending some time there, he decided to return home westabout. His track also passed through the Torres Strait and around the southern tip of Africa, but after crossing the Atlantic, the *Islander* was able to use the Panama Canal, which, of course, did not exist at the time of Slocum's circumnavigation. Pidgeon developed into a first class seaman

Harry Pidgeon, the first man to circumnavigate twice alone, aboard his home-made yawl Islander. (*Courtesy of* Yachting *magazine*)

and had few untoward experiences except for grounding on a lee shore near Cape Town (see Chapter 7) and having his rig damaged by a steamer that came too close to investigate him.

Pidgeon made a later circumnavigation in the same boat in 1932-1937, but on this voyage he had a crew for a small part of the time. In 1947, he even attempted a third rounding of the world in his *Islander,* this time doublehanded with his wife, but the old yawl was wrecked by a tropical storm in the New Hebrides.

While the *Islander* was completing her first voyage around the world, an entirely different kind of boat, an early British racing cutter named the *Firecrest,* skippered by the French singlehander Alain Gerbault, was setting out from Gibraltar to cross the Atlantic on the first leg of a circumnavigation. The crossing was very slow, 101 days, and was fraught with gear failure, but nonetheless Gerbault was the first recipient of the "Blue Water Medal," an award for meritorious seamanship presented by the Cruising Club of America. The circumnavigation continued from New York in 1924, after the *Firecrest* had her rig changed from gaff to Marconi. She, too, passed through the Panama Canal, and at Balboa, Gerbault met Pidgeon, who had almost completed his circumnavigation. The two singlehanders, as well as their boats, made an interesting contrast; for Gerbault, a former flying ace and tennis champion, was dashing and egotistical, while Pidgeon,

A *wintertime view of the yawl* Islander, *moored with four lines to minimize possible damage from the ice. (Courtesy of* Yachting *magazine)*

A rare snapshot of Alain Gerbault in the cabin of his cutter Firecrest. *(Courtesy of* Yachting *magazine)*

a photographer from the American midwest, was plain, modest, and re-served. Their vessels will be compared in Chapter 3.

Gerbault pushed on for the South Seas, where he eventually settled and wrote books extolling the natives' way of life and disapproving of the white man's civilization, but not before he took the *Firecrest* entirely around the world. He followed a similar track to Pidgeon's, but after rounding the Cape of Good Hope, he proceeded north for France and suffered a damag-ing grounding at the Cape Verde Islands. In July, 1929, he arrived in his native country and received a hero's welcome, with many accolades and awards, including the cross of the Legion of Honor.

The fourth solo circumnavigation was made by Edward Miles, an Amer-ican "do-gooder," who set out alone in 1928 on a "goodwill voyage" to spread the message of brotherhood throughout the world. Miles' direction of travel was entirely different from that of the previous circumnavigators, as it was eastabout, and his track passed through the Red Sea rather than around the tip of Africa. Two facts may detract somewhat from the im-portance of the voyage as a pure sailing feat, the first being that circum-navigation was made in two different vessels with a lengthy interval of time between boats, and the second being that the boat that traveled the greater distance by far had substantial auxiliary power, and it was used quite a lot. Both vessels were schooners about 37 feet long named *Sturdy*, which were built by Miles himself. The first boat burned up as a result of a gasoline fire near the Suez Canal, and because of that experience, Miles fit the *Sturdy II* with diesel power. He built her in Memphis, Tennessee, and then shipped her to Suez to take up where her predecessor had left off.

Slocum's accomplishment of circumnavigating alone by way of the Strait of Magellan in a westabout direction was duplicated by another retired ship's captain, Louis Bernicot, in 1936-1938. This Frenchman had a slight advantage over Slocum, perhaps, in that his vessel, the 41-foot sloop *Anahita*, had an engine of very low power, but that should not at all detract from Bernicot's fast voyage, which was an exemplary feat of seamanship. Bernicot had his share of heavy weather and actually capsized enroute to Cape Horn. Although he did not claim it in his book, *Voyage of the Anahita,* he told one circumnavigator that his boat made a 360-degree roll. Fortunately, she was well ballasted and righted immediately without breaking her Marconi mast. Some years after his voyage around the world, Bernicot was killed as the result of an accident on the same sloop.

An entirely different kind of circumnavigation was made by Vito Dumas from Argentina in 1942-1943 aboard the double-ended ketch, *Lehg II.* His track passed south of the three stormy capes (Good Hope, Leeuwin, and the Horn) and also south of Tasmania in an easterly direction. Of course, this was a short route around the world, and the winds were almost always astern, which accounts in part for the speed of the voyage (271 sailing days), but it was made in cold, barren waters where the almost unbroken fetch and boisterous winds can produce seas that are often extremely dangerous for small craft. Dumas was the first recipient of the Slocum prize, awarded, by the Slocum Society, for a truly outstanding solo voyage.

After World War II, another rugged double-ender, the *Stornoway*, sailed alone by Alfred Peterson, an American, circled the globe in an original way. She made the usual east-to-west rounding, but by the way of the Red Sea, in the opposite direction of Edward Miles. Peterson had few troubles, but most of them occurred in the Red Sea, where he experienced a serious grounding, was held prisoner for a short while, and had his boat plundered by pirates. He reached the east coast of America, from whence he started, in the summer of 1952, completing a voyage of nearly four and a half years.

Before Peterson arrived home, another circumnavigator, Marcel Bardiaux, was setting out on one of the most remarkable solo voyages of all time. In a home-built, 31-foot, racing-cruising sloop, this Frenchman, who was a former kayak champion, took about eight years to make a westabout rounding. The astonishing aspect of this voyage was that Bardiaux sailed his little boat, *Les 4 Vents,* around Cape Horn in the beginning of winter against the prevailing winds. The sloop capsized twice when approaching the Horn, and the experience will be described in Chapter 8. Bardiaux was not the first singlehander to round Cape Horn "the wrong way," however, for this had been done about twenty years earlier by Alfon M. Hansen, a Norwegian, sailing the double-ended cutter *Mary Jane*. Soon afterwards, though, Hansen was wrecked and drowned on the southern coast of Chile. It is also possible but improbable that Crenston (mentioned earlier) sailed around the Stormy Cape in a westerly direction.

Another Frenchman, but one who has based himself in America, Jean Gau, made two circumnavigations alone, the first in 1953-1957 and the second from 1962-1967. Gau had earned his money between voyages as a chef in a large New York hotel. His vessel and home was the 30-foot Tahiti ketch, *Atom*, which has not only carried him twice around the world, but also about a dozen times across the Atlantic. As one would expect, Gau and his *Atom* have had many adventures, including surviving the full force of two hurricanes, a lee shore stranding, and a capsizing by a freak wave. The latter experiences will be described in Chapters 7 and 8.

Until very recently the smallest boat to be sailed by one man around the earth was the *Trekka,* a 21-foot, fin-keel yawl designed by J. Laurent Giles. She was very capably skippered by a young Briton, John Guzzwell. Like many of his circumnavigating predecessors — Slocum, Pidgeon, Miles, and Bardiaux — Guzzwell built his boat with his own hands (Slocum actually rebuilt his boat). The *Trekka's* voyage, beginning and ending in Victoria, B.C., Canada (1955-1959), was in a westerly direction via Torres Strait, the Cape of Good Hope, and the Panama Canal. John wrote me that the same suit of cotton sails, costing "the ridiculous price of £29.10.0," carried him all the way around the world, which is indicative of his superb seamanship. His most exciting and frightening adventure came when he temporarily left the *Trekka* to join Miles Smeeton and his wife Beryl, in sailing the ketch *Tzu Hang* from Australia to England via Cape Horn. Almost all sailors know the story of how the ketch pitchpoled in the Roaring Forties when about a thousand miles from South America. The *Tzu Hang* was left dismasted, seriously holed in her decks, and in a near-sinking condition. Miles Smeeton gives great credit to Guzzwell for his seamanship and skillful carpentry in helping to save the *Tzu Hang*, jury-rigging her, making repairs, and helping sail her 1,350 miles to Coronel, Chile.

Another very small boat, a 25-foot, Vertue-class sloop named the *Cardinal Vertue,* was sailed solo by William E. Nance, an Australian, around the world eastabout (1962-1965). The most remarkable aspect of this voyage was that she was sailed across the Pacific through the blusterous latitudes of the high forties and then around Cape Horn. Nance's greatest troubles came earlier, however, on the passage from Cape Town to Melbourne, Australia, when his steering vane was damaged, the mast broke above the

Youthful circumnavigator Robin Lee Graham aboard his Lapworth 24, the Dove. *(Courtesy of* Yachting *magazine)*

spreaders, he was nearly washed overboard, and his boat suffered a series of knockdowns while rounding Cape Leeuwin. The voyage began in England, but the circumnavigation was completed at Buenos Aires, where he had stopped almost exactly two years earlier.

Since 1965, there have been a number of solo voyages around the world that have been highly publicized, such as those made by Robin Lee Graham, Francis Chichester, and Alec Rose. The former, a youth from California, is touted as the youngest circumnavigator. He was only sixteen years old when he started his westabout cruise (following a similar track to Pidgeon's) in the *Dove*, a stock Lapworth 24, and he was twenty-one years old when he concluded the voyage in *The Return of Dove*, a stock Luders 33. The Englishmen, Chichester and Rose, of course, were comparatively old men (66 and almost 60) when they completed their circumnavigations. They both made fast eastabout roundings, Chichester in about nine months (1966-1967) and Rose in slightly less than a year (1967-1968), passing south of the three stormy southern capes as Dumas had done. Unlike the Argentinian, though, the two Englishmen made voyages that were considered antipodal with the departure and arrival points being in England. As many sailors know, Chichester's boat was the 54-foot ketch, *Gipsy Moth IV*, and Rose's, the 36-foot yawl, *Lively Lady*.

Many other solo circumnavigations completed since 1965 are relatively

Alec Rose, the popular English grocer, who was knighted for his outstanding solo circumnavigation. (Courtesy of John Rock)

Francis Chichester aboard his Gipsy Moth III, *winner of the 1960 transatlantic race for singlehanders. (Courtesy of* Yachting *magazine)*

Alec Rose aboard his yawl Lively Lady. *Notice the long external chainplate straps and how the mizzen boom has been omitted so that it will not interfere with the self-steering vane. (Courtesy of* Yachting *magazine)*

unknown. For some reason they have received little coverage in the press and popular yachting magazines. Although these voyagers are not publicity seekers, they deserve recognition, and certainly their voyages should be of interest to other sailors. Some of these fine seamen are Frank Casper, Pierre Auboiroux, Alfred Kallies, Wilfried Erdmann, C.H. (Rusty) Webb, John Sowden, Leonid Teliga, Walter Koenig, and Roger Plisson. Casper, an elderly American and a retired electrical engineer, who will tolerate few electrical devices in his 30-foot double-ender, *Elsie* (see Chapters 5 and 6), has finally received some recognition in the form of the Cruising Club of America Blue Water medal for his circumnavigation made almost entirely alone (1963-1966) and for his many solo transatlantic crossings. Auboiroux, a French taxi driver, made a rapid rounding of the world alone via the Red Sea (1964-1966) in a 27-foot sloop, the *Neo Vent*. The German merchant seaman Alfred Kallies made his voyage via the usual Panama Canal-tip-of-Africa route (1965-1969) in a 25-foot double-ender, the *Pru*. Another German, Wilfried Erdmann, made a somewhat similar circumnavigation alone (1966-1968) in the *Kathena,* and after his return home, his accomplishment was for some time overlooked by the press and the German Sailing Association.

Rusty Webb, an Englishman, followed the traditional route (1966-1968) in his 58-year-old ketch, the *Flyd,* and he had some notable adventures, which included a dismasting and sailing about 1,500 miles under a jury rig. His grounding and remarkable repair to the *Flyd* will be described briefly in Chapter 7. It was reported that Webb died at the helm of his ancient craft a few years after his circumnavigation.

John Sowden, an American, and Leonid Teliga, a Pole, rounded the first half of the world in partial company with each other. At least they frequently met in ports, sometimes intentionally and sometimes accidentally. Their tracks coincided from Casablanca to Fiji by way of the Panama Canal, but after that they parted company, with Sowden and his 24½-foot sloop, *Tarmin,* spending some time in Indonesia, while Teliga and his 32-foot yawl, *Opty,* made a fast, non-stop passage to Dakar, Africa, and then crossed his outward-bound track slightly over two years after his voyage had begun in 1967. Teliga suffered horribly from cancer and died not long after his circumnavigation (see Chapter 7). Sowden finished his voyage in the summer of 1970, after about three and a half years of cruising. While in Capetown, incidentally, Sowden met Rollo Gebhard, a German single-hander who was on his way around the world (1967-1970), following a very similar track to Sowden's in the 24-foot sloop, *Solveig III.* Both Gebhard and Sowden were constantly plagued with engine problems, and they met while having their auxiliaries repaired.

Walter Koenig was a German voyager who circumnavigated alone (except for the final leg of his voyage) but never received the recognition he deserved. As the Slocum Society put it in their journal, *The Spray*, "The world very much ignored him." His voyage, made between 1965 and 1969 in a 25-foot converted lifeboat, the *Zarathustra*, followed a westabout route from Germany through the Panama Canal and home via the Red Sea. He had a difficult Atlantic crossing with a dismasting, but, like Peterson, his troubles were far greater in the Red Sea where he became severely ill, had engine troubles when the auxiliary was badly needed, was fired upon by Egyptians, and was nearly jailed in Saudi Arabia. The worst news by far came when Koenig had his illness diagnosed as leukemia, and he was given only a short time to live. He courageously finished the voyage with the company of his wife and died soon after returning to Germany.

A little-publicized solo circumnavigation was made by the French house painter, Roger Plisson, who followed the Panama Canal, Torres Strait, tip-of-Africa route (1967-1969) in a 24-foot home-made sloop, the *Francois Virginie*. Plisson was very inexperienced when he started the voyage but rapidly developed into a good seaman. He experienced some very heavy weather in the Bay of Biscay and much later off the Cape of Good Hope, losing his mast on both occasions, but was able to raise a jury rig and make port for repairs.

The amazing 'round the world race for singlehanders, the "Golden Globe" race of 1968-1969, produced the first non-stop solo circumnavigations, those of Robin Knox-Johnston, Bernard Moitessier, and Nigel Tetley. The former, a British merchant service officer, won the Golden Globe prize and £5000 for being the first around and back to England, whence the race started, in his 33½ foot, double-ended ketch, the *Suhaili*. His time was about ten and a half months. Tetley's time for a complete circumnavigation in the 40-foot trimaran, *Victress*, was a lot faster, a record 179 days, but the multi-hull broke up soon after she crossed her outward-bound track, and the singlehander had to abandon her. He was lucky to be rescued by a ship that was directed to him by an American plane.

It has been argued that Moitessier was actually the first person to complete a non-stop solo circumnavigation. His rounding, however, was not really antipodal, for after almost circling the globe, he decided not to finish in England but to keep going and terminate the voyage in the South Seas, where, he said ". . . you can tie up your boat where you want and the sun is free, and so is the air you breathe and the sea where you swim. . . ." So Moitessier is credited with the longest non-stop solo voyage, about one and a half times around the world. His boat was the 40-foot steel double-ender, the *Joshua*, and her track, like that of the *Suhaili* and *Victress*, was east-about, south of the three stormy capes in the "Roaring Forties."

Of the nine contestants who started the race, only Knox-Johnston rounded the world and sailed his boat back to England. Most of the competitors retired because of boat or gear failure, and others simply changed their minds because of ill health or coming to a full realization of the time, effort, and hardships involved. Donald Crowhurst, sailing a sister ship to the *Victress*, planned an elaborate hoax whereby he would cruise around in the South Atlantic for the time it would take to circumnavigate and then sail back to England ahead of his competitors to collect the prize. A gnawing conscience, solitude, and other pressures seemed to unbalance his mind, and, apparently he ended his life with a suicidal jump off the stern.

Despite the many failures to finish, which one would expect, the competition did produce the three non-stop circumnavigations already mentioned, and two Englishmen who withdrew, William Leslie King and Chay Blyth, completed circumnavigations some time later. The former, a retired submarine commander, capsized in his specialized, lug-rigged, *Galway Blazer II* (see Chapters 3 and 7), but he set out again on what proved to be another futile attempt the following year. Refusing to give up, King tried again for the third time in 1970, and this time he succeeded in completing a circumnavigation in 1973, although he nearly failed as a result of colliding with a sea creature near Australia. This experience and King's remarkable repair of his vessel will be described in Chapter 7.

Unlike King, who stuck with the same vessel, Chay Blyth, a former paratrooper and transatlantic oarsman, got sponsorship and had a new 58-foot steel ketch built, which he named the *British Steel*. The astounding thing about Blyth's circumnavigation is that it was made the "wrong way," that is to say, along the Roaring Forties route but east to west, against the prevailing winds. Yet, in spite of having to sail to windward, the voyage was made in the fast time of 292 days (1970-1971).

Other circumnavigators (or near circumnavigators) not mentioned so far, who made all or most of their passages alone are as follows: Bill Murnan, American (1948-1952), east to west from California to New York in the stainless steel, Seabird yawl, *Seven Seas II* (Chapter 3 and 8); Jacques Yves Le Toumelin, French (1949-1952), east to west via Panama Canal in the 33-foot, double-ender, *Kurun;* Joseph Havkins, Israeli (beginning 1954), east to west via Panama Canal in the 23-foot sloop, *Lamerhak II;* Michael Mermod, Swiss (1961-1966), east to west from Peru to France in the 24-foot lifeboat, *Genève;* Adrian Hayter, New Zealander, England to New Zealand (eastward) in the 32-foot yawl, *Sheila II,* and then England to New Zealand (westward) in the 26-foot folkboat, *Valkyr* (Chapter 3); Alan Eddy, American (1963-1968), east to west via Panama Canal in the 30-foot Seawind ketch, *Apogee* (Chapter 7); Tom Blackwell, British (1968-1971), in the 58-foot ketch, *Islander* (Chapter 6); Wolf Hausner, Austrian, east to west via Panama Canal in the catamaran *Taboo* (1966-

The handsome, Albert Strange designed, canoe-stern yawl Sheila II, *singlehand-edly sailed from England to New Zealand via the Red Sea by Adrian Hayter. (Drawing courtesy of the executors of Uffa Fox, deceased)*

1973); Goran Cederström, Swede, east to west via Panama Canal in the 27-foot sloop *Tua Tua* (1971-1973); Chris Baronowski, Pole (1972-1973), west to east via Cape Horn in the 45-foot ketch, *Polonez* (Chapter 6); Ambrogio Fogar, Italian (beginning 1972), east to west via Cape Horn in 38-foot sloop, *Surprise* (Chapter 8); and Edward Allcard, British (ending in 1974), east to west via Cape Horn in the ancient, 36-foot ketch, *Sea Wanderer* (Chapters 2 and 3). Two others I have heard of but have no details about are George Darling and Len Skoog. Two recent circumnavigations of remarkable speed are those of Kenichi Horie and Alain Colas (Chapter 3). The former, a Japanese, sailed his 29-foot sloop, the *Mermaid III*, around the world non-stop from west to east via Cape Horn in the amazing time (for a small monohull) of 276 days. The French sailor, Colas, claimed a new solo record by rounding the globe in 168 days in his trimaran, the 67-foot, *Manureva*, formerly *Pen Duick IV* (see Chapter 3).

The latest solo circumnavigations I have heard about were made by Japanese sailors Ryusuke Ushijima and Yoh Aoki, who sailed west to east via Cape Horn. Ushijima sailed the 30-foot ketch *Gin-Gitsune*, while Aoki sailed the homemade plywood yawl *Ahodori*. The yawl is reported as being about two inches shorter than John Guzzwell's *Trekka*, and so it would appear that she is presently the smallest boat to solo circumnavigate. She is also the smallest to round Cape Horn.

Modern Transoceanic Races

Since the early transatlantic solo races between Andrews, Lawlor, Blackburn, and Eisenbraun, there have been a few informal races between yachtsmen making east-to-west tradewind crossings to the West Indies. A typical competition of this kind occurred in 1958 between the famous singlehanders, Peter Tangvald (Chapters 2 and 7), who later circumnavigated occasionally alone, and Edward Allcard, mentioned in the previous paragraph. Tangvald, in his yawl, *Windflower*, won the race and the prize of one dollar by beating Allcard in his smaller boat, the *Sea Wanderer*, over the course from Las Palmas, Canary Islands, to Antigua.

A more formal transatlantic solo race, from England to America, was held in 1960. It was the brain child of Colonel H. G. Hasler, a World War II hero, who had led an attack on German ships in Bordeaux harbor from tiny "cockleshell" boats. After the war, Hasler had taken to solo sailing, and he developed a new, almost revolutionary boat and rig for simplified singlehanding. The result of his experiments was the famous, highly modified folkboat, the *Jester*, which will be described in Chapter 3. After many discussions and negotiations, Hasler persuaded a prominent London newspaper, *The Observer*, to sponsor the race and the Royal Western Yacht Club to handle the start and other important matters. In America, the Slocum Society, the organization devoted to encouraging long-distance passages in small boats, gave the race publicity and helped in handling the finish. The contestants were Hasler, himself, in his 25-foot *Jester;* Francis Chichester, a pioneer in solo flying, in the 39-foot sloop, *Gipsy Moth III;* Valentine Howells, sailing the more conventional folkboat *Eira;* Jean Lacombe in the smallest boat, the 21-foot *Cap Horn;* and David Lewis, an adventurous doctor who was interested in the medical and survival aspects of the race, sailing the 25-foot *Cardinal Vertue.*

All of the competitors had their share of rough weather. Chichester encountered above-hurricane-force winds on one occasion (see Chapter 8), and Hasler, pushing far north, hunting for easterly winds, weathered a lengthy and what he called "boring" gale. He mentioned "driving the poor little thing [*Jester*] into a filthy breaking sea with four reefs down." Howells suffered a severe knockdown that resulted in the loss of his chronometer, and he put into Bermuda temporarily. He had already lost electric power for proper time checks (and lights), because he was forced to jettison a huge damaged battery (Chapter 5). Lacombe weathered a severe gale lying to a sea anchor, and later he was taken in tow for a short while by the Coast Guard because of a threat from a hurricane and high seas. Dr. Lewis lost the top of his mast soon after the start in Plymouth, but he returned under jury rig and set off again (see Chapter 7). He experienced several blows during the race but none so hard as the gales he encountered on his return trip from America to the Shetland Islands. The race results were: Chichester, first, taking 40 days; Hasler, second, 48 days; Lewis, third, 56 days; Howells, fourth, 63 days; and Lacombe, fifth, 74 days. Times were slow by modern standards, but each competitor felt rightfully proud of his accomplishment, especially Hasler, who had done much to prove his theories.

The next solo transatlantic race, which has come to be known as the OSTAR (Observer's singlehanders' transatlantic race), was held in 1964. This was won in a little over 27 days by a newcomer, the Frenchman Eric Tabarly, sailing an unusual, 44-foot, hard-chined, plywood ketch, the *Pen Duick II.* After his victory, Tabarly became a national hero and was made a Chevalier of the Legion of Honor. Chichester, again sailing his *Gipsy Moth III,* came in second and bettered his previous time by about ten days. All the other participants in the 1960 race also competed again. Valentine Howells took third in a new boat, the 35-foot steel sloop, *Akka,* and Hasler in his *Jester* took fifth in elapsed time, being beaten by about one day by the *Lively Lady* and Alec Rose, who was later to become famous for the solo circumnavigation previously mentioned (Hasler beat Rose on corrected time). Dr. Lewis finished seventh in a heavy catamaran, the *Rehu Moana,* which had previously made a voyage to Iceland (Chapter 7), and which later would carry the Doctor and his family to the South Seas. Still later, Lewis was to gain more fame for his attempted solo rounding of Antarctica (Chapters 7 and 8). Lacombe finished ninth, beating six other competitors, although he was sailing the smallest boat, the 21-foot *Golif*.

By 1964, the OSTAR had become a well-established event which would be held every four years. It grew so popular that the 1968 race had thirty-five entries. On this occasion, there were many more multihulls and some large monohulls built especially for the race. Tabarly entered a new 67-foot trimaran, a radical concept for ocean work, the *Pen Duick IV*. In this particular competition, she had little chance to show her potential, however, because she collided with a ship soon after the start and had to withdraw (Chapter 7). Later, of course, she went on to break a great many speed records for offshore sailing craft (see Chapter 3). Many of the large, specialized craft, including the winner and second place finisher, were largely paid for by sponsors. This meant that participants sailing unsponsored craft often had to go into considerable debt or spend their life savings in order to get a competitive boat. One man spent so much money simply fitting out a boat he already owned that he had to sell his home to pay expenses.

The winner was an Englishman, Geoffrey Williams, making his crossing in about four and a half hours under twenty-six days in the 56-foot, sleek, low-freeboard ketch, *Sir Thomas Lipton*. The fast, 49-foot, South African ketch, *Voortrekker* sailed by Bruce Dalling was not quite a day behind to take second place on elapsed time and first on corrected time for the monohull award. A most unusual craft took third place. She was the 40-foot, schooner-rigged proa, *Cheers*, which will be described in Chapter 3, sailed by an American, Tom Follett. The winning skipper, Williams, had radio communication with a shore-based computer that suggested favorable courses, and evidently this was advantageous, as he was routed north of a storm that a lot of boats did not avoid. Many of the competitors retired from the race mostly because of mast or rudder failure, but two multihulls broke up, and one monohull sank after it was taken in tow following a dismasting. Eight out of thirteen multihulls failed to finish. In most cases this was because of various design failures, but one trimaran skipper, Eric Willis, became seriously ill (from contaminated drinking water according to one report), and he had to be taken off his boat, the *Coila*, after two medics were parachuted down to assist.

This race had a woman participant, a 26-year-old West German secretary, Edith Baumann, but unfortunately her boat, the *Koala III*, was one of the two multihulls that came apart in heavy weather. Edith was by no means the first female ocean-sailing singlehander, for Ann Davison had sailed from

Las Palmas to the West Indies alone in her 23-foot *Felicity Ann* in 1952-1953. Much later, in 1969, Ingeborg von Heister crossed the Atlantic alone in the trimaran, *Ultima Ratio,* and returned in 1970. The following year, Nicolette Milnes-Walker sailed across the Atlantic in her 30-foot sloop, the *Aziz,* becoming the third woman (not the first, as was often claimed by the press) to cross the Atlantic alone. In 1969, Sharon Sites Adams became the first woman to cross the Pacific alone, from Yokohama to San Diego, taking 75 days in her 31-foot ketch, the *Sea Sharp II* (Chapter 2). She had already sailed from Los Angeles to Hawaii singlehanded in her first *Sea Sharp,* a 25-footer, in 1965. In recent times, transoceanic solo passages by females are not so uncommon, for three women, Marie-Claude Fauroux (Chapter 3), Teresa Remiszewska (Chapter 7), and Anne Michailof, completed the 1972 OSTAR, and Clare Francis (Chapters 4 and 5) made an outstanding Atlantic crossing in 1973.

A transpacific race for singlehanders was held in 1969. Organized by the Slocum Society and the Nippon Ocean Racing Club, the race started in San Francisco and finished in Tokyo. Of five participants, only three finished the race, though Rene Hauwaert eventually completed the course. The winner was Eric Tabarly, sailing the interesting light-displacement monohull *Pen Duick V,* which will be described in Chapter 3. His time was only thirty-nine and a half days, about eleven days better than the next boat to finish. Second and third places went to Jean-Yves Terlain and Claus Hehner sailing 30-foot and 35-foot stock boats respectively. A very capable American singlehander, Jerry Cartwright, was forced to retire because of a severe blow to his head received when he was thrown from his bunk during a knockdown (see Chapter 7). Despite being extremely incapacitated by the injury, Cartwright made it to Hawaii without assistance.

Although the transpacific race had few participants, transatlantic solo racing had become so well accepted that the 1972 OSTAR had fifty-five entries. It was the year for multihulls, huge monohulls, and particular glory for French sailors. Tabarly's former trimaran, the *Pen Duick IV,* sailed by Alain Colas, was first in the remarkable time of twenty days and slightly over thirteen hours. A fantastically huge, 128-foot monohull, the *Vendredi 13* (see Chapter 3), skippered by Jean-Yves Terlain, was less than a day behind, while a 53-foot trimaran, named *Cap 33,* sailed by another Frenchman, Jean-Marie Vidal, was third with a time of about five hours more than twenty-four days. Brian Cooke, an Englishman, sailing Chay Blyth's former *British Steel,* upheld Britain's reputation by finishing fourth, and U.S. representative Tom Follett (of *Cheers* fame) sailed the trimaran, *Three Cheers,* to fifth place. Actually, Bill Howell in the catamaran, *Tahiti Bill,* probably would have taken fifth had he not collided with a Russian trawler near the finish (see Chapter 7).

The first authenticated Atlantic crossing by a lone woman was made by Ann Davison, shown here in the protected cockpit of her 23-foot sloop Felicity Ann. *(Courtesy of Patrick Ellam)*

The deep-draft seakindly hull of the Felicity Ann *relegated to an ignominious display outside the New York Motorboat Show. (Courtesy of* Yachting *magazine)*

The speedy 46-foot trimaran Three Cheers *designed by Dick Newick and single-handed by Tom Follett, who is shown at the helm. (Courtesy of Dick Newick)*

It is almost impossible to cross an ocean at any time without encountering some bad weather, but on the whole the 1972 race had light to moderate winds. After some fresh wind in the first week, the strongest blow was a short-lived gale produced by a fast-moving front, and then there were the usual sudden, isolated squalls. As a result, there were cases of gear failure and a number of dismastings. Some remarkable repairs were made that will be described in Chapter 7.

Undoubtedly, the greatest tragedy of the 1972 OSTAR had to do with the withdrawal of Francis Chichester, who was in poor health. The veteran singlehander, then seventy years of age, radioed that he was not feeling well and decided to retire from the race. He was sailing his *Gipsy Moth V* home to Plymouth when he was intercepted by a French weather ship offering assistance. Chichester declined the offer, but during the communications exchange, the *Gipsy Moth's* mizzen was damaged by the ship, and then some help really was needed. It came in the form of Chichester's son with others, who were brought to the *Gipsy Moth* by a helicopter and naval vessel. The real tragedy of the affair came when the weather ship collided with the *Lefteria*, an American yacht not in the race, which was coming to Chichester's assistance. The *Lefteria* sank and six crew members lost their lives. Of course, Chichester was distressed by the accident, but in no way could he fairly be blamed. As it turned out, this was his last voyage, for he died not long afterwards. But even before he landed at Plymouth, old, exhausted, and ill, he was reportedly planning another spectacular solo voyage. His spirit simply could not be suppressed.

In this brief history of singlehanding, every solo voyage obviously cannot be described, for there are far too many, and of course, not every one of them is known to the author. The following list, however, will at least partially acknowledge some other important solo sailors, who have not been mentioned thus far. Some of these will make their appearance later in this book, and the chapters in which they appear accompany their names. The list is as follows:

Rudolph Frietsch, John C. Voss (Chapters 4 and 5), Thomas Drake (Chapter 6), Fred Rebell (Chapters 2 and 5), J.V.T. McDonald, Franz Romer, Otway Waller (Chapter 6), R. D. Graham (Chapter 4), Marin-Marie (Chapters 2, 5, 6 and 8), W. B. Reese, William Weld, Francis Edward Clark, Ludwig Schlimbach, Henrick Garbers, Hans de Meiss-Teuffen (Chapter 7), John Caldwell, Joseph Peterson, Clyde Deal, Dr. Alain Bombard (Chapters 2, 4 and 7), Dr. Joseph Cunningham (Chapter 3), Dan Robertson (Chapter 3), Mike Bales (Chapter 3), Peter Hamilton (Chapter 3), John Goodwin (Chapter 3), Dr. Hannes Lindemann (Chapters 2 and 4), Axel Petersen, C. de Grabowski, Henry Wakelam, Mike Ellison (Chapter 7), Bob Bunker, Michael Butterfield, Geoffrey Chaffey, Derek Kelsall, René Blondeau, John Letcher (Chapters 3, 6 and

Frank Mulville's Iskra, *one of the singlehander's seagoing boats. (Courtesy of* Yachting Monthly)

Donald Ridler at the helm of his 26-foot, home-built Erik the Red, *which carried him from England across the Atlantic to the West Indies and back. (William Kimber & Co. Ltd.)*

The 22-foot trimaran Klis *sailed solo in 1967 by Bernard Rhodes from the Canaries to the West Indies in the remarkable time of 20 days. (Courtesy of Dick Newick)*

7), John Roberts, Paul Johnson, Bernard Rhodes, Alex Carozzo, Nich Clifton, Chris Loehr (Chapter 8), John Pflieger (Chapter 7), Pierre Dubernat, Malcomb Reid, Geoffrey Godwin, Henry Gilbert, Francis Brenton (Chapter 4), George Farley (Chapter 7), James Willis, William Verity (Chapter 2), Tom Harrison, William Wallace, Bill Watson, Rudi Wagner, Johann Trauner, I.L. Jenkins, Tony Norris, Ed Boden (Chapter 3), Jim Mathews, Fred Wood (Chapter 7), Peter Flokker, Loick Fougeron, Hugo Vilhen (Chapter 3), Tom Corkill (Chapters 2 and 8), Kensaku Nomoto, Martin Minter-Kemp, Noel Bevan (Chapters 5, 6 and 10), Bertrand de Castelbajac, Nigel Burgess, Andre Foezon, Bertil Enbom, Dave Englehart (Chapter 2), Stephen Pakenham, Colin Forbes, Bernard Rodriquez, Ake Mattson, Michael Richey (Chapters 3 and 4), Donald Ridler, D.M.R. Guthrie (Chapter 7), E. Grenapin, Fred McCallum, Barry Nelson (Chapter 4), Francis Stokes (Chapters 2 and 7), Raymond Rawls, Alexander Welsh (Chapter 2), Steve Dolby (Chapter 7), Gerard Pesty, Alain Gliksman, Franco Faggione, Jim Ferris, Marc Linskii, Mike McMullen (Chapters 4, 5 and 7), Jack Brazier, Joel Charpentier, Yves Olivaux, Guy Piazzini, Pierre Chassin, Bruce Webb, John Holton, Guy Hornett, Wolf Kirchner, Jock McLeod (Chapters 3 and 5), Richard Clifford, R. Lancy Burn, Philip Weld, Pat Chilton, Eric Sumner, Zbigniew Puchalski, Heiko Krieger, Christopher Elliott, Andrew Spedding, David Blagden (Chapter 8), Robert Salmon (Chapter 7), Sandy Munro (Chapter 7), Bob Miller (Chapter 7), Murray Sayle (Chapter 7), H. A. McAulay, M. Boyle, Tony Murdock, Martin Wills, Richard Konkolski, Peter Crowther, Gary Adams, Eric Hall (Chapter 4), James Crawford (Chapter 5), Tony Skidmore (Chapter 6), Colin Irwin (Chapter 3), Mike Kane, Henry Pigott, Tristan Jones, Graeme Dillon, Ben Dixon (Chapter 7), Colin Darrock (Chapter 5), Frank Mulville (Chapter 2), Jean-Claude Protta (Chapter 5), Max Gravelean, Sven Lundin, and Borje Wase.

My apologies to those I have overlooked.

2 / MOTIVES, PERSONALITIES, AND
PSYCHOLOGICAL ASPECTS

What compels a sailor to go singlehanding? Day sailing or taking a short cruise alone is perfectly understandable. Quite often there are problems in finding a crew; sometimes, in this crowded world, there is a desire to get off by oneself for a short while; or perhaps there is simply the fun of meeting the challenge of sailing unaided. Less understandable, however, is the urge to cross oceans or make extended passages alone. In fact, solo voyagers are sometimes thought of as being some combination of a recluse and an eccentric. I have even heard it said that such sailors are crazy or that they are complete "screwballs."

Undoubtedly, a few singlehanders have had some mental problems. Donald Crowhurst, for example, had certain instabilities that very well could have contributed to his demise. Yet, in all probability, there is no greater number of mentally disturbed participants in solo voyaging than in any other field of endeavor. It is true that singlehanded sailors are not normal in the sense that the average person hasn't the inclination (nor perhaps the nerve) to emulate them, but I think it is safe to say that the vast majority of ocean-going singlehanders are completely sane. A noted psychoanalyst-sailor, who made a study of singlehanders, Dr. John C. Lilly, has said: "A mentally ill person by definition can't successfully cross an ocean singlehanded." Perhaps this statement should not be taken too literally, because solo voyages have been completed by mentally disturbed sailors who have had more than their share of luck. But the singlehander with a sickness of the mind is subject to serious errors in judgment and perhaps a complete breakdown under severe stress. Certainly the odds in his case are against the successful completion of a lengthy and difficult passage.

This chapter, first of all, will touch on the various motives of single-handers, and secondly it will point out the primary psychological factors with which the solo seaman must contend. Those factors can present serious problems, but the isolated sailor is better able to cope when he has an understanding of them, and when he knows how others have dealt with the difficulties.

Personalities and Motivations

When lone sailors are asked about their reasons for singlehanding, they will give a variety of answers, some actual samples being: "To prove to myself that I could do it all alone"; "Because I like to sail"; "I longed for new scenes"; "Restlessness was nagging me"; "To put theory to the test"; "I simply had to"; "The best way to find peace"; "Because I bloody-well wanted to." Reasons are difficult to express, and the truth of the matter is that the sailor himself may not fully understand his exact motives. There are ostensible and conscious reasons, but most likely there are also sub-conscious and perhaps very complex motivations deeply buried in the mind. Of course, it is obvious that solo voyagers are very individualistic, and thus motives are highly varied, but nonetheless, there are probably some basic, commonly shared desires that give impetus to the singlehanding predilection. If it is possible to simplify and generalize on this involved subject, motivation factors might be put into ten categories, some of which (or possibly all of which) are shared to some extent by those who go to sea alone. They are listed as follows: (1) practical purposes, (2) self significance, (3) curiosity, (4) recognition, (5) independence, (6) escapism, (7) adventurousness, (8) competitiveness, (9) solitude, and (10) the mother sea.

The first factor, practical purposes, is the ostensible, conscious reason (or reasons) for making the singlehanded voyage. In some cases it may be the really significant motive, and in other cases it may only be an excuse for setting forth. This factor is present in many voyages but not in all of them. Practical purposes are often related to testing or proving a theory, gathering research material, or for tangible gains such as winning a prize or monetary rewards. Of course the unavailability of crew is another factor, but this will be examined under category (9). Notable examples of theory testing are the voyages of Dr. Alain Bombard, Dr. Hannes Lindemann, and to a lesser extent Jean Lacombe. All of these men set forth in rubber sailing boats for the primary purpose of studying and testing theories and equipment related to survival at sea. Although some aspects of these voyages are controversial, they nevertheless provided some very valuable information for shipwreck victims and offshore castaways. Bombard and Lindemann especially endured extremes of privation and suffering deliberately for the sake of mankind. More will be said of these theories later. Two others who were dedicated to experimentation and putting theories to test were Dr. David Lewis, who, when he sailed alone, was interested in the medical, psychological, and survival aspects of singlehanding, and H. G. Hasler, who was intrigued with the idea of developing the perfect boat for singlehanding.

There were others with ostensible motives that seemed for the most part to be excuses for extended and difficult solo passages. Francis Chichester, for instance, wanted to break all sorts of speed records, but his powerful competitive spirit seemed secondary to a compulsion for adventure. William Verity originally crossed the Atlantic alone in a 12-foot boat to show that the Irish monk, St. Brendan "could have" reached the Americas 500 years before the Vikings, but this reason sounds a bit far-fetched. William Andrews, Hugo Vihlen, and others wanted to set records for the smallest craft to cross the Atlantic, but there must have been deeper and stronger drives involved. Ann Davison became the first woman to cross an ocean alone because, as she explained, she wanted something to write about, and Marin-Marie wrote that he wanted to "get in touch with his subject" for the painting of seascapes. These were superficial incentives, but there were more, perhaps many more, underlying motivations.

The other factors related to motivation have little to do with pragmatics. They are urges or strong feelings that are sometimes difficult for the singlehander to explain. Some may not even be recognized; they might be buried deeply in the subconscious mind.

Factor number two, self significance, has to do with finding one's place in the world and acquiring a sense of belonging. Of course the attempt to discover one's identity is by no means unique for solo voyagers, but singlehanders may have special talents or attributes as seamen, explorers, innovators, handymen, leaders (by inspiring others), theorists, experimenters, artists, transcendentalists, or what have you. There is a need to put these attributes to use. Perhaps the singlehander discovers in singlehanded sailing what he thinks he is uniquely suited for, his most appropriate course of action, the best means of expressing himself. He may not be understood by the entire world, but his rewards are great self satisfaction and acceptance by his own kind. This motive is strong in singlehanders who have highly developed skills or specialized knowledge, examples being Slocum, Pidgeon, Guzzwell, Chichester, Casper, and so forth. Their particular skills have (or had) to do with boatbuilding and/or navigation. This expertise is not the reason for a voyage, but merely a means of accomplishment that must be exercised.

The tenacious Dr. David Lewis after his attempt to circumnavigate Antarctica alone. (Courtesy of Margo Mackay)

John Guzzwell wrote in his book, *Trekka Round the World,* "I visited friends in Jersey, but my two years absence had made me a stranger amongst them, and I felt I did not belong there. Out sailing with one of them my old dream of making a long voyage alone returned to me. I was confident I could do so, providing I had a suitable boat. The best idea was to build my own, and with my skill as a joiner, I was sure I could do so." Plainly we are told that the singlehander felt out of place, that he needed a feeling of belonging, and he needed to put his skills to work, not as an end but as a means to his dream. Here are manifestations of factor two, although there were undoubtedly other motives that drove Guzzwell to his remarkable solo circumnavigation.

Factor number three, curiosity, is the desire to see for oneself. This urge may be stimulated by heroes, but it cannot be satisfied vicariously by reading or hearing about the experiences of others; it must be firsthand knowledge learned through physical effort. There is a compulsion to see what it is really like alone at sea. Not only does the singlehander want to experience the pleasant moments, but often he is curious, perhaps subconsciously, about the more difficult periods. He may wish to test himself, secretly or not, to see how he will stand up to fatigue, loneliness, fear, and hardships, to see if he can manage his vessel by himself in heavy weather at sea. J.R.L. Anderson wrote of Japanese singlehander Kenichi Horie's motives: "He sailed because he had to and he had to sail because he wanted to. That simple passion of wanting to know, to experience, to see for yourself is among the hardest things in the world to put into words."

The need for recognition (category number four) seems fairly uncomplicated. It is a desire for fame, for public acclaim, a love of the limelight. The reason for this need, however, is more complex. It may be the manifestation of a genuine sense of superiority, a requirement of the ego, or a stimulant necessary to extract one's best effort; but in a few cases, it might be the mollification of an inferiority complex, the need to build up one's image in the eyes of others. There seems to be little doubt that William Andrews and some other cockleshell voyagers, especially those of the late 1800s, had a large share of this motivation. The voyages of Andrews, for instance, were well advertised, and he delighted in the large crowds seeing him off and the publicity he received after the ventures' completions. The following is Andrews' account of his greeting by the Spaniards after his Atlantic crossing in the tiny sneakbox, *Sapolio*:

"Two men supported me on their shoulders, others had my legs, and still others were pressing up behind, and starting on, we were soon at the health officer's quarters, where I signed my name to some document and was soon placed on top of the crowd again, and proceeded to the residence of the Governor, Felix of Carazons, Salas. It was not the most enjoyable ride I ever had, but as they were continually shouting 'viva *Sapolio*', 'viva Captain Andrews', and 'viva Americano Colon', while I endeavored to reciprocate by shouting, 'viva Huelva', 'viva Colon', 'viva Palos', 'viva Rabida', 'viva Hispaniola', etc., I did not mind the awkwardness of the ride. Looking back at the heads that filled the streets for a mile, I did wish for a photograph of the scene, as I then considered that I had reached the pinnacle of my miserable existence." Of course, all men like recognition, but Andrews seemed to revel in it.

The thirst for fame, however, is by no means limited to the old-time singlehanders. Nicolette Milnes-Walker, a psychologist who crossed the Atlantic alone in 1971, frankly admitted her love of publicity. As she told yachting correspondent Frank Page, "It is marvelous to be famous," and, "It is very attractive to have public recognition." On the other hand, it is only fair to say that a great many singlehanders abhor publicity. In fact, solo voyager Alexander Welsh reportedly knocked a press photographer overboard in an effort to preserve his privacy.

The independence factor, category five, is commonly found in the habitual solo voyager. He must have the greatest possible freedom and the ability to have some control over his own destiny. What greater freedom can one have than to be alone at sea, beholden to no one, with no responsibilities other than to oneself, without a time schedule, and free to wander wherever one wishes? Of course a price must be paid for this vagrant pelagic life: the lack of roots, absence of family, lack of companionship, and perhaps a guilty feeling of running away from one's duties. But there are those who abhor depending on anyone and also having others depend on them. For these people there is tremendous satisfaction in self-reliance. This kind of need for independence is typified by Gerbault when he wrote, "I want freedom . . . I am in no hurry . . . I am a-roving, and a rover has no definite plans . . . Now, every minute of the day, I am thinking of departure, and of the great joy called living, when I shall be again alone on the sea."

A motive closely related to independence is escapism (category six). This is a reaction against the routine life ashore that is so often full of tensions, pressures, boredom, and artificialities. There is often a longing to return to nature. Sometimes the desire to escape from discontent is freely admitted, as in the case of Fred Rebell, who ran away from his problems in Australia. In other cases, there is a reluctance to admit escape for fear people might think it a "cop out" from society. Sometimes rather amusing reasons are given for leaving problems behind, as in the case of Peter Tangvald, a circumnavigator who often sailed alone. Evidently, Tangvald had more than his share of marital problems, and his description of leaving his third wife may or may not have been made with tongue in cheek. He wrote, "I had to choose between her and the boat, she said. Any sailor will know that it is a lot more difficult to get a new boat than a new wife, so I bought a one-way ticket for her to Norway. . . ."

It is seldom, if ever, wise to take up voyaging for the sole purpose of escape, for quite often the dissatisfaction which causes the yearning to leave cares behind really comes from oneself. As singlehander Edward Allcard put it, "People who are unhappy here and go somewhere else are usually unhappy there too. It's a thing from within. I don't think anybody can escape from themselves."

The seventh factor, adventurousness, is probably shared to some extent by all singlehanders. It is a characteristic of those with a restless spirit, which some psychologists feel may result, partially at least, from latent wandering instincts inherited from primitive man. For the afflicted sailor there is an urge to travel, to visit new places, a need for change in routine, a desire for new experiences, excitement, and probably an unconscious wish for some element of danger. As solo sailor Tom Corkill put it, ". . . the bigger the risk, the bigger the adventure." Nearly all adventurers feel that they must physically and even emotionally lead the fullest possible life. Some sailors readily admit to having this characteristic, while others do not.

Chichester wrote, "The same old restlessness was nagging at me. . . . I found myself craving more excitement." On the other hand, Harry Pidgeon said, "I avoid adventure as much as possible." Nevertheless, no one would have chosen the kind of life Pidgeon led without having an adventurous spirit. The very fact that voyages are made alone indicates a possession of this spirit to some degree. As singlehander Bill Howell wrote, "If you love adventure, whatever you do is much more adventurous if you do it alone."

In one form or another, competitiveness (factor eight) is often an element in the motivation of singlehanders. Competitiveness may take its normal form, the desire to win a race or set a record, or it may be, in some instances, the reverse side of the coin, a desire to avoid competition. In the latter case, there may be an urge to reap the rewards of competition with little risk of being beaten. The solo voyager can often experience a similar kind of satisfaction and glory as that felt by a winning competitor but without entering a race. Then too, if he does enter a formal distance race, the matter of who wins is of minor importance; the real glory is in successfully completing the course.

One could suspect that Chichester had such motivations, because he invented races in which there were no actual competitors. He tried to break records of his own and others. He raced against the "magic" number of 200 miles a day, and he competed against the runs of square-rigged vessels, the ghosts of clipper ships. But despite this, I am inclined to agree with J. R. L. Anderson who thinks of Chichester as a true competitor, one with an urge for trying to break records and extending man's physical limitations. He really used competition as a spur to get the best from himself; and his competitive ventures were most satisfying when they were done alone. Chichester had little desire for participation in team efforts. As he expressed it, "I don't do a thing nearly as well when with someone. It makes me think I was cut out for solo jobs, and any attempt to diverge from that lot only makes me a half-person."

Within the competitive urge sometimes there is a strong element of nationalism. This is a pride in one's country so powerful that it actually becomes a motivating factor. Of course, there are times when the factor is merely used as an excuse for a solo feat, but now and again it can be a major motive. A case in point is the voyage of Robin Knox-Johnston, who sailed around the world alone non-stop partly because he ". . . could not accept that anyone but a Briton should be the first to do it." Evidently this was not a mere tongue-in-cheek remark, but a sincere expression of his patriotism. Another remark that gives evidence of intense competitiveness is the one Robin made after an accident during which battery acid was splashed in his eye. He wrote, "I debated turning back for Durban, but Commander King and Bernard Moitessier were in the race. I was in the lead and stood a slight chance of winning, and I felt that this would be worth giving an eye for, so I carried on."

Solitude (category nine), of course, is very much a factor in the life of a singlehander. He may enjoy it or he may not. Many solo sailors prefer congenial companionship, but they cannot find the right crew. Difficulties with crew are common. Pidgeon, Casper, and many others had such problems in this regard that they preferred to sail alone. Although apprehensive at first, they soon became used to managing by themselves, and life became more free and simple. Other singlehanders go off alone, because it is a necessary condition of a competition they wish to enter. If they have a dislike of solitude, however, it is not sufficiently strong to prevent them from embarking. One young singlehander, Dave Englehart, told me that he actually went cruising solo because of his fondness for people. He suggested that his life style gave him a greater opportunity to make new acquaintances, especially with congenial types. In a sense it broadened his social horizon.

Then there are those singlehanders who actually like being alone, at least for certain periods of time. Many of these sailors have tendencies towards introversion. There may be a need for inner reflection and contemplation that can only be achieved through isolation. For some there may be spiritual value in being alone, a feeling of closer contact with God.

Sailing alone may increase one's appreciation of the experience, even sharpen perceptual sensitivities. Transatlantic soloist Francis C. Stokes

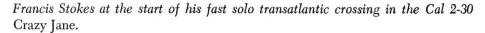

Francis Stokes at the start of his fast solo transatlantic crossing in the Cal 2-30 Crazy Jane.

wrote me, "Unless your crew is extraordinarily congenial, the experience shared will be diluted, less vivid and less well remembered. Solitude sharpens awareness of small pleasures otherwise lost."

In some cases the love of solitude may be a reaction against crowding, the population explosion on shore. Perhaps there is an urge for complete and utter privacy. H. G. Hasler has said, "The only pleasure I get at sea really is becoming isolated. I get a tremendous pleasure out of existing in a world that only goes as far as the horizon. I shrink from contact."

Our last category, number ten, has a rather strange title, "the mother sea." It has to do with the sailor's natural emotions in regard to the sea and his vessel. Part of his feelings are deeply buried in the subconscious. They may very well relate to genetic instinct, the sort of thing that tells spiders to build webs or birds to fly south in the winter. Of course, life itself originated in the sea, and water in one way or another has always been essential to man. Perhaps the deep love of the sea possessed by some sailors, the "sea fever" described so well by John Masefield, is in some part the awakening of an instinctive affinity with the mother element. As Robert Manry explained it, "There is an inherited something in the protoplasm of my body cells that feels an agreeable kinship with the sea."

But sometimes the sea's attraction is more a fascination than a love, and there are definitely times when sailors have a downright fear of the sea. In this case, the boat rather than the water may become the mother element, in a sense the protective womb. This feeling can even extend to the life raft. When David Shaw (not alone, but shorthanded) weathered a lengthy gale in his 37-foot yawl, he became extremely fatigued and developed a strong urge to assume the fetus position in his rubber raft. He described his feeling as being "absolutely straight Freudian because the raft also has a long cord that is attached to the ship. But I envisioned curling up in this thing. It was strictly back to the womb." As H. G. Hasler has written, "Nothing induces a womb complex more strongly than looking out of a hatch at an angry sea just under your nose."

The affection some sailors have for their boats is well recognized, and perhaps some parts of this emotion are instinctive. John Guzzwell has written, "A boat seems to have a soul and character of her own. Perhaps it is because of this that boats are usually thought of as being feminine." Single-hander Frank Mulville expands on this thinking when he says, "A boat is a living thing — full of eccentricities, perversities and endearing quirks. It vibrates with life and gives off sympathy and understanding." In fair weather, the boat may be like a companion or a girl friend, but in a hard chance she may seem more like a defending mother. Even in the heaviest weather offshore, the true seaman with confidence in his craft experiences a unique sense of security. Far from a lee shore with the vessel hove to and all hatches battened down, a snug cabin may seem more protective than a private fortress on land.

There seems to be no motivational common denominator for all single-handers. Too many contrasting individuals are involved. One sailor may be almost entirely motivated by just one of the ten factors we've been discussing, while another may, to some degree, be affected by all the factors. Nevertheless, it seems safe to say that all singlehanders possess at least some of these motivations in various combinations. The nearest thing to a common denominator could be, perhaps, a mixture of these motivations that are closely related to what J.R.L. Anderson calls the "Ulysses factor," the exploring instinct in man. This instinct derives, for the most part, from a primitive need to discover, pioneer, have adventures, investigate, and satisfy one's curiosity through physical effort. Anderson tells us that all men have the Ulysses factor to some extent, but in modern times, when there are few frontiers left to explore, the instinct is often strong in flyers, mountain climbers, offshore sailors, and especially in solo voyagers. This instinctive need is usually best satisfied through individual achievement and not through large-scale team effort.

Furthermore, most solo voyagers probably share what might be called a romantic optimism, the kind of idealistic outlook that allows them to make light of the bad times — the gales, hardships, fatigue, loneliness, worries, and fears. The singlehander thinks mainly of scudding before the trade winds with the warm sun on his back and his dream ship sliding off before foam-flecked seas of the deepest blue. He also dreams of landfalls on tropic isles with palm-fringed lagoons and native girls bedecked with flowers. Most, if not all, seagoers have such romantic visions, but those of the solo voyager are so intense and frequent that anxieties are put aside, obstacles are overcome, and dreams are turned into reality.

Psychological Factors

Regardless of the solo voyager's motivations, he will be exposed to certain psychological hazards that could have a great affect on the success of his voyage. The most usual problems of this kind arise from loneliness, fears, and hallucinations.

Loneliness is a common hazard to singlehanders, of course, but is seldom extremely serious, and surprisingly, many singlehanders claim that they are never deeply affected. As said earlier, there are some who enjoy or actually need periods of isolation. For them, singlehanding allows an escape from social inhibitions and the claustrophobia of overcrowding. Also, the isolation affords a unique opportunity for contemplation, reflection, obtaining a broader perspective, and perhaps spiritual or at least philosophical meditation. Others, who are not seeking escape from people, are often not adversely affected by the loneliness of singlehanding, for their isolation is completely self-inflicted. They expect solitude, and they don't experience the strong feelings of abandonment and despair so often suffered by castaways. Then, too, there is a definite difference between solitude and loneliness. It is possible to be lonely when surrounded by people, and this feeling of being alone is probably the most painful kind. As Marin-Marie wrote, "To be alone in the midst of a crowd is much harder to bear than to be a thousand miles from the nearest human being." More recently, solo racer Mike McMullen said, "It is only in big cities where no one is your friend that real loneliness is found."

All of this, however, is not to minimize the problem of loneliness. Slocum was badly afflicted at times; so was Ann Davison, Alain Bombard, Robin Lee Graham, and many others. In a letter to the well-known seaman and author, Humphrey Barton, Mrs. Davison wrote, "I agree with you that singlehanded sailing is not all it might be. The utter aloneness is rather apt to get one down. Didn't know I was quite so gregarious." The youthful Robin Lee Graham expressed his reactions by saying, "Loneliness was to ride with me for a thousand days, and throughout the longest nights. At times it was something I could touch."

There are ways to combat loneliness. One of the best is to keep busy, and this is not difficult for the singlehander, because there is always something that needs doing aboard a boat. Many singlehanders find it helpful to imagine that they have company. The boat can become an intimate companion, porpoises and birds are company, and the pets carried by a few solo sailors provide a kind of outlet for affection and communication. Gerbault's books became his "best friends." Slocum conversed with the moon, and he made "the porpoises leap" and the turtles "poke their heads up out of the sea" when he sang "Johnny Boker" and "We'll Pay Darby Doyl for his Boots." Sharon Sites Adams also fought the loneliness problem with imagined conversations and vocal outbursts. She wrote, "I talked and talked. I talked to the boat, to the gooney birds, to the moon and all the time to my tape recorder — it became my friend. I said 'hello' to a lovely star every night. I even screamed."

Incidentally, modern electronic devices such as tape recorders, radio-telephones, and even receiving radios may give the modern singlehander some form of temporary relief from loneliness. Aside from Sharon Adams, others have made good use of tape recorders. For example, Robin Lee Graham constantly recorded his own voice and played it back, and H. G. Hasler, who carried no radio, by the way, used his recorder to play tapes of jazz pieces "whenever morale needed boosting." Two-way radio communications between shore or other boats has afforded some relief from loneliness for modern singlehanders, especially those in ocean races when there are congenial competitors nearby. As a matter of fact, radios have been of real practical value in some cases, as for example, when Chichester, in 1964, obtained advice over his radio phone from a boatbuilder on how to repair a serious leak, and when Chay Blyth received soldering and engine repair instructions in a similar manner during his circumnavigation. Thus electronic communications can afford the kind of contact that can bring real security as well as ease loneliness, a psychological advantage the old timers didn't have. Navy psychologist, Dr. Benjamin Weybrew, in considering the advantage of radio contact for men in space has said, "The fact that astronauts can communicate with the outside world may be what holds them together in the long run."

Fear, to some degree at least, is experienced by most singlehanders. Dr. David Lewis, in collaboration with the Medical Research Council in London, made a study of the medical and psychological factors affecting the singlehanders competing in the 1960 transatlantic race. His findings showed that only one out of five contestants never felt "acute fear," although the degree varied with each individual. In general, there were two types of fear, initial tensions and anxieties lasting for the first few days, and then a very rational apprehension resulting from potentially dangerous situations, such as during a gale or when approaching a coast in bad visibility. Interestingly, Dr. Lewis found that quite often the singlehander does not remember the extent of his fears. He concluded that, "Observations noted *at the time* are the only valid ones." Of his own reactions, he wrote, "I honestly forgot that I had been frightened at all during one gale, until I looked up my notes."

Dr. John C. Lilly, in his studies of the mental aspects of singlehanding, noted that a critical period of fear during a solo voyage often occurs near the "point of no return" (PNR). This is the point beyond which it is easier to go on than turn back. It would not necessarily come near the middle of a passage but might come early if, for example, the vessel were running before the trade winds and when turning back would mean a difficult beat to windward. Actually, the point is likely to come very early, because it is really a state of mind, a mental PNR, when the singlehander considers such matters as the effort he has expended in planning and preparing for the cruise and the possible humiliation of turning back for no very good reason. At any rate, whenever it occurs, the mental PNR is a significant moment for the cognizant sailor. Often he has a powerful feeling of anxiety and indecision. Donald Crowhurst agonized over whether to continue or not. In his logbook he wrote, "Racked by the growing awareness that I must soon decide whether or not I can go on in the face of the

Complex psychological pressures caused the voyage of Donald Crowhurst to end in tragedy. (Peter Dunne/Sunday Times)

actual situation. What a bloody awful decision — to chuck it in at this stage — what a bloody awful decision!"

Continuing beyond the PNR may bring some relief in the sense that a difficult decision has been made, but this is the time when many a single-hander will have the strongest feeling of being entirely on his own, when he will have the fullest realization that he cannot count on receiving any outside assistance. Thereafter, barring storms or emergencies, this kind of apprehension may gradually subside as the sailor becomes increasingly habituated and the passage nears its end.

Fears in one form or another are perfectly normal for the solo voyager. The danger is in letting fear turn into panic, which could seriously hamper judgement. According to studies made by Doctors Bombard and Linde-mann and others, panic and loss of morale are the chief causes for the perishing of castaways adrift at sea. Bombard wrote, "Statistics show that ninety percent of the survivors of shipwreck die within three days, yet it takes longer than that to perish of hunger and thirst." Some psychologists even think that it is possible to literally die of fright. Most of the time, however, castaways who do not survive simply give up and stop fighting for life or perhaps kill themselves by jumping overboard. Actually, experienced seamen are rarely troubled by extreme panic, although I have heard of a few cases where fear caused greenhorns or slightly experienced sailors to lose their sense of reason.

It is not easy to fight fear, but a major weapon is self confidence. This is best assured by careful preparation, attention to one's health, seeing that the boat is sound and well equipped, learning all one can about the proposed route and weather conditions, polishing the techniques of singlehanding, preparing for all possible emergencies, and gradually building experience.

Another weapon is prayer and faith in God, or at least a belief in an exterior force which, to some extent, controls one's destiny. Some singlehanders become very superstitious, but usually this affords far less comfort than religion. Chay Blyth, whose circumnavigation was one of the most strenuous, had this to say: "Ten months of solitude in some of the loneliest seas of the world strengthened every part of me, deepened every perception and gave me a new awareness of the power outside man which we call God. I am quite certain that without God's help many and many a time I could not have survived to complete my circumnavigation." The religion of most singlehanders is not overly fatalistic, however. It is decidedly not a conviction that God or a superior being will protect the solo sailor no matter what blunders are committed in seamanship. It is more a belief that, "The Lord helps those who help themselves." As Robin Knox-Johnston put it, "If you are trying to do a particularly difficult job, and failing time and again, the knowledge that the Lord will assist you if you help yourself keeps you going at it, and in my experience the job usually gets done."

It is not at all unusual for singlehanders to suffer from the false sense impressions known as hallucinations. These are imaginary perceptions or sensations, the "tricks of the mind," such as hearing voices that don't exist or seeing visions that are not real. Just how many solo voyagers have hallucinations is hard to estimate, since not everyone is willing to admit having them, presumably for fear people might suspect serious mental disorders. Actually, there is no reason to feel overly abashed by such experiences, because completely normal people can hallucinate under certain conditions, and the environment of the singlehander can be quite conducive to false sensations and even the false beliefs known as delusions, which are closely associated with hallucinations. Dr. Lilly, who made a study of this subject with respect to singlehanders, set up controlled experiments whereby he could cause normal people to hallucinate in a matter of a few days or even hours.

Many singlehanders have frankly admitted to hallucinations and a few have been very explicit on the subject. Slocum described in some detail his imaginary Spanish pilot from the ancient caravel *Pinta* who took charge of the *Spray* while her captain was ill. Dr. Lindemann told of his feeling of traveling backwards, of an imaginary negro servant, and a black horse that pushed his boat. Robert Manry described a phantom hitchhiker and a wild search for an imaginary island. The interesting but frightening illusion of levitation was described by Fred Rebell when he became disassociated from his boat and found himself "floating in the air" as much as a hundred or more miles away from his actual location. During one of these "flights" of fancy, he spotted a vessel which he later saw in actuality.

Incidentally, it is interesting that more than a few singlehanders have reported dreaming about or imagining a steamer approaching their boats, and shortly after this warning, the real ship, identical to the one in the dream, has made its actual appearance. One singlehander who underwent this experience told me he thought the explanation lay in pure coincidence. In other cases, the experience might be some form of hallucination, but a psychiatrist-sailor friend offered still another possible explanation: that it might be the phenomenon known as *déjà vu*, the illusion of having already experienced something actually experienced for the first time. In other words, when the sailor saw the ship in actuality, it could possibly be that he imagined he saw her previously.

Although many singlehanders have survived hallucinations with no ill effects, there is no question that such mental disturbances are potentially dangerous. They can seriously impair judgement and cause fear and irrational behavior that could prove fatal. Dr. Lindemann mentioned that several times he had the urge to jump overboard to reach some imaginary food, and others have turned over the helm at critical times to a phantom crew member.

As a result of considerable scientific research in recent years, a lot more is known now than formerly about the nature and causes of hallucinations. In the normal mentally healthy person, hallucinations can be a kind of substitute for dreams. Psychologists tell us that dreams are important for mental health, since they help us get rid of tensions and frustrations, resolve certain conflicts, and perhaps fulfill some secret wishes. If we are denied dreams through lack of sleep, we are subject to an alternative in the form of hallucinations, which are very near relatives of dreams. So close is this relationship, in fact, that Dr. Calvin S. Hall, director of the Institute of Dream Research, has written, "Dreams are pure and simple hallucinations. They are the hallucinations of a sleeping person." The difference between dreams and hallucinations is that the former are normal and restorative, while the latter are not normal and can be damaging. Thus adequate sleep is a necessary element in the avoidance of hallucinations. Mere rest will not suffice; it must be sleep, which, whether we realize it or not, produces dreams.

Dr. Lilly has told us that there are two types of hallucinations experienced by the singlehander: the first is the "fatigue" type caused by exhaustion and lack of sleep, and the second is what he calls the "surplus-energy" type, caused primarily by monotony. In reference to the latter type, psychiatrists may use the term "stimulus deprivation." There is no doubt that certain activities on a small boat at sea can be extremely monotonous for a singlehander. Hour after hour of steering is one of those activities, and Dr. David Lewis has suggested that self-steering devices have been most helpful to modern solo sailors in minimizing hallucinations. Of course self-steerers not only alleviate monotony, but also reduce fatigue. It may very well be that rhythmic motions produced by wave action can contribute to a tendency to hallucinate. Dr. Lewis wrote, "Possibly the rhythmic effect of monotonous activities tends to induce auto-hypnosis." At any rate, controlling the boat's motion as much as possible (with anti-rolling and anti-yaw measures) and especially varying activities seems to be helpful in minimizing hallucinations that are due to the effects of monotony.

One of the most striking examples of a fatigue hallucination was told by the South African boating writer, Frank Robb. According to Robb, who claims the story is completely true, a singlehander making a passage in the Caribbean Sea encountered rough weather that lasted four days and denied him much-needed sleep and rest. When the weather moderated, he was unsure of his position but soon spotted a fishing boat and an island with a protected harbor. He sailed in, passing a launch full of sightseers, and found a snug spot to anchor. After dropping the hook, he furled his sails, went below, and collapsed on the cabin sole into a deep sleep. Twelve hours later the singlehander awoke, went on deck, and found that, although the boat was anchored in eight fathoms of water, there was no land or boats in sight. His mind had simply invented the island and harbor in order to allow his body to sleep. His physical actions were completely controlled by powerful fatigue hallucinations.

The utter necessity of sleep for singlehanders was learned by Dr. Hannes Lindemann not only from medical research, but also from unique, first-hand experiences. During his transatlantic crossing in a 17-foot rubber foldboat, he was often unable to sleep except for brief periods. At certain times, when he could not make his boat steer herself safely before the large seas produced by the blusterous trade winds, he could only try to accumulate brief snatches of sleep between waves. He practiced a form of self-hypnosis called autogenesis, which was helpful, but still he hallucinated frequently. He found out that sleep was a "vitally important factor." He wrote, "The castaway should try to sleep, if only for a few minutes at a time. Seconds of sleep may save his life."

Incidentally, Lindemann's ideas about proper diet are also interesting (this will be mentioned later), especially his high regard for milk, which he thinks should be included, in canned form, in the emergency rations of all lifeboats. He said, "It [milk] helps control the factors in a hungry man's body chemistry that make for panic and delirium."

In summary, experts seem to agree that hallucinations in the normal person are primarily caused by fatigue, especially lack of sleep, and by monotony and solitude. Other contributing factors may be improper diet, certain illnesses (abnormal physiological conditions, for example), certain drug poisonings, and perhaps auto-hypnotic types of motion. Thus hallucinations are best avoided by getting plenty of sleep (eight hours a day if possible), resting, varying one's activities, keeping busy, relieving monotony as much as possible, keeping mentally active, possibly relieving or varying hypnotic motions, maintaining good health, avoiding drugs, and eating proper meals. The one factor a singlehander can't do much about is eliminating solitude, but a radio, tape recorder, pets, or simply talking to oneself may help.

Of course, a great many singlehanders have never been troubled by psychological problems, but others on particularly strenuous voyages have had considerable troubles with abnormal behavior of the mind. Thus it makes sense to know what one might expect and what preparations and preventive measures can be taken. One compensation for a difficult passage is the perfect right of the successful singlehander to be extremely proud of himself. By his accomplishment he has proven to himself that he can withstand alone not only awesome exterior forces of nature but also the more potent internal adversaries in the mind. The rewards of inner satisfaction and self assurance can be very great and everlasting.

3 / THE VESSELS

Boats specifically designed for solo ocean crossings have varied in length from 6 to 128 feet, and singlehanded offshore passages have been made successfully (and unsuccessfully) in every kind of craft imaginable. Thus it is evident that there are many and varied opinions regarding the choice of an ideal vessel for singlehanding.

Of course, the major influence on the choice of design will be the fundamental purpose for which the boat is intended, that is, whether it will be used for solo racing, leisurely cruising, or even for an attempt at breaking a record. The 6-foot craft, for instance, was specifically designed to be the smallest boat to cross the Atlantic, and, though most will consider this a pointless if not foolish motive, the project was a fascinating challenge for both the designer and skipper. Regardless of the intended purpose, however, virtually all singlehanders seek in varying degrees the following characteristics for their boats: safety and seaworthiness, handiness, seakindliness, comfort, and speed. To some degree the latter quality is needed on any boat, because even if she is not racing, she will have to make port during the time of favorable weather and before her supplies are depleted. The dilemma is, of course, that many of these desirable qualities are in opposition with each other when they are translated into design parameters. For example, speed necessitates largeness, but handiness suggests compactness; seakindliness is associated with heavy displacement, but the fastest passage-making suggests light displacement. Thus one characteristic will have to be emphasized at the expense of another, and major compromises or "trade-offs" must be made.

Solo Racers

The primary requirement for a solo racing boat is length, because a heavy, non-planing hull can rarely be driven faster than 1.35 times the square root of its sailing waterline length. Thus, in a fresh breeze, the longest boat should be the fastest. Since there seldom have been restrictions on size, and, thus far, not much emphasis has been placed on handicap awards in singlehanded ocean races, the question of size boils down to how large a boat one man can handle. Determination of the largest size has usually been derived from an estimate of the largest sail a man can handle. In the early 1930s, the British designer-sailor, Uffa Fox, wrote that one man "could reef or stow a 500-square-foot mainsail in all weathers but not a larger sail." After completing the 1960 singlehander's race, Francis Chichester decided that his mainsail of 380 square feet and Genoa of the same size was more than he could manage in heavy weather. It is interesting that today this hypothetical limit has grown considerably higher, for Jean-Yves Terlain, skipper of the 128-foot *Vendredi 13* handled working staysails of 930 square feet, and after the race he reckoned that he could have managed more. Leslie Williams, who did well in the 1968 singlehander's race, wrote that he thought he could handle conveniently in light winds a sail up to about 1,200 square feet.

With a sail-size limitation, the way to get the longest hull with the most sail area is by having a multi-mast arrangement, with each mast carrying a sail of the maximum size according to the limitation. The *Vendredi 13* was rigged with three boomed staysails of 930 square feet each on three masts of equal height. This concept produced what seemed to be the longest practical length of boat, having a fairly respectable sail-area-to-displacement ratio, that one man could manage at sea. The boat was quite successful in that she was the first monohull to finish. However, there are decided drawbacks in the design. These are lack of maneuverability, expense, low speed in light airs, unsuitability for normal use after the race, and general unhandiness. With respect to the latter, one should not be misled by Terlain's remark that he could have handled slightly larger sails. It was made by a remarkably capable seaman absolutely dedicated to winning the race even if it involved taking some chances, and we should bear in mind that his race was sailed in mostly light to moderate winds. Furthermore, Terlain actually did have considerable trouble handling his sails at times. On one occasion, when he was lowering his forward Genoa, the sail got away from him and slid overboard. It was too heavy for him to haul back on board, so he had to tie lines around the sail and winch them in a little at a time. The operation of recovering the sail took about two hours. Maneuvering such a large boat may not be a serious problem offshore, but in coastal and inland waters where there are shoals and boat traffic, the lack of manueverability for a singlehander could be positively dangerous.

As for the *Vendredi 13*'s minimal speed in light airs, the problem is that when there is little wind, speed primarily depends on the ratio of sail area to wetted surface. Although wave making is the main form of resistance

It is astonishing that one man could handle a craft so huge as the Vendredi 13 *when one studies this photo which, despite the exaggeration of perspective, gives a size comparison between the boat and people standing on her afterdeck. (Courtesy of* Yachting *magazine)*

when the boat is moving fast, the surface area of her submerged hull is what really slows her down in light airs. Of course, the wetted area of the *Vendredi 13* was enormous, and yet her sail area was comparatively small. Her designer, Dick Carter, expressed the fear that when there was little wind she would be all but "glued to the water." Although this was putting it a bit dramatically, perhaps, the big schooner did lose the honor of being first to finish because of light airs that didn't suit her near the end of the race. Additionally, there is no denying that her three-masted rig lacked efficiency on most points of sailing.

Another difficult aspect of the *Vendredi 13* was the problem of construction. Her hull had to be kept reasonably light but strong and rigid. Then too, cost was an important consideration. The solution was a foamed-core, fiberglass sandwich construction, which was strong, but heavier than was hoped for, and because of its extreme length, the hull was quite flexible. There were some rather alarming stories (perhaps exaggerated) about the hull whipping to such an extent that it once acted like a springboard and catapulted Terlain upward, knocking his head against the overhead. Fortunately, he was wearing a crash helmet.

Aside from resorting to super size, there is another direction the designer can take to achieve unusual speed. He can make the boat super-light and fairly flat-bottomed so that she will partially plane or, to some extent, seem to lift up and skim over the water's surface rather than plow through it. With this approach, the boat can often partially escape from her restricting wave system, and then speed is not quite as dependent on length. Semi-planing types include multihulls and some canoe-like monohulls of very light weight with ballasted fins.

The multihull concept has many merits, and it proved highly successful in the 1972 singlehander's transatlantic race, but it has at least one serious drawback for the heaviest weather offshore. As often pointed out, an un-ballasted multihull can capsize, but what is far more important, it normally can't self-right. Of course, a monohull boat having a ballast keel can capsize too (though probably not as easy as a multihull), but with proper beam (not excessive), keel depth, and weight of ballast, she will right herself unless badly holed. On the other hand, the normal catamaran or even trimaran may be far more stable in the inverted position than when upright.

A lot of thinking has gone into solving the multihull capsize problem, but as yet no entirely satisfactory system has been worked out. Some of the systems tried or suggested have been: masthead flotation tanks or inflatable masthead bags; sponsons above the rail; V-shaped hulls to inhibit heeling beyond the point at which the leeward side of the V becomes horizontal; ballast or ballasted fins; ballasted swing keels or lever arms which can be hauled out from the hull to cause a righting force when the boat lies on her beam ends; a method of hauling a float attached to the head of a hinged mast downward to turn the boat upright; and systems of flooding one hull of an upside-down boat to make her lie on her side and then, after attaching masthead flotation, clearing the flooded hull to allow righting. We are even beginning to see experiments with stabilizing hydro-foils and dihedral fins angled inward to cause lift acting upward in the interest of preventing excessive heeling. The use of ballast on multihulls has not been very successful because of the adverse effect of weight on per-formance. Masthead flotation is highly desirable, but solid tanks may cause considerable weight and windage aloft, and, furthermore, such floats can break off or even cause a dismasting in heavy weather unless the rigging is extremely strong and well engineered. Fins and foils also present struc-tural difficulties for severe conditions offshore.

Donald Crowhurst, who was an inventive electronics technician, devised a clever scheme for righting his trimaran, the *Teignmouth Electron,* which he entered in the 1969 around the world race for singlehanders. The system, which was never fully completed, consisted of a buoyancy bag lashed to the masthead that would be inflated automatically by a cylinder of carbon dioxide when the boat was heeled to a certain angle. The method devised to activate the CO_2 was to fasten electrodes on the upper topsides so that

Donald Crowhurst's trimaran, the Teignmouth Electron, *was literally loaded with sophisticated gadgetry to minimize risks in heavy weather.* (Devon News/Sunday Times)

they would complete an electrical circuit when they became submerged as a result of heeling. Actually, the system was quite complex, for Crowhurst used a bank of electrodes rigged and positioned in such a way that they could distinguish between spray or temporary immersion and a truly dangerous angle of heel. Mercury switches might have been an alternative to using the electrodes. At any rate, the inflated bag would prevent the trimaran from turning turtle during a capsize, but she would still have to be righted from the position of lying on her side. For this part of the operation, a pumping system was devised that would flood the upper float, theoretically pressing the boat downward and then turning her upright. Other gadgets used by Crowhurst were alarms that monitored unusual stresses on the rigging and sheet releases activated by abrupt changes in wind speed registered on his anemometer.

Ingenious as these anti-capsize systems were, they have some drawbacks. It is seldom advisable to rely too heavily on electricity at sea on a small boat during heavy weather because of the possibility of power failure or short circuits from wet wiring. Also, pumping and flooding methods that look fine on paper are often difficult if not impossible to operate when capsized in the worst conditions of weather offshore. Very generally speaking, it might be said that the more complicated a system is, the less practical or reliable it becomes.

Perhaps the most successful transoceanic racing multihull of all time is the *Pen Duick IV*, built for and skippered by Eric Tabarly and later sailed by Alain Colas. Though a pure racing machine, this 67-foot trimaran has twice been sailed around the world, once solo (after she had been renamed the *Manureva*). Among her speed records are a trade-wind Atlantic crossing of ten and a half days, the course record for the Los Angeles-to-Honolulu race, an Indian ocean record, the fastest time for the singlehander's transatlantic race, and a record circumnavigation. Several times the tri exceeded 300 miles in a full day's run, and once she ran 326 miles in twenty-four hours while being singlehanded by Colas. Tabarly claims that her top speed has been twenty-seven or twenty-eight knots.

Before the 1968 transatlantic race for singlehanders, Tabarly had become convinced that multihulls were the way to go for winning speed. He was concerned about the possibility of capsizing, but as he well knew, the chance of survival weather in June on the North Atlantic is slight, and he decided on a trimaran "as being safer than a catamaran, which tends to capsize more easily." Furthermore, the *Pen Duick IV* was given a broad beam of 35 feet to make her enormously stiff, although she had a very limited range of stability as compared with a normal monohull. The trimaran was designed by André Allègre and was built very lightly but strongly of aluminum. With many struts and stays and much tubing connecting her hulls, she was described by multihull soloist Bill Howell as looking like a "floating Sydney Harbour bridge." Stresses on any multihull can be tremendous in heavy weather, but Tabarly's boat perhaps had some special problems with her ultra-lightweight construction having to be able to withstand prolonged periods of rough seas at unusually high speeds. Despite her superb engineering, it was reported that there was considerable vibration of the floats entering waves, and some early photographs show a few cracks at the tubing weldments. Even so, she made two high-speed circumnavigations and successfully negotiated some heavy weather along the way.

The *Pen Duick IV* had many early tuning problems that were eventually solved or alleviated. The most serious one was her rotating wing masts which could not be adequately stayed. Eventually they were replaced by conventional spars, which seemed very sensible, because even if a wing mast can be kept straight, it cannot be reduced in area during heavy weather. Another problem, which I don't think has ever been completely resolved, is the difficulty of self-steering at alternating high and low speeds.

Vane gears on most multihulls often work well at low speeds, and they can be adjusted to operate very efficiently at quite high speeds, but the vane has difficulties during extreme accelerations and decelerations. Two partial solutions to the problem are towing a drogue linked to the helm and the use of a hinged vane-supporting boomkin that allows the gear to tilt up at high speeds. Incidentally, Alain Colas made a most remarkable underwater repair to his self-steering gear during the 1972 singlehander's transatlantic race when the wind was Force 8 and the seas were twelve feet high. He could not even wear a face mask because of the risk that it might be smashed when the waves threw him against the bottom of the boat.

One cannot help but be awed by the seamanship of Colas in managing such a large, complicated machine as the *Pen Duick IV* alone. Even with a crew on board, maneuvering such a craft can be highly involved and demanding. The jibing operation during the Honolulu race was described by Colas as being, "a great ceremony, an intricate choreography which calls for the whole cast (crew I mean) and sends them real wild all over the place, wire-dancing between main hull and pontoons, escalating or leaping gracefully here and there, panting and sweating in a Samson-like tug o'war with spars, canvas or winches."

Another interesting type of multihull is the proa, as exemplified by the *Cheers,* designed by Dick Newick. This boat finished third in the 1968 singlehander's transatlantic race and once was sailed 250 miles in twenty-four hours by her solo skipper, Tom Follett, yet she is only 40 feet long. She is actually quite similar to a catamaran, with two almost identical double-ended hulls, except that one carries the rig, accommodations, and lateral resistance appendages, while the other hull is merely the outrigger or "ama," and it is considerably lighter in weight. The ama is always kept to leeward, and to change tacks the booms of her stayless, two-masted rig are swung through arcs of up to 180 degrees, so that, in effect, she is tacked by sailing forwards and then "backwards." The lateral resistance appendages are two tandem dagger boards with rudders attached. If half lowered, a board acts purely as a lateral resistance appendage, but when fully lowered its rudder is exposed and can steer the boat. The rudders are linked to a whipstaff, which is controlled from amidships by the helmsman. The two masts and tandem dagger boards enable the boat to be balanced quite easily (especially so, since she does not heel very much). Thus no vane gear is required, and this at least partially alleviates the problem of self-steering on a planing multihull.

With her ama to leeward, the *Cheers* has considerable resistance to capsize because of her low rig, heavy main hull, buoyant ama, and beam of over 16½ feet. But if she should get caught by a sudden wind shift that puts the ama to windward, she could flip over with comparative ease. In

The unique proa Cheers *designed by Dick Newick and raced so successfully across the Atlantic by Tom Follett. (Courtesy of Dick Newick)*

Tom Follett on the bow of the Cheers, *casting off for his solo passage from St. Croix to England in 1968. (Courtesy of Fritz Henle)*

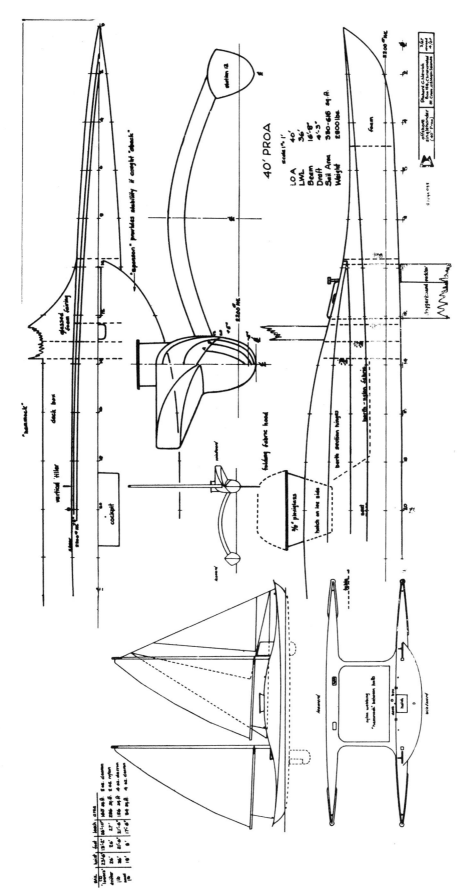

Plans of the 40-foot proa Cheers, showing her tandem daggerboards and sponson, which is always kept to windward. (Courtesy of Dick Newick)

fact, she once did this during early sailing trials. To safeguard against such an eventuality at sea, a sponson or flotation chamber was added above the rail of the main hull on the side away from the ama. In addition, her masts are sufficiently buoyant to discourage her from turning turtle. If she should happen to turn bottom side up, however, she has greater self-righting capabilities than the average tri or cat.

The obvious drawbacks of a boat like the *Cheers* are lack of accommodations and lack of maneuverability in crowded waters, mainly due to her inability to come about through the eye of the wind. In fact, her designer admitted that she needed a motor to be suitable for congested waters.

Putting aside specialized boats like the *Cheers* and *Pen Duick IV*, the following observations might be made about the good and bad points of the more normal types of multihulls as compared with normal monohulls: In general, multihulls have great initial stability but a poor range of stability. Tris generally have a greater range of stability than cats. The initial stiffness allows nearly level sailing and alleviates tiresome accumulative rolling, but it may cause a quick, jerky motion in certain seas. Furthermore, great initial stability involves more risk of capsize in heavy weather and imposes tremendous strains on the rigging. Multihulls are capable of great bursts of speed, but overloading can ruin their performance, and windward performance with ability to tack smartly is often (but not always) less than desirable, while self-steering may present greater problems than on monohulls. A tri and especially a cat usually demand extra care and attentiveness from a singlehander. If well-designed, multihulls can usually run off and sometimes surf very effectively in steep seas. Their shoal draft allows easy beaching if caught on a lee shore, and when unballasted, they normally will not sink if holed or capsized. On the other hand, as mentioned earlier, they are enormously stable in the upside-down position and may be difficult if not impossible to right. In fact, three people were forced to spend two months on the bottom of a capsized trimaran in the Pacific in the summer of 1973. Remarkably, two crew members survived the ordeal.

The third concept of achieving super speed, the very light, narrow monohull, has also been tried several times for solo ocean racing. A good example of this type, which has a canoe-like hull with a small, but deep, fin keel, is the Michael Pipe designed *Strongbow*, sailed by Martin Minter-Kemp in the 1972 transatlantic race. (See plans of the *Strongbow* on p. 72). She combines light displacement with long sailing length and a reasonably high sail-area-to-wetted-surface ratio, while offering the advantage of high resistance to capsizing. In the words of designer-author Douglas Phillips-Birt, she is "a highly specialized but basically healthy type of yacht." Although she did not finish better than seventh in the race, which is by no means bad for a boat of moderate size, she was hampered by the lack of adequate trials and time for tuning. At any rate, she has a great potential for speed, and indeed was said to have been clocked at over twenty knots on one occasion. Her speed is due not only to her length, 65 feet over-all, and her light hull, whose depth (excluding keel) is a mere 1½ feet, but also to her narrow beam, which is only 10 feet, 5 inches. Windward performance is enhanced by a very deep, narrow keel tipped with a streamlined bulb of ballast weighing five tons. Minter-Kemp praised the boat for her maneuvering ability, quickness in stays, stiffness, and seakindliness, although she did pound under certain conditions. Such a design demands a very high strength-to-weight ratio, and the *Strongbow* achieved this with cold-molded, plywood construction consisting of five laminations, some of which were laid diagonally. In addition, she was built with a steel structure nearly amidships which supported and connected the mast, keel, and shrouds. Nevertheless, it was reported that she broke a stringer, loosened a bulkhead, and took in water around her keel bolts. Such a hull can be under very considerable strain, especially at each end during heavy weather when moving at high speeds. Minter-Kemp described the motion of his boat as being "like driving a fast car on bad roads."

A somewhat similar but more extreme example of the light displacement canoe type is the *Sea Gar*, shown in Figure 3-1. This boat was never built,

FIGURE 3-1: "SEA GAR"
        design by Frank MacLear

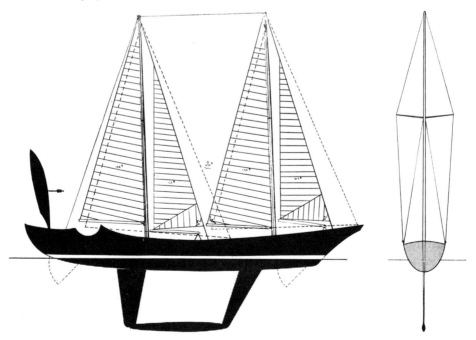

but she was designed by Frank R. MacLear before 1960 to compete in the singlehander's transatlantic race. She anticipated some of the modern developments with respect to solo racing despite the fact that she is based on an ancient craft, the gaumier, or Carib Indian dugout canoe.

The *Sea Gar's* dimensions are length on deck, 60 feet; length on the water line, 47 feet; beam at the deck, 8 feet; and draft, 12 feet. Her extremely narrow beam, only 6 feet at the waterline, will allow great speed to windward in steep seas, provided she is stiff enough to stand up to her modest sail area. Stability with little outside ballast (two thousand pounds) is derived from the leverage of her extremely deep keels. As can be seen in Figure 3-1, the keels are two high-aspect-ratio tandem fins joined at the bottom by a streamlined bulb of ballast. This keel concept has also been suggested by the hydrodynamicist and publisher for the Amateur Yacht Research Society, John Morwood. Such fins minimize wetted surface while providing high lift, and if the connecting ballast is properly shaped, it will mitigate "end losses" at the after fin, according to Morwood. In order to enhance stability during long tacks at sea, moveable ballast in the form of sand bags would be placed on racks on the windward side, and as a safeguard against being caught aback with the bags to leeward, they are rigged to slide overboard during an unlikely knockdown to windward.

For self-steering, the *Sea Gar* would have a wind vane gear, but, in addition, she would have tandem centerboards, one at the bow and the other at the stern, which could be trimmed for nearly perfect balance on any point of sailing. Her two-masted rig would also contribute to balance flexibility. Should the boat develop a weather helm, corrections could be made by trimming in the forward sails while easing off the after sails and/or raising the forward board while lowering the after one. This system allows almost infinite variations of trim.

As for sailing performance, MacLear estimates that the *Sea Gar* might be driven to windward at ten knots, reach at fourteen knots, and surf before high seas and strong winds at twenty knots. He estimates that the maximum speed-length ratio (speed divided by the square root of water-line length) for this type of boat should range between 2.2 and 3.5.

The obvious disadvantages of such a design concept are the extreme draft, which limits the boat to fairly deep harbors, and the restriction on accommodations and side deck space due to the narrow beam. Furthermore, there may be construction problems (as mentioned when describing the *Strongbow*), and of course, with any boat requiring shifting ballast, there may be some risk in getting caught with the weight on the wrong side. Even if that risk is minimized with an automatic jettison plan, such as that used by the *Sea Gar*, exhausting physical effort may be required to move the ballast to the windward side.

One boat that uses shifting ballast quite effectively is Eric Tabarly's monohull sloop, the *Pen Duick V*. She is somewhat similar to the light-displacement, deep-fin, canoe-body concept but for the fact that her beam is very much greater and her length was limited to 35 feet by the rules of the 1969 singlehander's transpacific race. Moveable ballast is in the form of water pumped to tanks on the windward side, and with the proper pumps, the time, if not effort, required to shift the water is not too great. In early trials, it took over twelve minutes to move the water, but after the installation of a large rotary pump, the pumping time was greatly reduced. Of course, most of the water might be allowed to flow by gravity to the leeward side just before tacking, but with that method there is a slight risk of being caught by an unexpected gust. It is safer to balance the moveable ballast more or less equally immediately prior to coming about. One annoyance to Tabarly was that his rotary pump leaked, and there was no bilge sump in the flat bottomed boat, which meant that water was often flowing up the sides of the hull and wetting his supplies at even small angles of heel.

The *Pen Duick V* is capable of high-speed planing in favorable wind and sea conditions, but at some sacrifice to comfort and range of stability. Although her broad beam of 11 feet, 4 inches allowed roomy accommodations in one dimension, the shallow depth of hull limited headroom, and her flat bilges caused severe pounding in head seas. Apparently her strong aluminum construction could withstand the slamming, but at a cost in discomfort and anxiety for the crew. One day during the transpacific race, Tabarly wrote in his log, "I've never known a boat to shudder like this before. Everything is vibrating, as though the whole rigging will come down at any moment." As for stability, the boat is very stiff, especially when her water ballast is being used, but she lacks the reserve stability and self-righting capabilities of a more normal monohull. This is mainly due to her considerable beam and light keel ballast of only 900 pounds.

Specialized Cruisers and Survival Aspects

The boats we have been discussing are highly specialized racers, and it is easy to see that they can demand major trade-offs, often with considerable sacrifice to important practical features, such as accommodations, moderate draft, seakindliness, and even self-righting ability. Those vessels designed especially for solo cruising require compromises also, but perhaps to a lesser extent, and, of course, quite different qualities are emphasized. As said before, speed is always important to some extent in order that the boat can make a passage in reasonable time and so that she can sail out of difficulties, such as clawing off a lee shore or making progress against a strong current, but, for a cruiser, the emphasis is more on safety and comfort. A few of the cruisers we shall discuss have been used for solo racing, but their skippers were more interested in successfully sailing the course in relative comfort, and they rarely had serious expectations of winning against the specialized racers, except perhaps in very heavy weather.

An ingenious early yacht of considerable size that was designed especially for singlehanded cruising is the sloop, *Barnswallow*. She was built in 1932-1934 by her owner, Paul Hammond, from plans of Starling Burgess. With a length of 39 feet on deck, a displacement of nearly 10 tons, and a mainsail area of 460 square feet, she was a sizeable boat for one man to handle, but she could be controlled from one central point, the forward part of her rather small cockpit. In this sense she might be considered a forerunner of the modern Hasler concept which soon will be described. Not only did her halyards and sheets lead to the cockpit, but also her ground tackle, roller furling headsails, and roller reefing gear for the mainsail. Some details of such systems will be discussed in Chapter 5. Plans of the *Barnswallow* are shown, and it can be seen that she has easy lines with a long shallow keel for steadiness on the helm while allowing accessibility to shoal harbors.

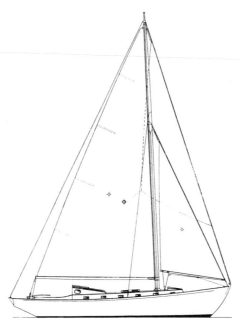

Plans of the Barnswallow *(above and to the right), designed by Starling Burgess, show her long keel of moderate draft for good directional stability and ease of entering shallow harbors. (Courtesy of the executors of Uffa Fox, deceased)*

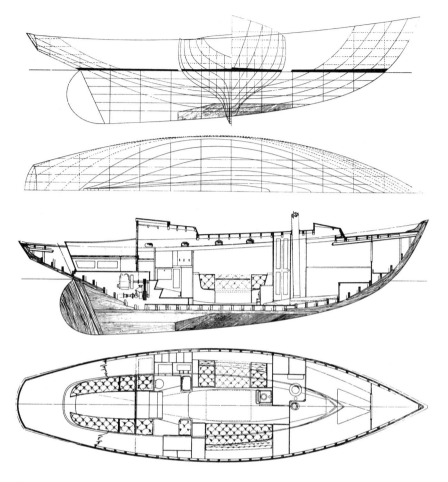

Paul Hammond's Barnswallow, *built especially for singlehanding, anticipated the central control concept. (Photo courtesy of the executors of Uffa Fox, deceased)*

Sailor-artist Marin-Marie, who crossed the Atlantic alone in the double-ender *Winnibelle,* was not able to control every evolution from the cockpit, but he rigged steering lines into the cabin and had a telltale compass overhead so that he could make helm adjustments without getting out of his bunk. Incidentally, Marin-Marie gave advice to Paul Hammond on the matter of self-steering with twin headsails, but Hammond developed a somewhat different system. (This matter of making a boat sail herself will be dealt with in Chapter 6.)

The central-control-point concept was carried almost to its ultimate by the famous "cockleshell hero" (Chapter 1) and innovative yachtsman, H. G. Hasler. His 25-foot *Jester* might be considered a real breakthrough in ease of handling and protection for a solo crew. This boat, which recently completed her seventh solo transatlantic passage, is a standard Scandinavian Folkboat below the water, but from the waterline up she is not quite like any yacht that preceded her. She is flush-decked, without a cockpit well, and with a kind of turtle-backed cabin trunk. The central control point is a circular hatch fitted with a folding pram hood, and from this position the boat can be steered and completely handled. Her one sail can be hoisted, trimmed, reefed or unreefed, and handed without ever the need of leaving the hatchway. From 1952 to 1959, she carried what Hasler called a "lapwing rig," but she was converted to a Chinese lug rig for the 1960 singlehander's transatlantic race. (These rigs and others will be discussed in Chapter 5).

The *Jester's* crew can operate the boat from either a high standing position in the control hatchway, which allows the upper torso and arms to be above deck, or a seated or low standing position, which allows the head only to be above deck. Lines for the sail adjustments are handled from the high position. The pram hood (similar to that on a baby carriage) is mounted on a rotatable ring around the edge of the circular hatchway, and the raised hood can be turned in any direction to give maximum protection or visibility. Normally, of course, it would be turned to windward in rough weather. Steering can be done with either steering lines or a whipstaff which works athwartships. A vane gear steers the boat most of the time on passages, and its control lines can also be handled from the hatchway.

Two large access hatches are on either side of the cabin trunk, but these are normally closed when underway. There is also a hatch in the foredeck, which is only opened in calm weather or when moored. Additional ventilation is supplied by ten small opening ports. The main accommodations, consisting of bunks, galley, and head, are located in the after half of the hull. This makes good sense when there is no cockpit well to restrict space below, because there is far less motion from pitching abaft amidships. The hull's forward half is used mostly for stowage.

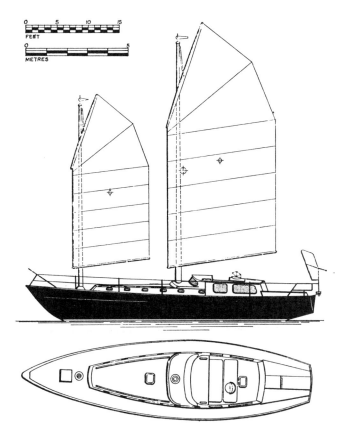

The Ron Glas, *designed by Angus Primrose and rigged for singlehanding by H. G. Hasler and Jock McLeod, represents the ultimate in crew protection, with nearly all evolutions manageable from below. (Courtesy of* Yachting Monthly)

Jock McLeod, an associate of Hasler, perhaps carried the concept of maximum crew protection one step further with his Chinese-lug-rigged schooner, *Ron Glas,* which he raced across the Atlantic in 1972. This boat had all halyards and lines leading under cover so that in wet weather all evolutions could be accomplished from below. McLeod wrote of his passage, "I never wore my oilskins at all. The only time I expected to wear oilskins was when securing or casting off in the rain, or going ashore, in other words in harbor and not at sea! I believe I have retained all the pleasures of sailing singlehanded and removed all the discomfort."

Aside from comfort and ease of handling, there is the important consideration of maximum safety, which is usually emphasized at some sacrifice to speed in a solo cruiser. Of course the extent of this emphasis will depend on the intended use of the boat. Short passages at carefully chosen times of the year in fair weather latitudes are quite a different matter from round-

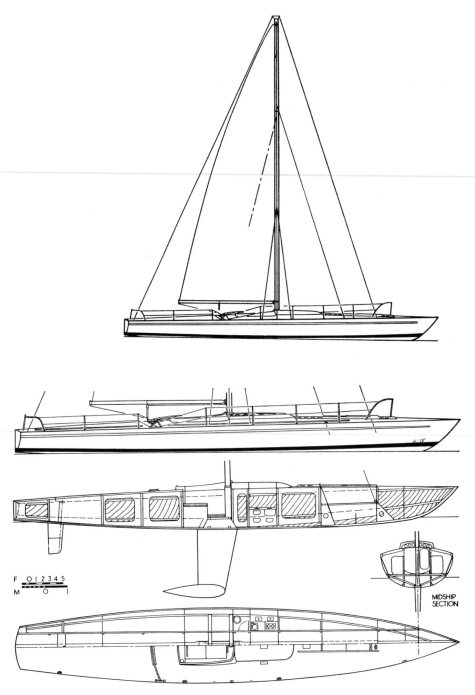

F O 1 2 3 4 5
M O 1

MIDSHIP
SECTION

The Strongbow, *designed by Michael Pipe and Paul Weychan, is representative of the narrow, ultra-light, deep-fin, monohull racer. Her dimensions are:* LOA, *65 feet;* LWL, *57 feet; beam, 10 feet, 5 inches; draft, 10 feet, 8 inches; displacement, 8 tons. (Courtesy of Michael Pipe)*

ing the Horn, passaging in the southern forties or fifties, or crossing an ocean during its season of storms.

Dr. David Lewis, for example, had to think in terms of survival in the worst possible conditions when he chose his boat, *Ice Bird*, for his proposed circumnavigation of the Antarctic continent, which he began in late October, 1972. His 32-foot sloop was heavily built of steel to withstand ice and the destructive seas produced in the latitudes of the "Screaming Sixties." She had two and a half tons of lead at the bottom of her six-foot-deep keel to provide a good self-righting capability, and the boat could be steered for long periods from below with visibility provided by a plastic dome in her sliding hatch-cover. Watertight integrity was maximized with such features as steel storm shutters for her cabin windows. As we shall see in Chapters 7 and 8, Dr. Lewis needed these survival features and then some.

Two other boats designed with maximum emphasis on survival are W. Leslie (Bill) King's *Galway Blazer II* and Colin Irwin's *Endeavor*. The former was specifically designed for a non-stop solo circumnavigation, and she participated in the Golden Globe Race of 1968-1969. The 42-foot hull was designed by Angus Primrose, while her rig and handling systems were based on the ideas of Hasler and Jock McLeod, utilizing the Chinese lug rig and central control position previously discussed. In the *Blazer's* case, however, there are two control hatches, one on the starboard and the other on the port side, for optimum comfort and visibility on each tack. All lines can be handled from either hatch. The boat is, like *Ron Glas*, schooner rigged with two unstayed masts carrying fully-battened lug sails. The foremast carries no headsails and is stepped far forward. A folding "A" frame is provided for a jury rig in case of dismasting, and King had an opportunity to use it, as he lost his foremast after a capsizing off Cape Horn in 1968 (this experience will be described in Chapter 7).

Like *Jester*, the *Galway Blazer II* has her accommodations abaft amidships. This is especially important in the latter's case, because her displacement is quite light (less than 10,000 pounds for her 30-foot waterline and 50 percent ballast ratio), and consequently her motion is often lively. Forward of the mainmast below decks is a vast stowage area and two flat, water tanks holding seventy gallons in the shallow bilge. Incidentally, it is highly desirable that such tanks of considerable width be divided with a plate in the center running fore and aft to minimize the free surface effect when the tanks are only partially full. Abaft the mainmast is the galley, chart table, a gimballed bunk, and an interesting padded chair that is adjustable to almost any angle of heel. Sir Francis Chichester had a gimballed athwartships-facing chair in his *Gipsy Moth IV*, but King's faced forward and could be locked in various positions of inclination.

Watertightness of the hull is of special concern to the singlehander, partly

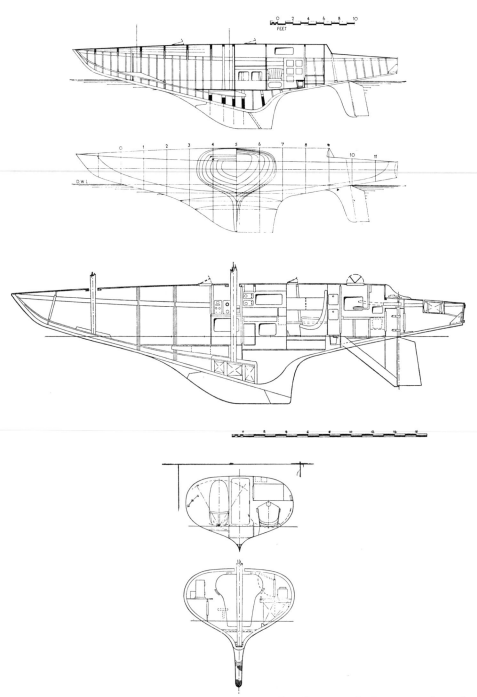

Plans of the Galway Blazer II, *a Primrose-Hasler design, which survived a solo circumnavigation that included being capsized and being stove in by a sea creature. Her dimensions are: LOA, 42 feet; LWL, 30 feet; beam, 10 feet; displacement, 4.5 tons. (Nautical Publishing Company)*

The H. G. Hasler designed Loner, *a midget ocean cruiser for singlehanded sailing. Her dimensions are: LOA, 14 feet, 5 inches; LWL, 11 feet, 3 inches; beam, 6 feet, 3 inches; draft, 4 feet; displacement, 3,000 pounds; sail area, 155 square feet. Her deep keel keeps the 1,200 pounds of ballast low and provides some windward ability for clawing off a lee shore in a blow. (Courtesy of* The Spray)

because if a through-hull fitting or its piping should happen to rupture, there is no one to help locate and repair the leak or help man the pumps. Chay Blyth had no holes in the bottom of his *British Steel* except for the propeller shaft, and Peter Tangvald became so alarmed when he discovered unsound bolts on a through-hull fitting, that he removed all plumbing and plugged the holes in the bottom of his *Dorothea*. Bill King had similar anxieties, and so the *Galway Blazer II* was left unpunctured below the waterline. Two bucket heads were installed, one to port and the other to starboard.

In her construction, the *Galway Blazer II* is immensely strong for her weight. She was built of laminated, cold-molded plywood, and her entire hull was rounded to resist the impact of heavy seas. Even her deck was extremely cambered and devoid of the conventional cabin trunk, which is subject to damage in the most severe conditions. It is just as well she was strongly built, for she survived a damaging blow from a whale or shark in 1971 (see Chapter 7).

Another specialized survival craft with the highly-cambered "whaleback" deck is the *Endeavor*, which was constructed for Colin Irwin to cross the Arctic above Canada and Alaska singlehanded. This is a similar route to the famous "Northwest Passage" followed by Roald Amundsen and his crew in the 70-foot cutter *Gjoa* back in 1903-1906, except that Irwin's route runs the opposite way, from west to east, partly to take advantage of some strong favorable currents. The last I heard of Irwin was that he had sailed about half way through the passageway and was spending the winter with Eskimos on Victoria Island.

The *Endeavor* is a highly modified Westerly Nimrod, a mere 18 feet long, designed by Ian Proctor. She, too, is rigged according to the Hasler concept with a Chinese lug sail and all lines leading to the central control hatch. In the rugged waters of the far north, there are times when Irwin must stay below, so even the anchor is carried aft with its chain running forward so that it can be dropped from the hatch. The whaleback deck gives enormous strength because of its elimination of flat surfaces, but special care has to be taken not to slip overboard when walking on it. Irwin uses a deck paint containing sand for skidproofing, and he is very careful about wearing a safety line when topside.

Of course, the *Endeavor* must be capable of withstanding pressures and abrasions from ice, but Irwin hoped to avoid the crushing forces of pack ice by staying very close to shore where he says the water is mostly open. His boat is fitted with a ballasted centerboard and a lifting rudder, which not only facilitates shore hugging but encourages the ice to lift the boat, rather than crush her, when the appendages are raised. They also allow the boat to be hauled up on top of the ice with the help of a special ice anchor and winch. The fiberglass hull is protected with an outside skin of three-quarter-inch mahogany planking, which is sheathed in heavy copper.

My friend, John S. Letcher, who is not only a singlehander but also an engineer and naval architect, has given considerable thought to the design of a "survival" craft. John's ideal, which he intends to build someday, will be built very strongly, but not necessarily heavily, to withstand groundings and collisions, and she will have a fairly long keel with a sweptback or sharply raked leading edge to minimize shock loading if it should happen to strike a solid object at a high speed.

This boat will also have sufficient flotation to keep her from sinking if she is holed. This feature is not as impractical as it might seem for a ballasted boat. In fact, several years ago a stock fiberglass 30-foot cruising sloop was fitted with foam flotation at very little sacrifice to volume for accommodations, and I remember seeing advertising photographs of her under sail with all seacocks wide open. Of course, another approach to flotation is with the use of watertight bulkheads and/or the use of tank-lockers, stowage areas built like buoyancy tanks that can be sealed with watertight doors. This locker-buoyancy system was utilized by Hasler for his design of an interesting midget ocean cruiser, the *Loner*. Still another means of supplying flotation is with the use of inflatable buoyancy bags. Such a system has been designed by Chris Burrows in England, and plans were shown in the magazine *Yachting Monthly* (January, 1974). Even a large life raft inflated below decks can add a lot of buoyancy to a small boat. Marcel Bardiaux used this method of helping to keep his 31-foot sloop afloat after she grounded on a coral reef near New Caledonia in 1954 (this incident will be described in Chapter 7).

Returning to John Letcher's ideal of a survival craft, another requirement would be recoverability from a roll-over. John feels that this calls for a beam which is fairly narrow by today's standards. He thinks that typically beamy modern hulls have a limited range of stability and a stable equilibrium position upside down. The limited stability range could encourage turning turtle during an extreme knockdown, while the stable equilibrium upside down discourages self-righting. Although John recognizes that a properly ballasted beamy boat will probably right herself, partly because of the free surface effect of water rising inside her hull, he believes that less beam (by today's norm) will help a lot in minimizing inverted stability.

A serious probable or at least possible consequence of turning turtle is loss of the rig. Even though well-found vessels and their crews stand a good chance of surviving a 360-degree roll-over, the rig is often totally wrecked, especially if it is a very tall, intricately stayed, Marconi rig. Perhaps the most original idea conceived by John Letcher for his survival craft is the concept of a "sacrificial" topmast. Figure 3-2 shows the load distribution on a typical Marconi rig during a roll-over, and it can be seen that the stresses are very much greater near the head of the mast. In fact, John tells us that the bending moments, compression, and shroud tensions are all proportioned to the fourth power of the mast height. It is apparent in the drawing that stresses are relatively moderate or small with regard to the lower part of the mast (i.e., lower when the boat is upright), thus this part could be designed quite easily to withstand the roll-over loading. On the other hand, it would be extremely difficult to design an unbreakable upper mast where the loading is so great. Thus John proposes to allow the upper part to carry away without damaging the lower part during a roll-over. This would be accomplished by having a mast composed of two spars, the upper one fitting into a socket at the top of the lower, and by having lighter rigging supporting the topmast. After loss of the topmast, sails especially cut for the lower spar are hoisted on permanently rigged halyards, the sheaves for which are located just below the topmast socket. The remaining lower portion of the mast will provide a low-aspect-ratio rig, but one that is fairly efficient for reaching port regardless of the wind direction. Of course the great danger of this concept is the possibility of the topmast carrying away while sailing in a fresh breeze and rough seas.

One of the most interesting and controversial aspects of designing for

FIGURE 3-2: SACRIFICIAL TOPMAST
concept and drawing by John Letcher

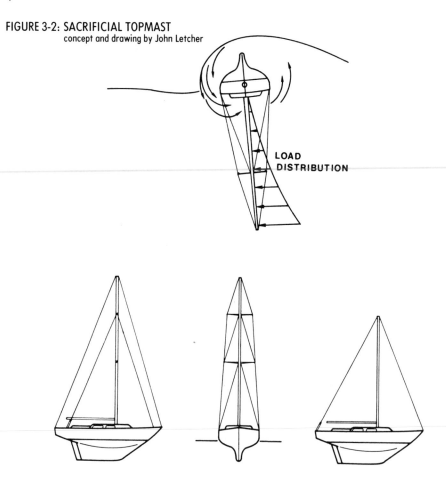

LOAD
DISTRIBUTION

survival is the matter of boat size. A great many offshore sailors will tell you that a very small boat is just as safe or even safer than a much larger vessel in a storm at sea. Their arguments usually bring up the example of the fragile corked bottle which will survive the worst possible storm in open waters.

While there is much truth in this reasoning, and a small boat has the greater proportional strength for a given construction material, there is little doubt that a cockleshell is more roughly handled by the elements over a broader range of conditions. Although glass bottles and perhaps even electric light bulbs are not broken by the waves, they are tumbled and rolled, and the cockleshell had best be prepared for the same kind of treatment. Furthermore, the midget seagoer will be violently treated much earlier than a larger craft when the weather deteriorates. The former will probably be subject to a knockdown or roll-over sooner, and she must heave to earlier. Additionally, she will most likely have a difficult time beating away from a lee shore in a real blow.

On the other hand, a large vessel handled by one man can also have many problems in heavy weather. She is difficult to handle; her gear is heavy and can cause injuries; her weight and size detract from maneuverability and cause crew fatigue; her deep draft makes her more subject to accidental groundings. Thus it seems that the medium-sized cruiser has many more safety advantages, for she is easily handled yet able to cope with a wide range of adverse conditions offshore or along a hostile coast. And just what is medium size? Exact dimensions are, of course, impossible to set. For a lower limit we might suggest the approximate overall length of 25 feet, but John Guzzwell made a very successful circumnavigation and weathered some extremely bad weather in a boat just over 20 feet long, and obviously there are many seaworthy and unseaworthy boats in every size. The upper size limit is even more difficult to set, because it depends on the weight and design of the boat, the capabilities of the man handling her, the extent of her cruises, and the character of the waters she will be sailing in.

The very smallest cockleshells are seldom chosen for offshore passage-making because they are considered the safest craft for the job. They are nearly always chosen for economic reasons or for the purpose of breaking a record. Although the smallest boat I ever heard of to make a short passage was a mere 4½ feet long, (she sailed along the coast of Ireland in 1822), the transoceanic record breaker is Hugo Vihlen's *April Fool*, which is just under 6 feet long. Obviously her voyage in 1968 was a stunt, but it was carefully planned, made a few contributions to survival knowledge, and produced some original design thinking. Her architect, Edwin H. Mairs, had to solve a lot of problems, such as the production of a hull that would have a volume sufficient for a man and the necessary stores for a three-month voyage; would have good directional stability, some windward ability, and a displacement suitable to her tiny sail area; and would have the safety features of watertight integrity, buoyancy, transverse stability, and longitudinal stability or resistance to pitch-poling. The latter was an especially difficult problem because of the *April Fool*'s extremely low length-to-beam ratio. Her beam of 5 feet was not much less than her length of 5 feet, 11 inches, which meant that she could somersault almost as easily as she could capsize.

The solutions and compromises involved in resolving these problems produce a unique hull that could be described as a deep-V, flat-cathedral

Hugo Vihlen in his tiny April Fool, *the shortest boat to cross the Atlantic. (Courtesy of Hugo S. Vihlen)*

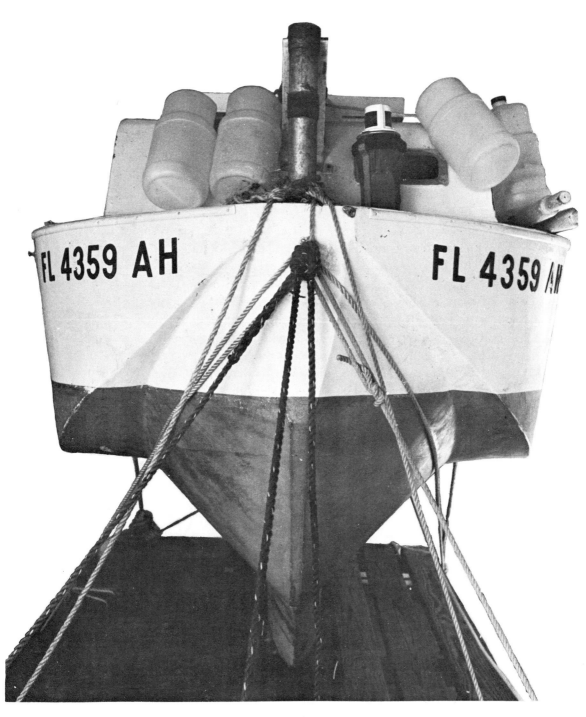

A bow view of the April Fool *showing her interesting semi-cathedral hull. (Courtesy of* Yachting *magazine)*

type (see Figure 3-3). The deep-V sections run along the centerline of the hull, while there are flat, rocker-bottomed, cathedral-type sponsons on each side. The term cathedral, by the way, has nothing to do with a church. It is a hull shape seen on some modern powerboats, and the term "cat-hedral" refers to negative dihedral, denoting flat surfaces that form a concave V. The *April Fool*'s deep-V sections give depth for lateral resistance, interior volume, and directional stability, while the cathedral-type sponsons provide transverse stability and bring reserve buoyancy into the broad, upper bow to resist pitch-poling. She has a long cabin trunk reaching almost from stern to bow with a long window on each side and two forward, a sliding after hatch, and a dome ventilator forward. The hull is lightly ballasted and provided with foam flotation. A single mast is stepped far forward, catboat fashion, and the rig is a Ljungstrom type (see Chapter 5), except that the sails are trimmed with twin booms mounted on a pedestal just abaft the mast, somewhat similar to Hasler's lapwing rig.

The *April Fool* took eighty-four days to sail from Casablanca, Morocco, to Florida. She behaved well enough during the voyage but proved difficult against a few headwinds she encountered, which is not surprising. In one sense, her passage was not the achievement of some of the other cockleshell ocean crossings, such as those made by the *Sapolio*, *Sea Serpent*, and *Tinker-belle*, because they did not follow the relatively easy trade-wind route, as did the *April Fool*. The latter's accomplishment was notable, however, in that it was so well planned, and it set an all-time record, which hopefully will discourage anyone else from trying to break it.

FIGURE 3-3: PLANS OF "APRIL FOOL"

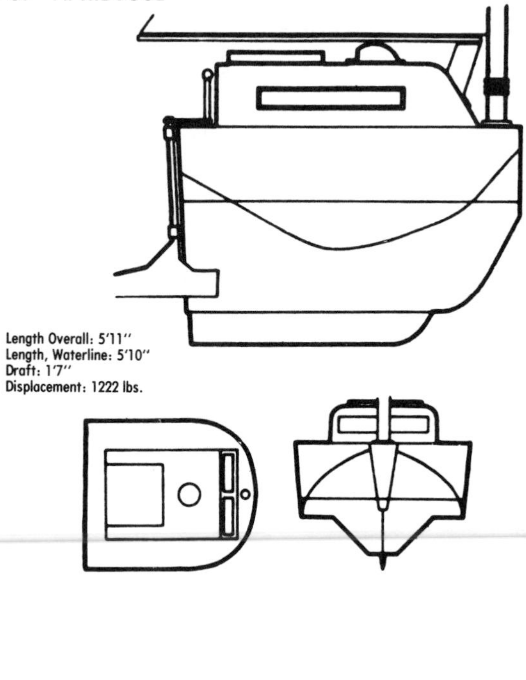

Length Overall: 5'11"
Length, Waterline: 5'10"
Draft: 1'7"
Displacement: 1222 lbs.

Standard Craft

Outstanding singlehanded voyages have been made in almost every kind of craft imaginable, yet there are a few favorite standard types. First of the circumnavigating vessels, of course, was the *Spray*, and she inspired many replicas. This was not surprising, because Joshua Slocum gave high praise to his vessel, and it is true that she had some good qualities for ocean cruising. Some of these are: an easy motion due to her heavy displacement, large volume and deck space for comfort, the ability to carry large quantities of stores with little harm to performance, and very good directional stability for self-steering. On the other hand, the old boat, which probably began her life as an oyster sloop in the early 1800s, had some shortcomings for singlehanded voyaging. She had gear of considerable size and weight for one man to handle; she was somewhat lacking in windward and light-air sailing abilities; and, although she was exceedingly stiff, she had a relatively small range of stability as compared with the normal modern monohull. Even her greatest contemporary champion, Kenneth E. Slack, who wrote the fine book, *In the Wake of the Spray*, admits that she was "Slow, clumsy, and unhandy beside the modern yacht. . . to sail such a craft amid congested harbors and steamer-ridden shores of these modern days requires a degree of skill far greater than the usual owner possesses. After all, there are few of us able to measure up to the standard of Captain Slocum."

Another popular early type was the *Sea Bird* yawl, a twenty-five-and-a-half footer designed for the *Rudder* magazine at the turn of the century.

John Riding at the helm of his 12-foot Sjo Ag *(Sea Egg), which he sailed halfway around the world. According to quite reliable reports, Riding and his little boat were eventually lost at sea. (Courtesy of* Yachting *magazine)*

FIGURE 3-4: SOME HISTORIC SOLO CRAFT

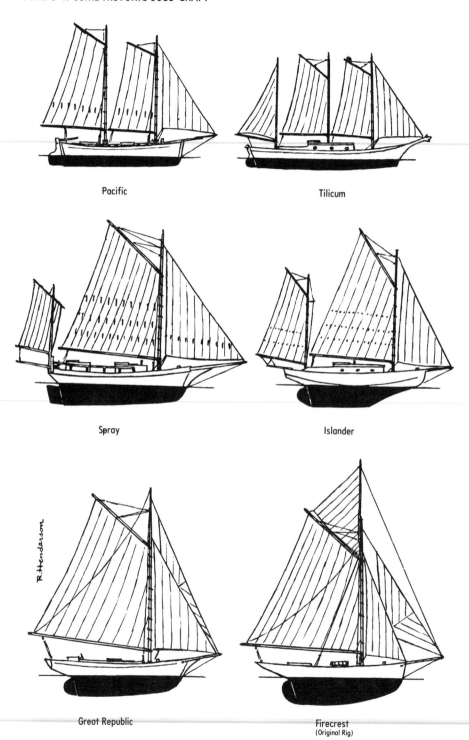

Pacific

Tilicum

Spray

Islander

Great Republic

Firecrest
(Original Rig)

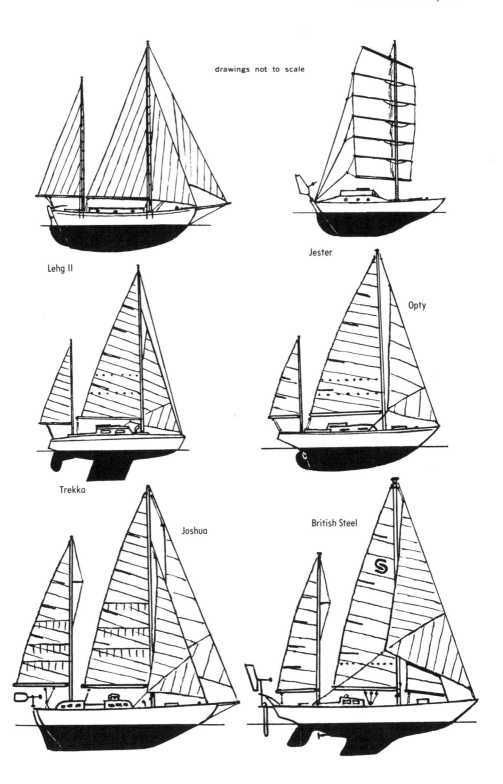

drawings not to scale

Lehg II

Jester

Trekka

Opty

Joshua

British Steel

Several people had a hand in her design, including C. D. Mower, L. D. Huntington, and Thomas Fleming Day, the editor of the *Rudder*. As Day wrote in his magazine, "I am not a designer, but I claim to be the author of this craft." Many seamen felt that the *Sea Bird* was not the most suitable type for offshore work, because she had hard chines and flat bilges. For given scantlings, flat sections are not as strong as curved ones, and boats with hard bilges can pound under certain conditions, but, despite this characteristic, the *Sea Bird* proved a very satisfactory offshore boat. In 1911, Day, together with two companions, sailed her across the Atlantic from Rhode Island to Gibraltar and from there to Rome. One of the *Sea Bird*'s crew, Frederick B. Thurber, told me that she had two main faults, insufficient area of her lateral plane for windward ability, and a high, square cabin trunk that caused some anxiety, as it took a battering from the seas. Incidentally, Robin Knox-Johnston had a similar problem with his *Suhaili*'s slab-sided cabin house, which was damaged by boarding seas. The *Sea Bird*'s freeboard was quite low by today's standards, and Thurber said that she was swept several times, but Captain Day claimed the chines were helpful in keeping spray off the deck in a moderate chop.

One of the *Sea Bird*'s outstanding features was ease of construction due to her V bottom, which minimized bending frames and planks. Several of these boats were home-built, and the most famous of them, Harry Pidgeon's yawl, the *Islander*, was sailed around the world two and a half times (two circumnavigations being made singlehanded). Actually, Pidgeon's boat was a larger version, 34 feet long, known as the "Seagoer" class. The famous circumnavigator liked his *Islander* so well that after she was finally wrecked on a South Pacific island during her third voyage around the world, he built another but slightly smaller "Sea Bird" type. Another home-built boat of this type that was sailed around the world, for the most part singlehanded, is William Murnan's *Seven Seas II*. She was built of stainless steel, and was very heavy when fully loaded. She was 30 feet long and, being a centerboarder, drew only 3 feet. Although she had very little freeboard, she weathered much heavy weather and often rode with a tire drogue over her stern (see Chapter 8). Both Murnan and Pidgeon claimed their boats would run off very well in heavy weather, although they would sometimes take water over the stern.

At one time during his voyaging Harry Pidgeon met up with Alain Gerbault in his *Firecrest*. The two circumnavigators inspected each other's vessels, and each admitted definite preference for his own. The *Firecrest*, an English racing cutter quite typical of the early 1900s, was an interesting contrast to the *Islander*. The 39-foot cutter, designed by Dixon Kemp, was narrow and deep with a plumb stem, prominent forefoot, and a long, overhanging counter. She was weatherly, could quite easily be hove to in heavy

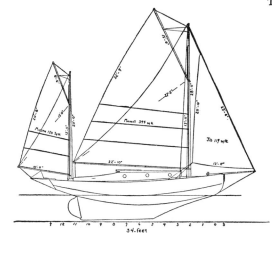

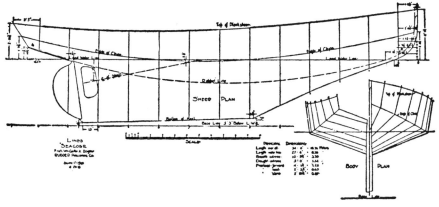

Plans of Pidgeon's Islander *show her hard chines, low deadrise, and cutaway forefoot. (Courtesy of* Rudder *magazine, part of Fawcett Publications)*

The Seagoer class Islander, *a larger version of the famous* Sea Bird *type. This craft, under the command of Harry Pidgeon, sailed two and a half times around the world. (Courtesy of* Yachting *magazine)*

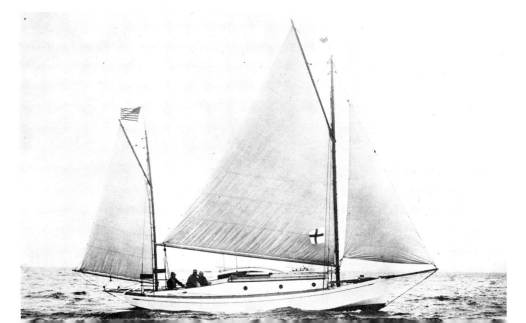

weather, and, although ardent when heeled, was fairly steady on her helm in consistent winds; yet she had some disadvantages for offshore single-handing. Among her faults were initial tenderness that caused her to "sail on her ear" when it blew and a tendency to bury her bow and hollow entrance. Furthermore, she would sometimes tend to gripe when running before heavy seas; and her long bowsprit was not conducive to maximum safety when it was necessary to work forward.

Other favorite vessels for offshore singlehanding include the double-enders. These vary from the heavy, full-ended Norwegian sailing lifeboats (Redningskoites) designed by Colin Archer, to the somewhat more fine-ended, canoe-stern types. An example of the latter was Edward Allcard's 34-foot yawl, *Temptress*. Famous Colin Archer types sailed singlehanded around the world are Al Peterson's 33-foot, gaff-rigged cutter, *Stornoway*, and Frank Casper's 30-foot, modern Marconi-rigged cutter, *Elsie*. And let's not forget Al Hansen's gaff-rigged *Mary Jane*, probably the first boat to be sailed by one man around Cape Horn from east to west (unfortunately she was later wrecked on the coast of Chile). Other craft that have circum-navigated singlehanded, which are quite similar to Colin Archer designs, are J. Y. Le Toumelin's 33-foot cutter, *Kurun*; Vito Dumas' 31-foot ketch, *Lehg II*; and Robin Knox-Johnston's 32½-foot ketch, *Suhaili*. The latter is said to be one of the William Atkin "Eric" designs based on the Colin Archer type. Other famous heavy displacement double-enders with generous beam and long, shallow keels are the "Carol" and "Tahiti" cruisers designed by John G. Hanna. The most famous of these used for solo voyaging is Jean Gau's 30-foot ketch, *Atom*, which was sailed twice around the world and about a dozen times across the Atlantic.

Some offshore sailors feel that the pointed stern is the safest type for running off before following seas, because there is no flat surface for an overtaking wave to strike when it comes from dead astern. The majority of designers today, however, seem to think that almost any kind of stern can be seaworthy if it is properly shaped. Overhang should not be excessive, and if the stern is a counter type, it should not be excessively flat, or it may pound. A vital feature of a proper stern is its buoyancy. An overly buoyant stern combined with a fine bow and deep forefoot may lead to broaching to or even pitch-poling in steep following seas, while a stern that lacks buoyancy may fail to damp pitching, or it may squat and be pooped by an overtaking wave. It is especially important that a double-ender be fairly full aft, because there is normally less volume in a pointed stern than in a counter or transom stern. Edward Allcard was pooped in his *Temptress* even though she had more volume in her stern than some double-enders, such as the "Tumlare" type. One advantage of either a pointed stern (but not an extreme canoe stern) or a transom type is the

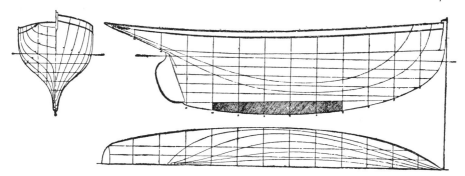

Plans of the Dixon Kemp designed Firecrest, showing her narrow, deep hull with plumb bow and overhanging stern, typical of the "plank-on-edge" English cutter type. She was 39 feet long overall and had a beam of only eight and a half feet. (Hawthorn Books, Inc.)

Alain Gerbault's famous cutter Firecrest in Le Havre, France, after her circumnavigation. (Courtesy of Yachting magazine)

allowance of an outboard rudder, which is a good feature on a deep-sea boat, because it permits some accessibility for inspection and repairs, and a rudder trim tab is easily attached for self-steering.

The heavy-displacement, double-ended type has a good reputation as a sea boat, but perhaps this is due primarily to its unusually robust construction and seakindliness. Disadvantages of the design are mediocre sailing ability, especially in light airs and to windward, lack of maneuverability in crowded waters, although the hull is usually quite well balanced for self-steering, and a less-than-desirable range of stability as compared to the typical modern yacht. Several of the double-enders have turned turtle, including the *Atom* (see Chapter 8) and the *Lehg II*. Granted, they were in extreme conditions that could have capsized any other craft of similar size, but where safety in ultimate storms is concerned, the higher the range of stability the better. A recent healthy development is the production of classic double-ended designs in fiberglass, which allows very strong construction but with a saving in hull weight that can be consigned to extra keel ballast. Three such designs are the "Westsail 32," produced in California; a 40-footer produced by the Colin Archer Club of Stockholm, Sweden; and the "Saga 34" of Norfolk, England.

Two other popular designs for singlehanding that are more modern but which might be considered classics, are the Folkboat and Vertue classes. Both these boats are slightly over 25 feet long with a moderate beam of little more than 7 feet, have transom sterns with outboard rudders, and have moderately long keels. The Vertue is heavier and is more intended as a sea boat, but the Folkboat has repeatedly proven herself offshore, and, although both craft have made very fast passages, the Folkboat might be considered the smarter boat on most points of sailing. The latter has considerable rake to her rudder, which results in less lateral plane and less wetted surface. There was a time when some sailors thought this feature was detrimental to self-steering, but this thinking is not so much in evidence today. In my opinion, a considerable rake aft often causes the rudder to operate more efficiently when the boat is heeled or rolling, at which times the resultant of force components working on the rudder is acting in a more lateral and thus more effective direction. It is also true that gravity tends to keep such a rudder amidships when the boat is unheeled. The really important concern with regard to self-steering is the directional stability of the hull, which is generally achieved through a reasonably symmetrical shape with somewhat balanced ends and an ample, but not necessarily extreme, length of keel, or at least a long skeg aft. Vertues and Folkboats have good directional stability, and in addition their rounded underbodies with slackish bilges and short ends make them comfortable sea boats for their size.

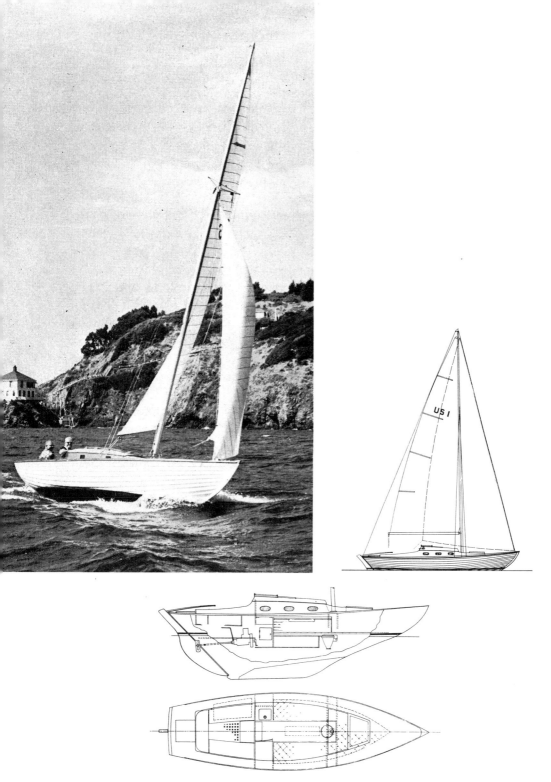

Plans of the handsome Folkboat, *which has made so many offshore passages. Her dimensions are: LOA, 25 feet, 2 inches; LWL, 19 feet, 8 inches; beam, 7 feet, 3 inches; draft, 3 feet, 11 inches; displacement, 2.15 tons; sail area, 262 square feet.* (Courtesy of The Skipper)

The Vertue was designed by J. Laurent Giles shortly after World War II and was closely based on his design of the gaff-rigged cutter, *Andrillot*, of 1936. Many of this class have made celebrated passages. Among those sailed singlehanded are the *Salmo* and *Speedwell of Hong Kong*, skippered respectively by A. G. Hamilton and John Goodwin; Dan Robertson's *Easy Vertue*; Dr. Joseph Cunningham's *Icebird*; and Ed Boden's *Kittiwake*; but the most famous of all is the *Cardinal Vertue*, which was twice sailed across the Atlantic in 1960 and later taken around the world via the "Roaring Forties" and Cape Horn by Bill Nance, an Australian. A wealth of detail about this class is given in Humphrey Barton's book, *Vertue XXXV*, which tells the story of his doublehanded Atlantic crossing and heavy weather experiences in the *Vertue XXXV* during the spring of 1950. Barton, who is a yacht surveyor and formerly a partner of Laurent Giles, suggests several ways of improving the standard boat for rugged offshore work. These modifications include a stronger doghouse and smaller unbreakable windows. Plans are shown in the book of a Vertue intended for extended ocean cruising, and she has slightly more freeboard than the standard boat, a lower, longer cabin trunk, and small round portholes rather than windows.

The Folkboat was the result of a Swedish design competition held in the early 1940s. The original concept had a long, overhanging stern, but later it was chopped off a bit to make a more seaworthy raking transom stern. Tord Sunden was responsible for the final design. Famous boats of this class include Hasler's highly modified *Jester* (already described), Valentine Howell's *Eira*, Adrian Hayter's *Valkyr* (Chapter 1), and Mike Bale's *Jellicle*, the latter having been sailed from England to New Zealand, for the most part singlehanded.

Very modern stock boats designed to take maximum advantage of the International Offshore Rule (IOR), which is the current dominating system of handicapping yachts for racing, are seldom ideal for offshore solo cruising. The reason for this is that such boats are designed primarily for speed with a full crew and also to rate well under a rule that is based on a series of measurements taken at or between specific points. This has tended to produce under the IOR a very-low-wetted-surface, "diamond"-shaped hull with considerable beam amidships, but with very fine ends. These boats are often given extremely short fin keels, which, together with the diamond hulls, result in poor directional stability in certain conditions. Other disadvantages are often a quick, lively motion; a bow that may have less than desirable buoyancy in head seas; and a keel shape that is not ideal from the standpoint of collisions with flotsam, grounding, or hauling out. Other deficiencies for offshore work found on many modern boats are: vulnerable rudders (either spade types or those mounted on weak, vertical skegs); large cockpit wells with drains that are far too small; little or no keel sump to hold bilge water; vulnerable windows; lack of a bridge deck or high companionway sill; flimsy construction; fittings that lack strength; and, sometimes excessively tall rigs. Despite some of these deficiencies, however, stock boats have been used successfully for singlehanding, but often after they have been modified and strengthened. Two stock IOR sisters of the "Aloa" class, designed by J. M. L'Hermenier, sailed successfully across the Atlantic in the 1972 singlehander's race, and one of these boats, the *Aloa VII*, was skippered by a girl, Marie-Claude Fauroux. She had no complaints about her boat, but the weather was moderate, and the "Aloa" is not the most extreme type. The rig is relatively small, and the fin keel is not extremely short nor is it sloped at the bottom. The rudder is an efficient one of high aspect ratio mounted on a skeg, but I would prefer that the skeg's leading edge be swept back a bit more for extra strength and less impact in case of collision with flotsam. The boat's ballast-displacement ratio is moderate, sufficiently high for reserve stability but not so high as to cause an excessively quick motion.

Desirable Features

This section will summarize desirable features for a solo cruiser. All of them may not be possible, or perhaps certain of them might have to be de-emphasized if the craft will be used for special purposes, such as racing, record setting, cruising in extremely heavy weather, but most features are nevertheless desirable and should be designed into the boat whenever possible, especially when she is intended for normal singlehanded cruising. For the sake of this discussion I have sketched a cruiser shown in Figure 3-5, that might be considered a happy compromise for solo passage-making at reasonable speed, in comfort, and with considerable emphasis on safety. The boat is not highly specialized, because she may be used for a variety of purposes. She will not be sailed singlehanded all of the time, and some of her life will be spent on inland waters as well as at sea.

This cruiser is of medium-size, about 35 feet long overall, because this size is not only reasonably economical, but also allows a good turn of speed with minimal handling difficulties, and she is large enough for ample stores, adequate comfort, and a high degree of safety over a wide range of conditions. She is of moderate displacement, not so light that her motion is excessively quick, nor so heavy that she lacks buoyancy or requires a lot of sail and heavy ground tackle that could be burdensome for one person to handle. Incidentally, I feel that a vessel's motion is of great importance to a singlehander, because it causes or at least adds to fatigue, and it increases the risk of falling (perhaps overboard). This boat's beam is fairly narrow

FIGURE 3-5: AN OFFSHORE SINGLEHANDER

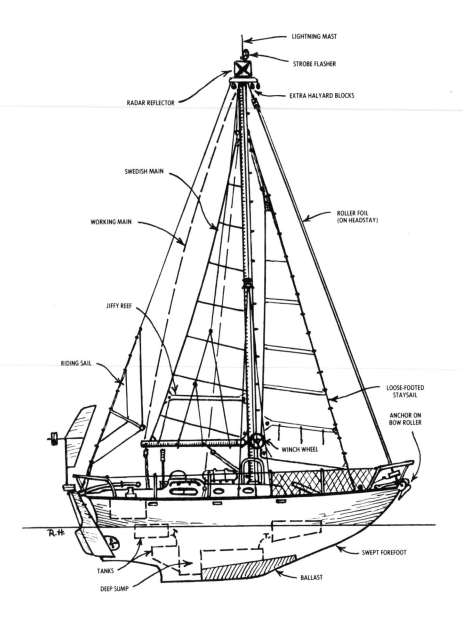

LIGHTNING MAST

STROBE FLASHER

RADAR REFLECTOR

EXTRA HALYARD BLOCKS

SWEDISH MAIN

ROLLER FOIL
(ON HEADSTAY)

WORKING MAIN

JIFFY REEF

RIDING SAIL

LOOSE-FOOTED
STAYSAIL

ANCHOR ON
BOW ROLLER

WINCH WHEEL

R.H.

SWEPT FOREFOOT

TANKS

BALLAST

DEEP SUMP

| APPROXIMATE | LOA—35' | BEAM—9.5' | DRAFT—5.7' |
| DIMENSIONS: | LWL—28' | DISPLACEMENT—17,000 LBS. | |

by today's standards to increase her inverted self-righting ability and give her an easier motion when she is rolling. The beam is not so narrow, however, that the boat is tender or overly subject to accumulative rolling.

She is fairly short-ended, because long ends tend to pound and may at times lessen directional stability, while a long waterline is essential to speed. Her overhangs are nevertheless sufficient for reasonable good looks and reserve buoyancy. The stern is a raking transom type, but the boat could be a full-sterned double-ender. Her rudder is outboard for good steering control (due to having a long arm between the rudder and the boat's turning axis), accessibility, and ease of using a rudder tab for self-steering. Her keel is moderately long for directional stability, but not so long as to produce an unresponsive helm. The keel's leading edge is swept back to lessen impact in case of a collision with a submerged object, but its bottom is fairly horizontal so that the boat will not pitch forward too much when grounded or slipped on a marine railway. Wetted surface is kept moderately low by means of the medium length of the keel and the cut-away lateral plane aft. This cut-away also affords some protection for the rudder heel during a grounding. Keel ballast is about 45 per cent of displacement, which should be ample for stability, but not so much as to cause an overly quick roll, since the boat has moderate beam and fairly slack bilges. Notice that some tanks are in the keel and that they are connected with higher tanks, so that at times, with a pump or gravity flow, the center of gravity can be moved slightly to modify, to some extent, stability and motion. There is also a deep sump in the keel for bilge water.

Freeboard is enough for reserve buoyancy, but not so high as to detract seriously from windward performance in a blow or make it too difficult for the singlehander to climb aboard the boat from the water. Regarding the latter action, it is a good idea to secure permanent steps to the transom, rudder, or elsewhere aft. The cabin trunk is well rounded, has small, unbreakable windows or ports, and there is a plexiglass observation dome in the companionway hatch which slides into a cut-out section in the hatch scabbard. The side decks are wide, uncluttered, and have a high toe rail. The cockpit well is small, but is as deep as efficient drainage will allow, because a singlehander needs all the security on deck he can have. There are numerous hand grips at strategic points and two pipe rails for security at the mast. Life lines are high and they support nets forward to protect the crew and prevent headsails from washing overboard when they are lowered. Although not shown, there are weather cloths or dodgers aft, open at the bottom for good drainage, and with heavy mylar windows for visibility. As can be seen, the boat will have an engine, because it can be most handy for battery charging and for maneuverability, particularly for a singlehander in crowded waters. The helm will be forward near the companionway so that the sailor can easily get below and reach equipment stowed just inside the hatchway.

Not a great deal will be said about the boat's rig, because this subject is discussed in Chapter 5, but a few comments may be appropriate here. It can be seen that the rig is what might be called a Bermuda cutter with the mast stepped almost amidships. This location inhibits pitching and provides a relatively safe location for working at the mast. A storm mainsail with its own track is shown hoisted, and the sail is dyed yellow for maximum visibility, particularly at night. The small staysail is self-tending, but boomless, because it is prudent for the singlehander not to expose himself to the hazard of being struck by a low boom. The main boom is quite high and short. It has a gallows frame, and its outboard end is well clear of the permanent backstay. A riding sail which will not interfere with the boom can be set on the backstay. There are mast steps and bright spreader lights useful for sail changes at night and which can be used for flare-up lights in the presence of ships. Notice, also, that there is a permanent radar reflector mounted at the masthead. Most halyards are led back to the cockpit, and there are lazy jacks to simplify lowering the mainsail.

Below, the boat has an L-shaped galley aft, because it is near the companionway, in a location of minimal motion, and its shape permits the singlehander to wedge and strap himself in. A chart desk is on the boat's opposite side, also near the companionway, with a quarter berth abaft it which can double as a seat. Just forward of the galley and navigation areas, there is a low bunk on each side of the boat. Of course, the leeward berth will always be used, but even so, it should be fitted with a bunk board, lee cloth, or safety belt. The area forward of the bunks contains the head, a work bench, and stowage space for sails and other gear. There could also be a couple of folding pipe berths forward for occasional guests or crew.

Many of the features discussed are obviously desirable for any boat, but they might be considered especially important for singlehanding. Extra care and thought should be used when designing, constructing, and rigging a solo boat. Of course, she should be strong, watertight, buoyant, and stable; but in addition, it is highly desirable that she have good directional stability, an easy motion, ability to lie-to comfortably, a layout that allows accessibility to gear from the cockpit, every possible safety device to avoid any kind of accident, and arrangements that make handling by one person as simple and easy as possible.

4 / PASSAGE PLANNING

Equally vital to the success of solo cruising as having a good boat is the care taken in planning a passage. This includes not only fitting out with proper stores and equipment but also, of course, selection of the ideal route and time of year for optimal weather and the minimizing of all hazards. Considerations concerning the route and time of a passage are the odds against storms, the percentage of calms and fair winds, the avoidance of ship traffic, navigation aids in coastal and inland waters, currents that can help or hinder, shoals or obstructions, fog and ice, the availability of good anchorages, and so forth.

Important Publications

Major sources of information for route planning are as follows: *Coast Pilots,* published by the National Ocean Survey, which cover U.S. coastlines; *Sailing Directions,* published by the U.S. Naval Oceanographic Office, which cover foreign ports and coasts (or the British Admiralty *Pilots,* having a very similar coverage); *World Port Index,* giving port information, published by the U.S. Naval Oceanographic Office; the U.S. *Pilot Charts,* issued monthly (or periodically in atlases) by the U.S. Naval Oceanographic Office, which show the average ocean winds, currents, storm tracks, and other important information; and the British Admiralty publication *Ocean Passages for the World,* which gives recommended routes, weather, winds, currents, and so forth. Obviously, charts and cruising guides of the places to be visited should be carried also. Two interesting and helpful charts for extended passages are the Admiralty charts 5308 and 5309 entitled respectively, *The World-Sailing Ship Routes,* and *Chart of the World Showing Tracks Followed by Sailing and Auxiliary Powered Vessels.* Of less value in the planning stage but important once the route has been determined are such publications as *Notice to Mariners* (prepared by the National Ocean Survey and U.S. Coast Guard), *Light Lists* (published by the Coast Guard and Defense Mapping Agency Hydrographic Center), *Tide Tables* and *Worldwide Marine Weather Broadcasts* (both published by the U.S. Department of Commerce), and *Radio Navigation Aids* (published by the Defense Mapping Agency Hydrographic Office).

Especially valuable are the pilot charts, for they divide the sea into five-degree squares and show the percentage of calms, gales, and the wind velocity and direction within each square. This information is based on many thousands of observations made during a period of more than 125 years, since the idea for pilot charts was originated by Matthew Fontaine Maury, the American pioneer in oceanography. Wind characteristics are shown graphically with the use of a wind rose in each five-degree square (see Figure 4-1 for a complete explanation). Short arrows of about equal length detached from the wind roses show the direction of the current, and numbers beside them show average current strength. Long, fine, unbroken, red lines show the tracks of some representative storms; while other red lines, made up of small circles, dashes, jagged marks, or dots, have to do with the limits of ice. Other lines and symbols on pilot charts show areas of fog, steamer lanes, lines of equal magnetic variation, lines of equal atmospheric temperature, location of ocean station vessels, lines of equal barometric pressure, limits of prevailing wind areas, reported icebergs, and more. Despite its great value in optimal routing and voyage planning, however, the pilot chart is not entirely a panacea for predictions, because it only gives percentages and averages of conditions that have occurred in the past. Offshore sailors should bear in mind the wisdom of H. G. Hasler, who made a remark to the effect that the winds do not read the pilot charts.

FIGURE 4-1: A PILOT CHART WIND ROSE

PREVAILING WINDS AND CALMS.—The wind rose, in blue color, in each 5-degree square shows the character of the winds that have prevailed within that square. The wind percentages are concentrated upon sixteen points. The arrows fly with the wind. The length of the arrow, measured from the outside of the circle on the attached scale, gives the percent of the total number of observations in which the wind has blown from or near the given point. The number of feathers shows the average force of the wind on the Beaufort scale. When arrow is too short, feathers are shown beyond its end. The figure in the center of the circle gives the percentage of calms, light airs, and variable winds.

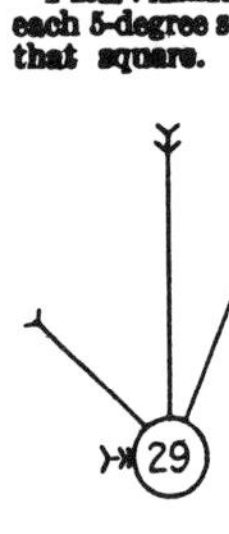

For EXAMPLE: The attached wind rose should be read thus: In the recorded observations the wind has averaged as follows: From N. 32 percent, force 4; from NNE. 20 percent, force 3; from W. 1 percent, force 6; from NW. 18 percent, force 2; calms, light airs, and variables, 29 percent.

```
0   10   20   30   40   50   60   70   80   90   100
```
SCALE OF WIND PERCENTAGES

In congested shipping areas, such as the English Channel or the approaches to New York City, the singlehander, especially, should make a careful study of traffic separation routes. These routes, which are recommended but not mandatory for ships, are found on standard charts and in navigation-related publications such as *Reed's Nautical Almanac*.

Global Weather and Currents

Most readers probably know about the general circulation of winds around our planet, but, for those who are uncertain of the basic pattern, a brief study of Figure 4-2 should be helpful. The illustration gives a generalized and simplified picture of the winds shown as they would be blowing if there were no land masses. The shaded bands are areas of high or low atmospheric pressure, with the concave hatch marks representing low pressure and the convex marks representing high pressure. The basic system results primarily from temperature differences and the earth's rotation. At the equator, where the globe is hottest, the air rises, leaving a belt of low pressure and calms corresponding to what meteorologists call the intertropical convergence zone (ITCZ) or equatorial trough, but more commonly known as the doldrums. Air that has risen in that region moves

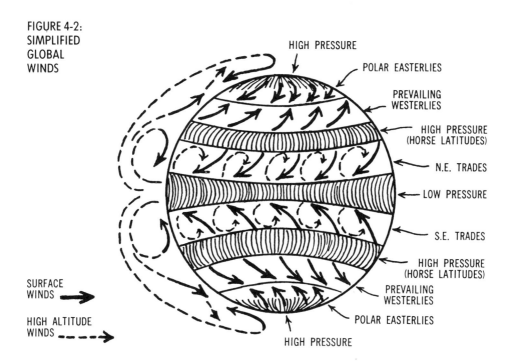

FIGURE 4-2:
SIMPLIFIED
GLOBAL
WINDS

HIGH PRESSURE

POLAR EASTERLIES

PREVAILING
WESTERLIES

HIGH PRESSURE
(HORSE LATITUDES)

N.E. TRADES

LOW PRESSURE

S.E. TRADES

HIGH PRESSURE
(HORSE LATITUDES)

PREVAILING
WESTERLIES

POLAR EASTERLIES

HIGH PRESSURE

SURFACE
WINDS ➡

HIGH ALTITUDE
WINDS ----➤

north and south, and much of it sinks to form high-pressure belts of light, variable winds, known as the horse latitudes, so called (according to one theory) because early ships carrying horses to the New World were often becalmed in those areas, and the animals were jettisoned when they died of thirst or starvation. The sinking air at the horse latitudes splits in two, with portions returning to the ITCZ to form the northeast and southeast trade winds. These are fairly consistent, strong, steady winds that were long used by commercial sailing vessels for trade, and hence their name. North and south of the horse latitudes the portion of sinking air that didn't return to the equator forms winds that move in the opposite direction to the trades, called the prevailing westerlies. Air that escaped sinking in the horse latitudes continues towards the poles, where it cools and sinks to form a high-pressure area and the polar easterly winds. The east-west components of the various wind belts are due to the Coriolis force, the deflection of a moving body to the right in the northern hemisphere and to the left in the southern hemisphere due to the earth's rotation.

The preceding description of the global winds is highly idealized and simplified, but in actuality, the systems are greatly altered by the existence of land masses and also the seasonal effect caused by the earth being tipped on its axis. The land not only blocks the flow of wind, but, more significantly, it causes uneven heating. As a result, fast-changing high and low pressure systems form inland, interrupting the continuity of the oceanic high pressure belts in the middle latitudes. These pressure systems add a circular, swirling motion to the winds in the region of the westerlies, and the wind tends to rotate clockwise around large highs in the North Atlantic and North Pacific Oceans, while rotating counterclockwise around highs in the South Atlantic, South Pacific, and southern Indian Oceans. The circulation of surface winds for the half year from approximately May to November is shown in Figure 4-3, while the half year from approximately November to May is shown in Figure 4-4.

These illustrations also show in a very general way, the location of semipermanent highs and lows over the oceans, the major wind systems, areas of variable winds, the position of the ITCZ, and regions of tropical storms. The most noticeable differences in wind patterns between Figures 4-3 and 4-4 are: the development of a closed (circular) and intense low-pressure system near the Aleutian Islands (the Aleutian low) during the northern winter and the strengthening of a low near Iceland (the Icelandic low) at the same time; the shifting northward of the ITCZ in the northern summer; and the reversal of winds in the Indian Ocean, China Sea, and north of Australia, which are known as monsoons. The latter are striking examples of wind systems produced by alternate heating and cooling of the land. In the northern winter, a high forms over southern Asia, and the monsoon

FIGURE 4-3: GENERAL PATTERN OF WEATHER AND WIND CIRCULATION
MAY TO NOVEMBER (APPROXIMATELY)

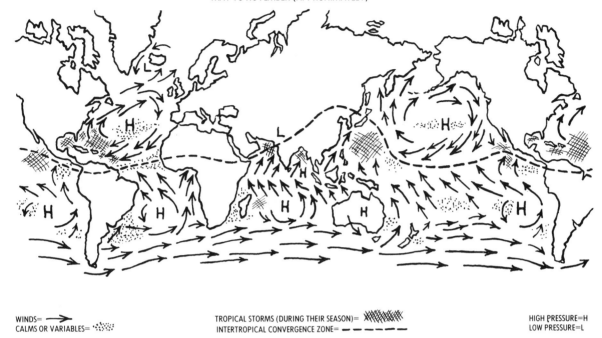

WINDS= ➝
CALMS OR VARIABLES= ∴∴∴

TROPICAL STORMS (DURING THEIR SEASON)= XXXXXXXX
INTERTROPICAL CONVERGENCE ZONE= ▬ ▬ ▬ ▬ ▬

HIGH PRESSURE=H
LOW PRESSURE=L

FIGURE 4-4: GENERAL PATTERN OF WEATHER AND WIND CIRCULATION
NOVEMBER TO MAY (APPROXIMATELY)

WINDS= ➝
CALMS OR VARIABLES= ∴∴∴

TROPICAL STORMS (DURING THEIR SEASON)= XXXXXX
INTERTROPICAL CONVERGENCE ZONE= ▬ ▬ ▬ ▬ ▬

HIGH PRESSURE=H
LOW PRESSURE=L

blows northeast toward the ITCZ north of the equator; in the northern summer, the heat forms an inland low, which draws the wind from the Indian Ocean high, causing the southwest monsoon north of the equator. South of the equator the monsoons have a westerly component in the southern summer and an easterly component in the southern winter (although at the latter time they are usually considered part of the southeast trades) due to the Coriolis force mentioned earlier. It is also plain to see that the westerlies of the southern hemisphere are unblocked by land masses; thus they are much stronger and more consistent than their counterparts in the north.

Some other, less noticeable differences between Figures 4-3 and 4-4 are the upward shift of the southern hemisphere westerlies during the southern winter; the building of the North Atlantic (Azores) high and the building (with a tendency to shift westward and somewhat north) of the North Pacific high in the northern summer; and a weakening of the Southeast trades in the western South Pacific in the southern summer partly due to opposition from the northwest monsoon east of Australia. It can also be seen that along with the seasonal shifting of the ITCZ, the trade-wind belts shift in a similar way. Their average limits in the higher latitudes shift from 25°N in January to 30°N in July for the northeast trades and 30°S in January to 25°S in July for the southeast trades. The trade-wind limits closest to the equator shift from about 2°N in January to 10°N in July (Atlantic) and 4°N in January to 12°N in July (Pacific) for the northeast trades. The southeast trade-wind limits nearest the equator shift from the following average positions in January: 0° (Atlantic), 4°N (Pacific), and 15°S (Indian Ocean) to July positions of 5°N (Atlantic), 8°N (Pacific), and 0° (Indian Ocean).

Cross-hatched areas in Figures 4-3 and 4-4 show the regions affected by tropical storms. They normally begin to occur in the early summer and become most frequent in the late summer or early fall of their hemisphere. These storms, which can be extremely dangerous, form over the ocean in or near the ITCZ. They drift westward, usually curve toward the pole of their hemisphere, and very often continue curving (or recurving) until they move in a westerly direction due to the Coriolis force and the prevailing westerlies. It should be emphasized that the illustrated regions by no means show the limit of areas subject to these disturbances, for individual storm tracks often proceed a considerable distance poleward, and they are sometimes very erratic. They are best avoided by cruising in the regions affected during the proper season only. Tropical storms are known as hurricanes in the West Indies - Gulf of Mexico - North Atlantic region and in the area just west of the Mexican coast; but they are known as typhoons in the western North Pacific and cyclones in the Arabian Sea -

Bay of Bengal - Indian Ocean regions. In the general vicinity of Australia and in the western South Pacific, they are called cyclones, but they are known as willy-willies off the Australian northwest coast. Although most of these storms reach their peak in the late summer or early fall and are almost nonexistent during the winter and spring, those in the western North Pacific can occur at any time of the year, but they reach their peak in August. The South Atlantic is free of tropical storms because the ITCZ in that area does not move south of the equator. Nevertheless, there are very strong winds called pamperos off the Argentine coast from July to September and sometimes later.

Although not as important to the offshore sailor as the winds, ocean currents are another factor to be considered. In a very general way these currents follow a pattern somewhat similar to the wind systems. North and south of the equator are the west-flowing north equatorial and south equatorial currents, which correspond to the trade winds. They are divided by a weaker easterly flow called the equatorial countercurrent in the very approximate vicinity of the doldrums. Farther towards the poles, there are great current swirls that rotate clockwise north of the equator and counterclockwise south of the equator, roughly similar to the way the winds swirl around the oceanic highs. We might consider that the North Pacific current and the Gulf Stream correspond with the prevailing westerly winds in the northern hemisphere; while a worldwide current called west wind drift corresponds roughly with the prevailing westerly winds in the southern hemisphere. The portion of the great current swirls that move toward the equator from the middle latitudes are the Canary and Benguela currents on the east sides of the North and South Atlantic Oceans, the California and Peru (Humboldt) currents on the east sides of the North and South Pacific Oceans, and the West Australian current on the east side of the Indian Ocean. Those parts of the swirls that move away from the equator toward the middle latitudes are the Gulf Stream and Brazil current on the west sides of the North and South Atlantic, the Kuroshio and East Australia currents on the west sides of the North and South Pacific Oceans, and the south equatorial current joining the Agulhas current on the west side of the Indian Ocean. In the northern part of the Indian Ocean during the northern summer, there is a monsoon current forming a large clockwise swirl that is a reversal of the circulation in that area during the northern winter.

Route Planning

The basic principle involved in route planning is to be in the right place at the right time for optimal winds and weather. The primary considerations are to avoid sailing into the regions affected by tropical storms during the dangerous seasons and to make passages in the higher latitudes during the warmer months (prior to or just after the end of the tropical storm season) when gales and extra-tropical lows, producing stormy weather, are at a minimum.

The classic routes around the world followed by most singlehanders (except for those who want the challenge of exceedingly difficult voyages) are the east-to-west trade-winds route, via the Panama Canal-Torres Strait-Cape of Good Hope, or the west-to-east route following the westerlies in the southern hemisphere. The latter is a lot faster but much rougher than the typical trade-wind route. In fact, a track that passes through the South Pacific in the latitudes of the Roaring Forties or Furious Fifties and passes south of Cape Horn can be positively dangerous for one man in a very small boat. Nevertheless, the eastward solo passage has been made successfully by such small craft as the 31-foot *Lehg II*, sailed by Vito Dumas; the 25-foot *Cardinal Vertue*, sailed by Bill Nance; and even by a 20-foot plywood yawl, the *Ahodori*, sailed by a Japanese sailor, Y. Aoki. The latter, I understand, suffered two capsizes. Of course, Bardiaux deliberately rounded the wrong way in his 31-foot *Les 4 Vents*.

If one were to attempt the easiest possible small-boat circumnavigation with a starting point on the U.S. east coast, he would leave for the West Indies in early June after the spring gales but before the hurricane season. It would be a good idea to hang around the West Indies where there are some protected harbors until after the hurricane season and then, in early November, to head for the Panama Canal.

Departing from England, a safe plan is to leave in August before the Autumnal gales, when the notoriously rough Bay of Biscay is relatively calm, and while there are still the fresh northerly winds known as the Portuguese trades. These will carry the voyager in minimal time to the Canary Islands, where he can wait until well after the end of the hurricane season before making a trade-wind passage to the West Indies and Panama Canal. From the Canal there is a relatively short but often quite windless passage to the Galapagos Islands. Moitessier and others recommend making the passage between December and February for the best use of winds and current. Continuing on to the central South Pacific, many voyagers stop at the Marquesas and then Tahiti using the southeast trades. These winds are usually fresh and steady in the eastern part of the Pacific, but in the western part unsteady winds are likely during the northwest monsoons from about November to March.

Starting the voyage from the U.S. west coast, some sailors might sail down the coast and thence to the Galapagos, but most will sail out to the Hawaiian Islands, taking care to stay in the southeast sector of the North

Pacific high. After a stay in Hawaii, the circumnavigators will usually head southward for the South Pacific Islands before or after the South Pacific cyclone season, which is approximately from mid-November until the end of March. Many voyagers with plenty of time wish to cruise through the South Sea Islands and perhaps visit New Zealand and east Australia, as was done by John Guzzwell and others. The most important consideration is either to avoid the areas affected during the worst of the cyclone season (during January, February, and March) or stay close to well-protected anchorages. It is also desirable to avoid the southernmost localities during the southern winter. Guzzwell recommended a February crossing from New Zealand to Australia for favorable winds, but one must stay below the zone affected by cyclones. A common route from the lower east coast of Australia to Torres Strait is inside the Great Barrier Reef, but it requires very careful piloting.

It is important to pass through the tricky Torres Strait when the monsoons are favorable, and, of course, where there will be minimal threat from willy-willies, which can form in the vicinity of the Timor Sea during the months between December and April. If one figured on an approximate three-month crossing of the Indian Ocean, a departure from the strait in June or July would provide the combination of southeast winds with the avoidance of Indian Ocean cyclones, which may begin as early as October. Although John Sowden reported an easy October passage through Torres despite having no auxiliary power, he had a lengthy stay in Indonesia and thus avoided exposure to cyclones at sea.

Obviously, the circumnavigator will have to decide whether he will travel up the Red Sea or round the southern tip of Africa. The latter passage can be extremely rough, but it is usually considered easier than the former. Among others, Al Peterson and Walter Koenig had extremely difficult trips up the Red Sea. Even when conditions are most favorable, between November and the end of February, when winds are fair in the lower half of the Red Sea, they are often calm and then northerly in the upper half. In addition, there is the heat, unmarked reefs, strong currents, often unfriendly natives, and so forth. Thus a passage across the Indian Ocean (via Cocos Keeling and Rodriguez Islands, normally) to Durban is most often preferred when the southeast trades are strong and when cyclones are minimal in the western Indian Ocean, from about June to October.

Rounding the Cape of Good Hope is seldom easy. Singlehander Jean Gau, who survived a capsize in that area (see Chapter 8), described the difficulties very well in an article published in *The Spray*. He wrote, "There is a reason for the bad weather in the neighborhood of jutting land masses. The greater the land mass, the greater the turmoil. As a result one can expect the worst off the 'Cape of Storms.' Moreover, in this region the presence of two currents, each one sweeping with great velocity in opposite directions, makes the southernmost tip of Africa one of the most difficult headlands to navigate. The westerly current along the shore is known as the Agulhas current. Nearer to the South Pole the Antarctic drift (west wind drift) runs eastward, pushed by the never ceasing westerly of these regions. It is amongst these perpetual storms that the highest waves in the world are to be found, particularly at the limit of the two oceanic currents where they reach the maximum height of 45-50 feet. By comparison, waves in the Pacific and Indian Ocean seldom reach more than 30-35 feet, those in the Atlantic 25-30 feet, while in the Mediterranean they do not exceed 15-20 feet. Fifty miles south of Cape Agulhas, in bad southwesterly weather the wind goes against the current and creates a very dangerous sea. The waves then have a tendency to become very steep when they meet an obstacle such as a ship. They break and fall on deck as heavy masses of dead water which can cause tremendous damage. It is one of those giant waves which on the night 26/27 February 1966 broke across *Atom*, causing it to capsize and lose its masts."

Despite Gau's gloomy description, though, the passage around Cape Agulhas and the Cape of Good Hope is relatively short, and a great many sailors have made it safely. Nevertheless, it is essential to be well rested and prepared, and a singlehander would do well to sign on a crew for the brief passage, although many have made it alone. The easiest time of rounding will most likely be near the middle of the southern summer when the weather is warm, there are good chances for favorable winds, and the westerlies, being farther south, are least likely to oppose the Agulhas current and create steep, dangerous seas. Favoring southeasters are common in the summer, but they can be extremely boisterous at times.

The passage from the Cape of Storms up the South Atlantic toward the eastern tip of South America is relatively easy. Once the southeast trades are reached, it is, in the modern vernacular, "a piece of cake" until the doldrums. A singlehander might want to break his isolation with stops at St. Helena and Ascension Islands, or he might take a more westerly course if bound for the West Indies and skirt the coast of Brazil. Jean Gau, who sailed the latter course, warns of the danger from floating trees, however, near the mouth of the Amazon during the rainy season (November-June). Of course, the West Indies should be reached well before the start of the hurricane season. A good time to head north for the U.S. east coast or for Bermuda, if one is going to England, is in May or June when winds have a southerly component and the American spring gales have diminished. From Bermuda to England, an initial course north of the rhumb line is advisable, because it is similar to a great circle track (the shortest distance) and gets one most quickly into the prevailing westerlies. Many stop at the Azores, but they face the probability of some head winds from there to England.

Race Strategy

One of the most common passages for singlehanders is that from Plymouth, England, to Newport, Rhode Island, not because it is an easy passage, but because it is the course for the singlehander's transatlantic race, held every four years and starting in mid-June (see Chapter 1). The principal difficulty of the course, obviously, is that it runs against the prevailing westerlies. There might be considered seven possible routes: (1) the far-northern, (2) great-circle, (3) rhumb-line, (4) Azores, (5) corner-cutting southern, (6) northern trade-wind, and (7) southern trade-wind (see Figure 4-5).

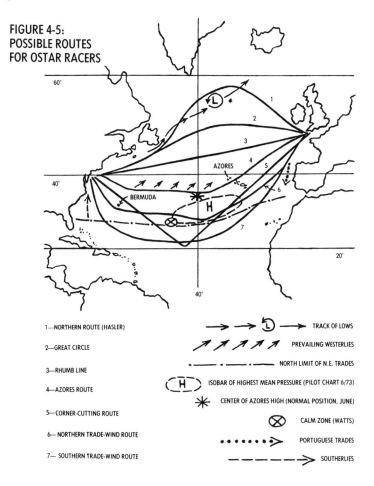

FIGURE 4-5:
POSSIBLE ROUTES
FOR OSTAR RACERS

1—NORTHERN ROUTE (HASLER)

2—GREAT CIRCLE

3—RHUMB LINE

4—AZORES ROUTE

5—CORNER-CUTTING ROUTE

6— NORTHERN TRADE-WIND ROUTE

7— SOUTHERN TRADE-WIND ROUTE

TRACK OF LOWS

PREVAILING WESTERLIES

NORTH LIMIT OF N.E. TRADES

ISOBAR OF HIGHEST MEAN PRESSURE (PILOT CHART 6/73)

CENTER OF AZORES HIGH (NORMAL POSITION, JUNE)

CALM ZONE (WATTS)

PORTUGUESE TRADES

SOUTHERLIES

The far-northern route is the one advocated and followed in 1960 and 1964 by H. G. Hasler after considerable research into the routes of early square-riggers and a study of the theories of Captains Hare and Becher. Hasler learned that many sailing ships leaving from Scotland and keeping north often beat those vessels sailing from the English Channel on early summer Atlantic crossings. Normally a procession of lows move across the upper North Atlantic from west to east, and they rotate in a counterclockwise direction. Hasler reasoned that if a ship could pass to the north of many lows, she would have a good percentage of favorable winds. His planned route in 1960 went as high as 55°N in mid-Atlantic, but he actually sailed even farther north. The strategy seemed to work quite well, as the *Jester* finished second in the first OSTAR race and fourth on corrected time (fifth on elapsed) in the second race (see Chapter 1). This was not bad considering that the *Jester* was only 25 feet long and carried a single Chinese lug sail, which is not the most suitable for windward work. There are, however, many drawbacks to the route, because it is considerably longer than a direct course; a fair amount of heavy weather may be encountered; there is often fog, especially in the vicinity of Newfoundland; the temperature is cold; and there is greater exposure to drift ice. Thus it is not surprising that the far-northern route is not popular, especially for boats that have good windward ability.

The great-circle or orthodromic route is the next most northerly course, and, nearly everyone knows, it is the shortest distance between two points on a globe, even though it appears as a curved track on a Mercator chart (the usual chart projection). The major drawback of a great-circle course from England to America is that there is a high percentage of head winds. In fact, the Admiralty chart for sailing ship routes shows a route just south of the great-circle course that is labeled "seldom possible." Despite this discouragement, however, many of the racing singlehanders, including those who have done well, have made passages that follow fairly closely to the great-circle route. In actuality, a true, great-circle course from Plymouth to Newport is not possible, because of the necessity of passing south of Newfoundland. Furthermore, the danger in that area from drifting icebergs makes it advisable to keep far south, perhaps as low as 45°N latitude or lower when nearing Cape Race, to reduce the risk. The average limit of drift ice actually reaches slightly farther south than 38°N in June.

The rhumb-line or loxodromic route is the one next farther south, and it is the straight line course on a Mercator chart. This course, too, gives a high percentage of head winds, but it is the next-shortest distance across, being only slightly over a hundred miles longer than the great-circle route. One minor advantage in sailing along the rhumb line (when winds permit) is that it is possible to hold a steady compass course, whereas with the great-circle route, the course must be changed continually. The usual means of determining one's course changes by the great-circle route, incidentally, is by using a gnomonic projection chart, which shows great-circle routes as straight lines.

The Azores route naturally passes near the Azores, usually between Flores and Fayal, then down about to latitude 36°N, and straight across, until turning more northward when northeast of Bermuda. Although this route is about 600 miles longer than a straight course on the Mercator chart, it has fewer headwinds on the average. One problem with the Azores route is that more calms are apt to be met. Actually, this will depend on the location of the Azores high, the center of which should be avoided, as the winds there are apt to be very light and flukey. According to the *Mariner's Weather Log* (published by the U.S. Department of Commerce), the normal position for the Azores high is centered near 35°N and 40°W during the time of the race. Sailor-meteorologist Alan Watts, however, mentioned a "zone of maximum calm at about 26°N and 48°W" in an article he wrote for *Yachting World* just before the 1972 race. Watts' calm area is considerably south and west of where one would expect to find the normal Azores high, but the high often shifts its position a great deal from month to month and also from year to year. Moreover, the isobar of highest pressure often covers a considerable area. Thus it seems that the chances of meeting some calms along that route are fairly high.

The trade-wind routes are, of course, much farther south, which adds a great deal to the distance but assures a much higher percentage of favorable fresh winds and advantageous currents. Eric Tabarly described what he thought was the most northerly practical trade-wind route as passing south of the Azores, down to about latitude 28°N, and then passing south of Bermuda before proceeding northward. This track, however, still passes into or near the horse latitudes, and so the risk of meeting calms is not a great deal less. A more southerly trade-wind route, down to about 24°N or a few degrees farther south, as recommended by the Admiralty *Sailing Ship Routes* chart, gives much greater assurance of fresh, favorable winds. The trouble with this plan is that the favorable conditions seldom justify the extra distance that must be sailed. It is a relatively pleasant passage and makes sense for cruising, but usually not for racing.

Alan Watts suggested the possibility of a corner-cutting, trade-wind course, whereby one would depart from the southern trade-wind route near the Azores and sail directly for a point at about 22°N and 46°W, and then directly for the finish. This course would theoretically get one below the mid-Atlantic zone of calms, and a distance of almost 900 miles would be cut from the deep southern route, but there are other areas of light winds, part of the horse latitudes, such as one near Bermuda, that might be difficult to avoid. In addition, the winds are not as fair and the current not as favorable when corner-cutting.

Simply put, those are the most essential factors relating to the weather that the OSTAR contestants must consider in planning their courses. The choice is not easy, because there are a great many variables. Although we tend to think of the prevailing westerlies as zones of somewhat steady winds, they can be extremely fickle in the northern hemisphere, as individual alternating low and high pressure systems and fronts move across the Atlantic from North America upsetting the regularity of the system. Quite often, there is a fair percentage of favorable winds where there are supposed to be head winds. For this reason, as well as the distance factor, the more direct routes seem to have paid off the majority of times thus far. Winners Chichester and Tabarly followed courses between the great-circle and rhumb-line routes in 1960 and 1964, while winner Williams was slightly below the great circle, and runner-up (on elapsed time) Dalling kept fairly close to the rhumb line in 1968. Winner Colas and runner-up Terlain were near the great circle in 1972, but the third-place finishers in 1968 and 1972 stayed closer to the Azores route.

In recent times, commercial ships and naval vessels often use what is called optimal track routing, whereby estimates are made of the most desirable routes that will avoid adverse conditions and minimize time for passage. These estimates are based on long-range weather forecasts translated into prognostic wave charts, showing the direction of waves, as generated by the winds, and isopleth lines, showing mean wave heights within bounded areas. Of course, wave information is of greater importance for powered vessels than sailboats, which are primarily concerned with the wind, but the weather forecasts and storm conditions are obviously important to sailors also. An OSTAR racer might profit enormously, for instance, by advance notice of an approaching low and its probable track, so that he could skirt its north side to get favorable winds, or perhaps head farther south to avoid it. Normally, a sailboat needs forecasts of the longest practical range, unless she has equipment that can receive updated detailed weather casts, because her passage time is relatively slow. The U.S. Naval Oceanographic Office and several commercial organizations give optimal routing based on five-day forecasts, but there is at least one forecast service, Irving P. Krick Associates of Palm Springs, California, that makes predictions for a month ahead. It should be kept in mind, however, that short-range forecasts usually insure much greater accuracy.

Ships will very often carry weather facsimile equipment that can reproduce up-to-date synoptic weather charts several times a day, but this gear is often bulky, expensive, and a great drain on electric power for a small sailboat. Nevertheless, Alain Colas carried a small facsimile machine, which he claimed was helpful, but two other competitors had problems with similar equipment. The previous transatlantic race winner, Geoffrey Williams, had radio communication with a shore-based weather service and computer, which gave him the best three of a possible 500 routes (according to one report), leaving it up to the skipper to make the final optimal choice. The 1972 competitors, however, were not allowed radio information that was not available to others.

One aspect of the strategy used by many of the racing singlehanders that seems rather puzzling is the fact that they often start the races with great gusto at top speed with the most suitable sails perfectly trimmed, whereas one would expect a racer to start off slowly and try to lull his rivals into complacency, giving them false senses of security. Then later, when out of sight, the racer could crack on sail and tune for all possible speed and possibly gain an advantage over a competitor, who is content to jog along comfortably, because he thinks his boat is faster.

Condition of the Vessel

A failure in gear, rig, or some part of the hull that might be considered a mere inconvenience aboard a fully-crewed vessel could possibly be a very serious problem for a singlehander. It is therefore the safest policy that the solo sailor's boat be given a thorough condition survey before she sets forth on a hard voyage. Some pains should be taken to get a well-qualified surveyor, who has had experience with the type of boat in question and the materials of which she is constructed. Two sources of obtaining generally reliable surveyors are: the National Association of Marine Surveyors, Inc., Box 65, Peck Slip Station, New York, New York 10038, and Lloyd's Register of Shipping, 17 Battery Place, New York, New York 10004. Even after the most thorough exam, however, it should not be assumed that the surveyor has picked up every fault. I have seen and heard of many defects that surveyors have overlooked. Thus it is most prudent for the owner to always be suspicious and keep his eyes wide open for possible troubles. Regardless of his technical competence, the surveyor should have sea experience, because only then can he have a full appreciation of the problems involved. As Ian Nicolson wrote in his book, *Surveying Small Craft*, "Anyone who has been through a big gale in a small boat is unlikely to make a slovenly surveyor."

Some of the more important hull features that should be checked on a fiberglass boat are the centerline joint when the hull is made from two halves, the hull-deck connection, sturdiness of bulkheads, security of chainplates, the stern and rudder tubes, thickness where fittings are secured, and areas of flexibility, especially flat areas in way of hard spots. Continued flexing in an area against which the hard edge of a structural member is pressed can fatigue and crack the fiberglass.

Take the case of singlehander Barry Nelson, who, in 1970, took a brief shakedown cruise in preparation for a solo circumnavigation in a stock 28-footer. Nelson had not gotten far, fortunately, when he heard the fiberglass crack, and soon afterwards his boat began to fill with water. He called for help and was promptly found by a Coast Guard helicopter, which lowered him a large-capacity pump. Later, a Coast Guard cutter took him in tow, but that action caused too much stress, and there was a massive failure of the towed boat's bottom. She sank so fast that Nelson had time only to save his wallet. Along with the boat, about $7,000 worth of gear bought for the circumnavigation was lost. The fiberglass failure was due to cheap, light construction, and considerable flexibility near a hard spot under a forward bulkhead. It is my understanding, also, that the boat's hull thickness was built up with liberal use of the "chopper gun," which simultaneously sprays chopped glass and resin onto the hull.

Let's face it, a lot of the cheap, stock boats, especially the smaller ones, produced today are not built for extended hard use offshore. In most cases, however, standard boats that are not too poorly constructed can be suitably strengthened by some of the following means: adding stiffeners in flexible areas; glassing over the bilge in way of thin, hollow skegs, which could possibly break off and cause flooding; bolting all fittings and connections; beefing up thin, vulnerable areas of the hull; strengthening the hull-deck joint; adding floor timbers and stringers in areas subject to great stress; strengthening and better securing the bulkheads; adding knees in the vicinity of chainplates; installing backing blocks under deck and through-hull fittings where needed; and so forth. Some details of fiberglass construction are illustrated in Figure 4-6.

As for boats built of other materials, it is important to inspect fastenings and weldments; sound thoroughly with a hammer for rot, voids, or wasting; examine carefully for corrosion and electrolysis; look for evidence of stress, unwanted movement, and leaks; examine for cracks, fractures, bulges, or dents; investigate any suspicious areas where there are misalignments, paint blisters, stains, or surface irregularities; and so forth. Regardless of the construction material, of course, such components as rudder, centerboard, mast step, partners, steering system, and all deck fittings should be thoroughly checked.

Special attention should be paid to watertight integrity. Check through-hull fittings to see that they are properly installed and that the valves are easily workable (plug-type seacock valves are preferable). Hoses should be attached with not one, but two, stainless steel hose clamps, whenever

FIGURE 4-6

HULL-DECK CONNECTIONS

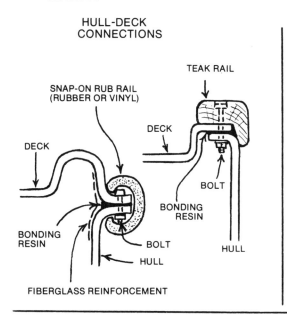

SNAP-ON RUB RAIL (RUBBER OR VINYL)

TEAK RAIL

DECK

DECK

DECK

BOLT

BONDING RESIN

BONDING RESIN

BOLT

HULL

HULL

FIBERGLASS REINFORCEMENT

FITTING ATTACHMENT

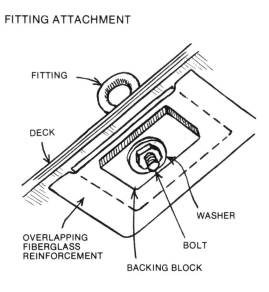

FITTING

DECK

WASHER

BOLT

OVERLAPPING FIBERGLASS REINFORCEMENT

BACKING BLOCK

FIBERGLASS HULL REINFORCEMENT (SUGGESTIVE OF LLOYD'S RECOMMENDATIONS)

HULL GRADUALLY THICKENED FROM AREAS A TO B, B TO C, AND C TO D. WEIGHT PER SQ. FT. OF D ABOUT 2½ TIMES A.

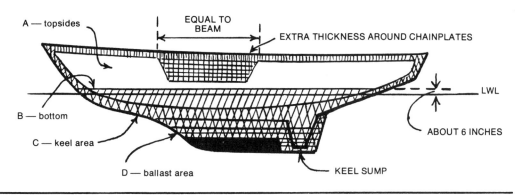

A — topsides

EQUAL TO BEAM

EXTRA THICKNESS AROUND CHAINPLATES

LWL

B — bottom

C — keel area

ABOUT 6 INCHES

D — ballast area

KEEL SUMP

HARD SPOTS AND TWO POSSIBLE REMEDIES

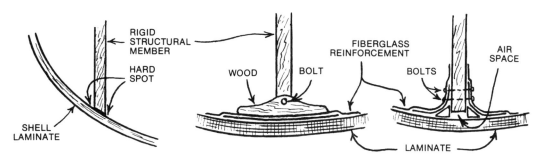

RIGID STRUCTURAL MEMBER

HARD SPOT

FIBERGLASS REINFORCEMENT

AIR SPACE

WOOD

BOLT

BOLTS

SHELL LAMINATE

LAMINATE

possible. Cockpit well drains must be large, and it is important that there be a high companionway sill and heavy storm slide to keep water from a flooded cockpit out of the cabin. Diaphragm bilge pumps are most often recommended, and they ought to be sturdy, large-capacity types, operable from below and from the helm. Windows must be of unbreakable glass or plexiglass able to withstand the smash of solid water on the leeward side during a knockdown. In fact, window frames and the entire cabin trunk should be of unquestionable strength. Likewise, hatch covers, dogs, and hinges must be capable of withstanding the heaviest weather. I believe that flush hatches are the safest kind. Be sure there are sturdy dogs on cockpit seat covers. There should be a means of blocking off all ventilators, even "Dorade" types, in the worst conditions. More than a few boats have faulty engine exhaust systems that allow water to enter the exhaust manifold from the outlet in heavy following seas. There should be a high loop in the line and preferably a cutoff valve at the outlet to prevent this.

The importance of a self-draining cockpit well of small volume cannot be overemphasized. On two occasions, I have seen keel boats with open cockpits fill and founder after knockdowns. Even if a cockpit is self draining, when the volume is large and the drains small, many boats can sink alarmingly low in the water when their wells are flooded. Commander R. D. Graham in 1933 made a singlehanded passage across the northern Atlantic and then from Newfoundland to Bermuda in the keel cutter, *Emanuel*, which lacked a self draining well, but he survived through exceptional seamanship, having an otherwise very able boat fitted with an effective pump, and having a great deal of luck. As the noted seaman-surveyor, Humphrey Barton, observed ". . . with her open cockpit there is no doubt that *Emanuel* was for a period in danger. A few heavy seas in succession bursting over the after part of the yacht would have sunk her."

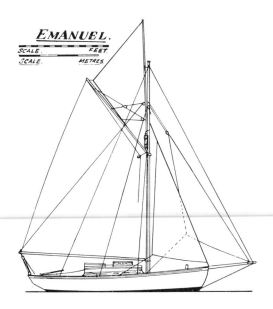

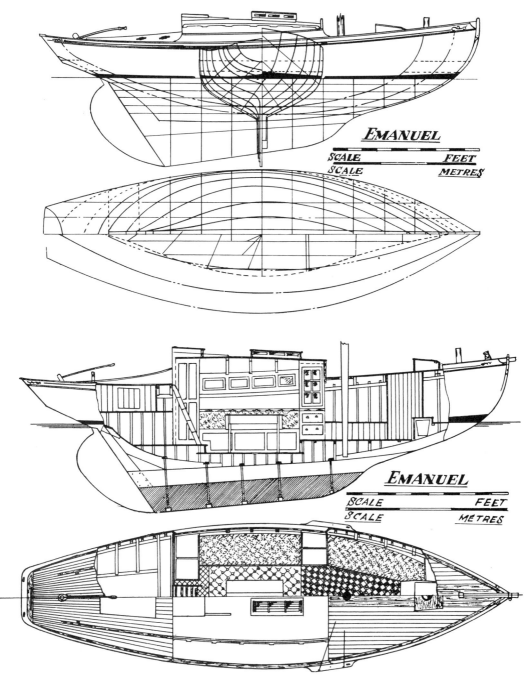

EMANUEL

SCALE _____ FEET
SCALE _____ METRES

EMANUEL

SCALE _____ FEET
SCALE _____ METRES

Above and to the left: Commander R. D. Graham's Emanuel, *which made a fast singlehanded crossing of the North Atlantic in 1933. The* Emanuel *was a splendid sea boat, but she lacked the important safety feature of a rapidly self-draining cockpit of small volume. (Photo from Wm. Blackwood and Sons Ltd.; drawings courtesy of the executors of Uffa Fox, deceased)*

One aspect of fitting out for offshore work, which is sometimes neglected, is the matter of securing heavy gear. Items such as anchors, batteries, tanks, and ballast should be fastened so that they cannot shift or come loose, even if the boat capsizes. As Edward Allcard has said, "Assume that one day the boat will turn upside down." When Eric Hall capsized in the Roaring Forties in December, 1970, while singlehanding his sloop, *Manuma*, he was almost seriously injured by a falling storm anchor he had stowed in the bilge. Batteries should have enclosed (but ventilated), acid-resistant boxes. A lesson can be learned from Valentine Howells not to lash the battery with lines that can shrink and crush the casing (see Chapters 1 and 5). There is a double reason for seeing that tanks are well secured, because a gasoline or LP gas tank breaking loose could cause a dangerous fire hazard, whereas a water tank could lose its precious contents. Incidentally, baffling in the tanks is important to keep the sloshing liquid from possibly bursting a seam. Take particular care with forward tanks, which are especially vulnerable to violent motion caused by the boat's pitching. Metal plumbing or fuel lines subject to fatigue cracking from moving or flexing should have their connections or vulnerable areas replaced with securely clamped flexible hoses. All loose gear ought to be capable of being stowed inside lockers whose doors have secure latches (not friction or magnetic fasteners). Fiddles around shelves are seldom high enough. If the boat has ballast in her bilge, it should be secured there, not simply wedged. Even ballast inside the keel cavity on some boats is subject to slight shifting, which in time can cause erosion. When the ballast is not bolted and consists of small pieces, it is a good idea to roll the boat violently to hear if there is any movement in the keel. Care should be taken to stow gear in lockers or the stern lazarette where it cannot fall under the handles of seacocks, fall against hoses or wires and possibly pull them loose, or become entangled in the steering quadrant and jam it. Cabin soles should be secured, but not so thoroughly that one can't gain access to the bilge at a moment's notice.

Wiring ought to be carefully inspected, because electricity is very often the first thing to fail during heavy weather at sea. Usually the problem is due to short circuits from wet wiring. See that the wiring is well secured, covered with waterproof insulation, and installed high out of the bilge, where it is least subject to becoming wet. It is vital that the wiring is protected with fuses or non-self-resetting circuit breakers to avoid overheating, which could possibly cause a fire or explosion if there is gasoline or LP gas aboard. Be sure that all switches are sparkproof. Incidentally, all wiring, piping, bolts, and, indeed, every part of the hull interior should be accessible. Quite often a ceiling or liner prevents accessibility, and if so, access holes should be cut, or else the liner or ceiling should be easily removable by loosening a few screws or with the use of a wrecking bar in a sudden emergency. See that the boat is properly bonded and grounded for lightning protection and the avoidance of electrolytic corrosion.

Needless to say, it is essential that the spars and rigging get a thorough going over. Rigging failures and dismastings are all too common, and these accidents are especially devastating for an offshore singlehander. Some important requirements are as follows: toggles at the bottom of all shrouds; a toggle at the bottom and top of the jib stay; the same arrangement for a permanent backstay if it will carry a riding sail; standing rigging a size larger than found on the typical stock boat; cotter keys rather than lock nuts on all turnbuckles; fairleads and keepers for all halyards to prevent them from jumping out of their sheaves; stops on halyards to prevent their eyes from being pulled into the sheaves; attachment of all halyard ends to keep them from going aloft; proper size pins and rigging fittings to prevent deformation or point loading and the shearing of cotter keys; all nuts and screw pins secured with peening or cotters; minimal holes drilled in the same vertical position on the mast; large holes (such as abandoned halyard exits) in the mast plugged whenever possible; all turnbuckles of the reinforced, open-barrel variety uniformly installed for ease of adjustment; tangs of sufficient weight to prevent bending or capsizing, and rigging pin holes drilled an ample distance from tang edges; spreader sockets extra strong (preferably not of aluminum); all metals on masts compatible or else carefully insulated against galvanic corrosion; wood spreaders inspected for rot and protected with ferrules to prevent splitting; spreaders positioned to bisect the angle they make against the shrouds and spreader tips securely lashed and wrapped to prevent chafe; sheaves a proper size and their diameters at least twenty times the diameters of the wire ropes they accept (see Figure 4-7); eye splices and tail splices carefully inspected and tested, especially when the latter run inside masts; thimbles for all eyes; the rejection of wire rigging that is kinked, corroded, or has "meat hooks" (wire snags); all rigging fittings (turnbuckles, toggles, swages, terminals, tangs, etc.) inspected with a magnifying glass and preferably with a dye penetrant and developer to reveal any possible hairline cracks from stress or corrosion or manufacturing defects; reel winches fitted with screw pin brakes and preferably winch wheels instead of handles (see Chapter 5); proper leads for all running rigging to avoid chafe; sail tracks through-bolted or otherwise securely fastened near the heads of stormsails; rigging installed to counteract the pull of stormsails; rigging designed to prevent excessive mast whip (double lower shrouds, fore stay, baby stay, or possibly running backstays); gooseneck heavy and designed to take stress when the boom is broad off; a proper main topping lift adjustable at the mast and able to double as a spare halyard; boom for roller reefing with a built-up diameter

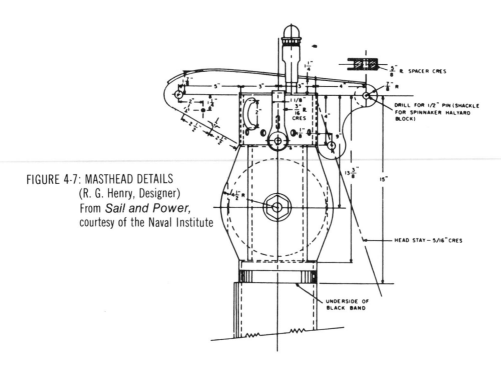

FIGURE 4-7: MASTHEAD DETAILS
(R. G. Henry, Designer)
From *Sail and Power*,
courtesy of the Naval Institute

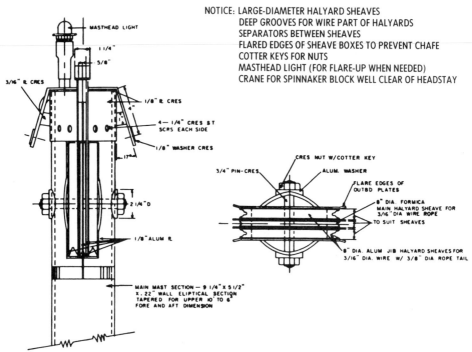

NOTICE: LARGE-DIAMETER HALYARD SHEAVES
DEEP GROOVES FOR WIRE PART OF HALYARDS
SEPARATORS BETWEEN SHEAVES
FLARED EDGES OF SHEAVE BOXES TO PREVENT CHAFE
COTTER KEYS FOR NUTS
MASTHEAD LIGHT (FOR FLARE-UP WHEN NEEDED)
CRANE FOR SPINNAKER BLOCK WELL CLEAR OF HEADSTAY

aft to prevent droop; a proper boom crutch, preferably a gallows frame; chafing gear, such as baggywrinkle, on offending parts of the rigging; a means of going aloft; turning blocks carefully inspected, because they must take double strain; all blocks extra strong and strapped; backstay insulators of the type that allow the shroud eyes to interlock in the event an insulator should break (see Figure 7-2); spars carefully inspected for dents, cracks, rot, or corrosion; electric wires aloft well secured and protected, preferably run inside the spars; adequate drains at the bottom of hollow masts; adequate tongue at mast heel and step deep enough to prevent any possibility of the mast jumping out or shifting; mast heel exactly square and fair to avoid unwanted mast hook; rigging designed to prevent compression bends (a minimum 12-degree shroud-to-mast angle preferable); sturdily attached masthead flotation with appropriate rigging on boats such as multihulls that can capsize and turn turtle (some multihull sailors would disagree on this item); head pendants on all less-than-maximum-luff-length headsails when they have halyards composed of wire with rope tails in order to allow at least three full turns of wire around the halyard winch when the sail is fully hoisted; stops on all tracks; a double track or switch for the storm trysail; weldments, riveting, or bolting of mast components examined for cracks, corrosion, looseness, and erosion; and all masthead fittings of substantial size, regardless of their weight and windage.

Further details of preparation for sea and boat inspection can be found in my earlier book *Sea Sense*. The American Boat and Yacht Council and Lloyd's Register of Shipping are two excellent sources of boat safety standards.

Provisioning and Fitting Out

In provisioning and stocking up for a voyage, a singlehander has an advantage over a large crew in that he need not carry a tremendous quantity of stores. Nevertheless, he must figure on taking longer to reach his destination than a fully-crewed boat would take, and it is of far greater importance that he is adequately nourished for the sake of good health, stamina, and physical fitness. It is probably better to overstock than understock, unless perhaps overloading will be very harmful to speed, because the lone sailor is less able to keep to a definite timetable. He might be delayed by a number of eventualities that would not so seriously affect a fully-crewed vessel.

Even in these days of vitamin pills, there is the danger of some ill effects from a long, steady diet of canned foods. Symptoms of scurvy are not as rare as one would think aboard small offshore boats. In his book, *Along the Clipper's Way,* Francis Chichester tells how one of England's most experienced yachtsmen, John Illingworth, developed more than a mild case of the disorder, and Chichester speculated that the first of the women solo voyagers, Ann Davison, also had some symptoms of scurvy, despite the fact that she took vitamins. Likewise afflicted was Vito Dumas, and he claimed that he might not have reached port had he not been able to dose himself with vitamin C. Singlehander Michael Richey wrote, "I have often wondered how much morale is bound up with nutrition, whether times of depression and lethargy are not the result of vitamin deficiency or even scurvy rather than psychological pressures."

Preventive measures against scurvy and other forms of malnutrition include not only the taking of vitamins and minerals, but also the eating of raw fruits and vegetables. Of course, the old anti-scurvy standby was lime juice for British sailors, hence the reason for their being called "limeys," but lemons have more anti-scorbutic value, and, according to Chichester, the customary ration of lime juice was the result of a mistake in language, because the West Indians called a lemon a lime. A small-boat voyager without ice is obviously limited in the kind of fresh foods he can take, but some excellent sources of nutrition that will keep well are: potatoes, onions, hard squash, cabbage, carrots, celery, garlic, oranges, lemons, grapefruit, and fruit or vegetables that will ripen after being picked, such as apples, tomatoes, and bananas. Dr. Hannes Lindemann, who made two Atlantic crossings, first in a dugout canoe (1955-1956) and then in a rubber-and-canvas foldboat (1956-1957), strongly recommends raw onions for the prevention of scurvy. Garlic is also valuable, he claims, for it keeps well under the worst conditions, and as compared with onions, garlic is a greater aid to digestion, although it contains fewer vitamins. Lindemann is also a great believer in the restorative powers of honey and red wine, while he thinks evaporated milk and beer are very important for calories and energy.

Clare Francis is one of many singlehanders who stresses the importance of high-energy foods. On her solo Atlantic crossing, she lost weight and became very weak until she began increasing her normal intake of carbohydrates. She recommends cake, honey, canned puddings, candy, and bread. Most bread will not keep for very long, but putting it in plastic bags with a desiccant will help a great deal. Of course, flour and yeast will keep a long time, and several singlehanders have baked their own bread, even in simple folding ovens.

Most singlehanders do not want to use refrigeration because of the electric power drain and the need to run a generator, which, of course, may use considerable fuel. Nevertheless, there are efficient holding-plate systems that can be operated by a compressor belted to the auxiliary engine, requiring that the engine be run as little as a half hour every other day.

Another system that requires no electricity but only a small flame to boil ammonia has often been used in rural houses, but it is seldom suitable for boats at sea because of the motion and heeling. Despite this, however, Marcel Bardiaux successfully used this type of refrigeration during his eight-year circumnavigation. His refrigerator's heating element, using kerosene fuel, was mounted in gimbals to minimize inefficiency caused by motion. From a safety standpoint, the arrangement should be satisfactory when only diesel and kerosene fuels are carried, but there could be risk of explosion when there is a continual flame low in the hull of a boat carrying gasoline or LP gas. Well-insulated ice boxes are perfectly satisfactory for short cruises. In fact, a large, portable, well-insulated, fiberglass chest with a gasketed top that is taped shut in such a way that the tape runs entirely around the seam will keep ice up to three weeks in temperate climates.

Aside from the picked fresh vegetables and fruits already mentioned, there are other nourishing foods that will keep for long periods without ice. Some of these are: nuts; cheese; rice; macaroni; beans (especially soy beans); lentils; cereals (wheat germ and granola); margarine; eggs; and dried fruits, such as dates, figs, raisins, apricots, and prunes. Cress and mustard have been grown by several singlehanders, but even easier to grow are bean sprouts, which can be kept in glass jars.

Fresh meat poses a problem, but animal protein can be supplied by powdered or canned milk (evaporated or whole fresh); salted butter; fresh eggs that have been greased or previously boiled for about 30 seconds for preservation; or canned meats, even though some nutritional value may be lost in the canning process. In addition, some smoked, cured, salted, or dried meats may be taken, such as certain smoked bacons, dried Burgundy ham, chipped beef, Lebanon bologna, meat immersed in brine, and so forth.

Fresh fish can be caught, of course, and sometimes fish can be eaten raw after being marinated in lemon juice or vinegar and onions. The plentitude of fish in the sea will depend on where one is sailing. Sometimes flying fish can be picked up off the deck regularly, but trolling at sea is often not effective. Robin Knox-Johnston says that a speargun is "essential." A novel means of catching fish is the method used by Alain Gerbault, whereby the circumnavigator used his own toes as tempting bait. He described dragging his foot in the water to attract a dorado and then spearing the fish as it sprang at his toes. The method could hardly be recommended for anyone with slower reflexes than champion tennis player Gerbault.

As for the water supply, the old rule of thumb is half a gallon per man per day, which is really ample for drinking, especially when beer, soft drinks, and canned juices are taken. The really important matter is to have the water supply divided between two tanks or portable containers in case some of it should go bad or one of the tanks should happen to leak through a rivet hole, seam, or elsewhere. Many voyagers have a catchment system that utilizes a groove on the main boom. This might be the groove that holds the slides at the mainsail's foot or a special channel made of wood strips secured to the boom. Usually the boom is topped up slightly so that rain water falling on the sail will run into the groove and forward to a bucket hung at the gooseneck. In some cases, however, a watertight hollow boom is allowed to fill and a plastic tube is led from an outlet directly to a water tank. It is important to let some rain wash the salt off the sail before beginning to collect drinking water.

Gear and portable equipment for long-distance cruising will, of course, include a very complete inventory of spares and tools. With his advantage of having more space for a given size of boat, the singlehander in anything larger than a cockleshell will have room for stowing almost anything he might need.

Portable gear and spares should include: heavy weather sails; fittings of every kind, especially winch handles, blocks, shackles, pins, turnbuckles, chains, and toggles; lines, sheets, rodes, and warps; emergency tiller, steering cable, rudder head fitting, and perhaps a substitute rudder; a stay or shroud of the longest length and an extra spreader; miscellaneous hardware and fastenings of every kind; spare anchors, including a drogue; sail stops, shock cord, and short lines; tackles, vang gear, preventers, and chafe guards; horn, lights, radio, and signal gear (such as flags, Aldis lamp, loud hailer, etc.); pumps, buckets, and bailers; bodily-comfort equipment, such as hats, sunglasses, awnings, warm clothing, foul weather gear, etc.; and, most especially, spare parts kits. These include: a sewing and sail repair kit (with thread, twine, marline, needles, fiddle, spike, palm, tapes, patches, beeswax, sail slides, hanks, sail shackles, leather, etc.); an electrical repair kit (with bulbs, fuses, electrical tape, copper wire, batteries, circuit tester, solder and soldering tool, radio parts, etc.); a plumbing kit (hoses to fit any through-hull fitting, hose clamps, spare parts for the head and all pumps, syphon hose, gaskets, nipples, packing, grease, diaphragms, flap valves, and tapered wooden plugs); a hull-repair kit (caulking cotton, bedding and seam compound, foam rubber, plywood sheets, common putty, cup grease, soft metal sheets, plastic steel, self-curing urethane putty, fiberglass tape and resin, canvas, epoxy adhesive, etc.); and engine-repair kits (gasoline engine: points, condenser, rotor, water pump, seal, impeller, distributor cap, coil, spark plugs, belts, etc.; diesel engine: injectors, starting-motor, solenoid, fuel filters, fuel pump, injector feed lines, etc.; and engine tools, such as gauges, spanners, and crank handle, a starting booster fluid, and lube oil). It is also important to carry spare parts for the stove, a patch kit for the inflatable raft, and, especially, extra parts for the bilge pumps and self-steering vane gear.

Some essential tools are: assorted sizes of screw drivers, pliers, wrenches, hammer, wood saw, hack saw with spare blades, wire cutter, bolt cutter, wrecking bar, hatchet, brace and bits, drill and bits, tin snips, chisels, files, plane, surform, clamps, vise, crimping tool for compressing sleeves on wire cables, etc. Pliers should include a large-channel type with adjustable jaws, needle-nose, and vise-grip. Important wrenches are: monkey, Stillson, end, socket, spark plug, and chain wrench. It is essential to have an end-wrench of sufficient size to fit the largest nut on the boat, and be sure to try the wrench to see that it will fit. One day I was caught out with a badly leaking stuffing box and found that my brand new, largest adjustable end-wrench would not fit, even though it was an identical size and make as a wrench used previously to tighten the gland. Later the new wrench had to be modified to make it fit. Apparently, there is sometimes a slight discrepancy between tools of identical make and model.

The ingenuity of some singlehanders can often overcome the lack of a needed tool or spare. Robin Knox-Johnston, for instance, made a clever roller reefing handle from a turnbuckle, and he made a feeler gauge for setting the spark on his generator by measuring off one inch of thickness of a writing-paper pad and counting the pages within the measurement. He found that two hundred pages made an inch, thus three pages gave him the required thickness of fifteen one thousandths of an inch.

Safety equipment and certain basic deck gear have not been discussed here, but they will be dealt with in the next chapter, which will consider the techniques of singlehanding.

Health and Survival Aspects

No less important than a well-found vessel is the singlehander's own fitness and preparedness for eventualities affecting his health. Although some fit young sailors set off with scarcely a thought about their health, it is certainly advisable for everyone to have a medical and dental check before leaving on a lengthy offshore passage. There may be considerable risk involved if there has been a past history of heart trouble, serious stomach ulcers, gallstone disease, suspected appendicitis, and so forth. At any rate, special health problems should be discussed with the doctor, and he should be consulted about medical supplies for the cruise. Two highly recommended books, written by sailor-doctors, which discuss first aid supplies and medical treatment when there is no professional medical assistance available, are *Advanced First Aid Afloat* by Peter F. Eastman, M.D., and *First Aid Afloat* by Paul B. Sheldon, M.D.

In addition to the usual bandages, gauze, adhesive tape, burn ointments, disinfectants, and other items found in first aid kits, there should be such supplies as: splints; hypodermic syringes; butterfly bandages; thermometer; catheter tube; enema gear; sanitary napkins (for serious cuts); dental kit; sutures; ace bandage; forceps; eye patch (Robin Knox-Johnston missed not having one); local anesthetic (Xylocaine, or Novocaine, and perhaps an ethyl chloride spray); seasickness remedy (perhaps Bonine, Marezine or Bucladin); ordinary pain killers (aspirin, codeine, or Talwin); severe pain killers (Demerol is often recommended); diarrhea medicine (Lomotil and Paregoric are recommended); laxative (Milk of Magnesia or Metamucial perhaps); and antibiotics (broad spectrum, such as penicillin, ampicillin, or Tetracycline, and special antibiotics for specific infections). Dr. Eastman's book deals with antibiotics in some detail. He also recommends two sulpha drugs for certain infections, Sulfadiazene and Azo-Gantrisin.

As Dr. David Lewis has warned, the singlehander must be careful in taking heavy doses of strong, pain-killing drugs that cause unwanted sleep or might adversely affect his judgment. At times, he might have to endure more pain than he wants in order to be alert during situations that demand careful navigation and seamanship. For a sailor who must stay awake, Dr. Sheldon suggests Benzedrine, but he warns that the drug should only be used for a temporary crisis, as continued use could result in cumulative fatigue and serious errors in judgment. It could also lead to hallucinating in certain cases.

Seasickness remedies such as Dramamine can cause extreme drowsiness in some individuals. The remedies in the previous list of supplies will rarely put a person to sleep, I have heard, but they may have different affects on different people and so should be tried when it is not vital to stay awake. In any event, it is important that serious seasickness is kept under control as much as possible, because dehydration can render a singlehander completely helpless. When repeated vomiting prevents the retention of liquids and oral seasickness remedies, an antiemetic, such as Compazine, can be taken by injection or suppository.

The old cliché, "an ounce of prevention is worth a pound of cure," is most appropriate for one who sails alone far from medical help. Proper diet and rest, of course, will help avoid many ailments. Wearing the proper clothing can avoid chills and overexposure that could lead to colds or various infections. Especially valuable are really waterproof foul weather gear (PVC or polyurethane-covered nylon is recommended), thermal underwear, gloves, towel scarves, and watch caps. Some singlehanders even carry wet suits. In hot weather, light clothing, wide-brimmed hats, awnings, and sunburn creams can prevent not only sunburn, but also certain skin problems and heat exhaustion (provided ample water and salt are taken). Other skin ailments, such as common salt water rash, can be minimized with careful attention to cleanliness, frequent washing in fresh water (provided the supply is ample), and the use of talcum powder or Desitin. Burns can be avoided with proper gimbals, pot holders, safe fuels, safety belts, and cooking while wearing foul weather gear in rough weather (John Letcher uses a long vinyl apron). Injuries from falls are best guarded against with sound safety practices and equipment (see "Safety Considerations" in Chapter 5). Exercise is vital to good health, of course, and the singlehander is usually active, but certain muscles and parts of the body are quite often neglected in small boats. Prolonged and continual sitting, for instance, may lead to drowsiness, stiffness of joints, and poor blood circulation, aside from the sore bottom known in modern parlance as "fiberglarse." It is well for the sailor to work out an exercise routine that puts to use the neglected muscles and keeps his blood flowing.

It is certainly advisable that the singlehander about to make a voyage give some thought to survival just in case he has to abandon his boat at sea. Basic life-raft requirements will be suggested in the next chapter under "Safety Considerations," but here some thoughts are presented on the gear that goes into the raft. Important items for a very complete survival kit are: signal mirror; flares (hand-held and parachute with Very pistol); orange smoke flares (for daylight use); small strobe light (the kind that is attached to a horseshoe buoy); freon horn; waterproof flashlight and spare batteries; dye marker; air pump and perhaps extra bottles of CO_2 for raft inflation; sea anchor; repair kit with screw-type wooden plugs for punctures; bailer; knife in sheath; fishing kit with hooks, line, lures, and a gaff or spear head; first aid kit with antibiotics, pain killers, and sea-sickness remedy; radio locator beacon; paddles; a short mast in two sections; radar reflector; a cloth (for sail, rain catching, or a spare canopy); emergency navigation kit with small plastic sextant, almanac, compass, pencils and pad, watch, pilot chart, etc.; marline; a coil of line; small tool kit with pliers, forceps, scout knife, wire, hacksaw blade, screw driver, etc.; life jackets; protective clothing (hat, long-sleeve shirt, etc.); sunburn lotion; Halazone tablets to purify water; matches in a waterproof container; plastic bags for distilling sea water by condensation, or a solar still; plastic bottles of fresh water; two sponges (one for bailing and the other for mopping up condensation); and emergency rations (including vitamin and mineral tablets, hard candy, yeast, canned milk, beer, pemmican, milk tablets, bouillon, garlic, peanut butter, raisins, etc.).

This sounds like a lot of gear, but most of it can be packed in a couple of heavy plastic ice bags (for waterproofing), and these can be put in empty sailbags containing a life jacket or two for flotation and stowed in a handy cockpit locker or in the lazarette. A sturdy lanyard should be attached to each bag. If any of the survival items listed are not kept in the bags, it is a good idea to write with indelible ink on each bag what is missing so that it can be obtained at once during an emergency.

A controversy has existed about drinking sea water ever since Dr. Alain Bombard made his celebrated solo Atlantic crossing in the inflatable rubber dinghy, *L'Hérétique,* in 1952 without food or water to prove that man can live off the sea itself. Certain French authorities on survival endorsed Bombard's theories, but many British and American authorities disagree and are adamant that a castaway should never drink sea water under any circumstances.

Actually, I think that at least some of the controversy stems from a misunderstanding of the French doctor. He never claimed that sea water could entirely replace fresh water as a drink, but rather argued that very small amounts could be drunk to augment fresh water or to replace it temporarily over a short period of time before dehydration has begun. He also reasoned that the amount of salt consumed by drinking sea water should not exceed the normal amount taken in when eating ordinary meals and using it for seasoning. He wrote, "I would consume the permissible daily intake of salt by swallowing it in sea water." Although Bombard admitted, "Everyone knows that sea water is dangerous," he claimed, "the essential thing, therefore is to maintain the body's water content at its proper level during the first few days before fish can be caught. The only solution is to drink sea water." But he warned, "It is essential not to wait for dehydration before drinking sea water." Bombard's fresh water came from catching rain, from condensation, and especially from squeezing the juice out of fish, which he did with a fruit press.

Dr. Hannes Lindemann, who seemed to make his Atlantic crossing in the foldboat partially for the purpose of disproving the Bombard theory, concluded that salt water should not be drunk unless there is sufficient fresh water on board. He wrote, "A small amount of salt water may be drunk as a salt replacement, but that is all."

Regardless of the controversy and the fact that some doctors feel Bombard has done more harm than good, the courageous Frenchman undoubtedly made some contributions. He demonstrated that it is possible to survive for long periods at sea without supplies of food and water (whether he did it because of, or in spite of, his theories), and, of course, that should give encouragement to all castaways. He showed that a sufficient catch of fish can supply a surprising amount of water (when a press is carried) as well as proteins and fats; while the eating of plankton, which he caught in a fine-mesh net, can supply enough vitamin C to stave off scurvy. Incidentally, Francis Brenton, who ran out of food while crossing the Atlantic in an outrigger canoe in 1967, also ate plankton as well as barnacles, eelgrass, and mushrooms that grew inside his boat. He suffered no serious ill effects

A demonstration by Joshua Slocum of his emergency still for producing a limited amount of fresh water. A fire under the bucket of sea water produces steam, which is then cooled by evaporation. (Courtesy of Yachting *magazine)*

from this diet, but it should be pointed out that many survival experts warn against eating plankton, because certain types have spines that may cause irritation, and there is a possibility that poisonous dinoflagellates could be consumed. Bombard caught fish with a home-made harpoon, and also had some success using hooks baited with flying fish that fell on board. He found that a light at night would sometimes bring "an absolute shower of fish."

In speaking of catching fish at sea, which can be difficult without the right equipment (a spear gun, for instance), some lessons can be learned from Poon Lim, who survived a record-setting 133 days alone on a life raft in the South Atlantic (1942-1943). Lim caught small minnows by baiting a hook made from a flashlight spring with a barnacle. Then he caught large fish, up to twenty pounds, on a large hook made from a nail, which he baited with a minnow. He put the large hook through the minnow's tail so that the bait fish remained alive and wriggling. For water, Lim caught rain in an awning suspended from four uprights at each corner of his square raft. Birds were occasionally snared when they lit on top of the awning.

In summation, a few general conclusions might be drawn from the studies of survival experts and the experiences of castaways:

Sea water should not be drunk unless, perhaps, a very limited amount (some say a pint a day) is drunk to augment an ample fresh supply. Salt intake should not exceed the amount normally consumed; and sea water should never be taken when a person is dehydrated. Even advocates of drinking sea water say that it should not be consumed for longer than five days at a time. When there is a lot of salt lost from the body through sweating, the occasional drinking of a limited amount of sea water will do no harm, and it may be helpful in replacing lost salt, provided fresh water is also drunk to clear the kidneys. John Voss drank a glass of sea water a day for his health, and Chichester occasionally did the same after a great deal of sweating in order to alleviate cramps in his leg muscles.

Fish, birds, and turtles are a fine source not only of fluids, but also of food. Their meat can be preserved by drying it in the sun. The eating of plankton is not recommended, as the risk of internal damage or poisoning is too great, thus an ample supply of vitamin C tablets should be carried.

If water is scarce, little, if any, food should be eaten, as digestion uses up body fluids. Some experts say that the consuming of protein requires the drinking of two pints of fresh water on the same day.

Sea water may be desalted with a chemical kit containing briquettes of silver aluminum silicate or with a solar still. The latter method seems most practical if room in the survival kit is limited. The still consists of an inflatable plastic sphere, which contains a black cloth that absorbs the sun's heat and causes condensation through evaporation of sea water in a storage compartment. The device is capable of producing about two pints of fresh water per sunny day.

Inflatable dinghies or rafts of heavy-duty nylon coated with hypalon or neoprene (synthetic rubber) are extremely durable, but they must be protected from chafe, as, for example, where the sea-anchor line leads over the bow. Dr. Bombard tells us that his dinghy needed slight deflation during hot days to allow for expansion of the air inside. He also thinks a wood flooring inside an inflatable dinghy is very important. Some of the better life rafts have an air chamber in the bottom for comfort and insulation.

Exposure and despair are the greatest enemies of shipwreck victims. Those who perish usually do so not because they starve to death or die of thirst, but because they lack proper protection from the wind, water, and sun, or because their morale breaks down, and they lose the will to fight for their lives. A canopy or cover and warm clothes provide the best protection from exposure, while the spirit can be bolstered with survival knowledge, having a definite plan of action, and keeping reasonably busy. Many standard life rafts contain (or at least should contain) survival manuals along with emergency supplies; and a pilot chart, with its showing of currents, prevailing winds, and steamer lanes, can be a splendid source for the planning of survival strategy.

After the castaway is rescued, he may drink a moderate amount of fluids but he must take solid food very gradually. Gorging himself with rich food immediately after the ordeal could cause serious illness, or even death.

A final word on abandoning ship is not to do it, unless it is certain the vessel is about to founder. Many times boats have been needlessly abandoned, because their crews felt that sinking was imminent, but days later the derelicts have been found afloat, even though their pumps were unmanned. Complete preparations should be made for abandonment during a serious emergency, but the actual drastic step should not be taken, perhaps, until the decks are all but awash.

Every offshore skipper of a fully-crewed vessel should take heed of Murphy's law, which states: "If anything can go wrong, it will," but for the lone sailor preparing to set forth on an extended voyage in rough waters, it will be most prudent if he thinks in terms of what my wife calls Henderson's law: "If anything *can't* go wrong, it may."

5 / SOLO TECHNIQUES

Successful singlehanding requires the highest caliber of seamanship. Not only must the solo skipper be a generally proficient sailor, but he should have, or at least develop, a good sense of order and care, extra vigilance, a high degree of patience, and considerable forehandedness.

The sense of order and care leads to an awareness of details in cruise organization; the recognition of correct procedures and proper sequence in boat handling; and immediate realization when any piece of gear is faulty, out of place, or subject to damage. Stowage and upkeep of all gear should be systematic and consistent.

Such orderliness and attention to detail, of course, must be accompanied by constant vigilance. The accomplished seaman has an ever-roving eye. He continually observes the sky; inspects his boat, rigging, and gear; and scans the water for boat and ship traffic and for flotsam.

Patience is important for a singlehander, because haste and lack of patience may lead to carelessness or oversights in boat management or navigation. Certain lapses in seamanship that might be inconsequential when there is a full crew aboard could well be serious for one who sails alone. A solo sailor should condition himself to taking all the time he needs to do a job right. R. T. McMullen, the famous British yachtsman who single-handed a heavy gaff-rigger in the 1870s, once declared in no uncertain terms that if an hour more were required "to take a perfect reef, another hour it should have."

Forehandedness has to do with the ability to anticipate, to know what might or probably will happen. I don't mean to imply that the successful singlehander must be clairvoyant, but rather that he should have sufficient knowledge, experience (which can be built up gradually), and familiarity with his vessel to perceive what problems could possibly develop. Then, of course, thought can be given to avoiding the problems and to coping with them if they should occur. Forehandedness is essentially planning ahead: laying out all gear that will be needed; stowing all supplies securely where they will be readily available; changing sails somewhat ahead of time; keeping well fed, fit, and rested in order best to cope with any crisis; and in general preparing the boat and oneself for any eventuality.

W. S. Kals, the boating writer and occasional singlehander, has given the sound advice that the best seamanship calls for an alternate plan. A good seaman thinks ahead and follows a plan, but he leaves himself an alternative just in case some unpredictable circumstance upsets the original plan. It is quite easy to see how this principle would apply to singlehanding in coastal or inland waters. If the sailor is headed for a certain port, for instance, and the weather deteriorates or head winds and a choppy sea should happen to delay his time of arrival until after dark, he should pick a secondary, more easily accessible anchorage as an alternative. Another example would be that when sailing into a difficult harbor entrance where the sails might be blanketed or strong currents could create a problem, the engine should be readied for instant use and gear organized for the possible need of dousing sails; or vice versa, if the engine were running but might not be entirely reliable, the sails should be ready for instant use. Likewise the anchor and rode and even docking lines should be prepared, for they could well be needed if something should go wrong with the original plan.

At sea, the alternative principle also applies. The offshore seaman carefully considers what change of course or tactic should be made in the event that he becomes ill, has major gear failure, or encounters dangerously heavy weather. These cases could possibly justify such alternative actions as heading for the nearest port or steamer lane or scudding before a storm rather than heaving to. As Kals reminds us, the great Captain Slocum changed his plan from an eastabout to a westabout rounding of the world after he had already crossed the Atlantic, which meant that he had to recross the ocean, because he was warned of pirates along his intended route.

A quality that every solo seaman should have is a healthy amount of wariness. Most singlehanders, especially those who cruise extensively, are bold and adventurous, for the occupation by its very nature takes a certain degree of courage, but the very best seamanship demands considerable caution. I remember when Eric and Susan Hiscock called at our home port, they stayed a day or so longer than they had intended because of a spell of threatening northeasterly weather. Actually, the weather was somewhat wet but quite mild, and most local sailors including myself would not have had any qualms about leaving for the next port at which the Hiscocks intended paying a visit. Yet the famous circumnavigating husband and wife team stayed put, not just because the weather was unpleasant and they were enjoying their stay, but because they were in strange waters in fairly uncertain conditions, and laying over was the sensible thing to do. There are probably few sailors who have covered as much of the earth with so few difficulties as the Hiscocks, and this is largely because of the cruising couple's outstanding seamanship, which includes an ample amount of caution. Of course the Hiscocks are not singlehanders, but they sail shorthanded, and their example serves us well.

Watch Keeping and Routine

The singlehander who cruises in coastal or inland waters from port to port may very often feel that what he does is relatively easy and insignificant as compared to the feats of the solo voyagers. This feeling may lead to his under-rating the problems involved. The truth is that, in many respects, coastal and inland singlehanding is more difficult than sailing offshore. The former activities normally require a much higher degree of vigilance and attention to the helm because of boat traffic and the imminence of shoal water. Then, too, the coastal sailor must be ever mindful of the possibility of being caught on a lee shore in heavy weather. Of course, the offshore singlehander also encounters these problems, potentially at least, when he makes a landfall, but he has much less exposure to them for a given amount of time under way.

When sailing alone on inland waters, it is important to keep a constant lookout. The helm can be left unattended while the sailor goes forward to sit in the shade or attends to one of the many chores that always needs doing on a boat, but he must condition himself to look around constantly for converging vessels, especially fast motor boats and steamers, which can approach so rapidly. He should not go below until well clear of all traffic and never remain in the cabin for more than a few moments when there are other boats in his vicinity. This kind of proper caution all but eliminates the possibility of sleep, and so it is advisable to make short runs when well rested from port to port. Of course it is possible to stand watch all day and night when alone, and many singlehanders have sailed for twenty-four hours or considerably longer without any sleep, but this greatly increases the risk. Not only is there the danger of falling asleep and colliding with another boat or running aground, but lack of sleep produces fatigue, which is perhaps the major (or at least one of the major) enemies of the singlehander.

Fatigue not only causes errors in calculations and judgments, but also leads to lethargy, carelessness, and downright laziness. The lazy sailor who neglects caution and attentiveness, who delays taking action when it should be taken, and who fails to double-check his seamanship and navigation, is simply asking for trouble. Aside from weariness and lack of energy, other symptoms of fatigue are forgetfulness and irrational behavior. The bone-tired sailor might, for example, strap on his safety harness and go forward to do a chore and then forget completely what he was going to do; he might struggle to stuff the large Genoa into the spitfire's bag; or wonder what's wrong when he tries to put his left shoe on his right foot. Very deep fatigue, of course, was discussed in Chapter 2, and it was seen that this can possibly lead to alarming and sometimes dangerous hallucinations. Stay-awake drugs may only increase any hallucinatory tendencies.

Although the inland sailor on protected waters usually has sufficient harbors so that he can make short runs and need not be seriously deprived of sleep, the coastal singlehander quite often is faced with longer distances between ports. In this case, he must sleep during an offshore tack or when hove to, if there is sufficient sea room. It is far safer to sleep during the daytime, when there is boat or ship traffic, than at night. Naps should be brief, perhaps no longer than an hour at a time, depending, of course, on the proximity of land, wind direction, weather, and so forth. A reliable alarm clock is a vital piece of equipment. As Bernard Moitessier can testify, failure of an alarm can lead to the loss of one's vessel (see Chapter 7). Of course, one has to be sure that he will wake up after the alarm sounds. It was reported that one singlehander during the 1972 transatlantic race carried three alarm clocks to go off in succession as a precaution against over-sleeping. It seems that prolonged periods of sleep are not really essential, and serious fatigue can be avoided with sufficient accumulation of short periods, when they include sound sleep and not merely rest.

When tacking offshore to snatch some sleep or rest, it is obviously important that the boat not change her course. Jean Gau, Harry Pidgeon, Vito Dumas, and other famous loners have grounded on coasts, because they were below when the wind shifted, or their boats failed to follow their intended courses for some other reason, such as the set of an unpredicted current. Wind shifts can be a real problem when vane gear steering is being used. Several partial solutions are: self-steering by sails rigged to flog or perhaps become blanketed and make a noise that will wake up the singlehander; an off-course alarm that sounds a buzzer when the boat strays too far from her compass course; an adjustable depth sounder alarm that warns of shoal water; or perhaps an autopilot that operates from the compass (self-steering systems will be discussed in the next chapter). None of these means, however, are a substitute for periodically waking up and having a look around. During the waking moments, there is the opportunity to check the compass course and lights, scan the horizon, read the taffrail log, check important gear, and observe the weather.

If the singlehander heaves-to for sleep, it is important that he know just how his vessel will behave and how much drift or leeway she will make. Of course this knowledge is gained from experience and trials in a variety of conditions. Heaving-to is normally accomplished by shortening sail, perhaps reefing the main or setting a storm trysail, and carrying a small jib aback (trimmed to weather) while the helm is lashed down. An easier method is to put the wind a little forward of abeam and then slack all sheets right off, but this causes the sails to flog, which is very harmful to them over a lengthy period of time, especially in a fresh breeze. Some singlehanders simply lie a-hull, that is lower all sail and let the boat drift beam-on (or nearly so) to the wind and seas, usually with the helm lashed down, when it is necessary to sleep and when continued sailing with the helm unmanned is too risky. An average boat lying a-hull might make as much as one and a half knots of leeway in moderate weather, but a modern boat with an abbreviated lateral plane might drift considerably faster in a blow.

When the drift is towards a shore that is not extremely far away, naps should, of course, be brief, and it may be advisable to put over a sea anchor. In fair weather, there is little reason for not using a type that holds the boat quite firmly, such as the parachute drogue or a large conic type, such as the old-fashioned cornucopia (see Figure 5-1). The famous small boat voyager and occasional singlehander, John C. Voss, invented a conic sea anchor that could be folded up for easy stowage, and this is also illustrated in Figure 5-1. For heavy weather, however, it may be advisable to use a drogue that allows more drift and affords more give to relieve shock loading, unless dangerously close to a lee shore, because a boat that is firmly tethered in such conditions may not be able to yield properly to the smash of the seas. This matter is discussed in Chapter 8.

Offshore, the singlehander can usually enjoy a more relaxed routine when he is far from transoceanic steamer lanes. In remote areas of an ocean, it is reasonably safe aboard a well-lighted boat to lead a more nearly normal life, sleeping at night and staying awake throughout the day. Although solo racers will awaken themselves quite frequently for the primary purpose of checking their course and the trim of their sails to maintain the best possible speed, the ocean cruising singlehander may sleep for lengthy periods at night, waking up only when there is a change of motion, unusual sound, or unwanted angle of heel. Seamen well acclimated to their way of life can often count on the alarm system of their own senses to arouse them when sails or gear urgently need attention. Many consider it safe enough to forego the alarm clock when far away from ships, but there should always be a radar reflector hoisted and bright navigation lights turned on. The question of what lights the singlehander should carry will be discussed in Chapter 7 under the section "Collisions."

FIGURE 5-1: SEA ANCHORS

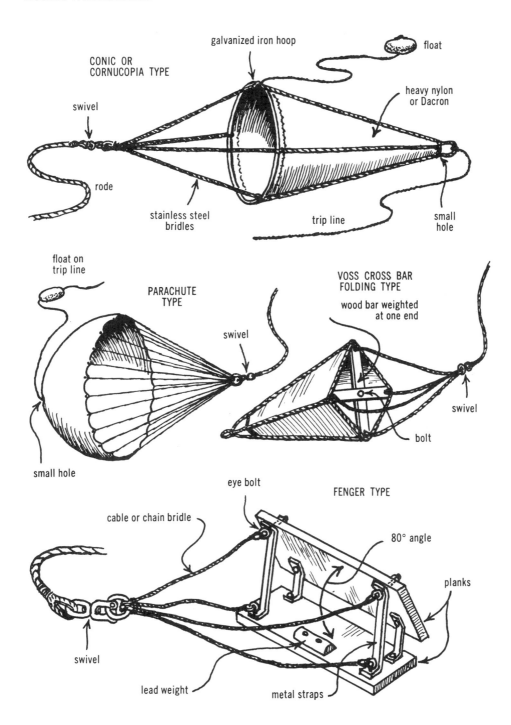

CONIC OR CORNUCOPIA TYPE

galvanized iron hoop

float

swivel

heavy nylon or Dacron

rode

stainless steel bridles

trip line

small hole

float on trip line

PARACHUTE TYPE

swivel

VOSS CROSS BAR FOLDING TYPE

wood bar weighted at one end

swivel

small hole

bolt

eye bolt

FENGER TYPE

cable or chain bridle

80° angle

planks

swivel

lead weight

metal straps

Aside from the matter of sleep and watch keeping, another vital part of the shipboard routine is meals. They must be nourishing and adequate to sustain strength and good health. Many singlehanders eat very little for the first few days at sea, presumably because of nervousness or seasickness. It often takes a few days to grow accustomed to the vessel's motion and to become used to the idea of being alone and completely self-dependent. Nevertheless, it is important to keep up one's strength and energy with adequate food. Also, if one is actively seasick, it is vital to continue drinking liquids in order to avoid dehydration. Of course, seasickness remedies are a help, but it is particularly important that the singlehander avoid taking a remedy that makes him drowsy before he has had time to sail clear of coastal waters.

For the sake of stimulating the appetite, it is a good idea to carry a great variety of food supplies. Aside from a wide assortment of canned goods, freeze-dried stores and even many fresh fruits and vegetables can be carried on extended passages (food stores were discussed in the last chapter). It is even possible to use refrigeration (see Chapter 4). Robin Knox-Johnston said of his stores: "If I were to do another voyage like this I would take a much greater variety of food. I relied far too much upon basics like bully beef and tinned vegetables, thinking that as long as I kept myself well fed I would not be too worried about variety. This was a mistake. I got fed up with the run of stews and bully and baked bean salads, and for several months ate less than I ought to have done through sheer lack of interest."

Food should not only be nourishing and varied but, as mentioned in Chapter 4, there should be some high-energy producers, such as honey, candy, and other sweets, because the singlehander is very apt to be extremely tired at times. Also, many singlehanders feel that there should be at least one hot meal a day and periodic hot drinks in cold weather. This is important for morale as well as the digestion. In rough weather, the single-burner "swing" type stoves that are gimballed two ways and burn sterno or lamp oil are a real blessing, and, needless to say, an unbreakable thermos bottle or two can be all but indispensable. Regular meals, with a breakfast, lunch, and dinner, seem to suit many singlehanders, but others prefer to eat only when they are hungry. Apparently an irregular schedule seems to do no harm, and the really important matter is a sufficient quantity and especially quality of food intake.

The rest of the daily routine for the passage-making singlehander relates mainly to hygiene and seamanship chores. Good health depends not only on food, rest, and sleep, but also on care of the body, which, of course, is vitally important for anyone entirely alone and beyond the reach of medical help. Minor ailments such as small cuts or boils should not be neglected because of the chance of a serious infection that could leave the loner partially incapacitated. Treatments should always be started early, and all preventive measures for possible illnesses should be taken.

Dr. Hannes Lindemann had a daily ritual (when weather permitted) consisting of what he called his "hygiene hour." At these times, he would strip himself of all clothing, expose his whole body to the sun for a short while, clean himself and remove all salt, treat himself for any afflictions, such as salt-water boils, massage and exercise any muscles that were not being used, dry his clothes, dust himself with talcum, and so forth. In regard to exercise, normal activities on a boat usually require ample use of most muscles, but certain muscles, especially on a cockleshell, may become partially neglected. John Letcher, who is an athletic singlehander and whose passages were made in boats larger than cockleshells, told me that he occasionally had problems with the weakening of unused muscles after a considerable time at sea, and he sometimes practiced calisthenic and isometric exercises.

Offshore sailors always have a great number of chores to do each day. Aside from regular checks of all parts of the boat and her gear, there is the normal cleaning, tidying up, putting things in order, and the inevitable repair and maintenance of equipment. Singlehanders often make a list of checks and jobs that need doing. A typical list would include such items as: oiling fittings; whipping or splicing lines; replacing a chafed line; taping cotter pins; drying out gear; replacing telltales; checking the bilge, water tanks, and batteries; rigging chafe preventers; repairing a flashlight; freeing up a sticking drawer; checking the steering vane; replacing a broken fitting; and so forth. In his book, *Gipsy Moth Circles the World*, Francis Chichester reproduced a typical work list, which he called his "agenda," and it contained seventy-one chores. He wrote, "This list is nowhere near a complete record of the work done on *Gipsy Moth* — it is rather a list of merely extra jobs. It omits all sail changing, radio work, adjustments to the self-steering gear, navigation, all regular work in the galley . . . Nevertheless, incomplete as it is, my agenda may give some idea of the human effort needed for singlehanded ocean sailing." Chichester's agenda may also convey the importance of self-discipline in solo passage-making. Carrying out all the necessary jobs promptly and in a careful manner not only is vital for sound seamanship, but also keeps one busy and provides therapy against anxiety, depression, and loneliness.

Rigs for Singlehanding

The suitability of a vessel's rig for singlehanding will depend on a number of factors: the size and displacement of the vessel; the purpose for which she will be used (i.e., racing, inshore cruising, normal offshore cruising, extremely difficult passage-making, etc.); and the size, strength, and age of the singlehander. A large, heavy boat will naturally require a lot of sail for respectable sail-area-to-wetted-surface and sail-area-to-displacement ratios. Such a boat will normally have a divided rig, since there is a limit to the size of a sail one person can handle. Of course, modern gear, such as the self-tailing, multi-speed winches found on contemporary yachts has extended the size limit considerably beyond the 500-square-foot maximum-sized mainsail conceived by Uffa Fox in the early 1930s (see Chapter 3). Nevertheless, heavy boats over the approximate length of forty-five or fifty feet will usually need to have their rigs divided into three sails. The most popular sail plans are the ketch and cutter rigs.

The larger boats having a basic three-sail rig will often be rigged as ketches, because with this rig the largest sail can be a manageable size without undue sacrifice to the total sail area. In addition, the ketch rig offers the advantages of a low center of effort for stability, ease of balancing the helm, ease of shortening sail in a sudden squall, a spar aft for setting a riding sail, and perhaps ease of setting up a jury rig in the event of dismasting. Disadvantages are relatively poor windward ability due to the mizzen being backwinded when close-hauled, blanketing of the mainsail by the mizzen when running, poor performance in ghosting conditions (unless, perhaps, the boat is very light or has a bowsprit which will allow an ample foretriangle for large headsails), greater maintenance of spars and rigging as compared with a one-masted rig, and often interference of the mizzen boom with a practical, high-aspect-ratio self-steering vane.

Concerning the latter problem, Robin Knox-Johnston had a complicated vane gear, looking much as if it were designed by Rube Goldberg, on his ketch *Suhaili*. It consisted of an elaborate metal frame supporting a vane on the boat's port side and another on her starboard side opposite the mizzen. Once during the *Suhaili's* circumnavigation, the gear on one side was seriously bent as a result of a knockdown. Sir Alec Rose solved the problem by omitting the mizzen boom on his *Lively Lady* and using the mizzen mast only to support a mizzen staysail. Of course, many large ketches, such as the *British Steel, Sir Thomas Lipton,* and especially *Gipsy Moth V,* with her unusual staysail rig, can have very short mizzen booms that do not interfere with the self-steerer. Bruce Dalling's *Voortrekker,* which finished second in the 1968 singlehander's transatlantic race, was able to have a minuscule mizzen and consequently a short boom by virtue of her very light displacement, which needed only modest sail area to produce high speed.

There are many advantages to the cutter rig for general-purpose singlehanding. The cutter provides a three-sail rig for easy management, but with only one mast. Sail is more centralized or concentrated amidships as compared with other rigs, and this factor often increases safety, because there is a wide working space with minimal motion near the mast, and the crew seldom has to venture onto the boat's extremities in heavy weather. Also, the mast amidships provides a wide base for efficient staying, while its weight in that location has a favorable effect on the moment of inertia to help alleviate extreme pitching. Another consideration that is seldom mentioned is the relationship of the centralized rig with boat's length of keel. Very generally speaking, a spread-out rig seems more appropriate for a long keel and a centralized rig seems more appropriate for a short keel. At least the boat with a very short fin keel may have problems with overly sensitive balance for singlehanding when her rig extends far forward and aft, especially if she has a bowsprit and overhanging mizzen boom.

Other plaudits for the cutter rig are windward efficiency due to high-aspect-ratio sails with effective slots between them, light-air ability because of the height of the rig and the large foretriangle for light-weather jibs, and heavy-weather ability for sustained beating against rough seas due to slot efficiency, pitch damping, and better mast support provided by the sails. Although the ketch rig enables sail to be shortened quickly in a sudden squall without sacrificing balance by simply dropping the mainsail, many experienced seamen feel that it is not safe to sail very long in heavy weather with a large headsail and no sail attached to the after side of the mainmast because of vulnerability to mast breakage. Of course, if the headsail and mizzen were dropped instead of the mainsail, then the mainmast would be better supported by the mainsail, but then power and ability to go to windward would be seriously impeded. In contrast, the cutter can reduce sail quite effectively and safely by dropping her jib, and the staysail with a slightly reefed main usually provides an efficient rig for prolonged windward sailing in a blow. Of course, the same would apply to a double-head-rigged ketch but her center of effort would normally be moved quite far forward.

Ordinarily a cruising cutter will have her staysail rigged on a boom, so that it is self-tending when tacking. It may be advisable, however, for an offshore singlehander to dispense with the boom because of the possibility, slight as it may be, of his being struck by the spar. With a proper sheeting and traveller arrangement, it is possible to make a boomless sail self-tending, but this may require an overly short, low foot on the staysail and perhaps a curved traveller. An ordinary double-sheet arrangement may be best for offshore work, because a boat is not tacked very often at sea. The boomless staysail with double sheets not only offers advantages in shape and fine-trim capabilities, but it will allow a slight amount of overlap, which will increase its power and efficiency.

For light-weather, inshore sailing where frequent tacking is involved, the singlehander will probably want to use a fairly large jib alone, without the staysail. In this case, it is well to have a removable staysail stay that can be released from the deck and brought aft to the mast where it will not interfere with the jib when tacking. This might be accomplished with a quick-release lever or with a slide on a centerline track (see Figure 5-2). The latter arrangement has an advantage in that the singlehander can control the operation from the cockpit. A line leading from the slide to a block just forward of the fore end of the track and thence back to a winch near the cockpit pulls the stay forward to set it up taut, and a piece of heavy shock cord can be rigged to pull the stay aft when the hauling line is slacked. A disadvantage of this plan is that there is a fair amount of clutter on the foredeck over which the sailor could possibly trip when he goes forward in the dark.

The quick-release lever necessitates a trip to the foredeck when the stay is released or set up, but the deck is relatively uncluttered. Several kinds of levers are available, but the one illustrated with the lever held to the stay with a slip ring seems very practical, because it avoids the weaker arrangement of a sheave for the stay and also a lever that lies on the deck when the stay is set up (as with the Highfield lever). A possible drawback in having the lever secure alongside the stay is that the staysail's tack must be high, especially when there is a lower turnbuckle; in any case, for the sake of visibility, the singlehander should always raise the foot of his jib or staysail, using a tack pendant if necessary. Incidentally, turnbuckles are very occasionally carried aloft for one reason or another, but I dislike this practice because of the difficulty of making adjustments and inspections. It is particularly advisable for the solo sailor to have his turnbuckles near the deck.

Two famous cutters used for singlehanding are Frank Casper's *Elsie* and James Crawford's *Angantyr*. The latter is over 60 feet long, displaces 35 tons, and carries 1,647 square feet of sail, and she demonstrates how handy the cutter rig can be even for such a large, heavy vessel. Crawford has sailed his boat solo across the Atlantic, and he occasionally manages her alone with apparent ease on crowded inland waters. I once saw the *Angantyr* with only one man aboard beat to windward under full sail through a small, crowded anchorage during a popular regatta. She seemed to weave her way through the anchored fleet of yachts and come about between them with no trouble at all. Of course, such boat handling is as much due to the skill and experience of the skipper as it is to the qualities of the vessel, her rig, and her gear.

The *Elsie* is much smaller, less than 28 feet on the waterline, but she is quite heavy for her size, and Frank Casper finds her cutter rig, with the mast nearly amidships, a very handy arrangement. He likes the large fore-

FIGURE 5-2:
SLIDING FORESTAY
AND RELEASE

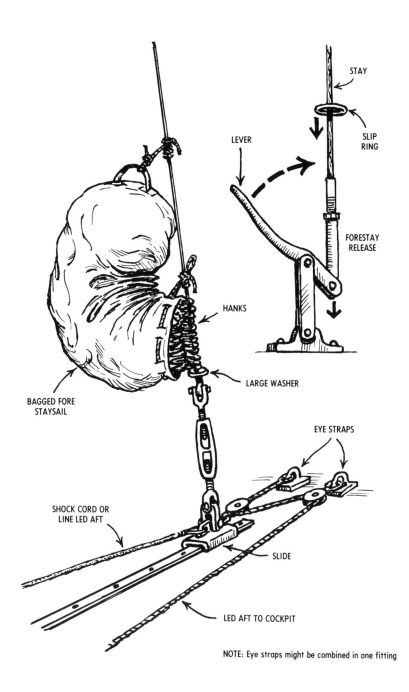

STAY

LEVER

SLIP
RING

FORESTAY
RELEASE

HANKS

LARGE WASHER

BAGGED FORE
STAYSAIL

EYE STRAPS

SHOCK CORD OR
LINE LED AFT

SLIDE

LED AFT TO COCKPIT

NOTE: Eye straps might be combined in one fitting

triangle for light-air jibs, and he told me that he finds the staysail very useful for self-steering (more will be said about this in the next chapter).

The sloop rig is probably more suitable for small boats of light displacement, however, because in the smaller sail sizes two sails are normally more efficient and manageable for a singlehander than are three sails. Furthermore, the sloop rig avoids the backwind problem with regard to the mizzen on a yawl or ketch, and it also avoids the problem of the staysail stay interfering with shifting large jibs when tacking on a cutter.

Extremely large boats may need three masts in order to divide the total sail area into sails of a manageable size. A prime example, of course, is the huge *Vendredi 13*, which carries three masts of equal size and three boomed staysails. This rig has certain practical advantages for one person on such an enormous boat, but it certainly lacks efficiency. In fact, H. G. Hasler called it "desperately inefficient, even to windward, with a quite excessive amount of mast and rigging for her sail area." Another drawback of the rig, aside from its lack of area and power in light airs, is the lack of efficient slots and disadvantageous upwash effect (bending of streamlines) due to the sails being so far apart. John C. Voss used a somewhat similar rig (ex-

Frank Casper at the helm of his sturdy double-ender Elsie, *which he has sailed around the world, singlehanded almost the entire way, and many times solo across the Atlantic. The* Elsie *has a high-aspect-ratio cutter rig that has advantages not always realized. (Harold Chasalow photo)*

In the rather special case of the Nootkan canoe Tilikum, *sometimes singlehanded by John C. Voss, the three-masted rig made a good deal of sense, partly because of her lack of stability and her ability to lie to a sea anchor with a riding sail set. (Courtesy of Provincial Archives, Victoria, B.C.)*

cept that his after sails were set on the masts rather than on stays) on his small Nootkan canoe, the *Tilikum*. In the vast majority of cases, the three-masted schooner rig is most unsuitable for small boats, but for the *Tilikum* there were some special advantages. She was very narrow and relatively unstable, thus she needed a sail plan with the lowest possible center of effort. In addition, she was the type of boat that would lie to a sea anchor streamed from her bow, and this often necessitated a riding sail which could conveniently be set on the aftermost mast. Another consideration was that she carried no self-steering gear, and so her spread-out rig provided a versatile sail plan for varying the boat's balance.

A rig that is especially suitable for singlehanded cruising is the ancient Chinese lug rig, as adopted and modernized by H. G. Hasler and Jock McLeod. Hasler's Folkboat, *Jester*, and the central-control-point concept were discussed in Chapter 3. The capability of handling all sailing evolutions from a single hatch was made possible by his experimentations with the Chinese lug concept on the *Jester* in the late 1950s. The type of rig he developed, illustrated in Figure 5-3, is basically a lug sail with full-length battens and multiple sheets to lessen sail twist and assist in reefing. It is a balanced sail, that is to say, its leading edge is somewhat forward of the mast, and this keeps the center of effort inboard to prevent weather helm when the sheets are started as shown in Figure 5-3. The sail illustrated is a more modern version than that used on the *Jester*, as the battens are all about the same length and the upper spar is peaked up higher for better

FIGURE 5-3: MODIFIED CHINESE LUG RIG

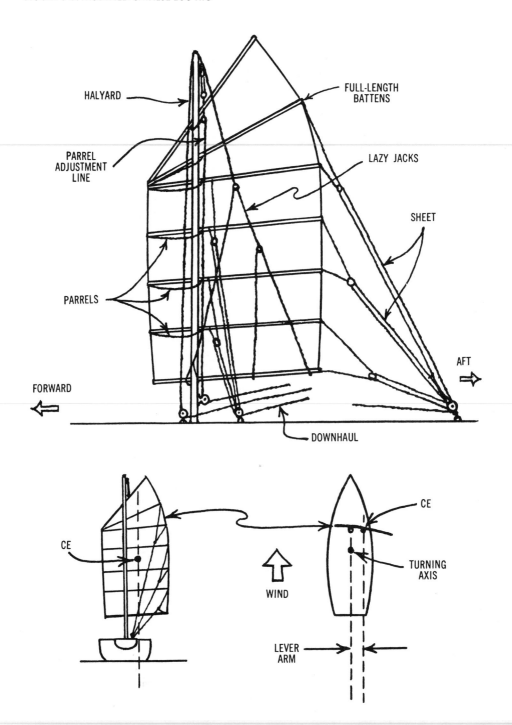

HALYARD

FULL-LENGTH
BATTENS

PARREL
ADJUSTMENT
LINE

LAZY JACKS

SHEET

PARRELS

AFT

FORWARD

DOWNHAUL

CE

CE

WIND

TURNING
AXIS

LEVER
ARM

efficiency to windward. Some of Hasler's and McLeod's newest sails have less balance, but they are usually used on two-masted schooner rigs, which minimize the problem of the center of effort moving outboard with well-started sheets, because the sails for the two-masted rig are narrower than that for the one-masted rig, and because a schooner sometimes can be sailed downwind wing-and-wing.

With the modern Chinese lug concept, the singlehander can hoist, trim, reef, and lower his sail by adjusting four lines led to his control station (see Figure 5-3). The normal procedure for reefing is to slack the halyard, which drops the lower battens down on the boom. The reefed portion of the sail is collected by lazy jacks, and the battens are held securely by tightening the downhaul and sheet. In some cases it may be necessary to adjust the parrel line also.

Despite the great convenience of this rig for singlehanding, there are some drawbacks. It lacks the speed in light airs and the weatherliness of modern Marconi rigs, and it might not be desirable for a singlehander who will sail his boat alone only part of the time. Another possible disadvantage is that the Hasler rig lacks stays and shrouds, which permits the mast to whip a great deal in some conditions. Although the lack of standing rigging prevents compression loading, a few of these masts have broken (see Chapter 7). An American designer who uses the Chinese rig, Thomas Colvin, prefers standing rigging carried fairly slack on his boats as a safeguard

Balance is easily achieved with the two-masted Chinese lug rig. This boat, the transom-stern dory, Erik the Red, *was built and sailed solo across the Atlantic by Donald Ridler. (From* Erik the Red *by Donald Ridler, William Kimber and Co., Ltd.)*

against mast breakage. It seems that the longer stayless masts have had the most problems with failures. The *Jester*, with her relatively short spar, has never had any mast trouble during seven Atlantic crossings in every kind of weather. Modern technology may provide the answer for large stayless masts. Dick Newick, designer of fast multihulls (*Cheers*, etc.) is presently making a lightweight mast of Kevlar, carbon fiber, and epoxy which he expects will have ample strength without standing rigging.

A minor problem with the Chinese rig is that there is an enormous pile-up of rope tails when the sheets are trimmed, and these can get under foot and possibly become fouled. One offshore singlehander, Colin Darroch, solved the problem by installing spring-loaded anchor rode reels for his sheets, and they would not only stow the slack line, but also, with the sheets cast off their cleats, would automatically slack and trim the sheets in gusty winds.

Before Hasler developed the Chinese rig he used in the 1960 transatlantic race, he also experimented with the Ljungstrom rig, which was patented in 1938. This rig uses a rotating mast having twin sails that lie together when beating and reaching but which spread apart and can be wung out on opposite sides of the boat when running. The sails are boomless, and they are wound up on the rotating mast when they are furled or reefed. Hasler modified the Ljungstrom plan to what he called a "lapwing rig" by adding two identical cantilevered booms to the twin sails. The system had some merits, but he finally rejected it for extended offshore work, primarily because of air becoming trapped under the sail and consequent ballooning when it was wound up on the mast in a strong wind.

Sail Handling Systems

One of the greatest problems for the singlehander is reefing and changing sails. Even casual cruising requires that different headsails of suitable size and cut be set for various strengths of wind, and, of course, mainsails and mizzens must be reduced or changed in heavy weather.

In current yacht racing the so called "jiffy" reef has become very popular, on American waters at least. This is merely a simplified, quick version of conventional "points" reefing except that the tack and clew reef cringles only are secured to the boom, and there are no points to tie up the bunt of the sail. Occasionally, a wire running between the two cringles is sewn into the sail to help remove excess draft (see Figure 5-4). The tack cringle is generally attached to a hook at the gooseneck, and the clew cringle is held by a single stout line which runs from an eye strap on one side of the boom, up through the cringle, down through a cheek block on the opposite

FIGURE 5-4: REEFING

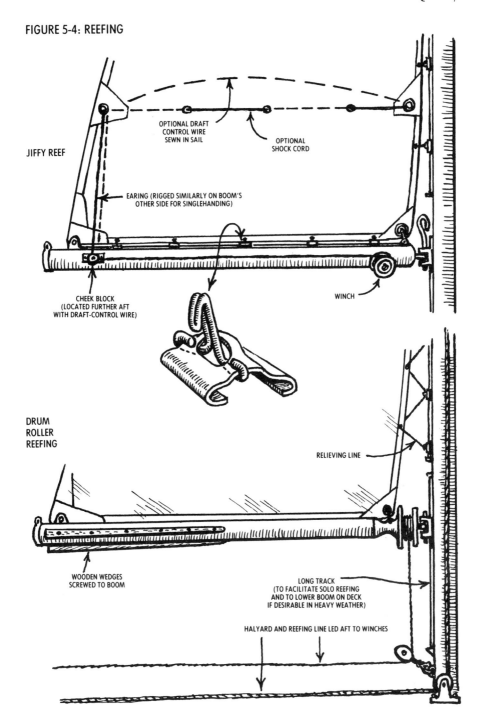

JIFFY REEF

OPTIONAL DRAFT
CONTROL WIRE
SEWN IN SAIL

OPTIONAL
SHOCK CORD

EARING (RIGGED SIMILARLY ON BOOM'S
OTHER SIDE FOR SINGLEHANDING)

CHEEK BLOCK
(LOCATED FURTHER AFT
WITH DRAFT-CONTROL WIRE)

WINCH

DRUM
ROLLER
REEFING

RELIEVING LINE

WOODEN WEDGES
SCREWED TO BOOM

LONG TRACK
(TO FACILITATE SOLO REEFING
AND TO LOWER BOOM ON DECK
IF DESIRABLE IN HEAVY WEATHER)

HALYARD AND REEFING LINE LED AFT TO WINCHES

side of the boom, and thence forward to a winch. The cheek block and eye strap are strategically located so that the line (properly called an earing) pulls the sail's leech aft as well as down (see Figure 5-4).

The method is suitable for a singlehander, but for lengthy passages I would prefer that there be at least a few reef points, or a lace line, or shock cord rove through grommets which can be pulled under hooks on the boom to hold up the loose bunt. In some cases, hooks may be secured to the slides on the sail's foot as shown in Figure 5-4. It may be advisable also to have a cheek block and winch on each side of the boom so that the lone sailor can take in a reef on the boom's windward side whether the boat is sailing on the starboard or port tack. In accordance with one recommended method, the sailor would slack the sheet a bit, go forward to the mast, adjust the topping lift so that it supports the boom, ease off the halyard, and pull down the sail until the tack cringle can be hooked at the gooseneck. Then he would tighten the halyard to take the slack out of the luff, belay the halyard, cast off the permanently rove clew earing, wrap it around its winch located at the forward end of the boom or on the mast, and snug down the clew cringle so that it is held fast to the boom. Last, he would slack off the topping lift. Later, the loose bunt can be tied up with the few reef points or shock cord. The harder it is blowing, the more the sheet will need to be slacked to let the sail luff and thereby ease the wind pressure on it. Of course, there may be more than one set of cringles for variable reefing, but each set will require another earing and another cheek block or set of cheek blocks in a different location.

A jiffy-reefing procedure often used on small stock cruisers is to haul up the clew before lowering the tack cringle. This method is all but essential when there is no masthead topping lift, but it requires complete slacking of the sheet and thus there will be wear on the sail from violent flogging. As mentioned before, it is highly desirable that the singlehander have a proper masthead topping lift for the sake of lowering or hoisting sail with the boom broad off, topping up when the boat is rolling, controlling the boom when reefing, and for possibly using it as a spare halyard.

Although roller reefing is not as popular as it was at one time, the system is far from dead. In fact, Clare Francis, who weighed slightly over 100 pounds, used it successfully on her solo transatlantic crossing in 1973. The only trouble she had with her gear came from its binding as a result of salt-water corrosion, but this problem was all but eliminated with lubrication. Of course, roller reefing systems should be properly designed, and often they are not on stock boats. Common deficiencies are undersized gear, an inadequate flange to hold the luff of the sail aft, a handle that slips off, too great a boom diameter near the gooseneck to allow for the build-up of luff rope when the boom is turned, and, especially, an incorrectly shaped boom to allow a proper sail shape after it is reefed. The best-shaped boom (seldom seen) has a wider diameter aft than forward to prevent excessive droop of the boom's after end when a deep reef is rolled in. If the boom is not made this way, its diameter aft can quite often be increased by fastening tapered wood strips to its after end. Marcel Bardiaux, who used roller reefing so effectively on his *Les 4 Vents*, had a bulge on the lower side of his boom so that after a reef was rolled in he could leave the boom turned with the bulge downward to flatten or remove camber from the sail, which usually is highly desirable in heavy weather.

With roller reefing, it is helpful if there is a long track for the gooseneck slide, because the singlehander can then lower the halyard until the slide is at the bottom of its track, and then turn the boom, winding the sail around it, until the boom reaches the top of the track. Next, the halyard is slacked again until the boom is down, and the process is repeated. In this way, the singlehander does not have to slack off the halyard at the same time he is cranking the boom around. Of course, the lower sail slides should be on a relieving line, and they should be removed before the reefing operation begins. The reefed sail's boom should be left fairly high on the gooseneck track in order that the luff can be easily tightened with a downhaul tackle. A taut luff will not only flatten the sail, but also will keep the camber forward for efficiency and to minimize heeling.

In Europe, a current fad is through-the-mast roller reefing, whereby a shaft from a universal joint near the gooseneck runs through the mast and the gears and turning handle are located on the forward side of the mast. There are some advantages to this system, one being that it eliminates tack setback (the wide gap between the sail's tack and the after side of the mast) and thus alleviates a slight loss of aerodynamic efficiency and a problem in rolling up the luff smoothly. I have heard quite a few favorable reports about the system. Indeed, British sailor-sailmaker, Bruce Banks, has called it "the most important gear development in recent years" (actually, it was developed before World War II). Through-the-mast roller reefing may be suitable for the singlehander, although I have heard of problems with the ratchet engaging the gears on one solo boat, and there is a disadvantage in having no sliding gooseneck. The singlehander will have to slack off the halyard and crank simultaneously, which might be difficult in heavy weather, or else perform each of these operations alternately for very brief periods. With a reel halyard winch that lacks a toggle screw brake (allowing gradual easing), the alternate method is probably preferable for maximum safety, but it will be a bit tedious.

Reel winches which self-store a wire halyard are slow when hoisting, and they can be dangerous, especially so for the singlehander. More than a few experienced sailors have been injured by a spinning handle as a result of the brake slipping or the handle slipping out of the operator's hand. In most cases, it is probably advisable that a lone sailor not use reel winches, despite their handiness. Nevertheless, in the case of internal halyards, where the mainsail will be deeply reefed, it may be desirable to have an all-wire halyard that is self-storing on a reel, rather than a wire halyard with a rope tail, because, with the latter system, the reefed sail must be supported by the relatively weak linkage of a wire-to-rope splice. With external halyards, however, the wire and rope can be joined by the stronger arrangement of two eye splices over thimbles. I once had a wire-to-rope splice pull apart inside the mast, and so I am a bit sensitive on this point. If reel winches are used, it is advisable to use a toggle-screw type (such as that made by Barient) by which the pressure on the halyard can be released gradually and/or use a winch wheel to obviate the need for a handle that can strike the operator. With the toggle screw, it is often possible to release the brake just enough that the boom can be turned while the halyard is eased automatically. A further suggestion for offshore sailors is frequently to wash the salt out from under the brake band for smooth, easy operation. (Of course, oil should never be used on the band.)

Internal halyards have their good and bad points. They reduce windage and noise resulting from slapping the mast, and they help prevent fouling, but, on the other hand, they are less accessible for inspection and repairs and large halyard exits allow the mast to fill with water rapidly in rainy weather or in the event of an extreme knockdown.

A handy arrangement for the singlehander is drum roller reefing whereby the boom is turned by a wire wound around a drum on the forward end of the boom. The wire is led from the drum to a block at the base of the mast and thence back to a winch accessible from the cockpit (Figure 5-4). With the halyard also led back to the cockpit it is possible for the lone sailor to reef without having to go forward. This system was used successfully on the *Barnswallow* back in the 1930s (see Chapter 3), and more recently it was used by sailor-sailmaker Ted Hood (but not primarily for singlehanding in the latter case).

The *Barnswallow* was very ingeniously rigged for easy handling by one man, but one feature in particular seems undesirable to me, and that is the excessive amount of wire rope and reel winches used. Of course, those winches eliminate the necessity for tailing a line when it is being pulled in, but reels are slow, backlashes can occur, and there is the danger of being struck by the handle, as previously mentioned. Nowadays, the singlehander need not be concerned if he has a problem with tailing, because there are self-tailing and self-cleating winches on the market (two examples are those made by Woolsey Marine Industries and Innovator Marine Products), and also there are spring-loaded reels which wind up sheets or halyards (such as those produced by Aye Industries).

A deep reef of any kind has its drawbacks, because the extreme reduction by either reef points or roller gear usually leaves a poorly setting sail with undesirable draft and shape. When it becomes necessary to reduce to a smaller area than a normal double reef, it generally pays to hand the sail and set a storm trysail, storm mainsail, or Swedish mainsail. The latter is a small main with a long luff but short foot and hollow leach for effective beating in strong winds. Its foot is secured to the boom, but often this does not necessitate removal of the lowered working mainsail, especially if there is a groove or track at the boom's bottom which can be rolled upright with a roller reefing gear. The storm trysail is loose footed, but its clew can be secured to the boom, or it can be belayed with separate sheets to avoid use of the boom, which can be a hazard at times. The trysail's foot should be cut high enough to clear the furled mainsail, and its head will come about halfway up the mast to a point, normally near a spreader, where a forward-pulling stay or shroud will oppose the after-pull of the sail's head. The trysail and perhaps Swedish main are most conveniently set on their own track, so that they can be left bent on at all times. The next most convenient system would be a short length of track for the storm sail with a switch at the top to lead the storm sail slides over to the main track.

Opinions are mixed on the merits of leading halyards aft to the cockpit. Some singlehanders prefer that everything is led aft, while others like the conventional system of belaying halyards at the base of the mast. With the drum roller reefing and the Chinese lug rig described earlier, it seems advisable to lead the main halyard aft, but with conventional roller reefing and jiffy reefing the main halyard should have its winch and cleat near the mast.

In my opinion, most headsail halyards should also be cleated at the mast, because the singlehander usually must go forward when lowering a headsail to gather it in, keep it from washing overboard, and tie it with stops or bag it. Normally he will slack the sheet just enough so that the clew can be pulled forward to the mast if it is an overlapping sail, then he will go forward and slack the halyard gradually, leading it around its mast winch and forward where he can control it, while he lifts up the foot of the sail (if it is low cut) and pulls it inboard while the sail is being lowered. Brian Cooke on the *British Steel* actually had his jib halyard led forward to a bow winch to facilitate handling the jib when it was being lowered. On the other hand, it is generally agreed that all spinnaker lines should be led back to the cockpit (the handling of this sail will be discussed in Chapter 9). Also, if a staysail has a boom, lazy jacks may be used, and then its halyard may be led aft. It should be kept in mind that leading halyards through blocks at the base of the mast and fairleads will increase friction somewhat, especially when the halyards are ropes running through small sheaves, but in most cases modern winches can supply all the power ever needed. Many singlehanders think it a good idea to rig downhauls to aid in lowering sails. A jib's downhaul can sometimes be led through its hanks when they are sufficiently large and down to a block at the tack.

A common method of handling headsail changes on a singlehander's boat is with the use of side-by-side twin stays. This rig allows two headsails to be hanked on simultaneously, and it is a relatively easy matter to lower a jib, transfer the halyard to the new jib, and hoist away. Of course two jib halyards can be carried, and sometimes, when it is desirable to keep the boat balanced or keep maximum way on, the new jib can be hoisted before the old one is lowered. The unused jib can be left permanently hanked on, stopped to the pulpit, or bagged. Often the bags are sausage-shaped and sometimes they are fastened with Velcro tapes (whiskery plastic tapes that stick when pressed together). Another possible advantage of twin stays is that there is a spare in case one should happen to break.

In theory, twin stays sound very workable, but in practice they have certain disadvantages, such as the difficulty in obtaining equal tension on each stay, sag and inefficiency caused by the luff not being on the boat's centerline, extra weight and windage, and the problem of getting the stays far enough apart so that they don't interfere with each other. Quite often when a jib is set on the windward stay it will sag to leeward and the luff will chafe against the leeward stay. There have even been cases of the jib hanks (even piston hanks) clipping themselves to both stays. This happened to Clare Francis, and she decided to do away with the twin-stay system. With sufficient practice, she found that sail changes could be made almost as easily with a single stay. Of course, with one stay, a replacement jib can be hanked on beneath the lower hank of the jib that is already hoisted, so that if a change is required, the hoisted jib can merely be unclipped as it is lowered; and then the new jib can be hoisted immediately after the halyard is transferred. Then, too, very-light-weather sails can be hoisted flying on their own wire luffs.

The problem of unequal tension on twin stays might be alleviated with the use of an inverted triangular plate with each stay attached to the top corners and a turnbuckle from the stemhead attached to the triangle's bottom corner (see Figure 5-5). A "U" bolt was used in a similar way by Mike McMullen on the 1972 singlehander's transatlantic race, but it broke and had to be replaced during the passage.

The *Strongbow* (see Chapter 3) has an interesting arrangement for simplifying jib changes. She has two widely spaced headstays that are secured some distance abaft the stem, and directly under the stays there is a large, self-draining locker that can be closed with a sliding hatch cover.

FIGURE 5-5: SAIL CHANGING
SYSTEMS

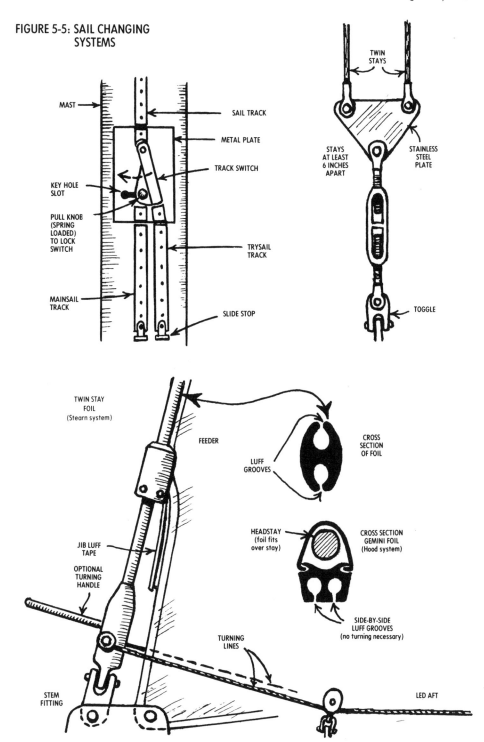

MAST

SAIL TRACK

METAL PLATE

TRACK SWITCH

KEY HOLE
SLOT

PULL KNOB
(SPRING
LOADED)
TO LOCK
SWITCH

TRYSAIL
TRACK

MAINSAIL
TRACK

SLIDE STOP

TWIN
STAYS

STAYS
AT LEAST
6 INCHES
APART

STAINLESS
STEEL
PLATE

TOGGLE

TWIN STAY
FOIL
(Stearn system)

FEEDER

CROSS
SECTION
OF FOIL

LUFF
GROOVES

JIB LUFF
TAPE

OPTIONAL
TURNING
HANDLE

HEADSTAY
(foil fits
over stay)

CROSS SECTION
GEMINI FOIL
(Hood system)

SIDE-BY-SIDE
LUFF GROOVES
(no turning necessary)

TURNING
LINES

STEM
FITTING

LED AFT

The jibs are tacked down inside the locker so that they can be lowered directly into it. The claim was made that a jib can be hoisted and sheeted in without the need to leave the *Strongbow's* cockpit.

A fairly recent development in yacht racing is the headsail luff support systems containing double slots. These systems, one developed by Ted Hood and another by Tim Stearn, use a streamlined aluminum extrusion, which either fits over an existing headstay or stands on its own (depending on the particular system), having two full-length grooves into which the bolt ropes of the jibs are fed. Foils are also made of plastic, and these have occasionally caused trouble by allowing the bolt rope to pull out of its groove, but I understand that plastic foils have recently been improved. The arrangement is handy on racing boats, because headsails can be changed without the need of lowering the sail to be taken off until its replacement has been hoisted, but the system may also prove useful for the singlehander, especially when the foil is used with roller furling (to be described later), after it has been sufficiently time-tested. With the proper feeding mechanism at the bottom of the extrusion, it is conceivable that the lone sailor could hoist sail from the cockpit or mast without the need to hank or unhank a jib. Furthermore, the singlehander can carry two jibs simultaneously, a large one for light weather and a small one for heavy weather. With this arrangement an increase in wind that requires a change down in headsail size means that the sailor only has to lower his large jib, and there is no need to hoist the replacement. There may be some difficulty in lowering because of the two sails sticking together, but teflon luff tape will help overcome friction in the groove.

Perhaps the greatest drawback of a slotted-foil-stay system, aside from occasional feeder jams, is that when a sail is lowered there are no hanks to hold the luff on board, and the sail can slide overboard, although it will not be lost entirely because of being secured at the tack. The singlehander can alleviate the problem by having ample nets rigged from the forward life lines. Of course, slugs (cylindrical sail slides) that fit inside the groove can be sewn to the jib luff to retain advantages of hanks, but then automatic feeding will be sacrificed unless perhaps the slugs could be stored in an attachable magazine. There have been breakage problems with stainless steel rod headstays and also some fitting failures in the aluminum systems, but so far, I have not heard of any aluminum foils breaking. With the latter material, crystallization does not seem to be such a problem, but aluminum foils can be bent by a severe blow from a spinnaker pole.

There is a special problem in lowering a jib that is tacked to the end of a long bowsprit because of the danger that the singlehander might fall overboard. Of course, there should be a sturdy safety net rigged from the bowsprit shrouds, but even so, a long sprit is precarious to work on. Alain

Gerbault once fell from his but was lucky enough to catch hold of the bob-stay and haul himself back aboard. In the old days, boats with long bow-sprits were often fitted with traveler rings by which the tack of a hankless jib could be hauled inboard for sail changes. The same thing might be accomplished by the more modern method of using a slide on a track.

Robin Knox-Johnston used the more simple arrangement of leading a line from the jib's tack through a block on the end of the bowsprit and then aft. Of course, this method failed to hold the tack close to the sprit when tension on the tack line was released, but apparently that was no great disadvantage. Robin wrote in his log, "The procedure for changing sails was as follows: Let fly the tack. This allowed the storm jib to come inboard and I unshackled it. Next slack away the halyard until the sail is on deck and unshackle it, and lastly unshackle the sheet. I then shackle up the peak, tack, and clew of the 'Big Fellow' and hoist it up halfway on the halyard. This is to keep it clear of the water once I haul it forward on its tack. With the tack made fast I haul the sail up taut and then trot aft to adjust the sheet." It should be said that this was not all there was to the procedure, because the *Suhaili* had a triple-head rig, and the "Big Fellow" was actually a large flying jib forward of a working jib, which in turn was forward of a boomed staysail. The working jib could be released from the bowsprit with a Highfield lever, and it was usually taken in when the large flying jib was set. Robin wrote that he always set one jib before handing the other in order to provide a lee and also to maintain balance throughout the operation.

An obviously valuable arrangement for a singlehander is the roller furling concept, whereby a sail can be rolled up on its own luff. Standard rigs utilize a head swivel and roller drum below the tack which stores a furling line (see Figure 5-6). To set the rolled-up sail, the furling line is cast off

FIGURE 5-6: STANDARD ROLLER FURLING

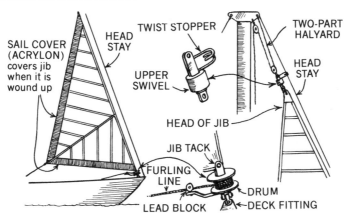

and the sheet is pulled, which causes the sail to unwind; to furl again, the sheet is cast off and the furling line is hauled on, which causes the sail to wind up. Quite often, sail can be reduced by partially rolling up the sail, although some manufacturers of the gear do not encourage this.

Roller furling comes in a variety of forms: conventional wire luff, rod luff, standard conversion kits, grooved foils (previously discussed) which fit over headstays, twin headsail gear, and even electric furling. The latter is very handy for large craft, but I, for one, would never depend on electric gear in heavy weather at sea, and furthermore there is the obvious problem of draining the batteries. Any electric furling should be backed up by a manual system. Stainless steel rod luffs, too, might involve some element of risk, since more than a few have broken, apparently as a result of stress corrosion. Their advantage is the minimizing of luff sag, which is often a problem with conventional wire roller furling, but standard rods are very difficult to lower if the jib should need to be changed or repaired. Occasionally, rod roller jibs are carried with no other stay, but this is a very dangerous practice because of the possibility of the rod breaking. There should always be an additional wire headstay to back up the system. Some rods are grooved like the aluminum foils so that jibs can easily be lowered, but then there is the problem, mentioned earlier, of keeping the hankless sail from washing overboard unless sail slugs that fit into the groove can be sewn to the luff. Such a system is provided by FaMet Marine of California.

The conventional wire luff system shown in Figure 5-6 can be quite satisfactory if it uses a two-part halyard, as illustrated, with a powerful winch to reduce luff sag, but, for lengthy passages at sea, the gear must be rugged and well engineered. Very often extremely taut wire halyards passing over small-diameter sheaves have broken. A disadvantage in any roller-furling system is that a partially furled sail is inferior to a sail that is made for a specific purpose and strength of wind. With a roller sail, cloth weight, camber, shape, construction, and location of the center of effort cannot be changed best to suit various conditions. Furthermore, in heavy weather there are often great strains where the leech and foot cross the rolled up sail.

Roller-furling twin headsails were used for singlehanding as early as 1930, when Otway Waller devised the system, primarily for self-steering in following winds. Paul Hammond, on his *Barnswallow*, later modified the rig, and, in recent years, Wright Britton has improved on the system with his "Roller Jeni Wings." Britton's rig seems to be a well-engineered and versatile arrangement, for the twins — two identical headsails sewn to the same roller luff wire — can be carried with their clews locked together, and their tacks fastened together near the stem to produce, in effect, a single, roller-furling jib; or the tacks can be secured to a point just forward

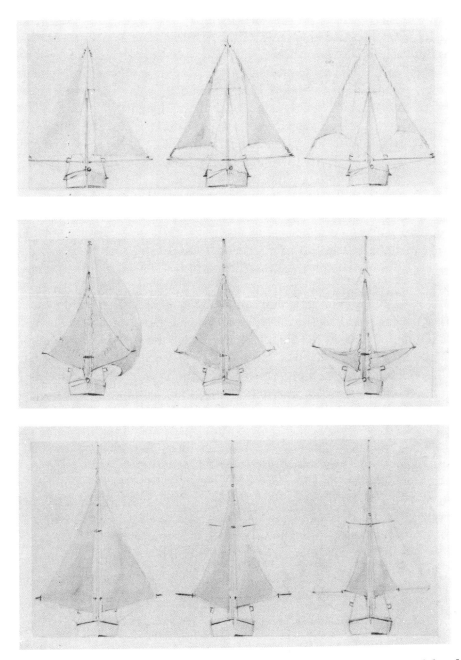

Three early systems of rigging twin headsails sketched by artist-singlehander Marin-Marie. His method used on the Winnibelle *is shown in the middle, while Otway Waller's used on the* Imogen *is at the top and Paul Hammond's used on the* Barnswallow *is at the bottom. The latter two systems use roller-furling gears to reduce sail. (From* Wind Aloft, Wind Alow *by Marin-Marie)*

of the mast to produce a balanced wing-and-wing rig for downwind sailing (see Figure 6-8). More will be said about this system in connection with self-steering in the next chapter.

Roller furling is even used for mainsails occasionally. Frank MacLear (the designer of the *Sea Gar*, described in Chapter 3, and of the *Angantyr*) has done much research and experimentation on a boomless roller mainsail. The MacLear rig sets a mainsail on a rotatable luff wire just abaft the mainmast, and the sail sheets to three permanent backstays, one on the boat's centerline and one on each quarter. Three sheets are led through blocks on adjustable sliders mounted on the backstays well above the deck. Advantages of the rig for shorthanded sailing are: elimination of the main boom, a particular benefit for the singlehander; and ease of hoisting, handing, and shortening sail. Disadvantages are: less than optimal sail shape on certain points of sailing; a higher-than-normal clew, with a relatively wide gap between the luff and the mast; extra stress on the backstays; slapping of the sail against the mast when furled; difficulties of lowering if necessary; possible malfunctioning of roller gear; possibility of ballooning or unfurling in a gale; and some problems in properly spreading the sail when running. The rig is still being improved, however, and after it has reached the peak of its development, its advantages may well outweigh its shortcomings for shorthanded cruising. An interesting new development that alleviates some of the problems associated with roller furling is the P. T. Jackson rig, which provides for furling inside a specially made mast. The system was described in *Yachting* magazine (October, 1974).

Much of the modern gear that has been discussed can improve efficiency and simplify operations on any yacht. Innovations and refinements, such as head foils, internal halyards, roller-furling mainsails, and so forth, may be advantageous for the singlehander who cruises short distances in relatively protected waters, but those who make distant passages offshore should be extremely cautious about fitting out with gear that is very complex and sophisticated. If such equipment is used, it is important that the singlehander use the specific brand that has proven most reliable, that he learn how to service and repair the gear, and that back-up systems can be rigged in the event of failures or irreparable breakages.

Difficult Operations and Heavy Gear

Many operations involved in singlehanding a boat are difficult or strenuous, and anything that can be done to make them easier will not only make sailing more enjoyable, but also will make it safer and reduce the hazards of fatigue. Sail handling has been discussed in the previous section, but there are other tasks that can be arduous or complicated when alone. Some of these are docking, picking up a mooring, breaking out the anchor and bringing it aboard, bending sail, and bringing the dinghy on board.

Most jobs that are difficult for one person to handle can be simplified if they are well thought out. As said earlier, planning ahead is the key to successful singlehanding. Take the job of bending on a mainsail, for in-

A dramatic painting by Marin-Marie of the Winnibelle *running before a squall with her twin headsails set. (From* Wind Aloft, Wind Alow *by Marin-Marie)*

stance. It might seem impossible for one person to feed a foot bolt rope into a grooved boom near the mast while he simultaneously pulls aft on the clew at the other end of the boom. Ordinarily, this is a two-man operation, but it is simple for one person to perform when he ties a line to the clew and runs it through a block at the outboard end of the boom and back to the mast. Such a solution would seem obvious, but it is all too easy, when one normally sails with a crew, to overlook what can be done alone with simple devices such as blocks, purchases, fairleads, Spanish windlasses, and so forth.

When a self-steering gear is not rigged during a short cruise or day sail, tasks often become difficult because the helm cannot be left unattended for very long. Of course, the helm can be lashed or otherwise secured, and a boat that is reasonably well-balanced under sail or that carries a consistent torque under power will hold a steady course for a short while; but if the singlehander is working a long distance from the helm, he will often have to make many trips back and forth from his working station to the cockpit to readjust the helm. One solution to this problem, without resorting to self-steering arrangements, is to rig steering lines which can be led to any work area. With a tiller, this is usually a simple matter of running the lines from the tiller through snatch blocks on each side of the cockpit and then forward. Wheel steering makes the problem more complicated, but most boats have (or at least should have) a means of rigging an emergency tiller. On our present boat, the square head of the rudder post, which accepts the emergency tiller, is just abaft the wheel (under a screw-on deck plate); thus there is a problem with the wheel interfering with the tiller. There is plenty of room abaft the rudder post, however, so it is a simple matter to put the tiller on backwards and then rig steering lines to it. With this arrangement, the helmsman has to remember to steer the opposite way to which he ordinarily would with tiller-steering, but this is not difficult because the backwards tiller works the same as does a wheel. One has merely to think of turning the helm the way he wants the bow to go.

An auxiliary engine is invaluable for a singlehander cruising on inland or coastal waters, despite the fact that a few purists refuse to use any power but sail. Peter Tangvald, for instance, once unbolted his balky engine from its bed, hoisted it on deck, and pushed it overboard. He claims that engines often give a false sense of security, and he cites the example of a boat that was wrecked because her engine failed in the middle of a dangerous pass leading to a harbor near Tahiti. There is great truth in what Tangvald says, but if the skipper understands the failings and limitations of his auxiliary power and learns not necessarily to depend on it in a crisis, then the engine can be extremely helpful. Of course, the boat that was wrecked should have been motorsailing through the pass, or at least had her sails ready for hoisting, but she had her sail covers on and so was helpless immediately after her engine quit.

A properly used and cared-for engine is a tremendous convenience in bringing a boat up to her mooring, maneuvering in tight places, docking, breaking out the anchor, motorsailing against rough seas to reach port before dark, charging up the batteries, and, of course, supplying power in a calm. For lack of a reliable engine, circumnavigator John Sowden spent two days drifting around in a calm when only fifteen miles from his destination at Suva, Fiji, where there was a dangerous pass that had to be negotiated. In my opinion, it is not sissy or unseamanlike to use auxiliary power when it is helpful. On the contrary, proper use of the engine in certain conditions can be the most seamanlike action to take. The important matter, however, is not to become overly dependent on the auxiliary and to learn to handle the boat in all conditions under sail alone.

The engine greatly simplifies breaking out a heavy or well dug-in anchor. The singlehander can haul his boat up to short scope, belay the rode, then go back to the cockpit and drive the boat ahead under power until the "hook" is broken out. He can then put the gear in neutral and go forward to pull up the anchor and cat it or bring it on board while the boat drifts slowly to leeward. The catting operation might have to be done in two steps if the boat drifts too close to a neighboring vessel or an obstruction. If too much effort is required to shorten scope, the anchor line often can be led aft near the engine controls, so that the solo sailor can take in slack as he slowly drives the boat ahead under power. It is interesting to note that the *Barnswallow* had her anchor rode permanently led aft to the cockpit, and her standard anchor, a large Danforth, stowed in a low hawse pipe, so her skipper seldom had to go forward.

Under sail, hauling in the anchor line is more difficult, since the sailor will often have to beat up to his anchor if he cannot haul his boat up to it. For this, it is often best to use a small, high-cut headsail that can be backed but will clear the head of the singlehander kneeling on the foredeck. Normally, the sailor will sheet in his mainsail and control the headsail from the foredeck while he gathers in slack from the anchor line or chain. This seems like a formidable operation, but it is not quite as difficult as it sounds, because the boat will all but come about by herself when she fetches up on her anchor line, which will become taut and pull the bow around through the eye of the wind. When she sails off on the opposite tack, the sailor can gather in slack, but he has to be extremely careful not to get his fingers pinched when the line becomes taut again.

Of course, another way of handling the problem of taking in scope on a heavy boat in a strong breeze is to use a winch or windlass, but this can be tedious. Very often, after the anchor line has been heaved on and the boat

begins to move, her momentum will reduce the effort of hauling in the remaining line and it can be pulled in hand-over-hand. Once the rode is at
a short stay it is usually not too difficult to break out the anchor under sail,
but if it is really dug in, a windlass, powerful winch, and/or tackle might
have to be used.

Lifting the "hook" onboard is not as much of a chore as it once was, because the most commonly used anchors today, such as the plows (CQRs)
and Danforths have more holding power and thus can be lighter than those
of former times. In a good holding bottom with ample scope, a twenty-
pound, "hi-tensile" Danforth, for instance, can hold a boat up to 40 feet
long in all but storm conditions. There will be times, however, when heavy
storm anchors or old-fashioned fisherman types for use in thick weed or
rocky bottoms will have to be hefted onboard, and then the singlehander
may want some help in the form of mechanical advantage. He will seldom
need such formerly used devices as anchor davits and catheads, but he may
want to use a boom with a winch, or cat his anchor under the bowsprit, if
the boat has one. In recent years, the vogue has been a roller chock at the
stem head, which allows a plow anchor to be pulled up with its shank over
the roller. When it is necessary to bring a heavy anchor onboard with a
boom, the spinnaker pole, reaching strut, or staysail boom can be used. The
pole is secured to the mast (or stay or pedestal in the case of the staysail
boom) and supported with a lift. A tackle or line leading to a winch is
rigged from the outboard end, and the pole is swung out over the water
so that the anchor can be lifted clear of the topsides. After it is lifted
above the deck level, of course, the pole is swung inboard so that the anchor
can be lowered to the deck.

The same principle may be used to bring a heavy dinghy onboard. Quite
often the main boom is used with a tackle, perhaps the vang, rigged from
the boom's end or middle. The dinghy can be lifted with a bridle rigged
between its bow and stern. With a lightweight dinghy, the boom is not
always necessary. I have brought our Dyer Dhow onboard singlehandedly
by hoisting it with the main halyard after fenders have been rigged to protect the topsides.

A laborious task for a singlehander is freeing his boat after a grounding.
For the most part, the same actions would be taken aboard a solo boat as
on one fully-crewed, but, of course, more effort is required by one man,
and he cannot use methods that involve crew weight, such as putting
people on the bow to lift the after end of the keel, or putting them on a
broadoff boom to make the boat heel. The boat might be made to heel without too much effort, however, by lifting the swamped dinghy from the end
of the boom. Kedging off may be difficult for one person, but it helps to use
an anchor no heavier than necessary and a long, light anchor line that is

neatly coiled on the after thwart or stern sheets of the dinghy, so that it will pay itself out easily when the boat is being rowed away from the grounded vessel for the sake of setting out the kedge. If there is no dinghy or raft, a light anchor might be swum out after it has been lashed temporarily to a number of life jackets or buoyant cushions.

For boats with short keels or a lot of drag (depth) aft, it is often helpful to have a very light Danforth that can be thrown a good distance off one side of the bow so that the boat can be turned toward deep water. Then she can be heeled by sail or weights and be driven ahead and hopefully off the shoal under power and/or sail. It usually pays, especially for the singlehander, to take his time, plan ahead carefully, and be sure where the deep water is through soundings or a careful study of the chart. There are times when a lone sailor might want to wait for a rise in tide rather than exhaust himself trying to free the boat immediately. Obviously, the urgency will depend on whether the boat is being damaged, the state of the tide, and other factors.

It is important for the singlehander to have powerful winches or a windlass with suitable chocks and fairleads as well as proper ground tackle. Marcel Bardiaux had one very powerful winch that he could move to different advantageous locations, and once he found it indispensable for extricating his boat from a dangerous coral reef (the incident will be described in Chapter 7). After a hard grounding on rocks or coral, of course, the hull should be inspected carefully to see that it is not holed, so that the vessel will not sink in deep water after she is freed. Bardiaux's *Les 4 Vents* nearly sank after she was pulled free of the reef despite the fact that she was fitted with some flotation.

Other operations that can sometimes present problems for the singlehander are docking and picking up a mooring. The latter is seldom difficult with an engine, because the boat can be turned into the wind (or current when that dominates), and the approach speed can be controlled by backing down when close to the mooring. Then the singlehander puts his gear in neutral, walks forward quickly, and picks up the mooring float with a long boat hook.

Under sail, however, the procedure is more difficult, because speed cannot be controlled so easily. In most cases, where the current is not extreme, it is best to make the approach under mainsail alone (if the boat is maneuverable under this rig) while sailing on a close reach and aiming a few boat lengths to leeward of the pick-up float. Speed can be controlled by slacking or trimming in the mainsheet, and some control can be obtained by the degree and speed that the rudder is turned. The shoot into the wind just to leeward of the pick-up float must be almost perfectly timed, because if the boat has too much speed, she may overrun her mooring before the sailor has a chance to pick it up; or else if he does pick it up, he may not be able to hold it. On the other hand, if the speed is too little, the boat may stop short, beyond the reach of the singlehander, or she might lose steerageway as a result of her slow speed. Obviously, this maneuver takes practice and one must know his vessel. Heavy boats carry more way than light ones, and boats with tall rigs having a lot of windage stop more abruptly than those with clean, short rigs in fresh winds.

A method for picking up the mooring advocated by at least one experienced singlehander is as follows: A line, which will be called the mooring line, is run from the cockpit to a bow chock, then aft to the cockpit again outboard of the lifeline stanchions and rigging. The line's returning end is fitted with a large snap hook (see Figure 5-7). When the boat is brought up to her mooring, she is made to overshoot slightly so that the pick-up float can be grabbed from the cockpit. The snap hook on the mooring line is snapped into the eye on top of the float, and then the float is cast off. The boat is snubbed by hauling in on the hookless end of the mooring line, and then she is allowed to drift back to leeward of the float. Slack is taken in on the mooring line as she drifts back, and finally the singlehander walks forward, picks up the float, and properly secures the mooring pendant. It will be helpful if the pick-up float is fitted with a vertical staff that can easily be grabbed.

One disadvantage of this system is that when the boat has such a long distance to drift back, her bow will most likely blow off, despite tugs on the mooring line, and if the pick-up is made under sail, the sail may fill and drive the boat ahead. Obviously, the sheet must be well slacked and kept from fouling. Also, it may pay to drop the mainsail promptly while the boat is still head to wind, but only after the pick-up has been made. One occasionally sees a self-confident skipper shoot for his mooring and drop sails before the mooring is picked up, but in my opinion, this should never be done when there is only one person aboard. A special hook, called the Star Mooring Hook, which can be closed with a spring gate, controlled by a lanyard, can simplify the mooring pick-up. This device, illustrated in Figure 5-7, can easily be attached to a boathook. It is sold by West Products and other chandlers.

Another pick-up method is to make fast a short line with a buoy to the pick-up float. It would be reached for in the conventional way, with a boat hook from the bow, but having the extra buoy attached allows more room for error. The singlehander shoots for the pick-up float but errs very slightly toward having too little speed. Then if he finds he cannot quite reach the pick-up float, he can probably reach the extra buoy, assuming it has drifted a short distance to leeward of the float. Of course, one has to be careful that the line linking the extra buoy to the pick-up float is not too long, as

FIGURE 5-7: MOORING AND DOCKING AIDS

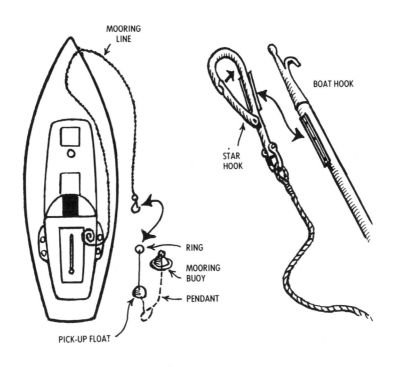

MOORING
LINE

BOAT HOOK

STAR
HOOK

RING

MOORING
BUOY

PENDANT

PICK-UP FLOAT

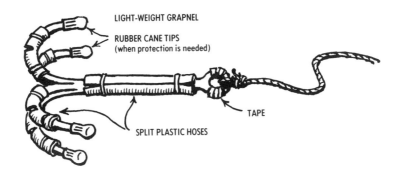

LIGHT-WEIGHT GRAPNEL

RUBBER CANE TIPS
(when protection is needed)

TAPE

SPLIT PLASTIC HOSES

it could be an obstruction to boat traffic when it is floating. Also, the buoy should be a prominent size and color so that it can be easily seen. Reflective tape (such as that made by 3M) stuck on the top of the buoy is a great aid to visibility at night.

Docking under sail in a large, heavy boat can involve considerable risk for a singlehander. It is far better to dock under power if the engine is reliable. Ordinarily, when the current is not a major factor, it is best to bring the boat alongside to leeward of a dock in order that the wind will keep her a short distance away from rough pilings, concrete, and so forth, which could mar her topsides. A recommended method, when there is no one on the dock to take a line, is as follows: A line is belayed at the bow, led through the bow chock on the side that will face the dock, and then led aft outboard of everything to the cockpit where the line is neatly coiled and hung on a winch or stanchion near the helm. Another line is belayed at the stern on the same side. This stern line will have an adjustable loop in its end and will be fairly short, perhaps eight to twelve feet, from the cleat to the loop, which also will be hung near the helmsman. After the bow and stern lines and fenders have been rigged, the boat is brought in almost parallel to the leeward of the dock, and the engine is reversed just before the cockpit is opposite a cleat, bollard, or piling on the dock. When most of the way has been lost the singlehander shifts into neutral, steps to the side of the boat, and puts the loop of the stern line over the piling or dockside cleat. With the other hand he takes the coiled bow line, jumps ashore, runs forward, and takes a turn around another piling near the bow. It is important that the bow line be secured promptly before the bow is blown off by the wind.

One often hears arguments that a single spring line should be rigged from amidships leading aft to the dock in order to bring the boat close alongside parallel to the dock, but this line can create extra complications for a singlehander. Contrary to what has been written by some advocates of the amidships spring line, a stern line of proper length will not swing the stern into the dock with any great force, because the lateral component of the stern line's pull will be at least partially counteracted by a turning moment caused by the stern line's aftward component pulling from the boat's quarter (see Figure 5-8).

Obviously, there are many different kinds of docking situations due to variations in wind direction, dock construction, height of tide, differences in current, whether or not there are people on the dock, and so forth. Each situation will require individual analysis, but the principles involved in the operation previously described are good ones to bear in mind.

It is usually not difficult to leave from the leeward side of a dock. One method for a boat that is to be backed away is to have one turn of the bow

FIGURE 5-8: FORCES WHEN DOCKING WITH A STERN LINE

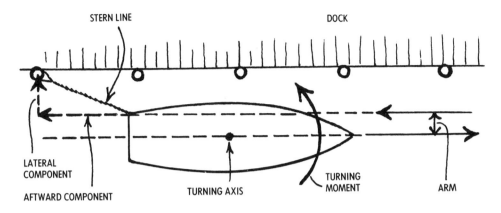

Turning moment illustrated (due to spread between aftward component and forward movement) partially counteracts tendency of stern to swing towards dock.

line around its piling and both ends of the line leading back to the cockpit. After the engine is started and spring lines and fenders taken in, the stern line is cast off, and then one end of the bow line which leads to the cockpit is let go. The bow line is hauled around its piling to fall free, and the engine is put in reverse, and the boat backs away. The singlehander takes in the line from the cockpit before he shifts into forward gear, because otherwise he might overrun the line when the boat goes ahead and possibly foul the propeller. Some modern boats do not back very well in a strong breeze, as their bows tend to blow off and the stern tends to round up into the wind, especially before there is sufficient sternway. If this is the case, it may be well to let the stern blow off a bit before casting off the bow line. Of course, another alternative is to warp the boat around so that she can leave bow first.

Small, light boats can be brought in on the windward side of a pier when it is very well padded and the boat is protected with fenders. This is a simple operation in a weak current, for the boat will blow against the dock. Departing is then a bit more difficult, because the boat will have to be pushed far out from the dock before she backs away. A commonly used method is to go forward on a spring line which forces the stern away from the dock, and this might work well unless the boat has a very cutaway forefoot with a lot of windage forward and her bow is easily blown off. A fender or so should be placed forward to protect against this, and the rudder might have to be turned toward the dock initially to keep the bow clear.

If it is necessary to sail up to a dock, the operation will be somewhat similar to picking up a mooring, but the approach should be made in such a way that the boat can always be turned aside at the last minute in case the speed is too fast. It is safer to err on the slow side, and quite often a line can be thrown to a person on the dock if the boat stops short, but speed should never be allowed to drop to the point where the boat loses all maneuverability and gets in stays. It is usually a good plan to make the approach with a small jib (high cut for visibility) so that it can be backed for the best possible maneuverability at low speeds. It takes real skill and familiarity with one's vessel to emulate Captain Slocum when he docked his heavy *Spray* in Gloucester's harbor so gently that "she would not have broken an egg," yet even Slocum could have occasional problems maneuvering in close quarters under sail, for in the same harbor he later "scratched the paint off an old fine-weather craft in the fairway."

In the event that there is no one on the dock to catch a tossed line, incidentally, a useful tool for the singlehander is a small, light-weight grappling hook covered with split plastic hoses and rubber tips on its prongs to prevent it from scarring the dock. The device can be used after the boat is brought to a stop close to a narrow pier, at which time the grapnel, being attached to a light line, is thrown over the far side of the dock so that it hooks onto the edge or some other projection, and the boat is hauled in and made fast.

Safety Considerations

Safety is a vital consideration on any boat, of course, but there is a somewhat different emphasis for the singlehander. On a fully-crewed vessel, for instance, horse-shoe buoys, man-overboard poles, and waterlights should be hung aft near the helmsman for the sake of a crew member who might happen to fall overboard. But such safety gear has limited value for one who sails alone, for if he goes over the side, there is obviously no one onboard to throw him the equipment. There is also no one at the helm to bring the boat back for a rescue. Thus it should go without saying that a singlehander must always move about the boat carefully and exercise extra caution in all activities. A great deal of self discipline is sometimes required to prevent overly hasty movements, dashes to the foredeck, the performance of tasks without safety lines in heavy weather, and casual or careless behavior in general.

Some suggestions for safety-related equipment and procedures are as follows:

- A life jacket or buoyant vest should be worn in heavy weather when close to shore or other vessels. Offshore in remote regions, some single-handers feel that a flotation device will just prolong the discomfort of drowning.

- Safety harnesses can be invaluable, despite the fact that some single-handers never wear them. A harness consists of a belt, with shoulder straps usually, and a moderately short, heavy lanyard with a large, strong snap-hook that may be clipped to the rigging or an eye to allow working with both hands in rough weather. There should be plenty of convenient places where one can clip on, and the singlehander should practice using his harness. Without learning to use it properly, a harness can be more of a liability than an asset. Incidentally, there are jackets on the market that have sewn-on integral harnesses. Some singlehanders use a jack wire which runs from the cockpit to the foredeck so that the lanyard's hook will have an uninterrupted fore-and-aft travel. Others use a long safety line which permits moving a good distance from a fixed clip-on point, but one must be careful not to become tangled with such an arrangement.

- Decks should be kept as clear as possible, and all smooth surfaces anywhere on the boat (especially varnished surfaces and the companionway ladder) should be skid-proofed with abrasive strips or by some other means. It may be advisable to mark obstructions that could be tripped over with reflective tape for night work under the spreader lights.

- Booms should be eliminated where they can be, and they should be kept as high as possible.

- Headsail sheets are best secured with bowlines rather than snap shackles that could strike a singlehander in the head.

- Sails should never be allowed to lie spread out on the deck, primarily because modern synthetics are very slippery to walk on.

- It is the safest policy for a singlehander to tow a floating line with a rescue quoit or a small, brightly painted buoy at its end.

- When the boat is rigged for self-steering, the towed line should be rigged to trip the steering vane or free the helm so that the boat will round up into the wind when the line overboard is pulled. A very simple method utilizing a wide-opening snap shackle is suggested in Figure 5-9.

- Boats with high freeboard need some permanent means of boarding, such as transom steps or perhaps footholds on the self-steering gear. In some cases a rail-secured, rolled-up ladder that has a release line hanging overboard may suffice.

- There should be two large-capacity, preferably diaphragm-type, bilge pumps, one operable from the cockpit near the helm and the other from below. The deck pump should be useable without the need of opening a

FIGURE 5-9:
TRIPPING THE VANE GEAR

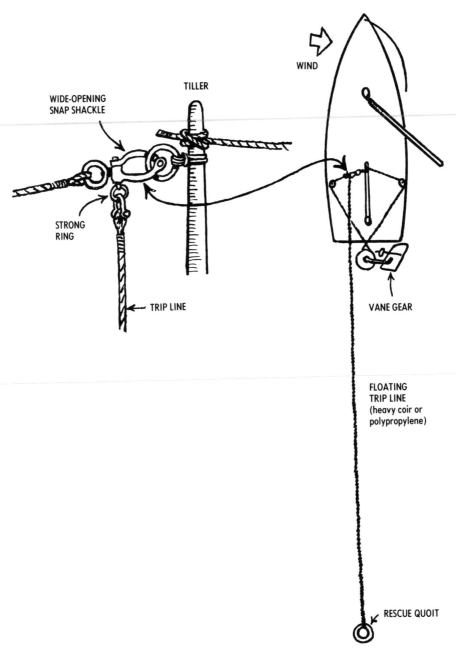

WIND

WIDE-OPENING
SNAP SHACKLE

TILLER

STRONG
RING

TRIP LINE

VANE GEAR

FLOATING
TRIP LINE
(heavy coir or
polypropylene)

RESCUE QUOIT

cockpit seat locker. In addition, it is advisable to have a portable pump and a couple of sturdy buckets.

• High life lines, well above knee level, running through well-bolted, closely-spaced stanchions between bow and stern pulpits are all but essential. Also it is important that there be a lower life line about midway between the top line and the rail. Life lines should be inspected every so often, especially if they are stainless steel wire running through plastic tubes, as they could possibly be affected by shielding corrosion (from lack of oxygen). Do not trust the average pelican hooks found on standard life lines, as I have seen these break on two occasions. Nets around the foredeck can be invaluable.

• A life raft is important on any offshore boat, but there is no need for a singlehander's raft to be large. A two-man or three-man raft should suffice. It is important that it be compartmentalized and fitted with a canopy, and carry emergency rations. A good inflatable dinghy may do (provided a canopy can be fitted), and it might be desirable to carry it on deck partially inflated and well secured with lashings that can be cut away instantly. Its painter must be secured to the mother vessel at all times, because inflated boats and rafts have blown away in heavy weather. If they are carried deflated, they should be well-protected with a waterproof cover, preferably rigid (normally a tightly sealed fiberglass canister), because rafts can deteriorate from being constantly wet and there have been cases of the CO_2 inflation not working as a result of rafts having been walked on. Periodic inspections, at least every two years, should be made by qualified examiners.

• Good visibility for the singlehander is vital. Measures to help his vision are red lights in the binnacle and above the chart table, high-cut sails, ample windows in spray dodgers, a plastic dome in the cabin top, and perhaps the use of an occasional wide view mirror. Incidentally, there is a small, circular, plastic lense called the "Lensor" (produced by Eberhardt Plastics and Company, Ltd., in Portsmouth, England) that can be fastened to the cabin window to add considerable width to the view. The device was written up in *Yachting Monthly* (January, 1973).

• Radar reflectors are especially important for the singlehander because of the amount of time he cannot stand watch. These devices, which are small geometric structures made of light metal or wire mesh with multiple, right-angle corners, reflect signals back to vessels using radar. A reflector can be hoisted in the rigging or preferably mounted at the masthead, but experts say that for greatest efficiency, the usual octahedral type should not be mounted or suspended with one point up (see Figure 3-4). Small battery operated "echo enhancers," which will make small craft much more prominent on the screens of radar equipped vessels, are said to be coming on the market very soon.

• Radar alarms have not yet been perfected for the singlehander's market, but they could afford considerable protection against being run down when there is no one on watch. Their function is to sound a loud alarm when they are swept by the radar beams of approaching ships. At least one sailor has used, with some success, the type of alarm used in automobiles to detect highway radar speed traps, and Hepplewhite Marine Ltd. of Sudbury, Suffolk, England, makes a radar detector for boats. It is my understanding, however, that the detector requires special tuning before use, and it makes a relatively quiet beeping sound; thus it might not be the complete solution for a sound-sleeping singlehander. Noel Bevan, the ingenious solo seaman who sailed the *Myth of Malham* in the 1968 transatlantic race, invented an omnidirectional masthead radar receiver that sounds an alarm in the cabin and can detect a ship as far away as ten miles. Bevan also devised another gadget, a hand-held device that he called a passive radar receiver. It is said to resemble a small square megaphone, and it produces hooting sounds with the use of a radar crystal and amplifier that can indicate the position of an approaching ship in fog or darkness. This is not like the portable "Whistler" radar that sends out its own signal, but it is similar to and evidently anticipated the Hepplewhite detector.

• Other alarms, already mentioned, which can be of considerable value are audible depth finders, such as the Cormorant "Safe-sail" (produced by ACC Design and Sales at Poole, Dorset, England) and off-course alarms, such as the Hestia model (produced by Brookes and Gatehouse Ltd. at Lymington, Hampshire, England). The depth finder has an audible alarm that can be set to sound at any depth up to 99 fathoms, while the off-course alarm can be set to sound when the boat departs from her proper heading by an angle greater than 20, 30, 40, 50, or 60 degrees. It is probably well not to set too small an angle at sea when it is rough or the wind is shifty if the boat is controlled by vane steering. It was stated that the home-made, off-course indicator used by Noel Bevan in the 1968 OSTAR was one of many "good alarms which nearly drove him mad."

• Radio-telephones are carried by many modern singlehanders, for they provide a contact with the rest of the world, which is a help psychologically, and a means of calling for help in the event of trouble. Furthermore, some races and individual sponsors require two-way radios. The trouble is that VHF (very high frequency) equipment has a very limited range, little more than line-of-sight, and long-range SSB (single sideband) equipment is quite expensive in addition to being a drain on the batteries and requiring complicated installation with a relatively long antenna and a ground plate. An alternative for rescue capabilities is an ELRB (emergency locator radio beacon), which is a small, waterproof, buoyant transmitters that send out distress signals automatically for about two days or longer.

Another alternative is a portable emergency radiophone that transmits and receives on 2182 KHz, the international distress frequency, Jock McLeod even used one of these sets, a Safetylink, in the 1972 transatlantic race to check his position occasionally from a passing ship, although, as he wrote, "One is not encouraged to have social chats on 2182."

• Visual distress signals, such as hand-held flares and those shot from a Very pistol, should be carried by every boat. It is also highly desirable to have a flashing strobe light, preferably carried at the masthead, which can be used as a flare-up light allowed under the Rules of the Road. In shipping lanes, it may be advisable to use such a light while the single-hander takes short naps at night, although the legality of this practice is questionable (more will be said about this in Chapter 7). Of course, a powerful flashlight or two with extra batteries must always be carried. Orange smoke signals are needed for emergency use in the daytime.

• An easy means of climbing the mast is all but essntial to the single-hander, because on long-distance passages he may have to go aloft for in-spections, to make repairs, and to look for shoals or distant landmarks. Permanent mast steps or ratlines are preferable, but a hoisted ladder or bosun's chair with a suitable tackle may suffice. (This too is discussed in Chapter 7).

• Collision mats are seldom carried, but as W. Leslie King and others have found out, they can be invaluable to the singlehander after a collision or serious grounding. A typical mat is triangular or square-shaped with lead weights or a piece of chain and corner lines that can be used to position and hold it over the damaged area of the hull and thus slow the rate of leaking (see Figure 7-1). A square mat is usually placed in the diamond position and is hauled beneath the water with the hogging line attached to the lower corner. Jock McLeod carried on his *Ron Glas* a mat made like a "pillow case" so that it could be stuffed full of blankets and the like. It had grommets all around the edges to accept multiple lashings. Collision mats have been out of vogue in recent years, but they could well come back into style because of the difficulty in performing emergency repairs on many of the modern boats with their fiberglass construction and liners that make it difficult to reach a damaged area from the inside of the hull. It could be worthwhile to carry a Simpson damage control gear, which will be de-scribed in Chapter 7. Other equipment relating to damage control will also be mentioned in that chapter. Tools and spare parts were listed in Chap-ter 4.

A few special safety considerations are needed in the case of a multihull, and most of these were discussed in Chapter 3. To reiterate briefly, a multi-hull may need sturdily attached masthead flotation with extra strong mast and rigging, automatic sheet releases, and some means of self-rescue in the event of a capsizing. Of course, all sponsons and amas must be very strongly attached, and there should be nets or webbing covering open spaces between hulls for obvious reasons. Sheet releases vary from simple cam-action jam cleats, which are mounted on hinged planks held down by shock cord, to the sophisticated electronic gadgetry devised by Donald Crowhurst (see Chapter 3).

A simple, swiveling, cam cleat can be held by shock cord or a thumb screw (see Figure 5-10). The screw may provide a somewhat more easily adjustable means of altering the resistance to sheet tension needed for releasing. A frequently used automatic release is the one made by Hepplewhite, which utilizes two mercury switches, one for port heel and the other for starboard, and may be set to free a sheet at any heeling angle. A disadvantage in electric gear, of course, is that there is some drain on the battery and perhaps some risk of a short circuit from wet wiring. Furthermore, Michael Ellison, who sailed the *Tahiti Bill* back to England after the 1972 transatlantic race, complained that the Hepplewhite would often release due to wave action rather than angle of heel from the wind. The jerking of the boom in rough weather can be a problem for mechanical-type releases.

If a multihull should happen to turn turtle in heavy weather offshore, self-rescue might be considered a two-step operation. The first is simply to survive on the bottom of the upturned boat until the blow abates, and

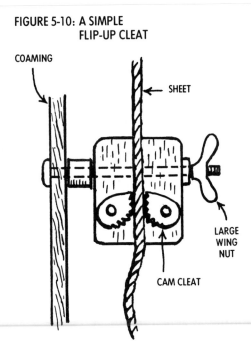

FIGURE 5-10: A SIMPLE
FLIP-UP CLEAT

COAMING

SHEET

LARGE
WING
NUT

CAM CLEAT

the second is to right her. Conditions must be ideal to right the typical multihull, especially a catamaran, because of her tremendous stability in the inverted position. The most effective means of righting at the present time seems to be the system of flooding one hull (an outboard ama on a trimaran) so that the boat turns on her side, then attaching masthead flotation such as an inflated life raft, and finally pumping out the flooded hull to allow righting. This method may require a rather complicated system of hoses, valves, and a large accessible pump, or two. Survival on the boat's bottom requires some hand grips and a means of reaching supplies. Bill Howell has a hatch in the bottom of his catamaran leading to food and water and also an opening in the trampoline between hulls to reach a life raft.

Navigating Alone

Navigation can present some problems for the singlehander, especially when he is close to shore. In crowded waters, it is often too risky for him to spend any time below at the chart table; so he must have his chart and all essential equipment available near the helm. A clear plastic case that is watertight and can hold a folded chart or chart book is invaluable. It may also be helpful to have a grid of parallel lines, printed on clear plastic sheet for placement over the chart (obtainable from leading chandlers or navigation supply companies) in order to obviate the need for parallel rules or protractors, as these can be difficult to handle while steering. Courses or bearings can be drawn on the plastic case with a grease pencil, and its markings can be rubbed off quite easily with a rag or paper towel. It is preferable that dividers are the bowed kind that are designed to be operated with one hand.

There should be a locker easily accessible from the helm where binoculars and navigation gear can safely be stowed. Shelves inside the companionway can be used when the helm is near the forward end of the cockpit. Quite often the chart case can be held up vertically against the after end of the cabin house with a piece of shock cord stretched between two eyes. On some boats with the helm near the companionway, the sliding hatch can serve as a chart table. The chart in use is taped or otherwise fastened to a piece of plywood or masonite on top of the hatch, and it can be slid in and out of the hatch scabbard in wet weather.

Sometimes the sailor who cannot leave his helm must make very rough checks without proper navigation instruments. A pencil with some notches might be used instead of dividers in an emergency; and if one puts a couple of rubber bands around the pencil so that it can be rolled across the chart without slipping, he will have a crude substitute for parallel rules. Robin Knox-Johnston wrote of a trick he used at times as a rough means of measuring distance off from a lighthouse or other tall landmark of known height when it appeared to be about one finger's width above the horizon. Ordinarily, of course, the distance-off by vertical angle method requires a sextant, but Robin could get a crude approximation by using his finger held horizontally at arm's length, which he found subtended an angle of about one and a half degrees. Also, a wide-spread thumb and little finger held at arm's length subtends an angle of about twenty degrees, while the hand's width subtends about ten degrees.

When bearings are taken by the singlehander, it is preferable that the instrument used contain its own compass when the main steering compass cannot be used for sighting, because it is obviously impossible to receive the boat's heading from a helmsman at the same moment the bearing is read. Of course, a hand bearing compass can be used, and this instrument is also handy to stow below near the skipper's berth so that he can check the course from his bunk, although an old-fashioned telltale compass hung from the overhead above the bunk is a still better arrangement. It is also highly desirable that the lone sailor's radio direction finder have its own compass, because the instrument usually cannot be brought very close to the ship's compass without inducing serious deviation errors. Likewise, the RDF can be affected by deviation, and it should be operated from a consistent location where errors have been recorded. Two popular RDFs with their own compasses are the Vecta (by Vec/Trak Research and Development Corporation), which uses pre-tuned, plug-in modules to avoid dialing and tuning, and the Brookes and Gatehouse Homer/Heron.

Although some veteran sailors, such as Peter Tangvald, claim they can sense shallow water by their vessel's change in motion and by visual and audible differences in the waves, a depth sounder can be very useful for sailing on-soundings when the instrument is working properly. The arrangement that has the indicator below and a repeater in the cockpit is a convenient one for singlehanding. A less costly arrangement is to have the indicator mounted on a hinged arm just inside the companionway so that it can be swung outside the cabin for visibility from the helm or inside the cabin for viewing from below. Pointer or digital indicators are probably easier for the singlehander to read than the flashing light indicator, which often has to be interpreted to some extent and can be obscured by direct sunlight. As said earlier, an audible alarm that can be set to sound off at a given depth can be valuable for the lone sailor making a landfall.

Accurate dead reckoning is difficult on any vessel, but it is especially so when one sails alone, because the boat may sail an erratic course when there is no one at the helm, and, very often, temporary course changes, from a windshift, for instance, will go unrecorded. The course must be checked and the log read as often as possible. The singlehander has to become intimately familiar with his self-steering device in a variety of wind and sea conditions in order to estimate accurately its ability to hold a steady course. Averaging yaws may not suffice, since the boat may swing in one direction and remain there for a longer period that she does in the opposite direction. An off-course alarm (described earlier) for major course alterations can be invaluable. Also helpful, as mentioned before, is a telltale or extra conventional compass below which is rigged in conjunction with a mirror so that a course change can be seen from the bunk. For quick reading, it is preferable that the compass have a five-degree card with only a few numbers and the cardinal points marked in large, bold letters. A hand-bearing compass with edge-reading facilities can also be satisfactory.

Speedometers may be used to measure distance on short runs, but they require time keeping, of course, and so are not as convenient or accurate as distance-recording logs. Most offshore sailors use taffrail logs towed astern. These are quite accurate, and they use no electricity, but their rotors are occasionally fouled with weed or bitten off by large fish. An extra rotor or two should be carried, and they are said to be less attractive to fish when painted black. Many experienced sailors can "guesstimate" without instruments the speed of their boats with surprising accuracy.

A DR computer similar to the "Hadrian" made by Brookes and Gatehouse can be very handy at certain times, since distance off course can be read from a dial at any time. However, the instrument requires a special log and electronic compass, it uses some electricity, and, of course, it does not consider the effects of current.

In recent years, several sophisticated offshore electronic navigation systems have been developed, such as Loran C, Omega, and Decca (the British developed system), but it does not seem likely that old-fashioned celestial navigation with the sextant, a time piece, and astronomical tables will ever be entirely replaced, at least not for many years to come. Electronic methods are relatively expensive, not as reliable, a drain on power, often lacking in consistent accuracy, and sometimes lacking in range.. Although it takes practice to make an observation with the sextant from the deck of a small boat, the method is reliable in clear weather, and calculations have been greatly simplified with the modern systems, such as those using HO 214, HO 229, and HO 249. There is even a tiny computer that can be programmed for these navigation methods and thereby all but eliminates laborious arithmetic. Of course, accurate time, necessary for longitude, is no longer the problem it once was.

Slocum often talked, tongue in cheek, about his chronometer, an old tin clock which he bought for one dollar and later "boiled," but the Captain could check his time from the early method of lunar observations. Nowadays, the offshore singlehander has accurate time with an electric watch, which operates from a tuning fork (or quartz crystal in expensive instruments), and a good portable radio, which gives time checks from the BBC (London), WWV (Colorado), WWVH (Hawaii), CHU (Canada), or other stations. WWV and WWVH, operated by the National Bureau of Standards on 2.5, 5, 10, 15, and 25 MHz, also broadcast high seas storm information for the offshore mariner.

During the 1960 transatlantic race, Valentine Howells lost power for his radio, and therefore proper time checks, because his battery straps shrank, crushing a huge battery, and, incidentally, dangerous chlorine gas was formed when the acid ran into the bilge. The lessons seem clear: to have a proper battery holding box and carry a portable transoceanic radio that can receive time signals with dry cell batteries and adequate spares. It is also advisable to carry a spare timepiece.

There seems to be a variety of opinion on the most suitable sextant for the singlehander. Some favor small, lightweight models for their ease of stowing and because they can be held a long time without tiring the arm, while others prefer heavier models (but seldom over five pounds) on a small boat, because they can be held steadier in a wind and the larger models are usually easier to read and operate. Micrometer screws for fine adjustments, rather than vernier scales, are generally preferred. More than a few singlehanders have used cheap plastic sextants successfully, but I have heard of slight distortion of the frame in the tropics and a few problems with mirrors and filters. One has to be careful that the cheap plastic sextant has proper sun shades to block out damaging rays, not always in the visible spectrum; otherwise, serious eye damage could result. The rotating, variable-density, polarized shades found on some of the newer sextants allow any shading variations with one simple adjustment.

Some sailors claim that sextants with bubble attachments are handy when the horizon is obscure, but even in weather that is quite calm it is difficult to hold the bubble steady on a small boat. An averaging device or plotting the sights on graph paper can help. In purchasing a bubble attachment, one should be sure the bubble is damped for marine use. There are unusual conditions where a bubble might be useful as a check. Such a condition could be the one experienced by Francis Chichester in 1964, during his Atlantic crossing in the *Gipsy Moth III*. One day, Chichester's sun observations were wildly erratic, up to 90 miles in error, he said, although he was an expert navigator, having written several textbooks on the subject. He finally came to the conclusion that there was a huge undetectable ground swell, due perhaps to a distant storm, that was giving him a false horizon.

A great aid in taking a sight alone, of course, is a stop watch that can be clicked at the instant the celestial body kisses the horizon. Some single-handers, however, find it sufficiently accurate to count off the seconds. Brian Cooke described his method as follows: "My drill is to take the sight then immediately count the seconds to myself while putting the sextant in a safe place; then looking at my watch and recording the time; then picking up the sextant and reading the altitude and noting this . . ." Ann Davison, on the other hand, found the counting method difficult, for she wrote: "Lurching through the companion hatch, clutching the sextant, I would murmur, 'One and two and oops and three, no four, and oh-oh, and six, where was I? and oh-damn,' and climb out again to take another sight." She resolved to buy a stop watch at the first opportunity.

Recently, it was reported that singlehander Jean-Claude Protta designed a very sophisticated chronometer that is attached to the sextant. A button, pushed at the moment of a sight, will stop the second hand, and after time has been recorded, another button will restart and automatically reset the hand.

Solo sailors vary tremendously in their proficiency as navigators. Some set off on a voyage with little if any knowledge of celestial navigation and hope that they will learn enroute, while others are masters of the art and insist on pin-point positions. Frank Casper, for instance, is such an expert that he uses lunars (à la Slocum) for time, and he once got a letter of thanks from the U.S. Naval Observatory for finding an error in the tables

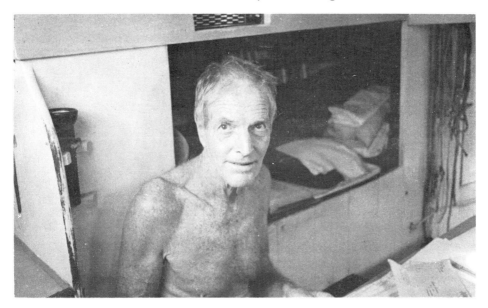

Singlehander Frank Casper, an expert navigator, shown at his chart table in the cabin of his cutter Elsie. *(Harold Chasalow Photo)*

of the *Nautical Almanac.* John Letcher has also worked out a reasonably accurate method of figuring time from lunars without use of the lunar tables which are no longer published in the *Nautical Almanac.* Then, in contrast, there is the case of Fred Rebell, who not only did not know celestial navigation before he set forth to cross the Pacific in a semi-open boat, but even attempted to make his own instruments. His sextant was constructed from a Boy Scout telescope costing one shilling, an iron hoop, and a hacksaw blade bent into an arc with the teeth serving as the degree scale. A taffrail log was made by inserting some twisted strips of aluminum into a broom handle, which served as the rotor, while the indicator was fashioned from a geared-down clock. This kind of equipment can hardly be recommended, but amazingly enough, it did work to some extent, and it illustrates the ingenuity of some singlehanders.

With the exception of self-steering, which will be covered in the next chapter, most of the standard techniques of singlehanding have at least been touched on in this chapter, but in reading an early (1924), delightful book on the subject by Francis B. Cooke, I find that I have neglected to mention the practice of reading on deck. Mr. Cooke wrote, "You may even lounge in a deck-chair with pipe and book, just casting a glance around every now and then to see that your course is clear." He then went on wisely to warn of the danger of becoming too absorbed in a book and neglecting a proper lookout. He advised against reading a novel with an enthralling plot and recommended such books as *Stevenson's Letters, Pepys' Diary,* or *Boswell's Johnson.*

Fred Rebell trying out his homemade sextant. (From Escape to the Sea *by Fred Rebell)*

6 / SELF-STEERING

An almost essential requirement for long-distance singlehanding is the ability to make the boat steer herself. It is obvious that the lone sailor must be able to leave the helm to perform many necessary chores and satisfy essential body demands, most especially to sleep.

Natural Ability

In the early days, natural course keeping was not quite the problem it is today, because, if I may be allowed a sweeping generality, most well-balanced cruising boats of former times had more consistent directional stability than modern stock boats of low wetted area. Men like Slocum, Blackburn, Tom Drake, and even Andrews could very often get their vessels to steer themselves on most points of sailing by simply adjusting the sheets and/or securing the helm, whereas this technique is seldom possible with fast, modern designs except for relatively short intervals while sailing close-hauled. Good course keepers like the *Spray* and Drake's *Pilgrim* derived their steadiness, for the most part, from their long keels, relatively symmetrical waterlines, favorable longitudinal relationship of the center of gravity to the true center of lateral resistance, high initial stability, and longitudinally spread out low aspect ratio rigs. On the other hand, the latest racing-cruiser has a short fin keel, either a wedge-shaped or diamond-shaped hull (see Chapter 3), a very fine entry, a tall rig concentrated over the load waterline, and initial tenderness for the sake of a favorable handicap rating, and these characteristics discourage natural course keeping. Easy heeling affects the steadiness of the helm in modern boats for several reasons. First, there is a wide separation in the transverse direction of the sail's center of thrust and the hull's center of resistance, especially when the rig is tall and the draft is deep, and thus a strong turning moment is created, which varies with the angle of heel. Second, the waterlines on many modern hulls become highly asymmetrical with heeling. Third, wedge-shaped or fine-ended boats will often change their longitudinal trim when heeled, thus changing the relationship of the center of lateral resistance with centers of gravity and effort.

The singlehander and yachting editor, Alain Gliksman, who won the under-35-foot award in the 1972 OSTAR, described the difficulties of balancing a heeled boat designed to the International Offshore Rule with the remark: "I don't like the modern IOR boats because when they heel it is like trying to drown a cat — it keeps wanting to come up again; it gets wild and you are getting nowhere." The increasing use of skegs and rudders with some rake aft (rather than the usual forward rake of the typical spade rudder) has helped some of the newest boats, but still, most modern racing-cruisers need special assists for self-steering. Certainly the new breed of boat is a far cry from such naturally stable course-holders as the 35-foot schooner, *Pilgrim*, which Drake claimed would steer herself by the trim of her sails alone "for days and days and days on any point of sailing." Self-steering assists needed by the modern boats take the form of wind vane gears, auto-pilots, special self-steering sails, and sheet-to-helm connections.

Vane Gears

There are a number of vane gear systems, the most common being: (1) the trim-tab type, with the wind vane driving a tab on the main rudder; (2) auxiliary rudder types, with the vane driving its own separate rudder; (3) the pendulum-servo type, whereby the vane twists a vertical pendulum paddle, causing the waterflow to swing the paddle laterally and thus control the helm; and (4) above-water types, whereby the vane controls the helm directly and the self-steering device has no underwater parts.

Although vane steering had been used on model boats for some time previously, Marin-Marie is credited with being the first to use this kind of self-steering on a full-sized yacht, when the Frenchman made a transatlantic solo crossing in the motorboat, *Arielle*, in 1936. The boat was fitted with an electric automatic pilot, but this was seldom used except in flat calms, and most of the self-steering was accomplished with the use of a V-shaped wind vane connected to an auxiliary rudder mounted on the transom. A significant contribution to the art was made in 1955 when the English designer, Michael Henderson, fit his midget ocean racer, *Mick the Miller*, with a vane gear, which some observers claimed could sail the boat to windward better than could a good helmsman. The gear consisted of a small vane

The schooner Pilgrim, *sailed solo across the Atlantic by her creator Thomas Drake, proved to be a natural course keeper. (Courtesy of* Yachting *magazine)*

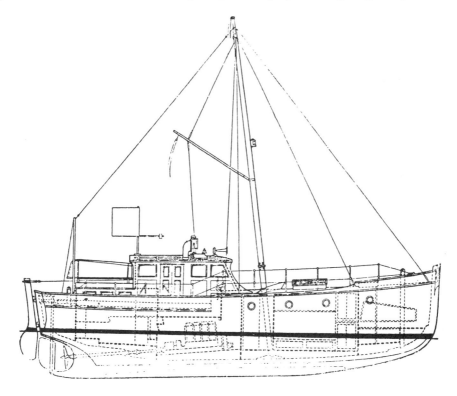

Marin-Marie's Arielle, *said to be the first full-sized vessel to use vane steering when she crossed the Atlantic in 1936. The vane mounted atop the pilothouse is connected to the outboard rudder mounted on the transom. (From* Wind Aloft, Wind Alow *by Marin-Marie)*

with a nearly vertical axis linked to an auxiliary semi-balanced rudder. Then in 1956, Ian Major made a double-handed Atlantic crossing in the 25-foot *Buttercup*, a twin-keel boat fitted with many innovations including a vane gear of the trim-tab kind. Another pioneer, who reportedly was working on vane gear designs as early as 1953, is H. G. Hasler. He used a trim tab on the outboard rudder of his *Jester*, and later he developed a pendulum-servo gear that is now being manufactured by M. S. Gibb Ltd. in England.

The simplest, or at least the most easily understandable, vane steering is the kind that has previously been designated as Type 4, the above-water gear. This controls the helm with the vane alone, and there are no under-water parts. A simple gear of this kind and its operation is illustrated in Figure 6-1. To put the gear in operation, the plywood vane is weathercocked into the wind, and the steering lines are crossed and attached to the tiller. When the boat strays off course, the vane changes its angle to the boat and pulls on the appropriate steering line to make the course correction as illustrated. Notice that there is a counter-balance weight on the vane that offsets the effect of gravity when the boat is heeled or rolling. The V-flaps

FIGURE 6-1: SIMPLE VANE GEAR FOR A SMALL BOAT

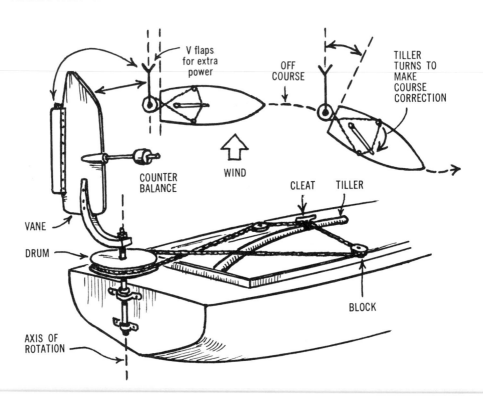

at the vane's trailing edge are not necessary, perhaps, but some authorities claim they add greater torque at low angles of attack and cause a quicker response.

The simple vane gear shown in Figure 6-1 is probably only suitable for a quite small, well-balanced boat. For a large boat using this system, the area of the vane would have to be very large in order to generate sufficient power, but the large size would be difficult to manage in heavy weather. When Francis Chichester used this type of gear in 1960 on his *Gipsy Moth III*, he alleviated the difficulty to some degree by making his vane, which he dubbed *Miranda*, from cloth so that it could be "reefed," in effect, in a blow. As compared with plywood, cloth is not as durable, but it can have

Francis Chichester's Gipsy Moth III *being steered by "Miranda," a large reefable vane having no special appendages underwater. (Courtesy of* Yachting *magazine)*

a bit of camber to increase the power. More recently the power of the above-water vane gear has been increased without the need of resorting to an extremely large vane area by utilizing such innovations as the dual-axis, vertically-pivoted vane acting as a pantograph, wedge-shaped or V-shaped vanes, similar to that of the *Arielle* (with the apex of the V pointing into the wind), and vanes with horizontal or nearly horizontal axes.

The latter types are especially popular, and one of the simplest gears, similar to the QME (Quantock Marine Enterprises) vane, designed by Peter Beard, is illustrated in Figures 6-2 and 6-3. It can be seen that the vane is weathercocked, and, when the boat strays off course, the vane will tip over on its horizontal axis, exerting a considerable force on the appropriate steering line. Notice in Figure 6-3 that when the counterbalance weight is to windward, on the starboard tack, the steering lines are crossed and we have what is called a reverse linkage, but when on the port tack with the weight to leeward the lines are rigged directly (uncrossed) to the tiller. The steering lines are changed over quite easily with a pair of snaphooks.

We used a QME gear on our well-balanced, 30-foot sloop, a fin-keel, spade-rudder Cal 2-30, and the device worked quite well in steady conditions when reaching and beating, but it was not so successful in light, shifty winds or when running. As a matter of fact, many types of vane gears fail when running, because of the weakening of the apparent wind on that point of sailing and also because of quartering seas slewing the stern off course and/or heeling the boat and because of the sudden acceleration when the boat begins to surf. Incidentally, it should be pointed out that a spade rudder often causes greater friction than a well-engineered rudder hung on gudgeons, but many spades are semi-balanced (with the turning axis somewhat abaft the leading edge), and this design partially alleviates the problem. Some real advantages of a small, above-water vane gear are that it is light in weight, easily detachable, and there is no need to deface the boat's stern with heavy, ugly brackets or special boomkins to support underwater parts. On the other hand, the above-water gear on a large boat will not normally be as effective or powerful as a well-designed gear having submerged appendages.

When the position and installation of the rudder allows it, the main rudder trim tab (Type 1) turned by the wind vane is an effective self-steerer. This type has been used successfully by Hasler, Howell, Nance, and many others, and a standard gear of this type of Hasler's design is made by Gibb Ltd., in England. The system seems best suited for outboard rudders hung on double-enders or transom-sterned boats. The basic principle of operation is quite simple. The vane turns a tab attached to the trailing edge of the rudder. Water flow on the tab forces the rudder in the opposite direction to which the tab is turned. In other words, if the tab is turned to

FIGURE 6-2: HORIZONTAL AXIS VANE
(similar to the QME gear)

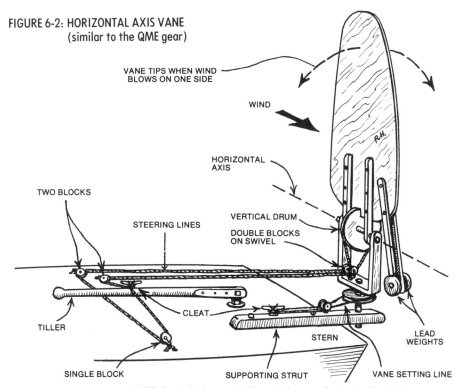

VANE TIPS WHEN WIND
BLOWS ON ONE SIDE

WIND

HORIZONTAL
AXIS

TWO BLOCKS

STEERING LINES

VERTICAL DRUM

DOUBLE BLOCKS
ON SWIVEL

TILLER

CLEAT

STERN

LEAD
WEIGHTS

SINGLE BLOCK

SUPPORTING STRUT

VANE SETTING LINE

NOTE: For clarity the steering lines are shown leading to the side of the boat
opposite the supporting strut, but in actual practice the steering lines would probably
be led to the side on which the strut is mounted

FIGURE 6-3: CROSSING THE STEERING LINES

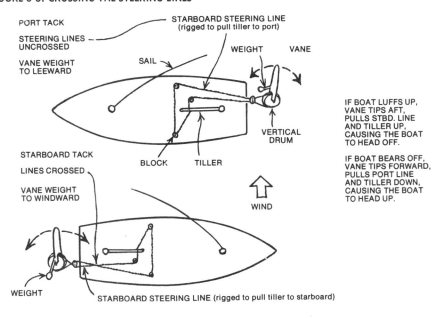

PORT TACK

STEERING LINES
UNCROSSED

VANE WEIGHT
TO LEEWARD

STARBOARD STEERING LINE
(rigged to pull tiller to port)

WEIGHT   VANE

SAIL

VERTICAL
DRUM

IF BOAT LUFFS UP,
VANE TIPS AFT,
PULLS STBD. LINE
AND TILLER UP,
CAUSING THE BOAT
TO HEAD OFF.

IF BOAT BEARS OFF,
VANE TIPS FORWARD,
PULLS PORT LINE
AND TILLER DOWN,
CAUSING THE BOAT
TO HEAD UP.

STARBOARD TACK

LINES CROSSED

VANE WEIGHT
TO WINDWARD

BLOCK   TILLER

WIND

WEIGHT

STARBOARD STEERING LINE (rigged to pull tiller to starboard) port, the rudder is forced to starboard. In practice, the system is more complex, since there are many subtleties in the engineering of a particular rig that can affect the performance. A direct vane-to-tab linkage has been used successfully on occasion, but, in many cases, such a linkage can cause oversteering and yawing problems. Quite often, reduction linkage is used to reduce the tab response, such as the simple, slotted-bar linkage shown in Figure 6-4, which creates a mechanical advantage and angle differences between the vane and tab. Ordinarily, of course, the helm is left to swing free with the main rudder trim tab simply initiating the steering, but in certain cases, when sailing at high speeds, the helm might be lashed, leaving the steering to the tab alone.

Auxiliary rudders (Type 2) are sometimes used when the main rudder is inboard and difficult to fit with a trim tab. In this case, a secondary rudder, controlled by the vane, is often mounted outboard, generally on the transom and/or stern pulpit. Occasionally, an auxiliary rudder is permanently mounted inboard on its own skeg, as in the case of *Mick the Miller*, and this system can be very effective. It has at least one drawback, however, in that a non-removable auxiliary rudder always adds somewhat to the underwater drag, even though it can be kept quite small when semibalanced. On the other hand, a stern-mounted auxiliary rudder, which is not too heavy, can be designed for easy raising or removal when not in use. Of course, removal will eliminate drag, harmful weight aft, unsightliness, and possible vulnerability to damage in heavy weather. Incidentally, an advantage of any auxiliary rudder is that it can serve as an emergency back-up in the event that the main rudder should fail. Some authorities recommend that auxiliary rudder self-steering gears be fitted only on smaller boats (perhaps under 40 feet long), but power can be increased by balancing the rudder blade or adding a trim tab to the trailing edge. Three production self-steering gears of the auxiliary rudder type are the "Automate," made in England; the "Polaris," made by James F. Ogg and Associates in California; and the "RVG" (Riebant Vane Gear), also made in California. The former gear is a neat portable system intended only for boats "up to 19 feet" long on the waterline, but RVG claims they have sizes suitable for boats up to 50 feet long on deck. To put this type of system in operation, the main rudder is secured, usually in a position that will correct for any weather helm, and then the vane is aligned with the wind and locked to the auxiliary rudder.

It seems that most of the well-known modern singlehanders sailing sizeable boats, including circumnavigators Chichester, Rose, King, Blackwell, Baronowski, and others, use pendulum-servo self-steering gears (Type 3). The reason for this is that in recent years these gears have been made highly reliable, they have great power and sensitivity, and they can be readily

FIGURE 6-4: TRIM TAB GEAR

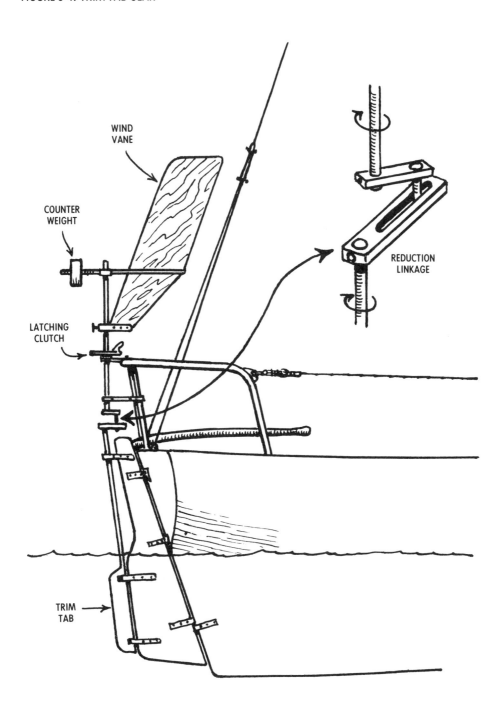

WIND
VANE

COUNTER
WEIGHT

LATCHING
CLUTCH

TRIM
TAB

REDUCTION
LINKAGE

fitted to the popular counter sterns. Furthermore, most standard types are not outrageously expensive, nor does the boat require modifications, as in the case of a permanent, inboard, auxiliary rudder with skeg.

Figure 6-5 shows a simple, step-by-step diagram of the gear in operation. This illustration shows no structural supports, as are customarily shown in manufacturers' drawings, because these often add to the complexity and make it difficult to visualize the operation. In step A, the vane turns because of the boat straying off course or the wind shifting (the vane always tries to point into the wind). The turning motion is transmitted through a reverse linkage, in this case a crossed belt or slotted bar, as illustrated, connecting the vane to the underwater pendulum suspended over the stern. The pendulum is twisted (step B), and since it is hinged on a longitudinal axis, the water flow forces it to swing to one side (step C). This motion turns the quadrant at the top of the pendulum and thus pulls the appropriate steering line, which leads to the tiller (step D). Although the procedure may seem like a Rube Goldberg arrangement, it is really quite efficient. I have been sailing with an Aries vane gear, which uses a pendulum-servo controlled by a small, horizontal-axis vane, and I was quite impressed with the way it steered a heavy, 36-footer (with a moderately long keel) under a variety of difficult conditions. There have been many good reports about the Aries, which is made by Nick Franklin (Marine Vane Gears) in England, and also about the Hasler-Gibb gear (previously mentioned), which uses a vertical-axis vane similar to the one shown in Figure 6-5. Still another popular and relatively inexpensive pendulum gear is produced by Gunning in England. Its vane axis is horizontal, and there is the unusual feature that several different sized vanes can be fitted for different strengths of wind. Indeed, Noel Bevan is said to have carried seven vanes (some spares) on his *Myth of Malham*, but Clare Francis (Chapter 1) tells us that she used a general-purpose vane on her Gunning gear, which obviated the need for frequent changes.

Many specific self-steering gears with their operational details can be seen in the Amateur Yacht Research Society's book, *Self Steering*, edited by John Morwood, and also in John Letcher's fine book *Self-Steering for Sailing Craft*. Neither of these books, however, considers in much detail the various alternative ways of attaching the gear to the vessel or the matter of linkage with wheel steering. Attachments must be made in the strongest possible manner, but many sailors rightfully object to boring more holes than necessary and weighing down their sterns with supporting structures that resemble a child's "jungle gym." A lot of planning should go into the attachment of the gear, not only for strength, freedom of movement, neatness, and simplicity, but also for flexibility of adjustment after trial and error. It is often a wise plan, if possible, to mount the gear

FIGURE 6-5:
OPERATIONAL PRINCIPLE OF
THE SERVO-PENDULUM
VANE GEAR

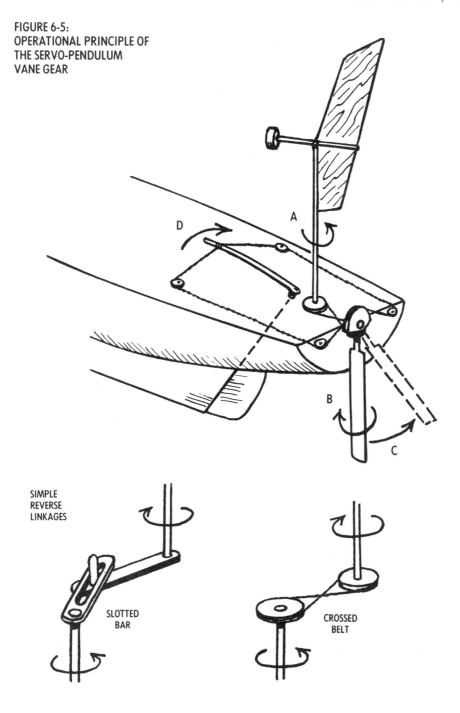

A

D

B

C

SIMPLE
REVERSE
LINKAGES

SLOTTED
BAR

CROSSED
BELT

in a temporary way in order to test it before the final installation. Many of the individual manufacturers will have ideas about methods of attachment and also about rigging for wheel steering. Marine Vane Gears, for instance, makes a special drum with a clutch that is secured to the wheel for the acceptance of steering lines (see Figure 9-2). The lines may be easily disengaged in a moment by simply pulling a knob to free the wheel for normal sailing, an important feature when sailing in crowded waters. On some boats an emergency tiller might be rigged when the vane gear controls the helm, but unless the wheel steering system works very freely, excessive friction might cause a problem.

A vane gear's power and sensitivity is very much dependent on the mitigation of friction. Whenever possible, it is advisable to use ball bearings and plastic bushings where this is commensurate with strength. Constant

The interesting double-ender Aleutka, *designed, built, and sailed by John Letcher (and sometimes singlehanded by his wife Pati). This boat was used for a variety of different self-steering experiments, the results of which appear in Letcher's book* Self-Steering for Sailing Craft. *(Courtesy of John Letcher)*

lubrication is needed also, because of the salt-water environment. I have heard about and seen quite a few cases of vane gears malfunctioning because corrosion or salt deposits jammed the moving parts. Of course, steering lines, too, must be led fair and run through firmly-attached blocks of suitable type and size.

Automatic Pilots

An entirely different approach to self steering is with the use of auto-pilots. As said earlier, Marin-Marie used an early model in his *Arielle,* and it worked surprisingly well over a long period of time (except when an important spindle unexpectedly expanded from overheating). Auto-pilots are far more suitable for powerboats, however, than they are for offshore sailboats, because of the electrical drain. Mechanical power is obtained from an electric motor that controls the rudder. Of course, the generation of electricity is no problem for a powerboat underway, but a sailboat under sail must deplete the charge stored in her batteries.

Just how great the electrical demands will be depends on many factors, such as the particular model of the auto-pilot, the size and weight of the vessel, her balance and yaw characteristics, sea conditions, other electric equipment, and so forth. A large vessel that is difficult to steer will require an auto-pilot with considerable torque output, but a small, well-balanced boat might use one of the small, inexpensive, self contained and low-powered models intended primarily for tiller steering, such as the Signet, Tiller Master, or Sharp's Tiller Mate. Battery charging requirements could possibly vary between the need to charge every six hours and every two days. Of course, an engine-driven alternator or independent generator can be used, but then there is the need to carry quantities of fuel on a long passage, and many sailors object to the noise of a generator. It has been suggested that using the auto-pilot's motor to operate a trim tab instead of the entire main rudder would save a tremendous amount of power, but, as far as I know, this system is seldom, if ever used.

The motor is sometimes activated by a very small plastic vane, but usually by a compass, in which case the boat is automatically held on a compass course. Needless to say, there is an immense difference between a compass-controlled and a vane-controlled course. In the latter case, the steadiness of the course depends on the degree and frequency of wind shifts, and when beating to windward the boat should sail at near maximum efficiency, perhaps better than if she were controlled by a helmsman. On the other hand, the compass control will keep a steady course, but the boat will seldom be sailing at peak efficiency. In fact, a sudden wind shift could put her aback or cause a jibe when running. Except perhaps in extreme wind shifts, there is no real need for an off-course alarm on a properly operating compass-controlled auto-pilot, but with any kind of self-steering, of course, it is essential for the singlehander to keep a lookout, continually in crowded waters and periodically in the open sea.

The disadvantage of battery drainage may become less and less of a problem as a result of modern experiments with charging devices that use such readily available energy sources as the wind and water. Attempts have even been made to utilize the vessel's motion, heat from the cabin stove, and solar energy, but the most promising results have come from underwater free-wheeling propellers and wind generators. A few competitors in the 1972 OSTAR had auto-pilots, because the rules allowed them, provided the electricity was produced by natural means and not by engine or chemical charging. The *Vendredi 13* was fitted with special free-wheeling propellers coupled to generators, but the Amateur Yacht Research Society reported that the system was not entirely satisfactory. On the other hand, Gerard Dijkstra, sailing the 71-foot, *Second Life,* which was dismasted during the race, claimed adequate satisfaction with his propeller-driven alternator, and it is my understanding that Bruce Webb later developed a similar arrangement for his 47½-foot *Gazelle.* These boats are said to use engine-shaft clutches and equipment produced by Sharp and Company in England. Michael Ellison, who sailed the *Tahiti Bill* home after the singlehander's race, suggested that rather than using a rotating propeller, a bicycle wheel with paddles might be placed between the hulls of a catamaran to generate power.

A wind-operated alternator was used by Martin Minter-Kemp on his *Strongbow,* and evidently it was satisfactory until about the middle of the transatlantic race, when the three-foot-diameter aluminum fan blew away during a squall. Fan-type or propeller-type windmills are not only vulnerable to strong winds, but also need a lot of open space in which to operate, and some can be extremely dangerous if they are not screened or located aloft or perhaps far astern, outboard. A friend of mine, Irving Groupp, has been working on what he calls a Savonius rotor (see Figure 6-6), a cluster of wind-rotated scoops, which would turn a generator or alternator. The scoops are mounted in tiers on a common vertical axis of rotation, but each tier is facing in a different direction as shown in the illustration. The advantage of such an arrangement is that it would require comparatively little space, would be relatively safe, might be easier to mount (possibly on a permanent backstay), and can be activated by wind from any direction, thus obviating the need for weathercocking. To my knowledge, this concept is presently just at the idea stage for boats, but it may have possibilities.

Very recently I read that singlehander Jean-Claude Protta has devised an auto-pilot used with a computer which uses so little current that it will operate up to two weeks on four flashlight batteries. Reportedly, the system will be produced by the Swiss firm Oxy Nautica.

Steering Sails and Sheet-to-Helm Connections

Many singlehanders have worked out completely satisfactory self-steering arrangements with special steering sails and/or by rigging sheets of special or standard sails to the helm. Although these methods forego a few of the advantages of vane or auto-pilot steering, they can avoid the use of expensive, complicated, and cumbersome equipment, and, of course, there is no electric power drain. Furthermore, with sail self-steering, trial and error experiments are often possible without the need of investing in costly mechanical gear that might prove less than entirely satisfactory.

As mentioned in the last chapter, the very innovative singlehander, Otway Waller, is given credit for inventing self-steering with twin headsails when

FIGURE 6-6: SAVONIUS-TYPE ROTOR

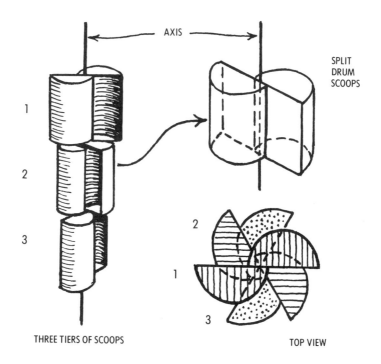

he sailed the 26-foot yawl *Imogen*, designed by Albert Strange, from Ireland to the Canary Islands in 1930. Shortly thereafter, Frederic A. Fenger, Marin-Marie, and Paul Hammond (see Chapter 3) devised different variations of the same system. In recent times, twin-headsail steering has been improved, standardized, and marketed by Wright Britton of Britton Yacht Systems (Chapter 5). Even in this age of highly-developed vane gears, twin headsails are a popular form of self-steering, partly because they work so well when running long distances, during tradewind passages for instance, when vane steering is least successful.

The basic principle of the twin-headsail rig is quite simple. Typically, two identical headsails (sometimes called twin staysails, or twin spinnakers, or twin wings) are boomed out on opposite sides of the boat, and their sheets are led back through quarter blocks to the tiller. When the boat strays off course, one twin pulls on its sheet harder than the other twin, which makes the helm correction and returns the boat to her proper course. (See Figure 6-7a). It is desirable to have the twins angled slightly forward so that their outboard edges are somewhat forward of their inboard edges, as illustrated. Waller used an angle of only ten degrees, but Fenger claimed, as a result of experiments with models, that twenty-three degrees was ideal.

FIGURE 6-7: TWIN HEADSAILS

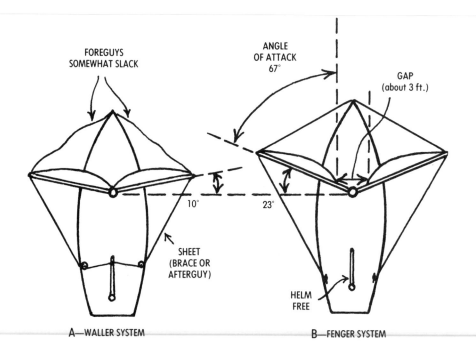

A—WALLER SYSTEM   B—FENGER SYSTEM

With this wider angle, and some space or gap between the luffs so that some wind can flow between the two sails, Fenger found that it was not necessary to secure the sheets to the helm (see Figure 6-7b). The gap between twin headsails may not be essential for course-keeping, however, because the Britton rig has the luffs of both twins sewn to a common wire with no gap, yet I was told by Wright Britton that a sheet-to-helm connection should not be necessary when the wind is aft.

John Letcher reported negative results in self-steering with his twins unconnected to the helm using a gap and the twenty-three-degree angle, but he conceded that angling the twins forward to form a wedge configuration contributes to stability. John feels, however, that the stability is gained at the sacrifice of considerable driving power. It is certainly true that with the twenty-three-degree angle, the thrust of the sails is not working in exactly the same direction in which the boat is moving with the wind dead aft, but, on the other hand, this configuration, with its sixty-seven-degree

Wright Britton's 40-foot yawl Delight *using the Britton "twin wings topsail" for greater speed in light airs. (Courtesy of Wright Britton)*

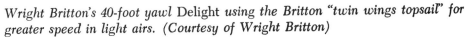

Francis Chichester appears to be rigging telescopic booms for self-steering twins on the Gipsy Moth III, *winner of the first OSTAR in 1960. (Courtesy of* Yachting *magazine)*

angle of attack causes some aerodynamic lift, which adds to the magnitude of the thrust even if it is from a less-than-optimal direction. Shroudless racing boats often ease their sheets so that their booms are well forward of athwartships with good results, and Fenger claimed that this practice on sailing canoes increased directional stability without loss of speed. As a matter of fact, Marcel Bardiaux made satisfactory speed in the trade winds with his twins angled as far forward as forty-five degrees, and he claimed his *Les 4 Vents* sailed a steady course with the helm left free.

One of the major differences among the various twin-headsail arrangements is the manner of their setting and handing. The Waller, Hammond, and Britton systems make use of roller-furling gear. Waller had the luffs and furling drums at the outboard ends of the poles, while Hammond had the tack of each twin and two drums located near his *Barnswallow's* stem. The Britton arrangement has a single roller drum controlling the luffs of both twins tacked down to the foredeck just forward of the mast (see Figure 6-8). With the roller gear, sail is reduced or furled by rolling the twins up on their luffs. Marin-Marie, however, found no need for roller furling, and he simply hoisted and lowered the twins with halyards in the conventional way. In some cases, the poles secure at fairly low points on the mast, and their outboard ends are hoisted aloft with their topping lifts so that they lie alongside the mast for convenient stowage when the twins are not being used. Other poles are secured to the mast quite far aloft so that the outboard ends may be dropped to the chainplates for convenient stowage. John Letcher's poles secure to the mast at the lower spreaders, which seems like a good idea, because the mast gets some bracing at that point from the lower shrouds. There is a neat arrangement with the Britton system whereby the inboard ends of the poles are fitted to vertical mast slides, and the inboard pole ends are down, perhaps about seven feet above the cabin top, when in use, but are up at the top of the slides so the poles may be stowed alongside the shrouds or mast when not in use (see Figure 6-8).

Some sailors who use twin-headsail rigs report severe rolling in following seas; thus the outboard ends of the poles must be kept high to prevent the possibility of dipping them in the sea. Of course, this requires that the sails be cut with high clews, and the inboard pole ends should not be carried too low, or else the poles will have a tendency to ride upward. In general, it seems best to keep the poles about horizontal or cocked upward very slightly. Occasionally, a storm trysail is hoisted and sheeted flat amidships to help damp rolling, but since the true wind is from astern the damping will be minimal. Incidentally, Captain Waller alleviated the rolling of

FIGURE 6-8:

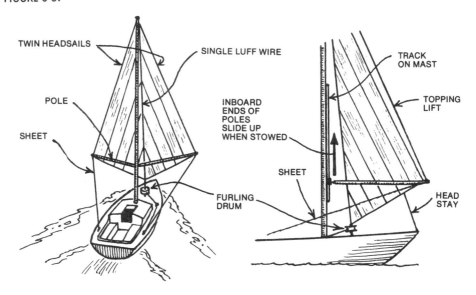

his *Imogen* by hoisting an anchor some distance up the mast, where it was secured to stop it from swinging. Evidently, this raised the center of gravity somewhat and reduced the metacentric height to affect the motion beneficially. John C. Voss once used the same trick with some success.

Self-steering with twin headsails works well when the wind is aft or slightly on the quarter, but other systems are needed when the wind is farther forward. Some of these systems are illustrated in Figures 6-9, 6-10, 6-11, and 6-12. Figure 6-9 is an easily-rigged method used by singlehander Tony Skidmore as his "sole means of self steering" on a 17,000-mile voyage in a 24-foot, fin-keel sloop. As can be seen in the diagram, a small staysail, a storm jib in Skidmore's case, is held slightly aback by a windward sheet led through a block at the shrouds, thence to a quarter block, and finally to the tiller, which is held almost amidships by elastic cord. When the boat wanders off course toward the wind, the weather sheet pulls harder than the elastic cord and pulls the tiller up to put the boat back on course. If she falls off too far, the staysail exerts less pull on the sheet, and the cord pulls the tiller down to make the course correction. In an article written for *Yachting Monthly* magazine, Skidmore claimed that the system worked for all points of sailing "from a close reach to within fifteen degrees of a dead run." The magazine's editor also tried the method and verified its effectiveness.

Many of the modern sheet-to-helm arrangements for self-steering make use of elastic lashings, and it is interesting that this wrinkle was used by Captain Waller back in 1930. He is said to have used rubber straps for exercising the muscles called "Sandow Developers," named after the popular strong man. Nowadays, of course, most sailors use elastic shock cord, although John Letcher writes that he prefers surgical tubing.

A somewhat similar method to Skidmore's is used by Frank Casper aboard his cutter, *Elsie,* and Figure 6-10 is based on a diagram that Frank sketched for me. The *Elsie's* staysail is fairly large and is set on a permanent boom. The windward sheet has an extra purchase, and sometimes the sheet is shifted aft on the tiller as shown by the dashed line in the diagram. In light weather when the wind is quite far aft, a jib is poled out to weather. Under these conditions, the circumnavigator carries his mainsail vanged down and trimmed flatter than normal to help prevent rolling. A vane gear is carried in addition to steady the boat in very rough seas.

A single staysail poled out on the windward side is often referred to as the weather-twin method of self-steering. With this system, the weather-twin's sheet is usually led to the tiller as shown in Figure 6-11. This windward sheet pulls the tiller up when the boat luffs, and the pull is counteracted by the strain of either shock cord and/or a jib or unboomed leeward staysail sheet attached to the tiller's opposite side, as illustrated. John Guzz-

FIGURE 6-9:
BACKED STAYSAIL
(Tony Skidmore)

FIGURE 6-11:
WEATHER TWIN

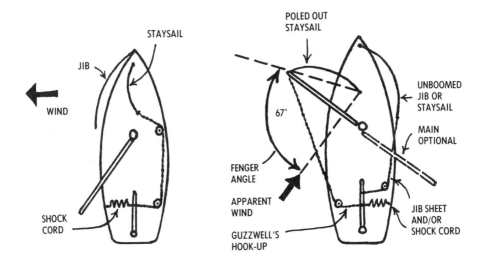

FIGURE 6-10:
STAYSAIL AND POLED-OUT JIB
(Frank Casper)

FIGURE 6-12:
MAINSHEET CONTROL
(John Letcher)

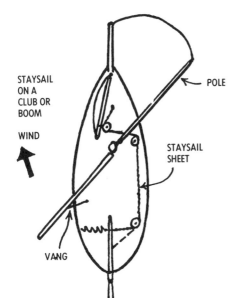

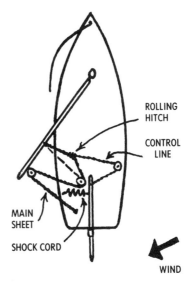

well, who used this latter kind of arrangement on his *Trekka,* secured the weather-twin sheet farther aft on the tiller than the leeward headsail's sheet to balance evenly the strain on the helm.

Frederic Fenger theorized that the angle of attack of the weather twin should be about sixty-seven degrees (see Figure 6-11), so that the wind flow is reversed, moving from leech to luff, and Stanley Bradfield tried this trim successfully on his double-ender, *D'Vara.* On this boat, the weather twin's sheet was secured to the tiller in the customary manner, but its pull was counteracted by an elastic rubber strap. Bradfield could carry full sail in addition to the twin, and he found that the system worked well in a variety of wind strengths on all points of sailing, from a dead run to nearly a beam reach. The *D'Vara* was hardly a typical boat, however, for she had an unusual main-trysail ketch rig, and she was designed by Harrison Butler to the metacentric shelf theory, which some designers still think produces an exceptionally well-balanced hull.

For brief periods of solo sailing, an ordinary staysail boomed out to weather with a standard spinnaker pole and carried with the mainsail broad off is a very simple means of self-steering before the wind. The staysail's sheet is led to the tiller's weather side, and its pull is counteracted with shock cord. I have even used a jib (rather than a staysail) successfully, which normally means that the headsail is not angled forward. Even so,

Designer and self-steering innovator Frederic A. Fenger singlehanding the 17-foot canoe Yakaboo *through the West Indies. (Courtesy of Wellington Books; from* Alone in the Caribbean *by Frederic A. Fenger)*

with careful adjustment of the shock cord, the method can be made to work on many boats, because a change of course into the wind causes extra pull on the sheet and a change away from the wind causes less pull, as the jib becomes partially blanketed by the mainsail. It is important, however, to rig a boom vang or preventer to avoid an accidental jibe.

Figure 6-12 shows still a different kind of sheet-to-helm self-steering, the connection of the mainsheet to the tiller. This method was used successfully by John Letcher on his solo and double-handed Pacific voyages. It can be seen that a line, which John calls the control line, leads from the tiller to a windward block and thence to one part of the mainsheet tackle where the control line is secured, normally with a rolling hitch. Notice that the part of the mainsheet holding the rolling hitch is bent or pulled away from being a straight line. The dashed line shows the sheet as it would be if the control line were not attached. This pull by the control line on the mainsheet is counteracted by shock cord or elastic led from the tiller to the leeward coaming. The system is based on the premise that most well-balanced boats will hold a steady course when close-hauled in a steady breeze. An increase in wind velocity will normally cause heeling and luffing up toward the wind, while a lull will cause bearing away. With the mainsheet-to-tiller system, a puff will put more pressure on the mainsail and pull on the control line via the mainsheet, thus pulling the helm to weather and correcting the course; while a lull will do just the opposite, increase the bend and allow the shock cord to pull the tiller to leeward. The method takes a good many trial-and-error adjustments, but John has used it on points of sailing from beam-reaching to close-hauled on a variety of boats in various strengths of wind, and he has written that "it has never failed."

It should be evident that there are many ways to "skin the cat" as far as self-steering is concerned. Other sail methods are to use a riding sail, set on the backstay with its sheet attached to the helm, or to secure the mizzen sheet to the helm on a yawl or ketch. A very simple method for temporary use, which need not take any extra sails or equipment, is to rig the jib sheet from its leeward winch to a quarter block to windward and thence to the tiller, which is held almost amidships by shock cord. This arrangement will be discussed in more detail in Chapter 9.

Self-steering is not the only challenge the singlehander faces, but its importance is illustrated by the remark made by Clare Francis when a reporter asked her a question concerning her motivations and the increasing popularity of the sport. She said simply, "People are sailing the Atlantic because of self-steering devices."

7 / EMERGENCY EXPERIENCES

On a fully-crewed vessel, emergencies can be difficult enough, but they will be infinitely more serious for the singlehander. This chapter and the next will recount a variety of actual, untoward experiences undergone by those who have sailed alone. Many of these stories are worth telling or retelling for the purity of adventure and the courage and/or endurance they display, but much more important, they contain examples of correct or occasionally incorrect action and teach valuable lessons in seamanship to all who make, or aspire to make, passages shorthanded.

Collisions

Perhaps the greatest hazard faced by a solo voyager is vulnerability to collisions. Obviously, he cannot stand watch all of the time, and considerable sleep and rest is essential for the preservation of strength, good health, proper spirits, and soundness of judgment. Thus the vessel must be left in charge of herself for a large part of the time during a passage, and then she is subject to the possibility of colliding with ships, other boats, flotsam, or even formidable marine life, such as whales. Actually the danger is not so great as it might seem when the singlehander takes the proper precautions, but there is always a certain degree of risk. Safeguards against collisions include: radar reflectors, echo enhancers (Chapter 5); flashing strobe lights; running lights aloft (now allowed by the International Rules of the Road); off-course alarms (Chapter 5); depth-sounder alarms; and perhaps radar alarms (Chapter 5). Of course, sensible precautions are the avoidance of steamer lanes and congested fishing banks, sleeping during the day when in crowded waters, and seeing that one's vessel is soundly constructed to withstand violent impact.

The most serious collision threat is probably from ships, and especially fishing vessels. Despite the fact that merchant ships stick closely to established traffic patterns and channels near large ports and to steamer lanes when offshore, modern ships move at high speeds, lack maneuverability, are sometimes under-crewed and lacking in adequate lookouts, and depend for much of the time on observation by radar, which is less reliable than the human eye unless visibility is very poor. Fishing vessels do not necessarily stick to established routes, even though fishing grounds and ports are generally well known. Some singlehanders are extremely concerned about the possibility of being run down by ships, while others seem casual to the point of being fatalistic. Robert Manry, for instance, spent much time sleeping during the day and standing watch at night. On the other hand, John Guzzwell wrote me concerning his voyage in the *Trekka*, "Don't know about being run down by steamers. I'm a heavy sleeper."

One singlehander who has given considerable thought to the risks involved in sleeping at night on a shorthanded passage is John Letcher. His interest in this subject is more than academic, since he was run down on two occasions, once by a steamer when alone and once by a fishing vessel when his wife was his shipmate. The following account, taken from his

A *signed photograph of Harry Pidgeon at the helm of his* Islander. *Notice the lamp boards on the mizzen shrouds, where they provide safe accessibility. (Courtesy of* Yachting *magazine)*

book, *Self-Steering for Sailing Craft,* describes the time when he was alone:

"From Hawaii I sailed *Island Girl* north to Alaska in 1964, arriving in Sitka early in September. I laid her up there for the winter, and early the next summer I returned for two unforgettable months of cruising and climbing in the fiords and islands of Southeast Alaska; then in mid-August, alone again, I sailed from Sitka to return to Los Angeles.

"The passage was fast, and in pleasure it suffered only from being in the wrong direction — from a remote, wild, exciting region toward a much less thrilling destination, not the way a voyage should be. Fair, fresh winds prevailed, the little black twins drove us over 100 miles almost every day, and the only uncomfortable experience was the northerly gale off northern California. At dusk of the 20th day we made a good landfall, picking up the lights of the coast near Point Conception. This cape is the dividing line between the chill, foggy Pacific Coast weather and the relatively warm, gentle climate of Southern California, so I felt we were almost in home waters.

"That night I saw the lights of many ships — one or two per hour — passing a little way inshore. We were running under twins, but by midnight the wind had almost died and progress — and maneuverability — had become very poor. One northbound ship appeared for a long while as if it were going to pass a little outside us, but rather close. I assumed they were seeing my lights, and was a little annoyed that they would pass so close. As their lights grew closer, and the muffled whine of turbines and the rush of the bow wave came across the water to me, I turned on my searchlight and aimed it at the ship. This was to let them know I was annoyed. Imagine my horror when the ship turned and came directly towards me! White over white, red beside green, the group of lights approached with an awful noise, growing by the second, and there was not the slightest chance of getting out of its path. As the pale bow loomed out of the darkness, I dived through the companionway and instantly there was a terrible jolt and a rending crash. In a few seconds of shuddering vibration the ship's side rushed past, then we were wallowing in the foamy, hissing wake as their stern light drew rapidly away. They never knew we were there.

"It turned out that there was no contact between our hulls. I believe that they were a little off their aim, so that their bow wave washed *Island Girl's* hull aside, but her rig rolled into the side of the ship. The mast was broken in three places, the forestay, headstay, and bowsprit were all broken, and the upward pull on the forestay lifted the deck and clamps so the sheer strakes were split on both sides almost back to the chain plates. I got away with my life and felt very lucky. *Island Girl* was towed to Santa Barbara and I refitted her there."

John Letcher on his Island Girl, *which he sailed solo from California to Hawaii and from Hawaii to Alaska using mostly sheet-to-helm self-steering. Later she was run down by a ship. (Warren Roll,* Honolulu Star Bulletin)

That was a truly frightening experience, but it may be of some comfort to others, who fear being run down by ships, to know that a boat can be fended off by the ship's bow wave (during a nearly head-to-head meeting) so that, unless the collision is dead on center, there is a good chance that there will be only slight, if any, contact between the two hulls. This increases the odds for survival tremendously, although the rig is very apt to be damaged. John told me that he dove below at the last minute before impact, because he considered that the cabin was the safest place to be during a head-on collision. Also, he said that the mast fell on the companionway and blocked it, and this emphasizes the advisability in having another hatch for an alternate exit. I agree with John that the cabin is the safest place to be when there is damage to the rig only, but with serious hull damage that would result in a rapid sinking, a safer location would probably be on deck near the life raft.

Being a very scientific-minded fellow, John calculated the probability of being run down by a ship on his 2,500-mile solo passage from Hawaii to Alaska. He reasoned that he could sail blindly back and forth continuously over those waters for over eighty years and expect to be run down only once in a thousand voyages. If daylight hours were assumed safe and nine-tenths of the ships stuck to charted lanes, the probability of collision for a single passage would be about 1/20,000.

Francis Stokes is even more optimistic. He wrote me that he guessed (very roughly) that his chances of being run down by a ship were possibly one in a million or one in ten million. Still he was not without worries, for he wrote, "Rightly or wrongly, one has a fairly persistent fear of collisions with ships."

Quite often, of course, when the weather permits, ships can be heard or smelled from downwind. The odor of smoke, the sound of whining turbines, the throbbing of diesel engines, the thrashing of screws when ships are light, and even the roar of bow waves can be detected by the singlehander in poor visibility or from his cabin when he is not sound asleep. These sounds often carry well at sea, especially in calm, foggy weather. In some cases, underwater sounds, the turning of a propeller, for instance, can noticeably reverberate through the hull shell. Many passage-making sailors develop a keen sensitivity for unusual sounds. They can sleep through a din of normal noises such as rattling blocks, creaking lines, and the gurgling of water flowing past the hull, but a strange, unexplained sound can wake them. This kind of sensitivity may at times seem almost clairvoyant, as in the case of Hans de Meiss-Teuffen, who crossed the Atlantic alone in 1946 aboard the 34-foot yawl *Speranza*. He entered in his log (on July 18): "Slept two hours, 1 a.m. to 3 a.m. Woke at three with the urge to have a quick look on deck. And there, only 300 yards off, a fishing motor vessel!" Needless to say, a singlehander should never count on any mental alarm systems to warn him, but there is some degree of comfort in knowing that they often work and that acute sensitivities are often developed by offshore sailors. As Michael Richey of *Jester* fame has written, "The experience of waking mysteriously at the right time seems to be a common one. It would be foolish to rely heavily on it, but it can certainly be taken into account."

Frank Casper told me that before he began sailing alone, an irresponsible crew member was nearly the cause of his being run down. On a passage between the Panama Canal and the Galapagos Islands, Casper and his single crew stood watch and watch, one sleeping while the other kept a lookout on deck. One dark night, while the skipper was asleep below, the crew decided to take a nap on deck. He closed the companionway doors and stretched out just behind them on the bridge deck. Casper, having the aforementioned seamanlike sensitivities, awoke to the sounds of an approaching steamer. He tried to rush on deck, but his sleeping crew lying against the companionway doors completely blocked that exit. Frank then ran forward and sprang through the forward hatch just in time to see the great bow of the ship bearing down on him. Rushing aft, he quickly started the engine, threw the helm hard over, and barely escaped a collision. Frank cited this experience as one of the reasons why he prefers to sail alone.

For all of us who sail when there is risk of collision with boats or ships, there is a valuable lesson to be learned from Casper's close shave, and that is to have the engine ready for instant use. This would usually mean having the main switch turned on, and the fuel and exhaust valves open; seeing that the bilges are clear of fumes (they should be anyway, at all times); seeing that the bilge water is below the level of the blower's exhaust hose when the fuel is gasoline; and running the engine for a short time at regular intervals to keep it in good working order.

There is little question that the standard legal running lights on small yachts are difficult and sometimes impossible to see from a large ship, especially when those lights are obscured by sails. One night when a steamer passed close to my small yawl, I heard a voice from the bridge call down, "You'd better get bigger lights than that, buddy." The International Rules of the Road now allow a boat under sail alone to carry, in addition to normal side lights, a twenty-point red light over a twenty-point green light at the masthead, sufficiently separated so as to be clearly distinguishable and visible for two miles. In the near future, a single lantern combining stern and side lights will be allowed at or near the masthead on small boats. Such arrangements help solve the problem of side lights being obscured by sails, and the options seem highly appropriate for singlehanders. Of course, when the solo sailor is awake and spots an approaching ship, he may want to use a "flare-up" light, that is to say, try to attract the ship's attention by turning on a bright flasher temporarily and/or shining a search-light on his sails. Incidentally, white sails are usually less visible or notice-able when lighted at night than those colored yellow, orange, or light red.

Some singlehanders use unusual lighting, often of dubious legality, but of high visibility. For instance, Jerry Cartwright carries a flashing, 360-degree, buoy marker light (Guest, No. 561) lashed to his boat's backstay, and the light is allowed to flash continually every night when he is asleep (it is said to last about 100 nights on the same battery). Although Jerry is not sure about the light's legality, he reasons that the extra safety it affords justifies its use, and he feels that on the high seas there is little chance that another vessel will mistake the blinker for a buoy. In checking into the matter of legality, he obtained unofficial opinions from two different Coast Guard station commanders, who said they would prefer that a small boat be seen and that such a flasher could qualify as a flare-up light allowed by the Rules of the Road. Cartwright seems somewhat dubious, however, about the legality of leaving the light on continuously.

An interesting point was brought up by solo transatlantic sailor Clare Francis, who believes in turning off her running lights and displaying a single white light when asleep. She reasons that if you are a sleeping single-hander and show running lights which indicate to the other vessel that he has the right of way, then you must be able to get out of his way. Of course, this situation would seldom arise unless the other vessel were a priv-ileged sailing craft, a slow-moving vessel that you were overtaking, or a ves-sel fishing, laying cables, and so forth, or your boat were displaying an addi-tional forward white light indicating she was under power. Nevertheless, Miss Francis considers that a single 32-point white light would hopefully lead the ship to assume the boat is "at anchor, fishing, or at least stationary" and thus cause evasive action to be taken early. Actually, the more legally correct lights for a singlehander off watch (under International Rule 4a) would be the running lights plus not-under-command lights, two 32-point red lights in a vertical line, one over the other, at least six feet apart. One well known singlehander who used these lights was Sir Alec Rose. The problem of designating that a boat is not under command will be dis-cussed further in Chapter 10.

One possible hazard of using unconventional lighting is the chance of attracting a ship by arousing her master's curiosity and then possibly being damaged by the ship. This nearly happened to Howard Blackburn several times during his solo Atlantic crossings. He usually carried white instead of colored sidelights because of their better visibility, but on several nights he was approached by steamers that came dangerously close. Even in the daylight, it is not unusual for ships to come right alongside. Harry Pidgeon, Francis Brenton, Francis Chichester, Bernard Moitessier, and others have had their rigs damaged by ships standing by.

Of course, bright lights will do little good when a ship is being steered by autopilot and has no lookout. Radar reflectors on small boats are definitely helpful but obviously only when the ship is radar-equipped and when the equipment is being properly used. An unusual way of getting a ship's attention was tried successfully by Chay Blyth. During his "wrong way" circumnavigation in the *British Steel*, Blyth carried explosives, which were fuse ignited and sounded like fairly heavy guns. Early one morning before dawn, near the Cape of Good Hope, he spotted a ship headed towards him. Blyth flashed his emergency lights and sounded his fog horn, but the ship did not alter course. When she was only about fifty yards away, the singlehander fired an explosive. With that, the ship suddenly sheered off, heeling sharply, and barely missed the *British Steel*. After the incident, Blyth entered in his log, "I'm shaking like a bloody leaf. I just can't control it. We've been close to being run down before but never as close as this."

Unless he heaves to at night, there is little a singlehander can do about preventing collisions with flotsam. The best he can do is to be sure his boat is strongly constructed to withstand violent impact, see that there is some means of keeping the vessel afloat if she should happen to be holed, and of course see that there is a proper means of abandoning and calling for help. A vessel can be kept afloat with permanent or even inflatable flotation, with watertight bulkheads, or by providing an effective method of plugging the hole, such as with a collision mat (see Chapter 5 and Figure 7-1).

Wooden boats seem a little more vulnerable to being holed than those properly built of heavy fiberglass, ferrocement, or steel. Peter Tangvald, for one, lost his old, but strongly-built, wooden cutter, *Dorothea*, during a West Indies passage in March, 1967, when she struck what was thought to be a large piece of flotsam, perhaps a floating tree trunk. The *Dorothea*, which had previously carried Tangvald safely around the world, promptly filled with water and forced her solo skipper to abandon ship in a seven-foot plywood dinghy, which is far from the safest kind of lifeboat. Peter had little time to get off his sinking craft, but he remained remarkably cool-headed, and plotted his position on the chart table with the inrushing water swirling around his legs. Then he quickly gathered together the gear, water, food, flashlight, clothes, compass, and so forth that he would need for his escape. His position was about forty miles southwest of Barbados, and Peter figured his best chance for survival was to head for the Grenadines, approximately fifty-five miles to leeward, making all the speed he safely could. He rigged a jury squaresail from an old awning, using an

FIGURE 7-1: DAMAGE
CONTROL

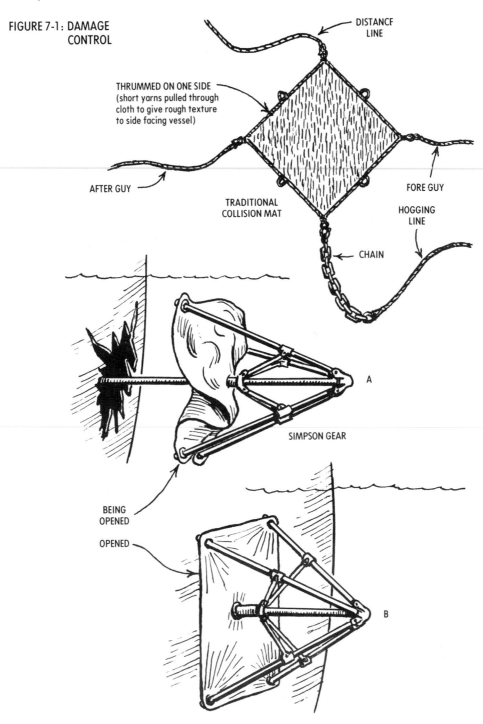

DISTANCE
LINE

THRUMMED ON ONE SIDE
(short yarns pulled through
cloth to give rough texture
to side facing vessel)

AFTER GUY

FORE GUY

TRADITIONAL
COLLISION MAT

HOGGING
LINE

CHAIN

A

SIMPSON GEAR

BEING
OPENED

OPENED

B

oar for the mast and a boat hook for the yard. A steamer passed close aboard in the middle of the night, and Peter repeatedly flashed SOS signals with his powerful light, but to no avail. After twenty hours of somewhat frightening sailing, which required the utmost concentration to keep the boat from swamping in the rough seas kicked up by the fresh trade winds, Tangvald reached Cannouan Island, where he landed in a nearly exhausted condition.

There are a few lessons to be learned from Peter Tangvald's experience. One, not often thought about, is that when a boat has a tight ceiling or inside liner, a damaged area may be inaccessible. Peter could not locate his leak or attempt to stop it, because of the permanent ceiling construction. Many modern boats are just as bad or worse with their fiberglass liners, which often make it difficult to reach the hull shell, fastenings, wiring, hoses, valves, and so forth. Also, there were at least two important items of equipment that Peter found he needed, namely a pocket knife and flares. A portable radio-phone transmitting on 2182 KHz would have improved his chances of being picked up by the steamer; and an inflatable boat would have served him well, but it is reassuring to learn that a well-designed dinghy, even one as small as Tangvald's, can survive in fairly rough seas when it is well handled.

One design feature found on many fin-keel boats, by the way, which increases vulnerability to damage in the event of collision with submerged objects, is the lack of sweepback to a keel's leading edge. John Letcher once hit a submerged floating log in his fin-keeler, *Island Girl,* and even though she was moving slowly, the impact was severe enough to loosen the strakes next to the garboards. The collision could have sunk the boat except that her bottom was covered with copper sheathing for worm protection, and this inhibited extreme leaking.

Multihulls may be more vulnerable to collisions with flotsam or relatively stationary objects than monohulls. Although the former have less displacement and thus carry less momentum, they normally travel at higher speeds and are often more lightly constructed. High speeds not only contribute to the extent of damage, but also, for a given period when there is no lookout, increase the chances that a collision will occur due to the rapidity of convergence with the stationary object. When Eric Tabarly crashed into an anchored freighter at night, not long after the start of the singlehanders transatlantic race in 1968, his trimaran, *Pen Duick IV,* was making fifteen knots. Tabarly had been standing watch but had temporarily ducked below to heat some coffee. Only about fifteen minutes elapsed between the time he carefully checked the horizon for ships and the time of the collision. The *Pen Duick's* unusually high strength-to-weight construction of aluminum allowed her to survive the impact, but she sustained a four-foot gash in one float, and her rig was damaged. Tabarly was forced to abandon the race and limp back to port.

In the 1972 transatlantic race for singlehanders, the catamaran, *Tahiti Bill,* sailed by Bill Howell rammed a slow-moving Russian trawler only about 100 miles from the finish line. The accident took place during daylight hours but in dense fog. The *Tahiti Bill* suffered a stove-in bow, but fortunately she had a watertight bulkhead that kept the hull from filling entirely. The Russians said they had not seen the catamaran when they looked at their radar twenty minutes before the accident. This points up not only the risks involved in sailing fast (though Howell was only making seven knots) without a lookout or in poor visibility, but also the fallibility of depending solely on radar to avoid collisions, especially when the screen is only checked occasionally.

Whales and Dangerous Sea Life

Many sailors venture offshore in small boats with very little thought about the possibility of being attacked by or colliding with sea creatures. This hazard seems to be the kind one would read about in a high-adventure or science-fiction story, but true reports of hull damage and even sinkings caused by marine life are not at all uncommon. The main culprits seem to be whales, killer whales, sharks, and, occasionally, swordfish.

Going back to an early singlehanded voyage, Bernard Gilboy was attacked by a swordfish during his Pacific crossing in 1882. The fish rammed Gilboy's double-ended schooner, the *Pacific,* at high speed and succeeded in putting its sword clean through the bottom of the hull. After giving the boat a shaking, the fish withdrew its blade leaving a spurting hole in the planking. The singlehander stuffed the hole with a wick and some rags, which stopped the leak surprisingly well. Another early singlehander who was attacked by several swordfish was Howard Blackburn during his Atlantic crossing in the *Great Republic* in 1901, but he thwarted the attack before his boat could be impaled by throwing coils of line on top of the fish and eventually driving them off. Blackburn's biographer, Joseph Garland, suggests, however, that such a tactic could be dangerous in that it might cause further provocation.

William Andrews, who feared almost nothing, was all but terrified of whales. During the latter part of his voyage in the *Sapolio* in 1892, not far from the coast of Spain, he encountered a pod of large finbacks, and he made the following remarks in his log: "At 5:30 a herd of fin-back whales came feeding straight for the boat, the wind being so light I could do nothing but keep on and take my chances with their flukes. I seized my shark tickler, rattled it on the boat, made a noise and yelled at them. All to no avail. On they came, with their mouths wide open and with blow holes big enough to crawl into. I commenced to tremble and feel shakey in the knees. When within fifty feet, O, how they made the water boil! I thought they would sound, and felt relieved; but no, I saw them coming under the boat, and as they rose to the surface and blowed all around me they were going in different directions, and so slowly. This they kept up for fifteen minutes, while I seized hold of a rope for safety, and seizing my paddle, used it very dexterously for a few minutes, thinking, from previous experience, that I might frighten them off. But no, still they glided under the boat, nicely or easily avoiding collision with each other and us. Finally, one slipped off, and I felt better; then another and another. One more curious than the others remained around for some time, when he slunk away after his beastly companions. I tell you, my friends, that I stood there holding the tiller trying to avoid those tons of bone and muscle, and without much headway on the boat, with the water boiling and foaming with the commotion they made, turning the boat every which way, completely beyond my control, and I wondering which way my course was, as the compass was whirling, too, they blowing their misty breaths in my face — I tell you again, friends, it wants nerve food a little better than I have with me." Andrews was certainly capable of vivid expression, at least when it came to his concern about whales.

At one time during his circumnavigation in the *Lehg II*, Vito Dumas sailed between two whales that were sleeping side-by-side. The 31-foot ketch actually tried to climb their backs. Dumas wrote that the bow lifted up and then slid off the shiny, slippery mound of flesh. Fortunately, the monsters did not wake up despite their being so rudely jostled, and the *Lehg II* slowly "elbowed" her way between them while the singlehander watched in awe.

Another singlehander, D.M.R. Guthrie, collided with a sleeping blue whale, the world's largest animal, while sailing his 30-foot sloop, *Widgee*, from Antigua to Bermuda in 1969. The impact was sufficient to roll the sloop over on her beam ends and awaken the whale. It thrashed the water in anger and narrowly missed striking the hull with its fluke. After the whale departed, Guthrie found a lump of torn skin and blubber caught in the rigging, and the rudder shaft was bent and jammed. Two days were spent working on the rudder, and repairs were finally effected by cutting away the jammed part with a chisel.

A school of small whales, identified as pilots, deliberately attacked Alan Eddy's 30-foot, Seawind ketch, *Apogee*, in mid-ocean during his circumnavigation. Possibly provoked by a collision with the ketch, the creatures repeatedly charged and butted her until the cabin sole was loosened, but the sturdy fiberglass hull built by the Allied Boat Company withstood the battering.

In contrast, Bill King's *Galway Blazer II* (Chapter 3) was severely damaged by a sea creature despite the boat's strong construction of molded plywood. The accident occurred in the waters just south of Australia in December, 1971, when a collision stove in the hull on one side just below the waterline. At first the singlehander thought that he had been rammed by a killer whale, and the assumption was not unreasonable, because the aggressive mammal has a record of occasional attacks on small craft. A highly publicized example was the sinking by killer whales of Dougal Robertson's schooner, *Lucette*, near the Galapagos Islands in 1972. Subsequent research into the holing of the *Galway Blazer*, however, led King to the belief that his vessel actually had been struck by a great white shark, a ferocious creature commonly found in those waters where the accident took place.

King's struggle to keep his boat afloat is an epic of seamanship and a remarkable example of endurance, for the singlehander was over 60 years old and not in perfect health. When the collision occurred, King was below, and he saw a circular portion of the hull spring inward and burst into jagged splits. He rushed on deck attempting to see what he had struck and then promptly threw the boat about onto the opposite tack in order to lift the damaged area out of the water. The sheets were trimmed in flat, and the boat was held off the wind to induce heeling. Occasional waves still washed through the hole, however, and it took considerable time and effort to clear most of the water from the bilge with a hand pump. Incidentally, I would like to stress an important point, that the heeling of a damaged hull should be accomplished with a method that minimizes headway, because forward speed will cause greater leaking and perhaps further damage.

After a tremendous struggle, the singlehander managed to stuff the hole with sponge rubber and nail a piece of Dacron cloth over the outside of the entire damaged area. This required that he hang upside down from the rail while his head was immersed and later that he lower himself over the side in a bosun's chair. While the job was being done, King had to break off from his work periodically to pump the bilge. Once the outside repair was accomplished, the damaged area, which still leaked, was attended to from inside the hull. King packed the hole with rubber strips, and he cut shores from a spare boom. These were placed against the sprung portion of the hull and held firmly by wedging their opposite ends against a strength member on the boat's other side. The *Blazer* was still making some water, and her skipper was forced to pump off-and-on throughout the entire night after the accident.

The next day further repairs were made. King made up and rigged collision mats which were held in place by thirteen ropes passed under the hull. In addition, he nailed on strips of sheet copper, applied seam compound and sticky tape and wedged in some more shores. It took about three days of work to all but stop the leaking. After this, King sailed 400 miles to Fremantle, Australia, with the boat moving sluggishly with the cat's cradle of lines under her bottom. He encountered some heavy weather, but the repairs held, and he reached port safely.

As a result of his experience, Bill King advises offshore sailors to carry such emergency repair equipment as a collision mat (see Figure 7-1), broad-headed nails, a heavy-duty stapling gun with stainless steel staples, and a wet suit for overboard repairs in cold waters. King recommends a triangular collision mat and one backed with foam rubber or thrummed as shown in Figure 7-1. Of course, it is doubtful that the nails and staples could be used effectively on most boats built of materials other than wood, but self-tapping screws could possibly be used on fiberglass hulls and softwood wedges or bungs on metal hulls. It seems advisable that all offshore boats carry a few small sheets of lightweight plywood, sheets of copper and lead, and poles or extra spars that can be cut into shores. King successfully used a sticky yellow tape (which he thought was mercury chromate) that could be made to adhere to a split under water. Of course, caulking compounds intended for use under water, such as those used on swimming pools or the kind of epoxy putty that hardens when submerged, could be very handy. Another leak-stopper that I have seen used effectively is a mixture of cup grease and soft putty. Globs of this waterproof mix should be smeared into a split or wide seam and covered with canvas, plywood, or sheet metal.

Recently, a unique damage control device has been invented by Barry Simpson in England (see Figure 7-1). It works on the principle of an umbrella, in that it can be thrust through a hole from inside the boat (while the device is folded) and then opened up, so that the unfolded fabric will cover the hole on the outside of the hull. The device is now being produced, and details on obtaining it can be found in *Yachting Monthly* magazine (June, 1974). Needless to say there must be immediate access to the hole, and a hatchet, ax, or wrecking bar may be needed to get through the ceiling or liner. The Simpson device might be easier to rig than a conventional collision mat, but the latter would probably allow easier jury repairs to the hole.

There have been many suggestions concerning defensive measures against sea creatures. Some sailors advocate trying to scare them off with sounds, such as explosives, engine or propeller noises, or the high-pitched sound from fathometers. The suggestion has even been made that the recordings of the sounds from whales or killer whales could be played through a transducer mounted on the hull, which might repel certain kinds of dangerous sea life. The main trouble with this defense is that sounds from a particular creature might attract members of the same species. For instance, the sound emitted by killer whales might scare off certain whales or sharks, but perhaps it could attract killer whales. Other sounds, such as explosions or even the noise of a propeller, might conceivably be irritants that could provoke an attack. In fact, M. J. Gilkes, who served with a whaling fleet, wrote that sperm whales in particular have a penchant for charging straight at the propeller of a whale-catching boat. Where whales are concerned, he recommends practicing Br'er Rabbit's strategy to "lay low and don't say nuffin."

Jerry Cartwright had a most unusual and frightening experience during the 1972 singlehander's race when he was listening to a BBC broadcast on the radio concerning whale extinction. The program played loud sounds of whales communicating, when suddenly a huge sperm whale surfaced alongside his boat. Fortunately it did not attack, but it gave the singlehander a good scare. Jerry felt there was a good possibility that the sounds had attracted the whale, for, as he wrote, "the timing seemed too perfect for coincidence."

Another controversial point is the effect on sea creatures of colored bottom paints. William Andrews often painted the bottoms of his boats black as a defense against whales. Bill King and others suspect that red and even white bottom paint can attract sea predators. Their reasoning is based on assumption that red is associated with blood and white with the foam whipped up by a wounded creature. An experienced charter boat captain, however, claims that, based on his own observations, some whales are repelled by red but attracted by blue bottom paint.

At present, it appears that the only sure defense against all kinds of sea creatures is the construction of one's boat. Strongly made hulls of heavy fiberglass, ferrocement, or steel probably offer the best protection, especially when they are well-rounded and well-stiffened with frames, bulkheads, stringers, and other structural supports. It seems important that any vulnerable skeg be strengthened and glassed over at its top in the bilge area in order to prevent an inflow of water in the event that the skeg should be broken off. Several boats have been sunk as a result of whales damaging their skegs. No matter how well his boat is built, however, the careful offshore sailor must be prepared for emergency repairs. Adequate shores could be vital. Frank Casper told me about his friend, John Goetzke, an occasional singlehander, whose wooden boat was attacked by killer whales. Six frames on the port and starboard sides were cracked, but Goetzke saved his boat by staying below and wedging numerous shores against the inside of the hull.

In a lighter vein, it has been said that nothing will make a whale disappear faster than producing a camera. One offshore sailor even suggested playing a tape recorder that reproduces the sound of camera shutter clicks.

Grounding and Lee Shores

Every blue-water sailor has a healthy respect for a lee shore, but it can be a special source of anxiety for the singlehander. When closely approaching or following a coast, he must stand watch almost continuously, because a sound sleep or even a period of rest below without heaving to could result in a grounding. Bernard Moitessier lost his *Marie-Theresa II* on the rocky shores of St. Vincent Island, West Indies, in 1958, when he took a nap after turning the control of his boat over to his self-steering gear. The singlehander relied on an alarm clock to awake him before he was too close to the island, but the alarm failed to ring or he never heard it, and Moitessier did not wake up until his boat was in the breakers. He escaped relatively unharmed, but the boat was pounded into a total wreck.

Jean Gau's beloved ketch, *Atom*, that had twice carried him around the world and had been his home for twenty-six years, was nearly lost on the beach at Assateague Island, Virginia, in 1971, right after she had weathered hurricane "Ginger." The singlehander did not even fall asleep, though he was dead tired after the storm. He had simply gone below for a rest and to listen to the radio when he was about fourteen miles off the coast, which lay to windward. That seemed a safe enough action, but while he was in the cabin, there was a drastic wind shift that put the shore to leeward. With his senses dulled by fatigue and being somewhat distracted by the radio, Jean was unaware of his impending predicament. At one o'clock in the morning, he heard the hissing of breakers, and he rushed on deck, but it was too late. The *Atom* was already in shoal water and she immediately grounded with sickening thumps. As a result of an unusually high tide, the ketch carried far up on the beach where she was left high and dry after the water receded. At dawn, Gau stepped ashore unhurt and set off on foot to look for help. Fortunately, he soon found it, more than he ever dreamed he would. The Coast Guard, National Park Service, U. S. Navy, native watermen, and other volunteers all contributed their efforts to free the stranded *Atom*. Her minor damages were repaired; she was pumped clear of sand and made watertight with caulking, plywood patches, and a fast-setting cement; a three-foot-deep trench was dug around her and then to the sea; she was pivoted so that her bow faced the water; and finally she was pulled free by a Coast Guard utility boat.

Slocum, Pidgeon, and Dumas all had similar experiences. Slocum hugged the shore too closely while sailing down the coast of Uruguay in December, 1895, and grounded on a sand bottom. Although the *Spray* was left high and dry at low tide, Slocum gives his readers no real details of how he managed to refloat his heavy craft. He said only that he dislodged her with the help of a "German and one soldier and one Italian, called 'Angel of Milan'." It can only be assumed that he kedged off at high water, since a heavy anchor had already been laid out with considerable difficulty.

Pidgeon ran his yawl *Islander* aground, because he fell asleep while too close to the shore not far from Cape Town, South Africa, in June, 1924. Fortunately, he grounded on a sand beach (narrowly missing rocks) in moderate surf. It wasn't long, however, before the wind freshened to gale force, and the yawl began to be tumbled over from one side to the other. Pidgeon cleverly prevented his boat from being seriously damaged by bending a line to his topping life, carrying it ashore, and securing it there. The line held the masthead steady and thus put a stop to the destructive tumbling motion. She survived the pounding, but was driven far up on the beach. When the weather moderated, the *Islander* was jacked up so that planks and rollers could be placed under her. Then she was pulled afloat with a powerful winch on a small steamer anchored a short distance off-shore.

Some particularly important lessons might be learned from Dumas' experience. Beating his ketch, *Lehg II*, along the coast of Argentina in 1943, the singlehander made boards of two hours each with the helm lashed. Perhaps an unpredicted current carried him too close to shore, but at one point when Dumas came on deck after a brief rest below, he saw breakers about 100 yards ahead. He had no knife with him to cut the lashing and wasted precious moments untying the tiller. By the time the helm was freed, it was too late, and the ketch grounded on a sandy beach. This points up not only the value of carrying a knife, but also the advisability of tying the helm with a slip knot or a loop that can be slipped easily off the end of a tiller or wheel spoke.

Wisely, Dumas stayed at the helm and left his sails drawing so that his boat would be driven far up on the beach. In calm water, this could well have been the wrong tactic, but there was a heavy swell and surf, which made it imperative for the boat to be securely beached so that she would not be continually lifted and dropped on the bottom. Dumas even unloaded the boat to lighten her in order that she would be left as nearly as possible high and dry. Several days later, the *Lehg II* was pulled free by a trawler with a long coir cable.

One of the most remarkable incidents involving salvage following a grounding was the case of Alain Gerbault's cutter, *Firecrest*, when she struck a reef after snapping her anchor chain in the Wallis Islands, just north of Fiji, in 1926. She pounded on the reef for about an hour and then suddenly fell over on her beam ends. Gerbault abandoned ship and began swimming for shore when, to his amazement, he noticed that the cutter was following him. The pounding had broken all her keel bolts, which caused the ballast keel to drop off. With almost all stability gone, the extremely narrow boat simply flopped on her side and drifted across the reef. She then lodged on a sandy beach.

To refloat the *Firecrest*, it was necessary to find the four-ton piece of lead ballast and float it across the lagoon, shore up the cutter, forge ten new bolts (some of which were over three feet long), move the ballast underwater and align it with the cutter's wood keel so that the bolt holes matched exactly, and then careen the boat after the ballast was bolted on so that she could be moved back across the reef into deep water. All of this had to be done on a remote island that had no facilities for such an operation. It took the help of fifty natives, two Chinese carpenters, the chief engineer from a passing tramp steamer (who had a forge and machine shop), and part of the crew of a French naval vessel. The heavy ballast had to be fitted to the keel twice, because the first time the bolts were too small in diameter, and they allowed water to spurt in through their holes. The whole operation took nearly two months, but the *Firecrest* was made almost as good as new.

The aforementioned singlehanders who saved their grounding vessels did so mainly because they had considerable help, but some others had little or no assistance. Two such examples were the circumnavigators Marcel Bardiaux and C. H. (Rusty) Webb. The latter fetched up on a coral reef off Barbuda in the West Indies in 1968. His 58-year-old, wooden ketch, the *Flyd*, was severely damaged with twenty-one holes in her hull. All by himself, Webb patched his boat with sheets of copper and canvas. This necessitated underwater work without diving gear over a period of fourteen days. Each copper patch required about sixty nails, which had to be hammered in while Webb held his breath beneath the boat. He said at first that he could only drive in one nail at a time, but that later he was able to manage two or three nails without surfacing. When repairs were finally completed, the singlehander sailed his patched-up boat more than 4,000 miles to England with the repairs leaking so much that he had to pump the bilge about every two hours.

Marcel Bardiaux also grounded on a coral reef, and he did so with such force that the impact threw him overboard and gave him a severe cut on the forehead. The grounding took place in 1954 on an incorrectly charted shoal that was out of sight of land and sixty-five miles from the nearest port, Noumea, in New Caledonia. Bardiaux's sloop *Les 4 Vents* was being badly damaged by seas that repeatedly slammed her against the coral, and it was obvious that she would have to be dislodged promptly while she was still watertight. The powerful singlehander immediately set to work kedging off. This required taking out on foot a heavy anchor and chain, which was carried and dragged over jagged coral washed by breakers. He used a portable windlass of his own design to drag the boat ahead until she was at short scope, and then the anchor had to be carried out again. This operation had to be repeated many times before *Les 4 Vents* could be pulled free. By then, she was so badly damaged that she was leaking seriously and seemed in imminent danger of sinking in deep water. However, the sloop had a number of buoyancy cans secured under her deck for the primary purpose of improving her ability to self-right, and these, together with a large rubber life raft which Bardiaux spread out and inflated below, supplied enough flotation to keep her from foundering. The Frenchman then sailed her, passing no less than twenty-seven vessels wrecked on the same reef, all the way to Noumea with the hull half-filled, and it was reported that he reached his destination with the decks awash.

A big factor in avoiding grounding and other mistakes in seamanship is the avoidance of extreme fatigue. Ben Dixon, who sails alone occasionally, told me that he nearly lost his sloop *Sundowner* when she dragged onto a lee shore, because he was so tired that he failed to set his anchor properly. To repeat what was noted earlier, deep fatigue leads not only to carelessness, but also to errors in judgement. Needless to say, the singlehander should get all the rest he can whenever he has the opportunity.

Rigging Problems

A frequently encountered problem on any passage-making vessel is rigging failures. Lines chafe through, halyards can jam in their blocks, tangles occur aloft, spreaders occasionally come loose, fittings fatigue from the constant motion, booms may break, and even dismastings are not uncommon. Of course, these difficulties are extremely trying for the singlehander, who must pull himself aloft to make repairs or must haul broken spars aboard and set up heavy gear and jury rigs alone. Effecting permanent and even makeshift repairs at sea by oneself calls for tremendous forethought, effort, patience, and often ingenuity.

The latter quality is evident in the experience of David Guthrie, the survivor of the whale collision mentioned earlier, who was alone in mid-Atlantic aboard his small sloop when the end of the main halyard ran aloft.

This necessitated a trip to the masthead in waters that were far from smooth. Guthrie had a large conic sea anchor aboard, and it occurred to him that he might be able to utilize its drag to assist him in going aloft. His plan was to keep sailing under a headsail and to attach a bosun's chair to one end of a spare halyard and secure the sea anchor to the halyard's other end. Then he would throw overboard the sea anchor, which would remain relatively stationary, and the boat's headway would pull the chair with Guthrie in it to the masthead. The plan also required that the single-hander carry aloft the end of a trip-line leading to the apex of the sea anchor so that it could be tripped to allow descending after the runaway halyard had been retrieved.

The idea was a good one, but its execution brought about some unanticipated problems. One was that the boat's speed of between four and five knots hoisted Guthrie entirely too fast, and a more serious difficulty occurred when the trip-line was found to be too short as a result of its having been led inadvertently under the stern pulpit. This mistake caused the trip-line to act before Guthrie was at the masthead, and down he came, fortunately with no serious injuries resulting. Once he was back on deck and the trip-line became slack, he was yanked aloft again by the strain of the sea anchor. After returning to the deck again, Guthrie was somewhat shaken, and having been "hoist by his own petard," he decided to postpone the experiment until the following day.

I never heard whether the halyard was eventually retrieved by this unusual method, but the plan definitely had merit and would have worked well had the boat been moving a bit more slowly and had the trip-line been longer. In fact, my cousin, Charles Henderson, used a similar method in going aloft after weathering a typhoon in the China Sea. He was not alone but was shorthanded, and he used a bucket secured to the end of a halyard that was dropped overboard as an assist in going up the mast.

Most singlehanders, of course, use more conventional methods of going aloft. Many have ratlines and/or mast steps, and these are not only useful for climbing the mast to make inspections and rigging repairs, but also for conning the vessel in clear waters where there are submerged reefs or other shoals. Marcel Bardiaux not only had steps, but also even had a way of rigging steering lines from the tiller leading up the mast so that the boat could be steered from aloft. Many singlehanders haul themselves up the mast with a tackle, and a few of the more athletic types climb up hand over hand for simple jobs aloft when the boat's motion permits. On a boat without mast steps or ratlines, however, it would seem to be an unnecessary risk for a singlehander to go aloft even a short distance without rigging either a bosun's chair or a ladder. I recall one story told to me by a strong young South African sailor, Frick Potgieter, who was watching John

Goetzke, approximately seventy years old, haul himself up the mast. The young man had offered to go aloft for Goetzke, but the latter refused help, because he said he often sailed alone and felt that he should keep in shape for the times when no help would be available. A small group of spectators was watching from a pier nearby, and Potgieter overheard a woman say, "Look at that young S.O.B. letting that old man climb the mast without even trying to help him."

The difficulties involved in going aloft when alone and in a rough sea were vividly described by Robin Knox-Johnston. In late January, 1969, aboard the ketch, *Suhaili*, during her non-stop circumnavigation, the large-reaching-jib halyard parted, and Knox-Johnston made several attempts to reach the masthead in order to reeve a new halyard. The first effort ended with an egg-sized bump on his eyebrow when the ketch rolled and swung him against the end of a spreader. The next day he tried again when the sea seemed a bit more calm. He hauled himself up with a tackle and had reached the upper spreaders when the boat started pitching severely. He waited ten minutes or so for the motion to stop, but to no avail, and meanwhile the jib on deck began to wash overboard. He decided to make a quick dash for the masthead. He wrote, "Both hands were on the tackle which I did not dare let go of or I would have fallen thirty-two feet. My legs couldn't hold on round the mast as the mainsail was in the way and I swung forward. I managed to cushion the return swing and fend myself off the mast with my feet, and I swung straight out towards the mizzen. Somehow I got caught the wrong side of the mainsail which stopped me being swung forward again and I was able to grab one of the back stays with a leg and then get a hand free for the same purpose — and there I hung, lurching wildly, until she eased up."

What a helpless feeling Robin must have had while swinging back and forth from the masthead, unable to use his hands and with no one on deck to steady him with a downhaul line. He managed to make it back to the deck uninjured, if somewhat shaken, but the new halyard was not reeved, and for some time thereafter the topping lift was used as a substitute for the halyard.

Robin's experience not only points out the added advantage of a strong topping lift that is controllable at the deck, but it also shows how handy proper mast steps can be for the singlehander. Robin might have had an easier time with the mainsail lowered so that he could have wrapped his legs or a life line around the mast, but, on the other hand, the hoisted sail might have been a considerable help in dampening the boat's rolling motion. Unquestionably, it is a good idea for anyone hauling himself aloft to have a quick and easy means of securing the fall of the tackle so that he can use his hands at a moment's notice. A commonly-used method is to pass the fall under the bosun's chair bridle and then secure it with a bosun's hitch (Figure 7-2) over a hook on the bottom of the tackle's lower block. For maximum security, I would prefer an extra half-hitch.

It was reported that three participants in the 1972 singlehander's transatlantic race, Mike McMullen, Phillip Weld, and Brian Cooke, used mast-climbing assists called jumars. These are metal clamps, used most often by mountain climbers, which attach to a rope and operate in somewhat the manner of a cam cleat, allowing the rope to move through the clamp in one direction, but preventing movement in the opposite direction. A jumar can be attached to a bosun's chair in such a way that it will accept and jam the fall of the hoisting tackle and thus hold the chair, at least temporarily, when the singlehander releases his grip on the tackle's fall.

Incidentally, Brian Cooke made a remarkable repair aloft on the *British Steel* during the 1972 race when a tang for a lower shroud broke. The tang was a stainless steel plate that was too thin and perhaps had its hole for the shroud's pin bored too close to the tang's edge. At any rate, the fitting broke between the hole and the edge, and Cooke felt compelled to repair it at night while in a confused sea following a blow. This involved five trips up and down the mast and working with one hand only (the other was needed to hold on). Evidently, Cooke made a figure-eight loop of wire around the mast at the spreader, though I am not sure how he avoided blocking the mainsail's track. The upper end of the shroud was then fastened to the wire loop. One of his greatest trials during the repair job was replacing a cotter pin with one hand in the dark while being swung around violently by the boat's motion. In many cases, a common shower-curtain ring can make a very handy temporary substitute for a cotter pin, since it can be inserted and snapped with one hand. I have just heard that Cooke unfortunately fell from the mast of his trimaran *Triple Arrow* during his attempt to set a solo speed record, the one sought by Francis Chichester, to sail 4,000 miles on a nearly straight course in 20 days. My informant tells me that Cooke fell more than 40 feet to the deck and crushed some vertebrae but miraculously made it home.

Chay Blyth is another singlehander who had more than a few rigging problems necessitating working aloft during his "uphill" circumnavigation on the *British Steel* in 1970 and 1971. On one occasion he wrote that he spent the "entire day" clearing up a tangle of halyards. After weathering a lengthy gale about midway between Australia and South Africa, he found that all of his headsail halyards had parted. Rectification required going to the masthead, about sixty-five feet up (one of the disadvantages of single-handing such a large boat), and threading tail lines (messengers) for the halyards through their sheaves. Blyth also said the operation involved cutting away a broken wire halyard, no mean job at such a height while trying

FIGURE 7-2: SOME RIGGING DETAILS

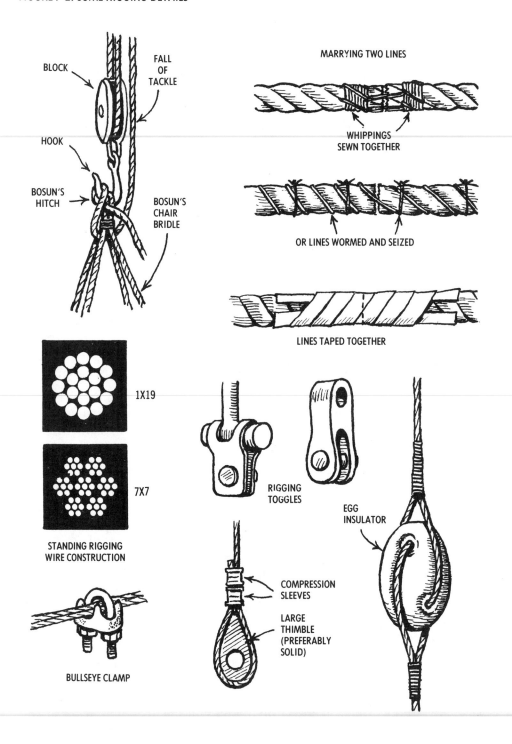

BLOCK

FALL OF TACKLE

HOOK

BOSUN'S HITCH

BOSUN'S CHAIR BRIDLE

MARRYING TWO LINES

WHIPPINGS SEWN TOGETHER

OR LINES WORMED AND SEIZED

LINES TAPED TOGETHER

1X19

7X7

STANDING RIGGING WIRE CONSTRUCTION

RIGGING TOGGLES

EGG INSULATOR

BULLSEYE CLAMP

COMPRESSION SLEEVES

LARGE THIMBLE (PREFERABLY SOLID)

to hang on for dear life. After this experience, he decided to replace the mizzen halyard *before* it parted.

Although Blyth climbed aloft to do this job, quite often a worn halyard can be replaced without climbing the mast by marrying (joining end-to-end by sewing, worming, and/or taping as shown in Figure 7-2) the end of the old halyard with the end of its replacement so that the new halyard can be reeved through its block simply by pulling it through from the deck. Incidentally, a very crude temporary halyard might be rigged for a storm trysail, perhaps, by throwing a line over a spreader. Chichester used such a method to clear his mizzen staysail halyard on the *Gipsy Moth IV* during her circumnavigation in 1967. After trying in vain to shinny up the mast, Sir

Brian Cooke aboard the 49-foot trimaran on which he hoped to achieve the goal sought by Chichester, to sail 4,000 miles in 20 days. (Courtesy of John Rock)

Francis tied a shackle to the end of a heaving line and threw it over a spreader. This line was then used to pull over the halyard.

The *British Steel* had some galvanized wire halyards which seriously wore or broke, and this brings up the question of whether stainless steel is not the superior material for rigging. Captain John Illingworth, noted authority on rigging, whose firm designed the rig for Alec Rose's *Lively Lady*, specified that her standing rigging be galvanized wire of 7x7 construction (seven strands of seven wires each). The argument for such rigging, instead of the usual stainless steel wire of 1x19 construction (one strand of nineteen wires), is that the 7x7 is flexible and can be bent into eyes and spliced. The stainless 1x19 wire, however, must use swaged terminal fittings, which are subject to failure as a result of cracks or other defects that are sometimes difficult to detect. On the other hand, properly done swaged fittings are considerably stronger than splices, there is less stretch in the 1x19 rigging, and highly reliable methods of inspecting stainless fittings have recently been developed. These inspections include checks with gauges (to detect flat areas and unevenness), magnets, dye or fluorescent penetrants, and even X-rays. For running rigging, flexible stainless steel wire of 7x19 construction can be bent into eyes and fastened quite reliably with compression sleeves, which can be clamped without difficulty by using a portable hand press. Of course, U-type bullseye clamps (Figure 7-2) can also be used in emergencies. As a matter of fact, Alec Rose had wire splices fail during his circumnavigation, and on two occasions he made very seamanlike temporary repairs with bullseye clamps after bending the wire in eyes around thimbles. Later, in Melbourne, Australia, permanent repairs were made with swaged eyes, and they were said to be entirely satisfactory.

The *Lively Lady* also broke a masthead tang, and designer-author Douglas Phillips-Birt tells us that this was probably due to crystallization and fatigue. Such failures are not uncommon on offshore craft that are subject to prolonged periods of motion, and every effort must be made to prevent or alleviate alternating movements and bending moments on the fittings. This is usually best accomplished with extensive use of rigging toggles, which may come in a variety of designs (see Figure 7-2), but which always function as universal joints to prevent metal fatigue. It is the safest policy to use toggles at the top and bottom of any shroud or especially stay that is subject to alternate motions and stress from various directions. In the case of the *Lively Lady*, Phillips-Birt suggests that Rose may have contributed to the tang's failure by putting "an unfair bending load" on it when he cast off one of his twin headstays (topmast forestays in British terminology) and led it aft around the spreader as an emergency substitute for a parted lower shroud. This was a necessary jury arrangement to safeguard against loss of the mast when the shroud broke at its upper splice.

Of course, the mast was also endangered when the tang failed, but Rose made a temporary repair by using a masthead halyard as a substitute for the broken headstay until he could reach the nearest port where a new tang could be fitted.

As mentioned in Chapter 5, twin headstays are often considered a boon to the singlehander, for in addition to providing backup mast support, they enable him to change jibs with a minimum of effort. There are drawbacks with the rig, however, due to possible jamming of hanks, chafe on the jib's luff, and difficulties in keeping an equal tension on each stay. One method of overcoming the latter problem, tried by Mike McMullen on his *Binkie II*, was with the use of a U-bolt to which each twin stay was attached at the stemhead (Chapter 5). Unfortunately the rig was not entirely successful, and the U-bolt broke during the 1972 transatlantic race. McMullen replaced the broken fitting with a spare, but it caused him considerable anxiety for the rest of the passage. He wrote, "I sailed with the constant threat of it [the U-bolt] breaking again, and had it happened I would have been hard pressed to finish." The use of a triangular plate at the bottom of the twin stays connecting them to a single turnbuckle has proven quite satisfactory in many cases (see Figure 5-5).

In the same race a woman singlehander, Teresa Remiszewska, who sailed the 42-foot yawl, *Komodor*, had many rigging problems, which included broken shrouds and stays. She made repairs with wire clamps and by substituting halyards for the parted standing rigging. One repair was indeed remarkable, especially when you consider that it was made by a singlehanded, forty-three-year-old member of the so-called weaker sex. In mid-ocean, Teresa noticed a crack in her wooden mast near the upper spreaders, and to help alleviate the problem, she removed the spreaders, resecured them at a lower position on the mast, and then shortened and readjusted the rigging to tighten the shrouds. The operation took an entire week, but the task was made easier by a rope ladder with wooden steps that could be hoisted aloft. This same kind of assist was used successfully by Brian Cooke when he repaired a broken masthead tang on his *Opus* during the 1968 transatlantic race.

The singlehander with the most rigging failures without loss of mast would have to be Alain Gerbault in the *Firecrest*, whose sails constantly ripped or blew out, running and standing rigging parted, and gear often broke or partially failed. These problems were primarily due to inadequate preparations, for his equipment was old and tired, even rotten, at the time he cast off. Of course, he had more than his share of heavy weather, and it could truthfully be said that the cotton sails used in Gerbault's time were not as strong as those made of modern synthetics. Nevertheless, a suit of cotton sails carried John Guzzwell around the world without any major failures over a period of about four years. Gerbault showed poor judgement in fitting out his boat, but we must give him credit for outstanding endurance and seamanship in overcoming many of his problems.

On one occasion, in the South Seas, he had to claw off a lee shore in heavy weather. When he had almost made enough offing, the mainsail split at a seam. Gerbault was forced to lower the sail and hurriedly sew up the seam before his boat drifted onto a coral reef to leeward. He just finished the job in time to avoid a serious grounding.

Another time, the end of his bowsprit broke, and Gerbault was forced to make a difficult jury repair. This involved cutting a slot in the end of the broken sprit, inserting an iron pin, and rigging a new bobstay. The latter was the hardest job of all, as it involved cutting a piece from the anchor chain and shackling it to the *Firecrest's* stem at a point just below the waterline. To accomplish this, Gerbault had to hang head down from the bowsprit while repeatedly being deeply submerged by the boat's pitching. He described himself as being alternately dipped and brought up "dripping and sputtering to repeat the dose again and again."

Gerbault's trials obviously show us the importance of having sound gear, plenty of extra fittings, and spare rigging, including extra chain suitable for emergency repairs. Furthermore, the experience with the broken bowsprit points up the value of having halyard downhauls, because when the break occurred, it was necessary to hand sail promptly to avoid losing the mast. Wind pressure held the mainsail so firmly against the rigging that Gerbault had to rig a purchase to the downhaul to lower it. He could not luff up to relieve the wind pressure on account of the slack headstay (due to the broken bowsprit), which gave no forward support to the top of the mast.

Another singlehander who experienced bowsprit problems was Bernard Moitessier, when, during his circumnavigation (Chapter 1), a ship approached to receive his written message, came too close, and damaged the rig of his ketch, the *Joshua*. The heavy steel bowsprit was severely bent, and it seemed impossible that one man alone at sea could make the repair. Moitessier tried, nevertheless, and after careful planning, used a four-part tackle, large winch, and a gin pole to pull the bowsprit straight. The repair attempt was a complete success, and the Frenchman wrote of his exuberance: "Incredible, the power of a tackle on a winch — I feel I am going to cry, it's so beautiful — the bowsprit begins to straighten out, very, very slowly. I am wild with joy!"

A totally different and less serious problem but one that can cause a singlehander no end of trouble, is the jamming of a halyard aloft. This is usually caused by the halyard jumping over the lip of its sheave and becoming jammed between the sheave and the shell of its block or wall of its sheave box. When such a jam occurs, sail can neither be lowered nor further hoisted, and forcibly hauling on the halyard only increases the jam. Robin Knox-Johnston, for one, experienced this difficulty in heavy weather during his circumnavigation. It was essential that the mainsail be lowered, because the *Suhaili* was threatening to broach, but the boat's motion made it impossible to climb aloft to unshackle the halyard. Robin solved the problem temporarily by slacking the luff of the roller-reefed sail by unrolling three turns off the boom and then hauling the outboard end of the boom up against the mast and frapping the mainsail to its spars. In his book, *A World of My Own*, Robin does not give details of the frapping operation, but I assume that he used the fall of a halyard to wind around the mast, boom, and sail, in effect, brailing the whole affair from the deck.

The jamming problem is best avoided by having a sufficiently deep groove in a sheave intended for wire with the narrowest possible space between the sheave and its housing, by using wire of a proper size, and by using fairleads to keep the halyards where they belong. In addition, there should be a separator between the side-by-side sheaves, and stops on halyards to prevent their eyes or end fittings from being pulled into their sheaves. Robin's experience also points out once again the value of a proper topping lift that is controllable from the deck.

Naturally, it makes sense for a singlehander to be as sure as possible that his rigging is sound and free of chafe before he gets underway. The rubbing of lines and sails cannot be stopped entirely, but it should be minimized with reinforcing patches on sails, baggywrinkle, fairleads, straps of shock cord, and constant vigilance. Before he embarked on his 'round-the-world voyage, Chay Blyth was so concerned about the prevention of chafe, that, in the boat yard in which his *British Steel* was being fitted out, he was given the nickname of "Chafe Bligh." It was this kind of attention to detail that helped him complete one of the most difficult voyages of all time.

Dismastings

The rigging failures described so far did not result in the loss of a mast, but sometimes when a vital fitting, shroud, or stay breaks, the whole rig will go by the board. This situation can be a desperate one for the singlehander, and it may demand the highest level of seamanship. The victim of such an accident must first of all clear up the wreckage and prevent the broken mast from battering a hole in the hull, and then he must either call for help, use his auxiliary power, or construct a jury rig that will allow him to limp to the nearest port. If he is rescued by a ship, he may have to abandon his boat, unless she is small enough to be taken aboard the ship. In some cases, the boat might be taken in tow, but this usually necessitates her being towed faster than her hull speed (about 1.35 times the square root of her waterline length for a displacement hull), and serious damage is apt to result. In fact, bandleader-singlehander Bob Miller lost his sloop, the *Mersea Pearl,* in just this way while she was being towed by a merchant ship at fifteen knots after a dismasting during the 1972 transatlantic race.

Unless a dismasted boat is quite near other vessels so that flares can be seen, she must depend on her radio to call for help. A boat equipped with a radio-telephone often uses her backstay for the antenna, and, of course, after the mast breaks, the radio is put out of commission. This happened to Bob Miller and also to Murray Sayle aboard the ketch-rigged *Lady of Fleet* in the same race. Miller was able to rig a jury antenna by erecting a nine-foot plank which he screwed to the topsides, while Sayle managed to salvage his antenna from the broken mainmast and rig it to the mizzen mast. Sayle was also taken in tow, but his boat survived being pulled at high speeds, primarily because she was a catamaran and could plane easily.

Another possible risk in using the backstay for an antenna is that the stay may be weakened by insulators. Sandy Munro, on the catamaran, *Ocean Highlander,* lost his mast for this reason during the 1968 singlehander's transatlantic race. Unbeknownst to Munro, the insulators used were about half as strong as those specified. It is a wise plan to use egg-type insulators (Figure 7-2) that prevent sharp bends in the wire and allow the part of the stay above and below the insulator to remain connected in the event that the insulator should happen to break. Also, incidentally, it is not the safest practice to bend a non-flexible 1x19 stay around in a loop to fasten it to an insulator. The better construction for looping is 7x7 wire (See Figure 7-2). Many offshore sailors carry whip antennas that are independent of the rigging, although they are less efficient, to avoid the problem of being unable to transmit after a dismasting. Those boats that are not equipped with radio-telephones should carry emergency locator beacons (Chapter 5), which continuously send out distress signals on emergency frequencies when the beacons are activated. One of these devices brought help to Alan Gick when his 19-foot *Cockle* was dismasted at sea after she had capsized in 1971, during an informal transatlantic race against two sister boats. This incident will be described in the next chapter.

Bob Salmon and his 24-foot sloop, *Justa Listang,* were taken aboard a ship after a dismasting following the failure of a shroud tang during the 1972 singlehander's transatlantic race. The rescue did not take place, however, until about four days after the accident, and Salmon had the opportunity to set up and use an effective jury rig. Having two spinnaker poles, he was able to make an A-frame by securing the end of each pole near the chainplates and clipping their opposite ends to a metal ring. Then he

Bill King's Galway Blazer II *under tow before the start of the "Golden Globe" race. (Nautical Publishing Company; from* Capsize *by Bill King)*

rigged a forestay and twin backstays that were secured to the same ring, and the A-frame was pulled to the verticle position with the backstays. His sail consisted of an inverted jib hanked to the forestay. It had no halyard but was set or handed by raising or lowering the A-frame. Salmon said the sail worked well downwind, and it helped steady the boat's motion, which was exceedingly quick with the sail down. Incidentally, the shroud tang that caused the dismasting failed in a mere Force 3 or 4 breeze after having survived much stronger blows, including a Force 9 gale. Thus it seems that metal fatigue was responsible, and again we are reminded of the importance of preventing fittings from bending with the use of adequate toggles or by other means.

Bill King also used an A-frame jury rig after being dismasted following a capsize in his Chinese-lug-rigged schooner, the *Galway Blazer II*, during the "Golden Globe Race" for singlehanders in 1968. Actually, King's emergency rig was a permanently-installed bipod of aluminum poles, hinged to the deck, which lay flat when not in use but could be hauled upright after a dismasting. During the capsize, the *Blazer* lost her foremast, but the stayless mainmast, made (like the foremast) of spruce sheathed in fiber-

The Galway Blazer II *under jury rig after her capsize and loss of foremast. Notice the A-frame supporting the headsail. (Nautical Publishing Company; from* Capsize *by Bill King)*

glass, was left standing. It was bent, but was partially useable. King's first job was to cut away the broken foremast before it pounded a hole in the hull, and then, after waiting for wind and seas to subside, he erected the bipod, which carried a small jib, and hoisted a few panels of the fully-battened mainsail. The latter sail was hoisted on the bent mainmast, but had that mast gone by the board, there were provisions for hoisting on the bipod a lug sail that could be used in conjunction with the jib (see Figure 7-3). The lower ends of the bipod were fastened to slides on tracks running for a limited distance fore and aft on each side of the boat in order that the jury rig's position could be shifted longitudinally for the best possible balance.

King had been capsized and dismasted by huge, confused seas following a gale in an area 1,100 miles southwest of Cape Town, South Africa. Fortunately he did not have to sail the entire distance to port under jury rig. He radioed for help and was towed the last 200 miles to Cape Town by the 52-foot ketch, *Corsair II*, which came out from Cape Town especially for the purpose.

FIGURE 7-3:
JURY RIGS

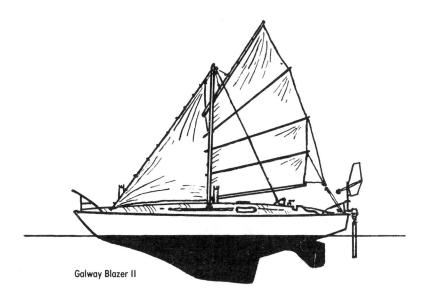

Galway Blazer II

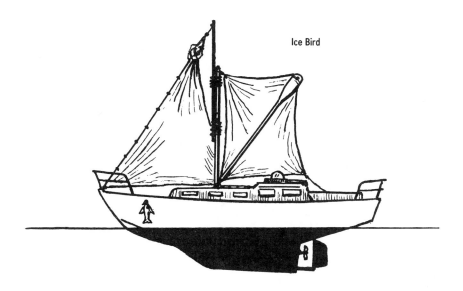

Ice Bird

Another of several boats dismasted by capsizing was Jean Gau's double-ended ketch, *Atom*, which was tumbled by a "freak" wave not far from the Cape of Good Hope in 1966. This incident will be described in Gau's own words in the next chapter. The capsizing left the *Atom*'s rig a complete shambles with both masts and her bowsprit broken and overboard but tethered by their rigging. After he had recovered from the initial shock of the accident, Gau set to work cutting away the rig, because the spars were pounding the boat and threatening to sink her. He worked in appalling conditions: in total darkness with the boat rolling violently and heavy seas washing over the deck, while hurricane force winds nearly tore off his clothes and took away his breath. For three hours he worked on the rigging with a hacksaw and pliers. At one point a wave tore the hacksaw from his hands and it was lost overboard. A South African sailor who spoke to Gau soon after the misadventure told me that the singlehander continued cutting the wire with pliers and a hacksaw blade held between his fingers. At any rate, the *Atom* was saved and she reached port under her auxiliary engine.

Gau's experience demonstrates another advantage of an auxiliary engine which is kept in good working order, and also shows the wisdom of carrying suitable tools for cutting away the rigging. There are times when a singlehander will not be able to bring a broken spar on board, and, if it is damaging the hull, it will have to be cut loose. Heavy-duty rigging cutters are recommended, but a good hacksaw can also do the job, and it is not a bad idea to carry a spare.

In a boat having the same kind of rig as the *Galway Blazer II*, Mike Ellison, during the 1964 singlehander's race, suffered a dismasting that was similar in some respects to Bill King's. Ellison's lug-sailed schooner, *Ilala*, lost her unstayed foremast in a confused sea following a gale. The whipping mast broke off about five feet above the deck. Although the mainmast was left standing, a previously broken halyard block limited the use of that mast. The block had fallen because its bronze eye had worn through. Ellison had difficulty climbing the mast because of the motion, and, according to one account, his rope ladder was too short to reach the truck. Nevertheless, he cleverly devised a way of hauling aloft, with a spare halyard that was insufficient to carry the full load of the mainsail, a new main halyard block with a strap around the mast. When the block was aloft, Ellison could pull on the new main halyard and tighten the strap so that it would not slide down the tapered mast. With this rig he could hoist four-fifths of the mainsail. Then with a long oar he erected a jury foremast that could carry three panels of the foresail. With this flimsy rig he limped 1,500 miles to Newport, Rhode Island, arriving there almost a month after his dismasting.

It would seem that large, unstayed masts are rather prone to breakage.

Mike Ellison commented, "A lot of homework will have to be done before large unstayed masts become reliable and generally acceptable." Yet the *Jester's* mast, smaller but unstayed, has so far survived seven transatlantic crossings. In steep, confused seas following a gale, which can cause violent rolling and possibly a capsizing, as in Bill King's case, it may be advisable to set substantial sail at once for the purpose of roll damping, steadying masts, and steering control. Ellison's experience also demonstrates the vulnerability of bronze fittings to abrasion, the value of mast-climbing equipment, and the wisdom of carrying spare halyards.

Many singlehanders have been dismasted, but few have suffered more from this problem than has Dr. David Lewis. He lost his mast (not for the first time) shortly after the start of the 1960 transatlantic race for singlehanders. A windward spreader failed on his 25-foot *Cardinal Vertue* and caused the wooden mast to break just above the spreader sockets (it may be remembered from Chapter 1 that this boat's mast broke in about the same location when she was owned by Bill Nance, but on that occasion, the cause was compression, according to Nance). Dr. Lewis got the broken mast aboard before it damaged the hull, and despite the boat's violent rolling, he shinnied up the mast stump and secured to its top a couple of blocks for halyards. The Doctor had religiously practiced climbing the mast before the race, and now his preparedness was paying off, because he had to climb the gyrating stump twice and lash the blocks in place while hanging on with one hand. With the mainsail scandalized and with a double-head rig, consisting of a trysail and a number three staysail, the *Cardinal Vertue* had a fairly efficient jury rig that allowed her to sail back to Plymouth, where the race had begun. A new mast was made in record time, and the Doctor set off again two days later to cross the Atlantic successfully and take a third place in the race.

Three years later, on a voyage to Iceland and back in the catamaran, *Rehu Moana*, with crew aboard, Dr. Lewis was twice dismasted. These accidents were due mostly to the fact that he was using unproven experimental rigs, and, of course, multihulls (especially cats) must have extremely strong rigging because they will not readily heel, and they cannot knock down sufficiently (without risk of capsizing) to spill the wind from their sails. As Dr. Lewis himself pointed out, "With a rigid object the stress increases as the square of the wind speed, and this applies to a cruising catamaran." A trimaran, especially one with submersible amas, will heel considerably further and spill some wind to relieve the stress somewhat.

Undoubtedly the worst dismastings the intrepid Doctor underwent occurred when he capsized three times on his attempted solo circumnavigation of Antarctica. Twice he was rolled over in late 1972 on the passage from New Zealand to Palmer Station, and the accident was repeated in early 1974 on a passage from Antarctica to Cape Town where the adventure was finally terminated. After each dismasting Dr. Lewis was able to make jury rigs and carry on alone despite incredible adversities.

On the first occasion, he was in the latitude of the "Screaming Sixties," to the south of that point on earth which is most distant from land. A depression had actually dropped the barometer's pointer off its scale (about 28 inches), and winds were estimated at 100 miles an hour, while seas reached heights of 40 feet. It was so cold that the temperature was below freezing inside the boat, which was appropriately named the *Ice Bird*, and the drinking water was frozen in its keel tank. In these appalling conditions, the 32-foot steel sloop was smashed and rolled completely over, through 360 degrees, by a breaking sea. She righted but was half filled with water, the mast was down and broken off about seven feet above the deck, the cabin house of one-eighth inch steel had a large split, and the forward hatch (not being flush) was wrenched loose by a shroud that fouled it.

Dr. Lewis literally had to fight for his life. The sprung hatch was pulled nearly closed with a tackle, and then there was the arduous task of emptying the bilge while water continued to spurt through the hatch and cabin split when the boat rolled. It has been said that there is no bilge pump as efficient as one scared man with a bucket, but Dr. Lewis needed more than six hours bailing with a bucket to clear the *Ice Bird*. Later, with frost-bitten hands, he unscrewed the turnbuckles and cast off the broken rig. When the blow abated, he set up a very inadequate jury rig consisting of a spinnaker pole supporting a knotted storm jib. The makeshift mast kept breaking away until it was all but worthless.

Two weeks after her first capsizing, the *Ice Bird* was rolled over again in a Force 11 storm. This time, however, damage was not so extensive, and there was less water in the bilge, partly because the ventilators were stuffed with rags. About one week later, the Doctor devised a satisfactory jury rig. A new mast was made of the heavy main boom, which was just under twelve feet long. Raising it was no easy task for one man with injured hands working on a violently rolling deck. The job was accomplished by fitting one end of the boom into the mast step on deck, while the other end rested in the erected boom crutch, and then rigging a line from the top of the boom to the bow and back aft to a halyard winch. Guys were rigged to hold the jury mast steady, and then it was winched up to the vertical position. The new spar was able to carry a trysail and jib. Under this rig, Dr. Lewis was able to sail 2,500 miles to Palmer Station, where he arrived at night, after threading his way through floating ice and rocks, to make fast alongside Jacques Cousteau's oceanographic vessel, the *Calypso*.

The third capsizing took place about 800 miles southwest of Cape Town. A new mast fitted in Antarctica went by the board, and again Dr. Lewis erected the boom. He even extended its length by lashing a spar to it as a sort of topmast. A long oar served as a sprit to hold out the peak of the jury mainsail. A fair-sized jib was also carried on a stay running from the stem to the topmast. With this rig and without the benefits of a self-steering gear or an engine, because they were inoperable, Dr. Lewis took three weeks to reach Cape Town. Surely the *Ice Bird's* passage from New Zealand to South Africa via Antarctica was one of the most remarkable solo voyages of all times, and Dr. Lewis must be considered not only an extraordinary seaman, but also one of the foremost experts on dismastings and jury rigs. More will be said in the next chapter about the circumstances of Dr. Lewis' capsizings.

Dr. David Lewis' Ice Bird with her jury mast after her third capsizing during the attempt to circumnavigate Antarctica. (Margo Mackay)

Sickness and Injuries

Life at sea in a small boat is a healthy one, but even the heartiest sailor is subject to sickness or accidents. A disabling illness or injury could be disastrous for a singlehander far offshore. Precautions against debilitation would obviously include: exercising special care when working the boat; carrying and using proper safety equipment (Chapter 5); keeping up one's health with good diet, rest, and proper clothing; carrying adequate medical supplies and instruction books; prior thought on avoidance and treatment of common physical ailments; and prior basic instructions from a doctor (or medical book) on self-treatment. Common afflictions are: injuries from falls; burns from cooking; injuries resulting from spar or fitting failures; cuts from using a knife or tools; rope burns; infections; salt-water sores; seasickness; sunburn; heat exhaustion; food poisoning; fever; sprains; toothache, etc.

Of course, it is highly advisable that a solo voyager have a thorough physical examination before setting forth, but it is amazing how casual about this sort of thing some singlehanders can be. For instance, Robin Knox-Johnston told an interviewer from *Rudder* magazine that he never conferred with his doctor or dentist before he left on his non-stop solo circumnavigation, which lasted ten and a half months. Even when the sailor enjoys uncommonly good health, a thorough physical can detect a latent malady that might occur at sea. A case in point is Peter Tangvald, an occasional singlehander, who suffered a heart attack offshore but fortunately when there was a companion on board. For five days, Tangvald lay in his bunk, crippled with pain and unable to work the boat.

A source of worry for some is the threat of appendicitis. More than one offshore sailor, before going on a cruise, has had his appendix removed, even when it had caused no previous trouble. This is an extreme precaution, however, that many people are not willing to take. There is the well-known case of William A. Robinson, who nearly lost his life from an acute attack of appendicitis after cruising to the Galapagos Islands, not alone, but shorthanded, in 1934. Nowadays, we have antibiotics that may cure, or at least inhibit, serious infections. It is of some comfort to read in Dr. Paul Sheldon's book, *First Aid Afloat*, "On antibiotic treatment alone in forty-one consecutive cases of later proven appendicitis at sea on ships without doctors not one life was lost." Dr. Sheldon goes on to say, however, that in some cases surgery might have to be done later. During his circumnavigation, Robin Knox-Johnston had a severe abdominal pain that he feared was appendicitis. It lasted for four days but turned out to be only indigestion, according to Robin. Had it been appendicitis, he would have been out of luck, since he was about a thousand miles from the nearest "decent" port, and, surprisingly, he carried no antibiotics.

Vito Dumas could have used some modern antibiotics (though he did have a disinfectant which was administered by injections) when his arm became horribly infected in 1942 during his solo circumnavigation. The arm became grotesquely swollen and almost unbearably painful. Dumas developed a high fever, and he became so desperate that he seriously considered amputation. In his book, *Alone Through the Roaring Forties*, he vividly described the predicament: "A decision had to be made. That night must be the last with my arm in this condition. Land? I could not reach land in time. If by tomorrow things had not improved, I would have to amputate this useless arm, slung around my neck and already smelling of decay. It was dying and dragging me along with it. It was septicaemia. I could not give in without playing my last card.

"There were several suppurating open wounds in the hands, but I could not localize the septic focus in this formless mass. With an axe, or my seaman's knife, at the elbow, at the shoulder, I knew not where or how, somehow I would have to amputate."

This hair-raising incident ended happily, though, for Dumas fell asleep (or passed out), and while he was unconscious, the infected arm burst open and drained itself. Amputation was no longer considered necessary, and several days later the courageous singlehander had almost fully recovered.

Pain killers as well as antibiotics can also be extremely valuable, if not essential. As Sir Alec Rose, who suffered from a bad back, has said, "nothing exhausts one so quickly as pain." Proper pain killers might have spared Leonid Teliga some excruciating suffering during his circumnavigation. During the voyage on his yawl, *Opty*, Teliga was struck in the abdomen with a boom, which reportedly helped develop or accelerate cancer. The brave sailor, who died not very long after he rounded the world, said almost nothing about his affliction; but his log reveals that the cancer developed rapidly and caused such terrible pain that he tried to seek relief by chewing on his blanket, and during one series of paroxysms he seemed to lose his mind for several days.

Although some pain killers are extremely effective, the singlehander must be careful that what he takes will not overly dull his sensibilities, cause unwanted sleep, or adversely affect his judgment. As mentioned in Chapter 5, Dr. David Lewis gave this warning when he compiled a list of medical supplies for the participants in the 1960 singlehander's transatlantic race. He wrote, "Morphia may so impair judgement that for a lone sailor who has to rely on himself, it is rather a means towards suicide than a treatment." Dr. Lewis suggested aminode hydrochloride for severe pain, but it would be wise for the singlehander to consult with his own doctor.

Minor pain killers should be taken for the relief of such ailments as headaches and bad teeth. More than a few singlehanders have been afflicted with persistent toothaches. William Andrews, for instance, was bothered to such an extent on his voyage in the *Sapolio* that he pulled out his own tooth with a pair of pliers. Obviously, a modern voyager would do well to carry a dental kit with proper instructions.

The determination and courage of some singlehanders to carry on when they have serious physical ailments is sometimes incredible. Aside from the cases of Teliga and of leukemia victim Walter Koenig, mentioned in Chapter 1, there are the unpublicized examples of Commander George Farley and Steve Dolby. The former, who was invalided out of the Royal Navy for diabetes, crossed the North Atlantic alone in the stormy month of September, 1966, aboard his 23-foot sloop, *Dawn Star*. He had the most difficult task of giving himself daily injections of insulin, which included boiling the needle, while the boat was tossed about by continuous heavy weather consisting of a procession of lows, four full gales, and a hurricane. On an earlier cruise, he almost lost his life when his supply of insulin went bad from excessively hot weather.

Steve Dolby, though nearly blind, has done extensive offshore cruising alone in recent years. He couldn't take a star sight because of his poor vision, and he could only read a chart if he held it a few inches from his eyes, yet the tenacious singlehander was determined to see whatever he could of the world from the deck of his own small boat before his condition worsened.

Of course, the example of Francis Chichester is well known. He was afflicted for many years with a number of serious ailments including lung cancer, but he refused to give up until almost the very end, which came soon after he retired from the 1972 singlehander's race.

Injuries from accidents are not uncommon, but fortunately they are seldom completely disabling. This was hardly true for Jerry Cartwright, however, when he was thrown out of his bunk during the 1969 transpacific race for singlehanders. Jerry turned in one night without securing his bunk board (actually a canvas screen), and when his 29-foot sloop, *Scuffler II*, was hit by a gust that caused her to round up and drop off a wave, he became airborne. Landing on his head against the bunk on the boat's opposite side, he sustained a serious blow, which resulted in a concussion (subsequent X-rays revealed a long crack around the right side of his skull). The next three weeks were a nightmare for Jerry. He suffered from deafness in one ear, vertigo, lapses in memory, and almost continuous nausea with prolonged periods of vomiting and consequently dehydration. It is a great credit to his courage, tenacity, and seamanship that he was able to carry on alone and reach Hawaii, where he was promptly hospitalized.

Jerry admits to making a mistake in not securing himself in his bunk. He wrote, "I forgot a prime rule of the sea—constant vigilance." Very often rules are obvious, and it is easy to give lip service to them, but how difficult it is to live by them with never a moment of laxity or carelessness. Experiences like Jerry's, however, remind us in a general way of the need for extra caution when alone and specifically of the need for proper, easily-operable bunk boards or lee cloths (perhaps even automobile-type seat belts), adequate hand rails above and below deck, safety belts, and lanyards with adequate places to snap on, skid-proof surfaces, and a minimum of clutter and fittings on deck that can cause tripping (see Chapter 5).

Of special value to a disabled singlehander is a reliable self-steering device. Cartwright said, "I remember feeling a profound sense of gratitude for that steering vane." (It was a Gunning pendulum type, by. the way.) Of course, there is one situation when the self-steerer could be a decided disadvantage, and that would be if the singlehander should happen to fall overboard. There is the story of one solo sailor who deliberately dove off the bow of his boat and surfaced in time to grab her stern, but taking such chances seems tantamount to playing Russian roulette. Even in calm weather, a self-steering boat could easily catch a puff of wind and leave her swimming master floundering in her wake.

Dr. Alain Bombard had a close call of this kind during his bold Atlantic crossing in the rubber dinghy, L'Hérétique, when he lost a cushion overboard and dove in to recover it, even though he took the precaution of lowering sail and putting out a sea anchor. After reaching the cushion, he turned around and saw his boat drifting away faster than he could swim. The sea anchor, which was a parachute type, had fouled its lines in such a way that it had collapsed and was causing little drag. Despite the fact that Bombard had been a champion swimmer, he could not reach the boat until, luckily, the lines became untangled and allowed the parachute to open. The safest policy for a singlehander who insists on swimming is not only to lower sail, but also to attach himself to the boat with a line and also to rig a boarding ladder, because there have been cases of swimmers who were too exhausted to pull themselves aboard. Of course, there is also the added danger of sharks, which can appear very suddenly.

No one knows how many singlehanders have accidentally fallen overboard while their boats were self-steered. There are probably not many of these accidents, but still, derelict boats of solo sailors are occasionally found, as in the case of the boat of John Pflieger, Commodore of the Slocum Society Sailing Club, who may have fallen overboard while sailing his Stella Maris from Bermuda to St. Martin in 1966.

One extremely lucky solo sailor was Fred Wood, who was knocked overboard when his boat, Windsong, accidentally jibed during a passage from Tahiti to Hawaii. Fortunately, Wood was a strong swimmer, and he happened to be only five miles from Christmas Island when the accident occurred. It took him seven hours to reach the island, and then he had to pick his way through a jagged coral reef before landing. He managed to keep away from the dangerous surf by listening to the differences in sound produced by the breaking waves.

As mentioned in Chapter 5, a means of reducing the hazard of being left astern by a self-steering boat after a fall overboard is to tow a long tripping line that will disengage the self-steering gear when it is pulled. Very often it is possible to grab a long line towed astern when it is floating and has a rescue quoit or buoy attached.

Good health and safety at sea very much depend on thoroughness in cruise planning and preparation. Physical conditioning, medical supplies, diet, safety equipment, and survival gear were discussed in Chapters 4 and 5. This chapter has presented the most common kinds of emergencies the offshore singlehander might have to face, although boat management in heavy weather has not yet been covered. This important problem and a selection of the true heavy-weather experiences will follow in the next chapter.

8 / ALONE AGAINST THE ELEMENTS

Every passage-making singlehander sooner or later encounters heavy weather. His boat-handling evolutions will not be exactly the same as those on a fully crewed vessel because of the need for more prompt action and one-step-at-a-time procedures. The helm can be manned for a limited time only. Sails must be shortened or removed early, and the boat must be made capable of fending for herself if the storm lasts for any length of time.

In a blow, the solo sailor simply shortens sail and lets his self-steering gear take charge, or in heavier weather he may strike his steering vane and heave to, quite often under a deeply-reefed mainsail or storm trysail alone, or with a storm jib aback (sheeted to windward) and the helm lashed down. Under gale or severe-storm conditions, he will often lie a-hull (see Chapter 5), that is to say, take down all sail and let the boat drift as she will. In this way, the vessel normally will find her natural position and retreat from the seas. The vast majority of modern sailing cruisers will lie a-hull about beam-on or perhaps with the stern slightly up to the wind and seas. Most vessels will forereach slowly while they drift off to leeward. They will tend to heel on the crests of the waves and right themselves or roll to weather when descending into the trough. The helm should be secured with shock cord or some other elastic material to relieve as much strain on the rudder as possible, and usually the helm is lashed down to inhibit excessive forward speed. The singlehander can then retreat to the shelter of his cabin, but the motion may be considerable. He should have numerous grab rails to grip and safety belts to hold him securely in the galley, at the chart table, or in his bunk.

Some of the numerous practitioners of the hulling tactic (lying a-hull) are: Marin-Marie, Jean Gau, John Guzzwell, Francis Chichester, Chris Loehr, Alec Rose, and Chay Blyth. It is interesting to compare this group of singlehanders, because their voyages range in time from 1933 to almost the present, and their vessels represent a variety of moderately deep, ballast-keel monohulls, the general type which perhaps is best suited to hulling. For the most part, this suitability has to do with the relatively high range of stability afforded by a ballasted keel of ample weight and depth. An excessively deep keel with great lateral plane, however, could be less successful, for it might overly inhibit leeway and cause the vessel to trip when she moves sideways.

Be this as it may, Marin-Marie successfully lay a-hull in a deep-draft vessel with great lateral plane during a violent Atlantic storm in early August, 1933. His 36-foot craft, the gaff-rigged cutter *Winnibelle*, was somewhat similar to the famous Colin Archer-designed Norwegian double-enders (Chapter 3), except that she had slightly less beam, greater draft, and a heavily-ballasted keel. With her rather high metacenter and short rig, the *Winnibelle* was naturally a vigorous roller, but despite this, her motion was tolerable when hulling under bare poles in a real blow. Marin-Marie wrote, "The *Winnibelle*, lying at right angles to the sea, was a great deal easier in her motion than she had been running before the Trades, when she had given me such hell, the bitch!" Wisely, he spread his mattress on the cabin sole to avoid being rolled out of his bunk and rested when he could, while the cutter lay beam-on with the helm lashed down, drifting at one and a half or two knots to leeward. Marin-Marie did not try to estimate the wind's velocity, but it was so strong that when he went on deck he could not stand up and could only move about on his hands and knees.

Jean Gau's *Atom* is also a double-ender, one of the famous "Tahiti" ketches designed by John Hanna (Chapter 3). She has considerable beam and displacement, but has, by modern standards, a rather modest amount

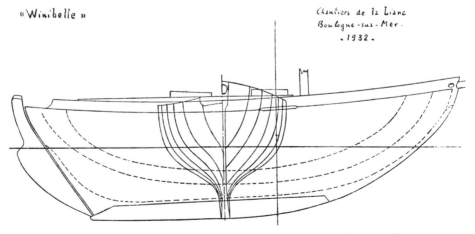

Plans of the Winnibelle *show the size of her lateral plane and wine glass sections. (From* Wind Aloft, Wind Alow *by Marin-Marie)*

Marin-Marie's Winnibelle *lay a-hull successfully despite her sizable lateral plane and tendency to roll when running. (From* Wind Aloft, Wind Alow *by Marin-Marie)*

of ballast on her long, moderately-shallow keel. In September, 1957, the *Atom* rode out hurricane "Carrie," the same storm that sank the large bark, *Pamir,* with a loss of eighty lives. The little double-ender lay a-hull with her helm lashed alee in 120-knot winds while her master closed himself in in the cabin and "slept, ate, read, and drew pictures." This is the storm tactic usually employed by Gau in extremely heavy weather, but it should be mentioned that on one occasion the method utterly failed, and the *Atom* was rolled completely over. This accident, which will be described in detail later in the chapter, does not necessarily disprove the merits of hulling, even for a Tahiti ketch. It simply demonstrates that the tactic can fail in particular weather and sea conditions. When the *Atom* capsized, she was in one of the world's most dangerous stretches of water, off the Cape of Good Hope, where a southwest storm of over seventy knots opposed the fast-moving Agulhas current causing unbelievably high, steep seas. Perhaps no tactic could have prevented the *Atom* from turning over in those conditions, but the beam-on position merely resulted in a capsize, whereas a position with bow or stern into the wind might have resulted in a far worse pitch-poling (somersaulting end-over-end). In 1971, this same boat survived five days of battering from hurricane "Ginger" when she was about 300 miles from Bermuda. Again she was left to her own devices, drifting off under bare poles, while Gau, then sixty-nine years old, stayed below eating, napping, and pumping the bilge. The latter activity reminds us of the importance of having a bilge pump operable from below.

In contrast to the heavy double-enders, the 21-foot yawl, *Trekka*, sailed around the world by John Guzzwell, is a light-displacement yawl with a fin keel and separated rudder attached to a skeg. In June, 1958, off the coast of Australia, she encountered a tropical cyclone that lasted for six days. She lay beam to the wind and seas with her helm lashed down and all sails furled while drifting to leeward at the rate of one knot, according to Guzzwell's estimate. In this manner, she rode the waves well, but gradually ran out of sea room. To reduce drift towards the lee shore, Guzzwell improvised a drag from two heavy warps and an eight-foot length of lumber. One warp was made fast to the bow and the other to the stern. They lessened the boat's drift, but her motion was not as comfortable as before, when she had no drag. It is interesting to note that after the wind had shifted and moderated, Guzzwell tried running off dead before the high seas under a storm jib while towing the drag astern, but the *Trekka* did not behave well and was nearly pooped by seas breaking over her stern. John lowered the jib, took in his drag, turned broadside to the seas, and lashed his tiller down; once again the little yawl rode the seas like a duck.

Francis Chichester had many heavy-weather experiences, but the one that sticks in my mind is the gale he encountered during the 1960 singlehander's race, which gusted up to 100 m.p.h. His boat was the 40-foot sloop, *Gipsy Moth III*, a racing-cruising type of moderate proportions designed by Robert Clark. She had a rather deep conventional keel, a cutaway forefoot, and a raking rudder attached to the keel. In the storm's early stages, Chichester described an appalling din, "a high-pitch screech or scream dominating. Plenty of spray peppering everything and seas hitting periodically with a bonk! Crash!" The sloop lay a-hull, stripped of all sail and with her main boom lowered and lashed to the deck. Evidently her motion was not too violent, for with the wind at an estimated ninety m.p.h. Chichester went below and had a meal of fried potatoes, onions, and three eggs, and then "went to sleep reading *The Tempest*." Later, however, when the wind increased even more, the *Gipsy Moth* began to forereach excessively and take quite a pounding from the seas. In an effort to slow her down, the singlehander streamed astern a large auto tire at the end of ten fathoms of anchor chain and twenty fathoms of warp, but still the boat reached ahead at about three knots. I am not too surprised that the drag failed to slow her more, because it might have tended to hold the stern up slightly and thus encourage forereaching. Nevertheless, the *Gipsy Moth III* weathered the blow satisfactorily.

It seems rather odd that in 1971 Chichester ran off before a sixty-knot blow in his larger and faster *Gipsy Moth V* instead of trying to lie a-hull. He told us in his book, *The Romantic Challenge*, that the boat behaved dangerously, knocking down repeatedly, while running before the wind at ten knots (once the speedometer showed twelve and a half knots) under a small storm jib sheeted flat, and then later under bare poles. He tried slowing her by heading up into the wind, but she would not turn past the beam-on position. Chichester expressed great concern about how anyone can manage a very fast monohull sailboat in such weather conditions. Apparently he lay with the wind and seas abeam only temporarily, and never really gave the hulling tactic a chance. Perhaps he was hesitant to do so because of the extreme knockdown he had experienced when lying a-hull in the *Gipsy Moth IV*. That boat, however, was said to be unusually tender. At any rate, we can only speculate on how the *Gipsy Moth V* would have behaved when left to herself under bare poles with the helm lashed down. It seems likely that she would have lain approximately broadside to the seas but would have forereached at a moderate to fairly fast speed. A tiny, flat, riding sail aft and possibly a heavy anchor hung at long scope from the bow might have been helpful in keeping her head up to or slightly above the beam-on position and thus inhibiting forereaching.

A clue to the hulling behavior of the *Gipsy Moth V* might be obtained from the experience of Chay Blyth's *British Steel*, when this boat lay a-hull between Australia and the Cape of Good Hope near the end of April, 1971. Both the *British Steel* and *Gipsy Moth V* were designed by Robert Clark, and although their rigs differed somewhat, their hulls were very similar in their lines and dimensions. It has been said that Blyth's boat was designed for going to windward, while Chichester's was for sailing downwind, but this distinction has probably been overrated, for both craft look very much alike in form and underwater profile, each having similar, abbreviated, fin keels and separated, skeg-mounted rudders. As a matter of fact, the *Gipsy Moth V* has slightly more draft, a feature conducive to good windward performance, even though she was intended to excel when sheets were well eased. Be that as it may, there are few significant differences between the shape of the two hulls. When Blyth drifted under bare poles beam to a wind exceeding sixty knots with steep seas, he did not express any great anxiety over excessive speed. His chief concern regarding the boat's behavior seemed to be her rolling and/or knockdowns, but he never mentioned her heeling past about fifty degrees.

Two strong advocates of hulling are Alec Rose, who sailed the 36-foot yawl, *Lively Lady*, around the world in 1967-1968, and Chris Loehr, a mas-

The slack bilges and moderately narrow beam of the Gipsy Moth IV give us a strong hint as to why Chichester found her to be excessively tender. (Courtesy of Yachting magazine)

ter mariner and sailmaker, who made several heavy-weather passages alone in the 28-foot sloop, *Lento*. Rose's boat is heavy and fairly narrow, with a spoon bow having little overhang, a deep forefoot, long, deep keel, counter stern, and slack bilges. Loehr's craft is a "Great Dane," quite a modern cruising design by Aage Utzon, but based on traditional concepts. She is fairly heavy with slack bilges and a moderate length of keel, but with a cut-away forefoot and a raking, outboard rudder. Concerning the hulling tactic, Loehr said, "I believe any ship will find its natural position in the sea. . . . There is something about nature you cannot fight. Just as your body quickly finds the most comfortable position when you sit down, so does a boat on the ocean." Alec Rose put it only a bit differently: ". . . it is safer to lay a-hull. That is to strip off all sails and let the yacht go with the sea and take up her own position." He went on to explain that the *Lively Lady* would lie with the wind just forward of the beam, with a list to leeward, and forereaching "slightly." He said the boat was often "thrown about unmercifully" but no more so than if other tactics had been employed. Furthermore, he wrote that he would lie a-hull "in the very fiercest storms."

Of course, not all singlehanders advocate the hulling tactic, at least not under all circumstances. In fact, even the strongest advocates would probably agree that there could be certain conditions that might make other tactics more expedient. One cannot be dogmatic where the fickle sea is concerned. One circumstance that could call for different tactics would be in the case of boats lacking in reserve stability, such as certain multihulls or shoal-draft centerboarders, which might more safely be kept end-to the seas. On the other hand, some of these craft might lie a-hull with their centerboards retracted under the right conditions. Bill Howell lay a-hull successfully in the catamaran *Golden Cockerel* (later called *Tahiti Bill*) with her daggerboards fully up during a lengthy gale when he was racing in the 1968 OSTAR. With her boards down, the multihull could have tripped and capsized, but with them up, she was simply thrown to leeward by the waves. In particularly steep seas with plunging breakers, however, even a boardless multihull can capsize as we shall see near the end of this chapter when the roll-over of the trimaran, *Clipper One*, will be described.

Other storm tactics used less frequently by singlehanders are lying to a floating sea anchor; and scudding, or running before the wind and seas with little or no sail hoisted. Most modern offshore sailors are not in favor of using a sea anchor (or drogue as it is sometimes called) unless, perhaps, the boat is small and of very shallow draft, or in the case when it becomes imperative to slow drift towards a lee shore. The reason for this is that many of today's deep-keel boats, especially those cut away under the water forward and with a lot of windage forward, will not lie to a sea anchor streamed from the bow. They simply fall off the wind, lie about beam-on, and try to forereach. A riding sail set aft may help, but it may impose great strains in the very heaviest weather and flog at times. Such a sail should be cut flat to inhibit flogging (which could destroy the sail) when the boat temporarily swings her bow towards the wind. A better tactic for a boat that will not keep her head up is often to stream the drogue astern, but some sterns are quite vulnerable to pounding or being pooped, and also there is the danger of excessive stress from shock loading and of the boat being overly tethered or held so firmly that she cannot give to the seas.

It would probably be helpful if an elastic type of anchoring system could be used, such as the experimental kind shown in Figure 8-1. Notice that the rode is nylon, and there are loops of heavy shock cord that will elongate and stretch under heavy loading. Also, the bag has slits which are held shut by plastic battens sewn into the cloth and a girdle of shock cord. When the bag is jerked by its rode, the slits should open wide to relieve the shock. The two bars at the bag's mouth, one of wood and the other of metal, are simply to avoid the usual iron ring, which complicates stowage. The bag design is merely an idea of mine, and thus far it has not been tested.

FIGURE 8-1: AN ELASTIC SEA ANCHOR
(To relieve shock loading)

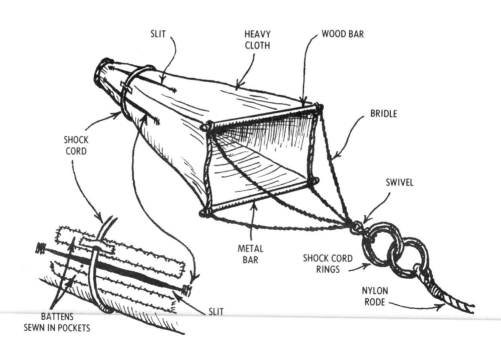

The open boat Elaine, *whose centerboard Fred Rebell utilized to make an effective drogue during his solo crossing of the Pacific in 1932. (From* Escape to the Sea *by Fred Rebell)*

A drogue can be extremely valuable on any small, shallow craft, such as a lifeboat, dinghy, or open boat that can be made to lie with its bow up, for such a craft should seldom be allowed to get broadside to breaking seas on account of the risk of rolling over. In the early days of offshore single-handing, many small-boat sailors, such as Gilboy, Andrews, Lawlor, and Blackburn, used standard sea anchors (see Figure 5-1). To relieve violent jerking strains, Blackburn used a spiral steel spring at the inboard end of his rode. This could even be used to advantage today, although we now have such shock absorbers as nylon, shock cord, and rubber snubbers. Care must be taken with the latter, however, to see that its metal thimbles do not chafe the rode.

A relatively modern example of a small boat using a sea anchor successfully is the case of Robert Manry in the 13½-foot modified centerboard dinghy, *Tinkerbelle*. During her Atlantic crossing in 1965, she rode out several blows with a drogue streamed from her bow. She kept her head to the wind and seas, but this position could be held only when her outboard rudder was unshipped. At certain times Manry found it helpful to hoist a scrap of sail aft on the permanent backstay to act as a riding sail.

Many times sea anchors have been improvised with some success. Fred Rebell, the amazing do-it-yourselfer who crossed the Pacific in the 18-foot open boat, *Elaine* (Chapter 5), made an effective drogue out of his centerboard. During a gale near the end of the passage between Hawaii and

California in December, 1932, the *Elaine* lay hove-to under a triple-reefed mainsail sheeted in flat. She was keeping her bow somewhat toward the seas but was shipping a great deal of water, and on one occasion she took a bad knockdown that half filled her. Rebell decided that he should lower sail and stream a drag from the bow, but he had no sea anchor. After racking his brain, he thought of the centerboard, which was a large, heavy metal plate. It must have been a job to remove the board during the storm's height, but Rebell extracted it from the well, rigged some sort of bridle, and launched the affair over the bow. It veered around crazily at the end of its rode but apparently succeeded in holding the *Elaine's* bow to the seas. I wonder, however, if there was not another, more subtle advantage to such a tactic. By removing the board, Rebell also raised it completely and, although he sacrificed some stability, he also removed a sizeable underwater appendage on which the boat could trip. Thus he could have increased his boat's resistance to being rolled down. At any rate, the *Elaine* came through the blow relatively unscathed.

As mentioned earlier, auto tires are sometimes used for drags. Bob Griffith (not a singlehander, but a remarkable seaman, who circumnavigated Antarctica in the 52-foot ferrocement cutter, *Awahnee*) told me that at times he carried as many as twelve tires. Solo sailor Bill Murnan carried an aircraft tire aboard his steel "Seabird" yawl, the *Seven Seas II*. He sometimes towed it astern edgewise but found that it caused greater drag when towed from a bridle in an upright position.

Running off before the wind under bare poles is a classic means of weathering a storm, but it may not always be suitable for a singlehander, because the tactic normally requires a man at the helm, and there is obviously a limit to the time one man can steer in very severe conditions. It has been suggested that a singlehander can scud before a storm with the self-steering vane controlling the vessel, but in the worst weather such a practice could be extremely dangerous. Of course, there are a number of requisites for scudding, even when the helm is manned. First of all, there must be ample sea room, because the vessel may move with considerable speed; second, she must be readily controllable while running. She must not yaw, squat, or root her bow excessively. Her performance will depend primarily on two factors: the nature of the seas and the boat's design characteristics, such as the fullness of her bow, length of keel, location of the rudder, kind of stern, and so forth.

A vessel that proved well suited to the scudding tactic under the right sea conditions was the famous *Spray*. Slocum ran her off before a gale near Cape Horn in 1896 while carrying a reefed forestaysail sheeted flat and towing two long hawsers. The helm was lashed amidships, and evidently the *Spray* was able to steer herself. There are not many modern yachts, however, that can safely steer themselves for any length of time before the heaviest weather offshore.

Bernard Moitessier devised a method of scudding at high speed before the exceptionally high seas of the southern Pacific, but the technique required his hand on the helm. His procedure in the very worst conditions, which he claimed was suggested from the writings of Vito Dumas, was to head off directly before the wind, stripped of all sail and towing no drags, until his boat was approached by a steep following sea. At this time he would head up slightly so that the stern was about fifteen to twenty degrees from being square to the seas. This attitude was held until the crest rolled under the quarter and the boat settled into the trough of the next following wave. The boat's slight angle to the seas, he claimed, would inhibit surfing and cause the boat to heel somewhat, which would also discourage rooting (having the bow dig in). He found it necessary to keep his boat moving sufficiently fast at all times for good steering control, normally close to but not exceeding (if possible) a speed equal to the square root of the waterline length. Moitessier stated that towing drags failed to slow his *Joshua* and merely hampered steering in those great seas of the high latitudes in the South Pacific. Both Dumas and Moitessier sailed ketch-rigged double-enders with long keels and outboard rudders, but the larger *Joshua*, built of steel, had less draft, less ballast, and a much taller rig than Dumas' wooden *Lehg II.*

Another solo skipper of a double-ender, Robin Knox-Johnston, used the scudding tactics in the huge seas of the South Pacific, but he usually towed a drag in the form of a 100-fathom, 2-inch, polypropylene warp. With her long keel and a tiny storm jib sheeted flat and set far forward at the end of her long bowsprit, Robin's 32-foot ketch, the *Suhaili,* was able, like the *Spray,* to keep her stern up to the seas with the helm unattended. The long warp was streamed in a somewhat unusual manner, for, although it was towed astern, it was streamed in a bight with both ends secured forward and leading down either side of the boat. The singlehander claimed that this method allowed more stretch in the line to provide "give" against the force of the seas, and, of course, the bight helped smooth the crests. A further benefit might be that if the helm should need attending, the drags would not hamper steering excessively due to their being secured far ahead of the rudder.

During his remarkable solo voyage from Australia to Antarctica in late 1972 and early 1973, Dr. David Lewis used a method similar to Moitessier's of scudding at high speed before gales. He ran off in his 32-foot sloop, the *Ice Bird,* under a tiny storm jib at an angle of about twenty degrees to the following seas. The tactic demanded that the helm be controlled, but Lewis was able to accomplish this by rigging steering lines that led into the cabin.

Unfortunately, in the worst conditions the technique did not succeed entirely, and in a late November gale, while running before waves about forty feet high, the *Ice Bird* was overwhelmed (see Chapter 7). She was smashed down by a breaking sea and rolled completely over. She righted immediately but suffered the loss of her mast and other damages described in the last chapter.

It is impossible to say, on that particular occasion, how the *Ice Bird* would have fared had she been hulling. She probably would have rolled over, but, with very little forward speed, perhaps the capsizing would have been less damaging. In at least one respect the *Ice Bird* may not have been entirely suitable for high-speed scudding, for her keel was of moderate length only, with the attached rudder not as far aft as it could have been (according to the drawings I have seen) for optimum steering control. Scudding in the kind of sea conditions to which Dr. Lewis was exposed undoubtedly requires continued careful attention to steering, and during a lengthy storm, a singlehander could surely become exhausted whether steering from the cockpit or below. After reaching Cape Town following his third capsizing (Chapter 7), Dr. Lewis said, "I was greatly influenced by Moitessier. I thought it right to run her off before the wind but I don't know . . ."

There are various interpretations of the term capsize, but to me it means a knockdown or roll-down at least to the point where the vessel's righting moment becomes zero or where her stability changes from positive to negative. At this point, she has lost her ability to self-right. She may hang momentarily between positive and negative stability and then slowly right, or she may "turn turtle" (roll completely upside down with her keel in the air) where she could possibly remain for some time (perhaps indefinitely, if she is a multihull), or she might make a 360-degree roll-over.

More than a few singlehanders have undergone the frightening experience of a capsize. In fact, such accidents were quite common in the early days when ocean crossings were made or attempted in cockleshell boats with little or no external ballast. Johnson, Gilboy, Andrews, Lawlor, and Blackburn all capsized at sea. Lawlor probably had the easiest time of it with his *Sea Serpent*, because she was fitted with about 600 pounds of lead on her keel, not enough to prevent a capsize, but very helpful when it came to righting the boat. Andrews, on the other hand, had no external ballast at all on his *Mermaid,* and, as said earlier, he reported no less than seven capsizings during his attempted Atlantic crossing in 1891. On one occasion it took him thirty minutes of struggling to right the boat.

The log of Bernard Gilboy's solo Pacific crossing, which was rediscovered and published not many years ago, gives the understated details of his turning turtle approximately 240 miles from the Fiji Islands on December 13,

1882. His 18-foot, double-ended schooner, the *Pacific,* broached-to while running when a sea broke under her quarter, and she promptly rolled over bottomside up. Gilboy, who had been aboard the boat continuously for nearly four months, suddenly found himself underneath the overturned hull. Extricating himself, he surfaced on the windward side, and managed to crawl onto her slippery, weed-and-barnacle-covered bottom. He struggled out of his heavy shirt and oilskin coat, which were weighing him down, and then set about figuring how to right the boat. This would be no easy job, because the masts and sails thrusting downward caused great resistance to being lifted, while the boat's broad beam made her very stable in the inverted position, and her shallow, unballasted keel contributed little as a counterbalance to assist in righting.

Gilboy had decided to dive under the boat and attempt to retrieve a line that could be used to help with the righting, when he noticed his sea anchor, with its line attached, floating to windward. The drogue was a sail-pattern type (similar in appearance to a squaresail), and evidently a bubble of air trapped under the canvas kept it on the water's surface. The singlehander caught hold of the drogue's line, the end of which was made fast on the forward deck, and hauled it up over the boat's bottom. This gave him something to pull on when trying to roll the hull upright. Gilboy positioned himself to leeward on the side of the hull opposite the line's attachment, and with his legs braced against the topsides, he pulled on the line with all his might. He tried repeatedly, but with no success. As his log stated, "It seemed to be a hopeless task." He persisted, however, and finally, "after an hour's hard work she began to right."

But Gilboy's difficulties were far from over. Although the half-swamped boat was now on her feet, the captain had great difficulty in keeping her upright. To lessen windage and top-hamper, he began to cut away the rigging and unship the masts, but before the job was completed, the *Pacific* capsized again. This time Gilboy had less trouble righting her, and he succeeded in unshipping the masts, which he lashed together and made fast, along with some other loose gear, to the drogue line. The spars and gear floated to windward and acted as a drag to hold the boat's bow into the wind and seas to help prevent another capsizing. Gilboy scrambled aboard and began bailing for all he was worth with a large sugar-cube box. Water seemed to wash into his cockpit hatch faster than he could bail it out. There was a large watertight compartment forward of the cockpit, but Gilboy had failed to plug its limber holes, and so the compartment was partially flooded. After a long period of exhausting work and great anxiety, the boat began to gain freeboard, and about dawn the next day she was finally cleared of water.

The crisis was over, but much food was lost or spoiled and the compass,

rudder, and mainmast were gone. Gilboy devised a reasonably well balanced jury rig by substituting for the mainsail a triangular sail, which was
hoisted to the head of the foremast, tacked down amidships, and boomed
out with an oar. The singlehander gamely struggled on for about a month
and a half longer, but, at the end of that time, his food and water were
almost gone, and he was weak and exhausted; he allowed himself to be
picked up by the schooner, *Alfred Vittery.* He was only 160 miles short of
his destination in Australia.

Modern monohull boats, of course, nearly always carry external ballast
on (or encased in) the keel, which not only increases the range of stability,
but also helps with self-righting in the event of turning turtle. Most ex-
ternally-ballasted monohulls that have had the misfortune to roll upside
down have remained in the inverted position no longer that a few minutes,
but occasionally a boat will become stabilized with her keel up.

Such was the case when the 19-foot *Cockle* capsized during her transatlantic race against two sisterboats, modified Hunter 19s, in November,
1971. Her singlehanded skipper, Alan Gick, was only about four days out
from Falmouth, England, in the Bay of Biscay, a notoriously rough area,
especially at that time of the year, when his little *Cockle* turned turtle. She
had been lying a-hull during a blow that produced relatively short, confused seas about twenty feet high, when she was hit by an unusually high
sea with a breaking top caused by the coincidence of two waves. Gick was
below at the time, and he was thrown to the cabin top as his boat rolled
completely upside down. Fortunately, the companionway hatch was closed
so that the cabin was not completely flooded during the knockdown, but
about half of the supplies and stores were flung or fell to the cabin top.

After recovering from his initial shock, Gick suddenly came to the frightening realization that his boat was not righting herself. Not even the steep
seas washing over her bottom could roll her upright. The water level inside
the cabin began rising, and the singlehander described his situation as similar to being inside a washing machine. He managed to don a life jacket
and then inflated a rubber dinghy, which he hoped would keep the *Cockle*
afloat. He had the strong feeling that she was about to sink, although she
had a certain amount of built-in flotation. Moments later, however, he re-
considered and deflated the dinghy in order that he could try to escape
from the cabin and use the dinghy as a life boat. After about twelve minutes of being upside down, which must have seemed an eternity, the little
vessel began to right. Her mast had broken, and the partial removal of its
stabilizing effect, along with the free surface effect from water that had
risen inside the hull, allowed her to roll back on her feet. The water level
inside the cabin was then less than half a foot below the bridge deck, but
Gick bailed frantically and evidently very efficiently, for he reported clear-

ing the boat within about half an hour. The broken mast and tangled rigging were afloat to windward, and they acted as a kind of sea anchor. Gick managed to float them far enough away from the boat to prevent their damaging the hull, which lay almost broadside to the waves.

The blow continued, and, before dawn the next day, the *Cockle* turned turtle again, but this time she did a rapid 360-degree roll-over. Again stores and gear were flung about the cabin, so Gick took hammer in hand and nailed almost everything movable to the cabin sole. When daylight came, he shifted his drag, consisting of the broken rig and a 150-foot warp, to the stern. The *Cockle* seemed to behave better tethered from her stern, but the blow showed no signs of abating, and Gick decided to call for help with an emergency radio beacon. Fourteen hours later an airplane spotted him and sent a ship to his rescue. Gick was eventually taken off, but the *Cockle* could not be hoisted aboard the ship on account of the bad weather. The singlehander wrote, "It was heartbreaking to see her drifting away into the darkness."

The other two competitors experienced the same bad weather, and one of them, Geoff Cath, also capsized (six times according to one report), but his rig remained intact. He and the third competitor, Nigel Harman, made it under their own power to Vigo, Spain.

Gick was at a loss to explain how his boat could have remained so stable in the upside-down position, since she had a ballast-displacement ratio of fifty per cent. One partial explanation could be that the shifting stores falling to the cabin top contributed to the inverted stability, especially before the water in the hull had risen and, of course, the boat's moderately broad beam contributed to the problem.

Incidentally, John Letcher, the previously mentioned singlehander-engineer-naval architect, told me that he made his twin-keeler, *Aleutka*, quite narrow because of his concern over high stability in the inverted position. At present, however, he has modified his former thinking somewhat and feels that the free surface effect of water rising in the hull would cause enough instability to justify slightly more beam.

Another possible contributing factor to the *Cockle*'s predicament was that her keel's center of gravity may have been relatively high due to its shape and distribution of ballast, and the flotation might have been concentrated at higher locations for better advantage when capsized. At any rate, Alan Gick's experience teaches us some valuable lessons:

(1) There is high risk in a very small boat crossing such a notoriously rough body of water as the Bay of Biscay at other than the most favorable time of the year.

(2) All gear, stores, and ballast must be absolutely secured to prevent shifting during the worst possible knockdown in heavy weather at sea.

(3)   It can be dangerous lying a-hull in such a boat in short and steep confused seas that have breaking tops of the plunging variety.

(4)   Consideration might be given to *sturdy* masthead flotation and suitable rigging to support it on all capsizeable boats having questionable self-righting characteristics (even monohulls) that might venture offshore.

(5)   There is not necessarily a need to be extremely alarmed if a well-ballasted boat with moderate beam does not right immediately after turning turtle, because, as water slowly rises inside her hull, the free surface effect and the lessening of the load waterline beam will be helpful to righting.

Another element of hulling worth considering is the extent of forereaching while lying a-hull in a boat having a short fin keel. It seems that most fin-keelers are more subject to tripping on their keels when hulling if they are allowed to make any more that a slight amount of headway because their lateral resistance depends on hydrodynamic lift caused by forward speed. Quite often by lashing the helm down (perhaps with a shock cord to alleviate strains on the rudder) and, in some cases, by setting a very small riding sail aft, headway can be minimized.

The foregoing is certainly not intended to be overly critical of Alan Gick, for his boat was well equipped and extensively modified for heavy weather offshore, and the singlehander acted in a cool, courageous manner. Actually, he knew full well that there were risks involved but didn't quite realize their extent. He confessed to feeling very humble at having to call for help, because, as he wrote, "Yachtsmen who set out on trips like this should not expect to be rescued." Nevertheless, Gick caused his rescuers minimal risks and his recounting of the experience provides some valuable lessons for those who aspire to offshore passages in very small craft. In fairness to the Hunter 19 class, it should be said that David Blagden made a highly successful Atlantic crossing in one of these craft, the *Willing Griffin*, in the 1972 race for singlehanders, and he survived some very heavy weather and knockdowns on his qualifying cruise prior to the race. Blagden was so confident in his boat that he wrote, "Such a small boat does stand the risk of being completely inverted under exceptional conditions, though the heavy keel with a fifty per cent ballast ratio would flip her up, almost immediately." We know from Alan Gick's experience, however, that this is not necessarily true.

The capsizing of monohulls having well-ballasted keels is nearly always caused by extraordinary wave action. Usually these waves are encountered during stormy seasons, in areas where there is tremendous fetch, and/or where there are shoals (not always charted) or strong currents that cause steep, plunging seas; then there are the "freak" waves that will soon be described. Probably the most notorious regions for producing dangerous seas are those in the high southern latitudes, especially in the general vicinities of Cape Horn and the Cape of Good Hope. Aside from Dr. David Lewis, other examples of singlehanders capsizing in those regions are: Marcel Bardiaux, Tom Corkill, Jean Gau, and Bill King. It will be remembered that the latter's experience was briefly described in the last chapter under the section, "Dismastings."

Marcel Bardiaux experienced two rapid 360-degree roll-overs while sailing around Cape Horn from east to west in 1952. He is generally credited with being the first singlehander to round the Horn against the prevailing winds and safely clear the shores of South America. This feat, accomplished near the beginning of the Antarctic winter in a mere 31-foot, homemade, racing-cruiser, has been described as the equivalent to climbing Mt. Everest. Of course, Al Hansen, in the double-ender, *Mary Jane,* had previously made an east-to-west rounding of Cape Horn, but soon afterwards he was wrecked and lost his life on the rocky coast of southern Chile. Bardiaux's boat, *Les 4 Vents,* was uniquely fitted for the passage. In anticipation of a possible capsizing, Bardiaux had secured flotation in the form of twenty-four five-gallon GI tins to the underside of the deck. He felt that these tins in conjunction with the lead ballast on the keel would immediately right the boat from an inverted position.

When Bardiaux rounded Cape San Diego, the southeast tip of Tierra del Fuego, to pass through Le Maire Strait on his way to the Horn, weather conditions were simply appalling. He was being set to windward by a nine-knot current flowing against a fifty-knot gale! Experienced sailors need little imagination to realize what short, steep, tumbling seas were created by such an opposition of wind and water flow. *Les 4 Vents* had made several boards to windward under a deeply roller-reefed mainsail, which Bardiaux could only set after dipping the sail in seawater to unfreeze it, when the wind freshened and backed to the southwest putting Cape Horn dead to windward. Bardiaux could make no progress to weather despite the powerful current, and so he hove to; *Les 4 Vents* was then thrown backwards by the breaking seas. In an effort to counteract this sternway, Bardiaux scrambled below to get his sea anchor. Moments later, a comber taken on the beam tumbled the cutter, throwing Bardiaux to the cabin top amid a shower of loose gear. A flood of water burst through the companionway, but the boat quickly righted herself. The singlehander struggled out of the cabin and slammed shut the companionway doors, but then *Les 4 Vents* turned turtle again. This time she did not right as promptly due to the shifting of equipment and stores, and Bardiaux was submerged in the icy water. When she did turn upright, the mast was still intact, but the storm trysail, headsails, and dodger were gone. The powerfully built Bardiaux remained on board by clutching the twisted dodger frame, which was bolted to the deck.

Les 4 Vents was half filled and listing badly, but Bardiaux streamed a long warp and fifteen fathoms of anchor chain, which seemed to steady the boat, while he manned the pump. When the bilges were mostly cleared, he hoisted a scrap of sail and made for what shelter he could find. Soaked to the skin and in subfreezing temperatures, the singlehander slowly worked his boat into countercurrents and smoother water along the coast. It was totally dark when he reached Aquirre Bay and dropped the hook with a scope of sixty fathoms.

Bardiaux was shaken but not deterred by his ordeal, and he set off again thirty hours later to beat past the Horn. On May 12, 1952, in a storm of hail and snow, the determined Frenchman left Cape Horn to starboard. He then stood about twenty-five miles to the SSW, came about, weathered Hermite Island (northwest of Cape Horn), and eventually fought his way through floating ice and strong winds into Beagle Channel. From there he proceeded to Cook Bay and out into the Pacific. Bardiaux's singlehanded near-wintertime doubling of the Horn in a small, homemade boat has to be ranked with the most astonishing of all sailing feats.

In many ways, *Les 4 Vents* was well-prepared for her venture, having buoyancy tanks, a small cockpit, a well-rounded cabin trunk, small portholes, bolted dodger frame, and so forth. But on the other hand, she had no deck-enclosing life lines, minuscule coamings, and a less-than-satisfactory means of blocking off the companionway.

When the weather deteriorates to survival conditions, it seems that the safest location for the crew is below, perhaps strapped in their bunks, but if it is necessary that someone be on deck for steering or some other purpose, he should be attached with a stout safety line. Not everyone has the strength of Bardiaux to hang on with his bare hands alone during a capsize or severe pooping. The safety line should probably be of considerable length, because otherwise the sailor might be held too long under water during a roll-over or extreme knockdown. Singlehander Ambrogio Fogar, sailing the 38-foot sloop, *Surprise,* was rolled over in the Tasman Sea during a cyclone in 1974. Only moments before she turned turtle, Fogar was washed overboard, but he remained tethered by a long safety line. He actually watched his vessel roll through 360 degrees from the end of the line. With sufficient ballast on her keel and moderate beam, the *Surprise* righted promptly, and Fogar was able to haul himself back on board.

Unlike monohull boats, unballasted multihulls most often capsize from wind force rather than wave action. An exception, however, was Tom Corkill's 25-foot trimaran, *Clipper One,* which turned turtle about 200 miles northwest of the Cape of Good Hope. She had been lying a-hull in a blow and was stripped of all sail, when a steep sea broke against her beam. It stove in the cabin side and threw the boat upside down. Corkill was below at the time, and after his initial recovery from the tumbling, he forced open the companionway hatch, took a deep breath, and swam down and out from under the upturned boat. With lungs nearly bursting, he bobbed up into a roaring gale. Clad only in shorts and a jersey, with the seas washing over him, he had to cling to the bottom of the craft for eighteen hours. An important factor that led to Corkill's rescue was that the *Clipper One's* bottom was painted with a bright "air-sea-rescue" orange paint that enabled the overturned vessel to be spotted by a ship.

Without special systems of self-rescue such as those described in Chapter 3, there is little chance of a singlehander righting a multihull, thus all precautions should be taken to avoid capsizing. Most of these were discussed in Chapter 5. In Corkill's case, perhaps the most effective measures would have been sturdy masthead flotation with extra strong rigging (although this is a controversial preventative); small, strong cabin sides and windows; the capability of lying end-to those particular seas; and the capability to avoid tripping. In respect to the latter, the *Clipper One* was heavily loaded and had taken on a considerable amount of water, which evidently shifted, and, together with the extra weight, caused her leeward ama to dig in. A proper bilge pump operable from the helm and also from below might have been helpful. The trimaran designer, Robert Harris, wrote, "It is also possible that had Corkill pumped out his *Clipper* before retiring she would have been buoyant enough to remain upright."

In the literature of the sea, one often finds references to "freak" waves. These are gigantic crests towering high above their neighbors. Occasionally, also, there may be abnormally deep troughs, sometimes referred to as "holes in the sea." Monstrous freak waves are fortunately rare; when they do exist, they are often formed by the mixing of several different wave trains (systems of related waves moving at about half the speed of the individual waves) during prolonged storms at sea, sometimes after a wind shift, or perhaps by the shelving of underwater shoals or the opposition of strong, offshore currents. Slocum and Gerbault met freak seas of considerable size, and each singlehander avoided being washed overboard by climbing aloft. One might think a safer place would be in the enclosed cabin. After spotting the approaching wave, Slocum had time to douse his sails and haul himself up the peak halyards, and Gerbault climbed his mast halfway to the truck. Each vessel was completely buried by tons of water, but neither capsized.

Jean Gau, however, was not so lucky. He met with a huge tumbling sea near the Cape of Good Hope that rolled his double-ender, the *Atom*, completely upside down. The capsizing took place during the singlehander's second circumnavigation, in 1966. The *Atom* had been lying a-hull under bare poles during a blow that gusted up to seventy-two knots in a region

Jean Gau's Atom *in happier days on the River Orb, Valras, France. (This photograph, contributed by James Tazelaar, will appear in his book* To Challenge a Distant Sea: The Life and Voyages of Jean Gau.)

noted for dangerous seas, when she was overwhelmed. Published writings by Jean Gau are presently all too rare, but the following is an excerpt, describing the incident, which appeared in the Autumn, 1966, issue of the Slocum Society's journal, *The Spray* (translated from the French in "Le Midi Libre," May, 1966):

"In the night of February 27th, at about 3 A.M., I heard a strange distant sound. It increased in intensity. It appeared to be the roar of a distant waterfall. Second by second it increased. I could not believe it was real. I wondered what would happen. As the roar increased, I instinctively grabbed the edge of my bunk. In a tremendous explosion the huge wave hit the starboard side and tons of water fell on deck. I was thrown against the deck beams and buried under all the objects which were on the starboard bunk opposite mine; navigation instruments, charts, etc. The cabin lamp went out.

"To my amazement and for the first time, *Atom* had capsized completely (keel uppermost). I had kept all the openings closed except for a small porthole at the end of the cabin. Through this opening a powerful jet of water entered the cabin, flooding everything. For an undefined period of time I felt paralyzed, awaiting the end. I knew that one day or the other, I would meet one of these monstrous waves which would bury me and my boat. I really thought that moment had arrived, but suddenly, thanks to its heavy keel, the boat righted itself. In a desperate effort, I took the decision, which appeared senseless at the time, to reach safety. I was nearly buried under wet blankets and other assorted objects, and it was only after I freed myself that I was able, although heavily bruised, to reach the deck. The sea around the boat was a raging mass of water, but what gave me a feeling of horror was to see that *Atom* had been dismasted. It was a frightful sight, the stumps of the masts sticking out of the deck. The mast, boom and the bowsprit with the sails still lashed on had carried downwind, but were held back by the shrouds and the stays. The dinghy which had been solidly lashed on the cabin top had torn its fastenings and disappeared.

"All this happened within a second, maybe less. The sight was so discouraging that I felt nothing more could be done. I made an effort to look at things calmly and thought it was not the time to sit there and do nothing. The boat was still afloat, and maybe there was still some way of reaching safety. *Atom* and I had been together for a great part of our lives and were destined to sail or sink together. She had saved my life several times, and it was now my turn to do all that was humanly possible to save her."

And save her life he did. Gau's remarkable feat of cutting away the smashed rig was described in the last chapter. After it was set adrift and no longer threatened to hole the *Atom*, the singlehander set to work pumping the bilge and repairing his drowned engine. The following day he succeeded in getting the auxiliary started, and on March 2 he arrived at Mossel Bay on the southern coast of South Africa. When an astounded witness to his arrival asked Gau why he sailed alone in such a little boat, the circumnavigator replied that he could not help it. "More than anything else," he said, "I love my boat, the sea and adventure."

9 / SINGLEHANDING FOR EVERYONE

We can't all be Slocums or Chichesters, and I'm sure that many sailors have no particular desire to emulate the masters. There seems little doubt, however, that many an avid sailor would enjoy an occasional sail or week-end cruise by himself just for the satisfaction of doing it alone or because the right crew is hard to find.

Let us suppose that you have a small stock cruiser (about 30 to 35 feet long) not specifically modified for singlehanding, and you want to take her out alone. You are new at singlehanded sailing and are a bit nervous about the possibility of getting into trouble and making a spectacle of yourself. The answer to this worry is thorough preparation and careful planning ahead.

To begin with, see that your boat is properly equipped. A few items of special importance for singlehanding are: sheets that are within easy reach of the helm; steering lines and/or a means of locking the helm; a proper, adjustable topping lift leading to the masthead (not a short strop securing the boom to the backstay); adequate clearance between the boom and backstay (not always the case); stowage compartments or lockers near the helm; decks clear of unnecessary gear or fittings that could cause tripping or fouling of lines; all engine controls near the helm; suitable headsails that allow good visibility; a steering compass that may also be used for taking bearings; a long, lightweight boat hook; and a handy place to stow the anchor (perhaps on the bow pulpit) where it will be out of the way but available for instant use. Before getting underway, locate and put in an accessible place every piece of gear that will or might be needed. For example, see that binoculars, chart, horn, sail stops, winch handles, and even personal items such as sunburn cream and dark glasses are near the helm. Shelves just inside the companionway and winch-base stowage compartments are handy for these items. While speaking of personal gear, by the way, let me urge the use of proper skidproof deck shoes and a knife with screw-driver and folding spike carried in your pocket. Pliers and a small adjust-able wrench in a leather case hung from the belt can also be useful, and by all means carry a spare sail stop attached to your belt or in a pocket.

Don't leave your mooring or marina berth until all lead blocks are in place, headsail sheets have been properly rove, the anchor and rode are ready for use, sails and lines that might be needed are conveniently stowed, food and drinks are in a handy location, all loose items are made secure so that they cannot fall during a knockdown, hat and foul weather gear are available, and so forth. The proper size of jib for one man to handle in the estimated strength of wind should be bent, and by all means see that it is high enough off the deck to allow good visibility. The sail may require a tack pendant. Be sure that everything is rigged so that lines cannot foul. The anchor, for instance, should not be stowed where the headsail sheets can foul it when coming about. In some cases, it might be advisable to rig a line that will act as a fouling preventer similar to the one shown in Figure 9-1. It is a good idea to tie the headsail sheets to the clew grommet with bowlines, but tie the knots in such a way that they cannot foul on the shrouds. The end of the line where it finally emerges from the knot should be facing away from the shrouds and not towards them. This is also ex-plained in Figure 9-1. A bowline facing the wrong way can foul even when shroud rollers are used, and the singlehander does not want to have to make a trip forward to clear it.

If your boat lacks a self-steering vane, rig simple steering lines as sug-gested in Chapter 5, which run from the tiller through blocks on each side of the cockpit and then forward. The ends of the steering lines can be secured to jam cleats mounted in the vicinity of the mast, or, if there are no jam cleats, the lines can be made fast to the grab rails or life line stanchions forward with simple slip-knots that can be released quickly. Jam cleats can also be mounted on the tiller, but I prefer two half hitches that can be slipped over the tiller end in order to free it immediately in an emergency. The important point to remember when the helm is lashed is that you must be able to release it *quickly* from either forward or aft because of boat traffic or for some other reason. If the boat has a wheel, the best plan is usually to fit the emergency tiller when the system works freely. Almost every boat with a wheel has this provision, or at least she should have. As said in Chapter 5, sometimes the emergency tiller will have to be rigged backwards (see Figure 9-2) in order that it will clear the wheel when there is a steering pedestal just forward of the rudder post head. Obviously, this arrangement necessitates reverse steering, with the tiller pushed down to make the boat turn downwind, and pulled up to turn the boat into the wind.

Before casting off, check the weather, wind, and tide conditions. Analyze

FIGURE 9-1: FOULING AND JAMMING PREVENTION

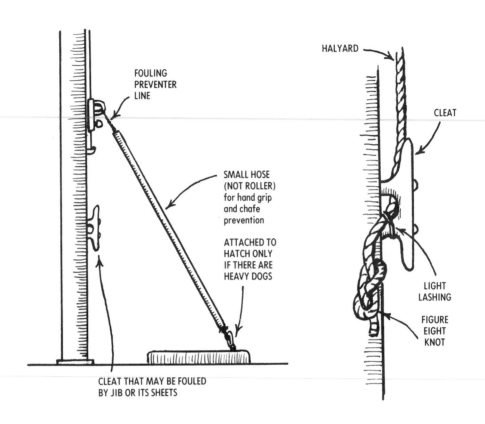

FOULING
PREVENTER
LINE

HALYARD

CLEAT

SMALL HOSE
(NOT ROLLER)
for hand grip
and chafe
prevention

ATTACHED TO
HATCH ONLY
IF THERE ARE
HEAVY DOGS

LIGHT
LASHING

FIGURE
EIGHT
KNOT

CLEAT THAT MAY BE FOULED
BY JIB OR ITS SHEETS

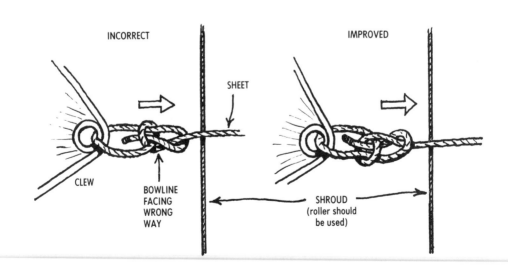

INCORRECT

IMPROVED

SHEET

CLEW

BOWLINE
FACING
WRONG
WAY

SHROUD
(roller should
be used)

FIGURE 9-2: SIMPLE TEMPORARY SELF STEERING

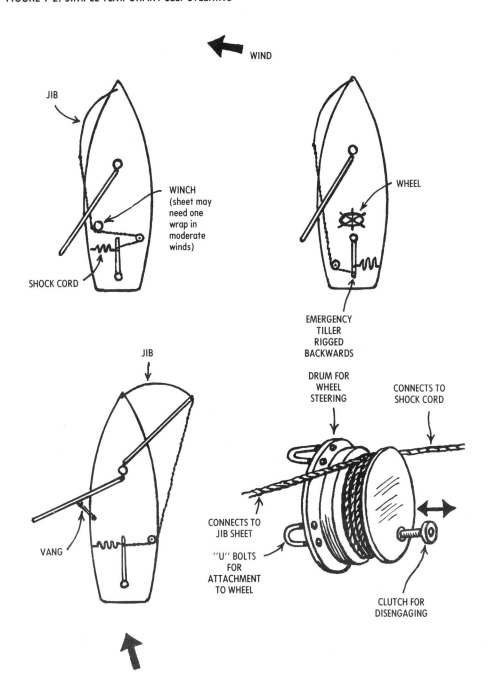

carefully just how your boat will be affected when she leaves her dock or mooring. Will her bow be blown off? Is the current setting her against the dock? Should she be warped around the other way or moved closer to the end of the dock? Which direction should be taken in leaving the mooring? These are the kinds of questions you should be asking yourself. Take your time in answering them, for a singlehander should avoid making hasty decisions.

A reliable engine, naturally, will simplify getting underway. After starting the engine, be sure it is warmed up and running smoothly before casting off. It is a good idea to doublecheck that the water intake and fuel valves are open, because sometimes the effect of these valves being closed will not make itself known until the boat is underway. In most cases, docking lines should be looped around their piling or dockside cleat and then led back to the cockpit for easier control when there are no people to help on the dock (see Chapter 5). If a dinghy is being towed, its painter should be fitted with cork floats so there is no possibility of its fouling the propeller. Also, all loose lines on the deck, such as jib sheets, ought to be belayed with their coiled ends in the cockpit so they cannot fall overboard and be sucked into the prop.

After you are well away from the dock or mooring and are running under power in open waters, try lashing your helm so that the boat will hold a reasonably straight course. In most cases the boat will have a slight tendency to turn to port due to having a right-hand propeller, assuming the shaft is on the centerline and is not angled to counteract the torque. It is a simple matter to secure the tiller by belaying the appropriate steering line, usually the port line when the boat has the normal tiller and customary torque. Of course, some boats have other means of locking the helm, such as a friction screw on a wheel, or a tiller "comb," which consists of a toothed, metal strip fastened to the deck running athwartships under the tiller that will accept a metal fin on the tiller's underside. I prefer steering lines, however, that can be released quickly from aft or forward. The boat cannot be expected to hold a steady course for very long, but long enough to allow you to move about getting the sails ready to hoist. While you are preparing the main halyard, untying stops, and so forth, it is important to look around. *The importance of keeping a continual lookout while singlehanding in crowded waters cannot be overstressed.*

When the sails are readied for hoisting, go aft, slow the engine, head into the wind, and relash the helm to hold the bow into the wind's eye. If the halyards lead back to the cockpit, the helm may not need lashing, but otherwise, of course, you must go forward to make sail. Customarily, the mainsail is raised first and then the jib. Keep a tension on the main halyard until just before hoisting, because in a choppy sea, a slack halyard can jump around to the wrong side of the spreaders, which could cause an awkward situation for a singlehander. By all means, see that the halyard ends are secured so that they cannot possibly go aloft. Some cleats are designed with a hole through their bases so that the halyard ends can be run through and knotted. This is a good plan, but keep the knot pulled a short distance away from the cleat and perhaps lash it there with light marline (see Figure 9-1), so that it won't interfere with belaying the line and perhaps cause a jam. If the halyards are internal, a figure-eight knot in the end will usually prevent the line from disappearing into the mast, and there is no need to run the line through the base of its cleat. But check on this to be sure the halyard cannot escape into the mast exit. Be sure that the halyards are properly coiled and hung after sail is hoisted.

Now you are under sail with the engine cut off. After figuring your course, the next action to take is trimming the sails for proper balance. The average, well-balanced boat normally will have her sails trimmed to carry a very slight weather helm when close-hauled in a moderate breeze, but when she is being singlehanded her sails should be trimmed for almost perfect balance, i.e. with neither weather nor lee helm. This probably will mean that the headsail will be trimmed slightly flatter than usual, and the mainsail cracked just a bit. Our boat requires that the mainsail be eased about four inches farther than normal in a ten-to-twelve-knot wind. If the boat is well balanced and her sheets properly trimmed, she should be capable of steering herself to windward for short periods, perhaps for fifteen minutes or longer under ideal conditions. Of course, a sudden gust, wind shift, irregular seas, or powerboat waves may knock her out of the groove, but the helm can be readjusted quite easily. This self-steering capability, even if only for brief periods, is of great value to a singlehander, because it frees him to move about attending to chores and his various needs.

It is more difficult to make a modern boat without a vane gear sail herself on a beam, broad, or quartering reach, but simple methods have been devised with sheet-to-helm connections such as those described in Chapter 6. An effective plan is to rig a small staysail set inside the jib, as shown in Figure 6-9. The staysail is backed slightly, and its sheet is led through blocks to the windward side of the tiller, while a shock cord is rigged to pull the tiller to leeward. When the boat luffs, the staysail exerts more force on the tiller to correct the course, but when she bears off the staysail exerts less force allowing the shock cord to make the correction.

An even simpler, but perhaps slightly less effective, method is to forego the staysail and merely rig the jib sheet to the windward side of the tiller. Take the leeward sheet and lead it from its winch to a lead block on the windward side of the cockpit and then back to the tiller. The sheet's pull is counteracted by the tension of shock cord from the tiller to the leeward side of the cockpit (see Figure 9-2). To hook up the lines, first straddle the tiller and hold it between your legs while facing forward with the boat on her desired course. Then, using your hands to pull on the shock cord and sheet, balance the tension between the two lines and tie them to the tiller, the sheet first and then the shock cord. I find it convenient to throw a couple of hitches over the tiller end for the sheet but to tie the shock cord on its own standing part with a rolling hitch for easy adjustment. The boat should then take over steering herself for temporary periods at least. If she starts to head up, the jib will pull harder and pull the helm up, which, of course, will cause her to bear off to the original course; but if she falls off, the jib will become partially blanketed by the mainsail and pull less hard, which will allow the shock cord to pull the helm down, thereby causing the boat to head up to her original course. The jib may have to be trimmed a bit flatter than normal so that it will be partially stalled when on course; if the boat begins to luff, the flow will become attached (rather than turbulent) causing greater efficiency and thus the jib will pull harder.

Some experimentation will be necessary in selecting the right size of shock cord and setting the proper tension, trimming the sails for best advantage, and determining the proper number of wraps of the sheet around the winch. In moderate conditions, one wrap around the winch may be about right, but in lighter airs it might be best not to use any wraps, especially when an emergency tiller is used, because, unless the wheel steering can be disconnected, the emergency tiller will have to turn the wheel, and this will obviously take more effort. One method of avoiding this extra effort is to attach to the wheel a steering drum such as the one made by Marine Vane Gears and illustrated in Figure 9-2. If the drum is used or the emergency tiller is rigged backwards (as mentioned earlier) or your standard tiller can be folded over to aim aft, then the leeward sheet will be led directly to the tiller and the shock cord rigged to windward. These matters obviously will vary with individual boats. When coming about, the jib sheet and the shock cord can easily be slipped over (or otherwise disengaged from) the tiller end, and then, of course, the self-steering system will have to be rigged for the new tack.

If the helm is manned, a boomed headsail with a traveller will allow you to come about very easily without touching a line, but it is not really difficult to singlehandedly tack the usual jib having double sheets when its overlap is not excessive. A 150 percent jib, one having an LP (a perpendicular from luff to clew) one and a half times as long as the base of the foretriangle, should slide around the mast by itself, and it will provide a lot more power than a self-tending working jib. Rollers around the shrouds will allow the jib to slide around the shrouds with minimal chance of fouling and chafing.

The normal procedure for tacking a double-sheet jib would be to wrap about two turns of the windward sheet around its winch and see that the winch handle is available, cast off the leeward sheet and take all but about three or four wraps off its winch, and turn the helm with one hand while holding the leeward sheet in your other hand. When the boat is almost head-to-wind, slack the leeward sheet, throw off the remaining turns from the winch, and, after the bow passes through the wind's eye, haul in on the opposite sheet hand-over-hand as far as possible. Then wrap about two or three more turns around the winch in use while alternately correcting the helm. Hold the helm steady with your leg or body, insert the winch handle and crank in the jib until it is correctly trimmed. A few hints are: see that the sheet being slacked is coiled or flaked down and clear to run; put only a couple of turns around the windward winch to begin with in order to avoid an override; let the sail blow clear of the spreaders before hauling it in; and look around for other boats before and during the operation.

Should you find it necessary to change headsails during your solo sail, the steering lines led forward will come in handy, because, when the head-sail is dropped and the boat is sailing "baldheaded" (before the new sail is hoisted), her balance will change, and you can correct the helm by readjusting the steering lines from forward, obviating the need to go aft. Rigging some form of net or lacing between the forward life lines will help keep the lowered sail aboard. The question of whether or not to lead the jib halyard back to the cockpit was discussed in Chapter 5. In my opinion, it is usually more advantageous to keep the halyard at the mast so that it can be more easily controlled when the jib is being lowered.

One handy method of lowering the jib is to back it, that is pull in somewhat on the windward sheet, or tack and let the sail go aback, and then lower it. Another method is to run off and let the mainsail blanket the sail. In this case, the sheet will have to be slacked with an overlapping jib in order that the clew can be brought inboard. As said before, carry a spare stop with you to secure the sail when it is down. It is often helpful to have stops or spare lashing lines rove through the cabin-top grab-rail forward. When lowering the sail, cast off the halyard and take all but one turn off its winch, then lead the halyard forward under its winch. While standing on the bow, slack away the halyard with one hand while pulling down and gathering in the jib with the other hand. When the sail is about half way down, you may find that you can let go the halyard and use both hands for gathering in the jib, but be sure the halyard is not fouled and that its bitter end cannot possibly go aloft.

The solo sailor with a single jib stay may find it easier to remove the lowered sail completely before hanking on its replacement, but the change can be made much more quickly, when it is properly organized, if the replacement jib is hanked on beneath the original jib before that sail is lowered. When it has been hauled down, the handed sail is unhanked (but the tack is left attached) and tied to the rail or life line with one or two stops. After the halyard is transferred, the new jib can be hoisted without further ado. Of course, new sheets and proper leads should have been provided for the replacement jib before it was hoisted.

The self-confident singlehander who wants to get the most in speed from his boat may even set a spinnaker in light airs. As most sailors know, however, the modern parachute spinnaker can be a contrary devil to handle, and even fully-crewed racing boats have had numerous problems with this unseamanlike sail. It seems most prudent, then, for the solo sailor to set the 'chute only when the wind is light and in waters that are fairly free of boat traffic.

Prior to getting underway, the spinnaker should have been properly prepared for hoisting, either turtled (folded and stuffed into a special container or bag) or stopped (rolled or bunched up and tied with easily breakable stops). The stopping method assures more control in a breeze, but, since the singlehander is only setting his when the breeze is light, the turtling method should suffice. If prior turtling has been overlooked, the operation can be done in the cockpit while underway without too much difficulty.

One method is to secure the head to something solid with a lashing (merely to hold it steady) and then, with the sail in the bottom of the cockpit in order to keep it from being blown by the wind, sort out the two leeches and bring them together to prevent the sail from becoming twisted when it is hoisted. Working down from the head to the foot, the two leeches are accordion-folded, and they can be held in place by stepping on them. When the entire length of the leeches has been folded, the loose bulk of the sail is stuffed into the turtle or bag, and then the folded leeches are neatly laid on top of the bulk with the head and two clews hanging out of the bag's top. I find it convenient to have a piece of shock cord in the bag's neck to hold it closed yet still allow the sail to be hoisted out of its bag. The bag can then be taken forward and secured to the pulpit. Of course, the halyard is attached to the head, and the guy and sheet attached to each clew.

An alternative to turtling the 'chute is the use of a "Spinnaker Sally," produced by Jack W. Fretwell, Jr., of Millwood, Virginia 22646, U.S.A., or a somewhat similar "Spee Squeezer," produced by Parbury Henty and Co., 44/45 Chancery Lane, London WC2A 1JB, England. These are spinnaker setting-handing devices that use interconnected plastic rings or a cloth sock to contain the 'chute when it is being hoisted or lowered. Complete operation instructions can be obtained from the producers.

After the turtled spinnaker is secured forward and lines are attached to its corners, the pole is hooked onto the mast and the lift and downhaul (foreguy) are attached. In light airs, I prefer to rig these lines to the pole's middle to permit end-for-end jibing (to be described soon) without the need of changing the downhaul's position, which would be required if the line were attached to the pole's end. The hook-up is illustrated in Figure 9-3. The outboard, spinnaker-pole end-fitting is generally hooked onto the guy, and, incidentally, there should be a lanyard adjustable at the pole's middle to control the end fittings' spring-loaded pins. After all lines have been attached, hoist the pole with its lift until it is almost horizontal, and then haul in on the guy until the tack (windward clew) of the sail is perhaps about three feet from the pole end and the pole is positioned slightly forward of being square to the wind. The secret in performing such a com-

FIGURE 9-3: SPINNAKER HOOK-UP

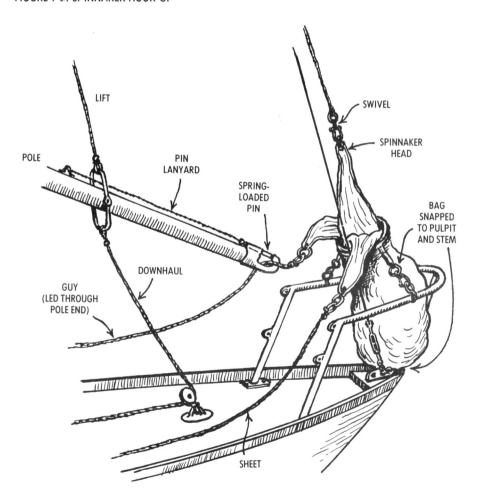

plicated operation singlehanded is to see that all elements are pre-set. This doesn't mean that they are set to positions of final trim but only to positions where the sail is most easily managed immediately after it is hoisted. Pull the sheet as taut as you can without pulling the spinnaker leech very far out of its bag. The sail is now ready for hoisting.

The spinnaker halyard is best led aft to the cockpit where the single-hander can steer by straddling the tiller or conveniently make helm corrections with his leg while he is hoisting the sail. The hoisting operation should be done rapidly to help prevent hourglassing. The sheet and guy should be belayed nearby to port and starboard. In any breeze at all, it may be best to keep the boat almost dead before the wind, so that the 'chute will be blanketed until it is completely hoisted. Then, with the sail up and after the sheet and guy have been partially adjusted, head up into the wind until the 'chute fills. Once on the desired course, final adjustments for proper trim can be made quite easily one at a time. In my opinion, it is best to lead the pole lift and downhaul as well as the halyard back to the cockpit.

Jibing can be a bit tricky, but pre-setting the various lines involved can help simplify the operation. Run off almost dead before the wind and square the pole, bringing it aft until it touches the forward shroud. Secure the helm, and go forward to the mast. After grabbing the sheet and holding it in the crook of your arm, unhook the pole from the mast and hook it onto the sheet which will become the new guy. The pole is now secured to both lines, but you now unhook the old guy, which will become the new sheet, and hook the free end of the pole to the mast. The lift and downhaul will have been pre-set, so you won't have to touch them. Be sure there is enough slack in the new guy to allow the pole-end hook to reach its eye on the mast. This is a mistake I have made more than once. It means an extra trip back to the cockpit unless the guy has been led forward. Now the 'chute is jibed, and you return to the cockpit to turn the helm slightly and jibe the mainsail. This method, commonly called end-for-ending, is the one I prefer, but no doubt the dip pole method can be used. This involves raising the pole to a high point on its mast track so that its outboard end can be dipped down and swung over inside the forestay. It is the easiest method in a strong wind, but in such conditions, setting a spinnaker alone can hardly be recommended.

Handing the 'chute is most easily accomplished when the boat is run dead before the wind so that the sail is blanketed. When the various lines are led aft, the whole operation can be done from the cockpit. Steering with your legs, ease the guy forward until the pole touches the forestay, and then cast off the guy entirely and let it run through the end of the spinnaker pole (be sure the guy shackle is tied closed if there is a fresh breeze). Next, cast off the halyard, and, with one or more turns around its winch (depending on the strength of wind), clamp the freed halyard between your elbow and side to hold it temporarily. Haul in on the clew with its sheet, and alternately lower the spinnaker while pulling it (with the sheet) under the main boom, which will have been trimmed in somewhat. As the 'chute is gathered in, it can be pulled into the bottom of the cockpit or stuffed down the companionway. The lowering and gathering-in operations can be done alternately (a bit at a time), by using one hand for each operation, or by letting the halyard run under your arm to free both hands for gathering in.

The noted writer on sailing alone, Francis B. Cooke, wrote, "A word of advice I would give to the single-hander is not to use the spinnaker. . . ." Those words were written over ten years ago, and times have changed somewhat. Today there are races for singlehanders in fairly large cruising boats, and it is not at all unusual to see the spinnaker being carried. John Guzzwell even carried a spinnaker along with self-steering twin staysails in light airs. With this he found that his *Trekka* would not only sail a lot faster, but also that she would continue to self-steer, and her rolling was greatly reduced. Nevertheless, it is well to bear in mind that, unless all operations are carefully prepared with ample forethought, the sail can give plenty of trouble to one who sails alone, especially in a breeze of wind and when there are rough seas.

If the wind is fresh, or you simply don't want to expend the effort of setting a 'chute, a wung-out jib works quite well. It can be boomed out or can be carried on the side of the boat opposite the mainsail without a pole. With the latter method, the boat is simply sailed by the lee, and the jib is allowed to jibe while the mainsail is not. The secret in keeping the jib drawing is to keep sailing very slightly by the lee. This requires a constant hand on the helm in order to keep the jib full without jibing the mainsail. I would strongly recommend the rigging of a vang or preventer line from the boom to some point forward in order to prevent an accidental jibe of the mainsail.

To boom the jib out to windward, rig the spinnaker pole as though you were going to set the 'chute, with one end of the pole hooked onto the mast and the other end raised with the pole lift. The windward jib sheet is run through the outboard end of the pole, and, after the leeward sheet is slacked, the jib can be hauled out to the pole end. This is a fairly stable rig, and the boat may even be made to steer herself in smooth water. Self-steering by this method was briefly mentioned in Chapter 6. The windward jib sheet is secured to the tiller and its pull is counteracted by a length of shock cord on the opposite side of the tiller (see Figure 9-2). Should the boat bear away and sail quite far by the lee, her jib will become partially blanketed, and the shock cord will correct the helm; but if she should head up above her course, the jib will exert a greater pull than the shock cord, and the sheet will make the helm correction. Don't neglect to carry the vang or preventer on the main boom.

When sailing alone in shoal water, care must be taken not to become so absorbed in the technique of sailing that piloting is neglected. It is important to know where you are at all times. The solo pilot should keep track of all buoys and channel markers passed as he goes along and keep his local chart at hand near the helm. As said in Chapter 5, a folded chart or chart book and a grid of parallel lines printed on a sheet of plastic (to obviate the need of parallel rules) are very handy, especially when the grid and chart can be fitted together and enclosed in a transparent case of stiff plastic. It may be helpful to carry a pad of tracing paper so that a simple sketch chart of an unfamiliar anchorage can be traced from the proper chart, with only the most important features noted. The purpose of this would be to have a simplified guide and thus obviate the need of taking the time to study the more complex navigation chart while entering the harbor.

The compass should be in plain view from any position around the helm, and it is helpful if it can be mounted on a pedestal so that bearings do not have to be taken with a separate instrument, such as a hand-bearing compass or pelorus. Binoculars kept near at hand, of course, are all but essential to look for channel markers or buoys, observe their numbers, and "read" the flow of the current. It is advisable that the singlehander keep himself well informed of the current, by the way, because an adverse flow could delay the time of arrival at his intended anchorage and perhaps cause him to arrive after dark. He should plan on entering an unfamiliar harbor in broad daylight, preferably when the sun is fairly high, if the water is clear and the bottom can be seen. Particular care should be taken to get in early if bad weather is making up. In areas of great tidal ranges, of course, the tide tables need careful study.

Whether coming to anchor under sail or power, I think it is usually desirable to lower the headsail. A handy wrinkle is to bag the jib but leave it hanked on. Then the bagged sail (still hanked on) can be swung forward and stuffed between the bow pulpit and the headstay high up, where it is out of the way, will not interfere with the anchor rode and bow chocks, and will not become covered with mud from the ground tackle when the anchor is weighed again. When anchoring under sail, the boat is normally rounded up to the wind. You walk forward to the anchor, and, after headway is completely lost, lower the hook, paying out the rode only after the boat drifts backwards and/or her bow blows off. Be sure the main sheet is well slacked and free to run so that the sail will not fill. If the boat is extremely cut away under water forward, her bow may blow off so rapidly that she will not make any sternway. In this case, it might be advisable to lower the anchor while headed downwind, usually with the mainsail sheeted in fairly flat to reduce speed and steering control lines led forward in case the boat tries to round up. I would not advise doing this, however, if the rode is chain, as it could scar the topsides or underbody when the boat overrides it. After sufficient scope has been paid out to make a fairly flat angle between the rode and bottom, the rode is snubbed so the anchor will dig in. If there is any doubt whether the flukes have a good bite on the bottom, it is a good idea to wait until the boat comes head-to-wind, then pay out more scope, and push the main boom far to windward, so that the boat is blown astern, causing the anchor to dig in.

There are several means of releasing the anchor from the cockpit, a simple method being to hang the anchor at the stem from a wood toggle that can be tripped with a line leading aft, as shown in Figure 9-4. One must be careful, however, that the boat is making sternway (or headway if sailing downwind) when the hook is dropped, because the rode can become fouled, of course, if it is dumped on top of the anchor. Many sailors prefer to go forward where they can give the rode more careful attention, pay it out gradually, and better snub it.

It is easier to dig the hook in under power. After the anchor has been lowered and the boat has drifted back against her payed-out rode so that she lies head-to-wind, the engine is momentarily reversed to be sure the flukes have a good bite on the ground. Then the singlehander puts the gear in neutral and goes forward to let out more rode, enough for a scope-to-depth ratio of five or six to one if there is sufficient swinging room. It is especially important that a solo sailor be securely anchored in a protected harbor with good holding bottom and where there is ample swinging room preferably away from other craft, for he certainly doesn't want to have to weigh anchor or take other corrective actions in the middle of the night should his boat or a neighbor's start to drag. If one wants to anchor by the stern in fair weather and light airs, it is a simple matter to drop the anchor astern from the cockpit and snub it while the boat is making headway. Should it be necessary to transfer the rode to the bow in the event it breezes up, the end of the rode should be run to the bow cleat before the line is cast off astern.

When getting underway, there is sometimes a problem in breaking out the hook. In light winds and when the anchor is not deeply buried, it might be broken out simply by taking in scope rapidly and then snubbing the rode when it is at a short stay, so that the boat's momentum does the work. In any kind of wind, though, the engine or sail power may have to be used unless one uses a windlass, which will be tedious when it is hand operated. Sailing out an anchor alone can be difficult (see Chapter 5), and it is usually preferable that the engine be used. If it is blowing so hard that scope cannot be taken in by hand, give the engine a temporary shot forward, put the gear in neutral, and then go forward to pull in the rode. Breaking the boat's inertia and starting her moving ahead will usually enable you to continue shortening scope hand-over-hand, but if not, you may have to make several trips back to the cockpit to alternately run the engine ahead and then go forward to take in scope. An alternative, mentioned in Chapter 5, is to lead the rode aft to the cockpit. When the rode is at short stay, of course, the engine is run ahead at whatever speed is necessary until the anchor is broken out.

It is a good idea to hoist the mainsail before getting underway when the boat is lying head-to-wind, but I usually do not set the jib until after the anchor has been weighed, cleaned, and secured. The reason for this is partly to keep mud off the sail, but also because a thrashing jib and sheets will interfere with stowing the ground tackle.

As said before, a reliable auxiliary is most useful, particularly for single-handing on inland waters, but the solo sailor should not become so dependent on it that he cannot manage under sail alone. Obviously, the auxiliary should be run frequently and kept in top shape, but even if it is highly reliable, in very vulnerable situations the sails should be ready for use in case of possible engine failure. Basic engine controls, such as the throttle and gear shift, are nearly always conveniently located near the helm, but other necessary controls are often located below or away from the helm. In my opinion, a singlehander should be able to start his engine without the need of going below or even leaving the helm. This means that the battery switch, blower switch, fuel shutoff valve, and so forth should be operable from the cockpit. This is often not difficult to arrange, because these controls can usually be installed inside a seat locker or within easy reach just inside the companionway.

Returning home from a solo cruise, one must be careful not to become careless through overconfidence at being in familiar waters. It is generally the safest plan to start the engine and lower sails, or at least the headsail, before entering the harbor. Head into the wind with the engine running slowly and the helm lashed. Allow plenty of room for rounding up and making headway to windward, because handing sail and, indeed, all evolutions take more time when one is alone. Be sure the topping lift is attached before lowering the mainsail. Furl the sails, tie them temporarily with a minimum number of stops, and leave the halyards attached for the time being (in case the engine should quit). The halyards should be pulled taut, however, even though they are left shackled in order to keep them from whipping around and fouling aloft. A suggestion is to lead the main halyard under a low mast winch (see Figure 9-5) so that it can be tight-

FIGURE 9-4: A SIMPLE ANCHOR RELEASE

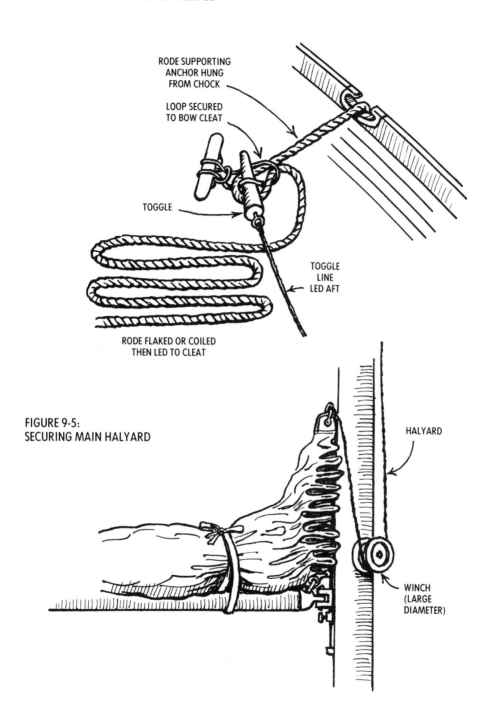

RODE SUPPORTING
ANCHOR HUNG
FROM CHOCK

LOOP SECURED
TO BOW CLEAT

TOGGLE

TOGGLE
LINE
LED AFT

RODE FLAKED OR COILED
THEN LED TO CLEAT

FIGURE 9-5:
SECURING MAIN HALYARD

HALYARD

WINCH
(LARGE
DIAMETER)

ened without pulling the sail aloft. If you will be docking, break out all fenders and docking lines well in advance. Of course, the boat hook will be needed for picking up a mooring, unless perhaps, your buoy is fitted with a wand. Have the boat hook handy anyway.

It is perfectly possible to pick up the mooring under sail alone in favorable conditions if you wish. This operation was discussed in Chapter 5. I would recommend a slow approach on a close-reaching course under mainsail alone, provided, of course, your boat handles well with this rig. The close-reaching course allows the mainsail to be trimmed or luffed for best control of speed. When close to the mooring the boat should be moving just fast enough for good helm control. In negligible current, the boat should be rounded up into the wind a boat length or two (depending on her displacement, primarily) from the buoy. Steady the helm and then quickly move forward with the boat hook to pick up the float attached to the mooring pendant. I find it easiest to reach for the pick-up line under its float rather than trying to spear the usual eye at the top of the float. By all means have a sturdy pick-up line, because if the boat is moving a bit too fast, you may have to snub her with the pick-up line before you have a chance to put the loop of the pendant over its bitt or cleat.

After some experience in day-sailing alone and a few successful overnight solo cruises, the beginning singlehander will develop a more intimate familiarity with his boat and a stronger confidence in his seamanship. Of course, this development will serve him well, not only in solo and short-handed work, but also aboard fully-crewed vessels and especially during emergencies. It could even lead to more ambitious projects, such as an extended inshore cruise or perhaps a coastal passage.

Needless to say, the more ambitious the cruise, the greater the need for careful and extensive planning. Weather maps, cruising guides, pilots, and tide tables should be studied in advance of the cruise to determine the best anchorages for the probable weather, and alternate courses and harbors should be selected for all possible conditions. Aside from the usual considerations in selecting a harbor, such as protection, depth, holding ground, and so forth, the singlehander should look for an anchorage that he can easily reach in daylight, one that is relatively uncrowded and free from traffic congestions, and one that is well marked with navigation aids for ease of entering and leaving. Obviously, there will be times when all of these conditions cannot be met, and the singlehander may have to compromise those of least importance. Cruising range can be extended by waiting for favorable winds, carrying extra fuel, and leaving a familiar port before dawn so that an unfamiliar port can be reached before dark. The solo sailor should never leave a harbor until he is rested, well fed, and has listened to a reliable weather report on his radio. On reaching a strange anchorage, it is always wise to slow down and to be certain that the channel, landmarks, navigation aids, and so forth are well understood before entering.

A passage along a coast with few harbors or a run across open water between two ports that are far apart may necessitate sailing all night. This can be done if the singlehander is thoroughly rested, having had at least eight hours of deep sleep just before leaving, but it may be risky trying to stay awake for periods longer than twenty-four hours, even though some solo sailors have stood watches for a great deal longer (Howard Blackburn once stayed at the helm for sixty-two hours, according to his biographer, Joseph Garland). Certain stay-awake drugs can help when taken very occasionally, but continued use could possibly lead to hallucinations. Remember, too, the adverse effect that fatigue can have on sound judgement, accurate navigation, and proficient seamanship.

To reiterate some points discussed in Chapter 5, the singlehander making a coastal passage might catch an hour or more of sleep by taking an off-shore tack or heaving to when there is sufficient sea room and no boat or ship traffic. Normally, snatches of sleep should only be taken during the day, but brief napping might be done at night under ideal conditions if the boat is well lighted. As said before, a vital piece of equipment is a reliable alarm clock. Prior to the passage, the singlehander should experiment with various methods of heaving to (lying a-hull, backing the jib, lying to a sea anchor, and so forth), and estimates of the boat's drift and headway should be determined for each method under a variety of conditions.

I hope this chapter has not seemed condescending to the veteran singlehander. It has been intended primarily for the beginner. Of course, most of the procedures dealt with are quite basic, but I believe the key to successful solo sailing is an appreciation for and adherence to sound fundamentals.

The occasional singlehander who sails only short distances may never aspire to an extended passage alone, but with enough experience in solo day-sailing and over-night cruising, there is no reason why he could not become a blue water voyager if he so desired. Many years ago, Jim Crawford, who later became an offshore singlehander, asked Harry Pidgeon a question about how he managed to sail around the world alone. The circumnavigator replied, "You can sail one day, can't you, Jim? That's all it is — one day after another."

10 / THE FUTURE

It seems very probable that in the future an increasing number of sailors will be cruising or at least day-sailing alone or shorthanded. To some extent, the increase will be due to factors that are causing a growth in the popularity of boating in general, such as the population explosion, more leisure time for the average person, more boats available through modern production, and a back-to-nature resurgence stimulated to a large degree by contemporary awareness of pollution problems and preservation of the ecology. Specifically, though, singlehanding may be expected to gain in popularity for certain psychological and practical reasons. The latter will have to do with the lack of availability of crew as more people obtain their own boats, and also the fact that boats with the newest gear should become increasingly easy to handle shorthanded or alone. Psychologically, solo sailing relates to an increasing desire for independence and individuality. This is not only a desire to escape or experience a change from crowding and the emotional pressures of contemporary life, but it is a reaction against our modern society in which people are often mere cogs in a large machine and identities are numbers fed to a computer. Another factor is that the tremendous number of solo voyages successfully made in recent years by all kinds of people, including women, teenagers, and old men, will inspire others to follow, and will add a snowball effect to the growth of singlehanding.

Despite the promise of future growth, however, there are some objectionable and unhealthy trends. Some of these are production of stock boats that are unsuitable for singlehanding and use of unwholesome boats for solo racing, federal regulations which could possibly discourage seamanly solo passages in small craft, the accentuation of solo racing, and increasing sponsorship of singlehanded voyages.

Many stock boats have undesirable features because craftsmanship and careful detail are lacking as a result of mass production; design emphasis is often placed on round-the-buoys racing (despite the fact that a small percentage will be used for that purpose); short-cuts and oversights are common in modern construction; and flimsy gear is more the rule than the exception. Having a sound vessel, an important requirement for any sailor, becomes essential when one sails alone, and especially so when cruises are made offshore. When the average stock boat is taken to sea, she should be given a thorough going over by a qualified surveyor. As said in Chapter 4 the hull can be strengthened by reinforcing bulkheads, beefing up or stiffening flexible areas, bolting or bonding hull-to-deck connections, strengthening the area around the mast step, glassing over the bilge in way of a vulnerable skeg to prevent flooding in case it should break off, and so forth. Rigging and fittings can be made a size larger than normal, and standard equipment should often be replaced by high-quality gear for best security. Of course, some stock boats are built to high standards and need little modification, but many are deficient, and a few are positively deplorable.

Unhealthy boats are also resulting from the great emphasis on solo racing, in my opinion. This has encouraged the building of monstrous, impractical, and expensive monohulls or multihulls. Multihulls have their good points, of course, but they are more subject to capsizing, and despite the accomplishments of Eric Tabarly, Alain Colas, and others, multihulls hardly seem the most suitable craft for extended offshore solo cruising. In fact, catamaran enthusiast Bill Howell once admitted, "I don't think an ocean racing cat such as I've got here is a singlehanded boat." Trimarans are better accepted for offshore work, but usually when there is a crew of more than one. Even the British tri enthusiast and author, D. H. Clarke, has written, "If you want to sail alone across an ocean in a trimaran, and you believe it is necessary to take as many precautions as possible to prevent a capsize plus gadgets to save you after you have capsized, then the only advice I can really give you is don't go by tri, go by monohull!"

A principal objective for transatlantic solo racing, put forth by H. G. Hasler in 1957, was "to encourage the development of suitable boats, gear, and techniques for singlehanded ocean-crossing under sail."

Few sailors could find fault with that philosophy, but many recent solo racing boats indicate that the development trend has strayed quite far from Hasler's original concept. Hasler himself would seem to agree with this, for he has been quoted, since the 1972 transatlantic race, as saying, ". . . not very much has been done to make boats easier or more comfortable to sail," and, "I thought that everyone would think as I did — that one would like to sail with the minimum of exertion and the minimum of fatigue, but this has not proved true." In regard to the huge *Vendredi 13*, Hasler described her as "a fascinating experiment in the wrong direction."

It is probable that the vast majority of singlehanders (or would-be singlehanders) and shorthanded sailors are neither "blood and thunder" adventurers in the extreme nor super-dedicated racers. The majority are quite ordinary sailors who are interested in safe, leisurely cruising, involving a minimum of risk and anxiety. Although they want a smart sailing boat with good speed, they want docility, seakindliness, and easy handling characteristics at a reasonable cost. In my opinion, this is the kind of boat that should be developed — not impractical, oversized, expensive, and overly sensitive craft that demand feats of endurance to make them perform.

Sponsorship is a controversial subject. There are good and bad points in being financed by an industry or newspaper to race or make a voyage singlehanded. The big advantage of this arrangement is that it enables qualified sailors without financial means to undertake such ventures. Arguments against sponsorship would include distasteful commercialism that detracts from the purity of the sport; the disadvantage in a competition of those who cannot acquire sponsorship; the encouragement in developing expensive, sophisticated gear that is beyond the means and desires of the ordinary sailor; and the added sense of responsibility and obligation to a sponsor felt by the singlehander.

The latter can be a very serious burden for many sailors. Hasler, for one, has written, "I have a considerable aversion to being sponsored. . . . For me it would be horrible to start a transatlantic race and feel that you had to do well in order to give your sponsors a return for their money. The greatest freedom I value is the freedom to give up off the Eddystone Light if you don't like it." Donald Crowhurst suffered over the sense of obligation he felt towards his sponsors, and some say that this was a major factor that led to his demise. He felt forced to make his voyage (in the 1968 round-the-world race for singlehanders) and to leave before he was mentally or physically prepared. Frank Page, an English yachting correspondent, wrote that "Crowhurst spent his last night on shore weeping in his wife's arms, but still unable to take the awful decision to call off the enterprise which involved so many other people relying on him." It might be argued that Crowhurst was mentally unstable, but any completely normal sailor can feel heavy pressures from responsibility to his sponsor that could adversely affect his best judgement.

As for the boats and gear made possible by sponsorship, they are usually very expensive and far beyond the means of the average unsponsored sailor. Of course, this makes possible the development of certain sophisticated gear and boats, but such gear and specialized, custom-made boats can give an unfair advantage to racing singlehanders with sponsors. In the 1968 transatlantic race, there were complaints and criticisms that the winner, Geoffrey Williams, had decided advantages with his specialized, low-freeboard ketch and her equipment, which included loran and radio access to a shore-based computer that provided optimum course recommendations. Sponsorship also produced the *Vendredi 13*, which is not only a highly-specialized boat designed to win a particular race, but a very impractical and hard-to-handle giant for ordinary singlehanding. As for future races, there has been talk of even larger craft, such as a four-masted schooner 236 feet long!

It seems the only sensible course is to put some emphasis on characteristics other than a boat's top speed, which, for the racers at least, has been blown far out of proportion. The accentuation of elapsed time for a racer might be de-emphasized in a number of ways: by limiting size and displacement; staggering starts; emphasizing separate prizes for monohulls and multihulls in different size categories; restricting sponsorship to discourage super-boats; placing the accent on corrected time awards resulting from a more fair handicap system; and, possibly, emphasizing seamanly performance awards. The main arguments against these measures is that development would be inhibited, and it is probably true that "far-out" ideas would be restricted. On the other hand, there might be more concentrated effort on practical vessels and gear, the kind that would be of use to the everyday sailor, who occasionally sails alone and often cruises shorthanded.

A form of handicapping has been used in the most recent transatlantic races, but the simple rating system used has been called unfair and totally unrealistic, and furthermore not much attention is paid to the winner of the handicap award. How many people knew that the *Voortrekker* won the award in 1968 or that the *Blue Smoke* won the monohull handicap trophy in 1972? Public interest seems to be in the order of arrival of the finishers. Staggered starts with the small boats starting first might take some of the attention away from the large craft, but what many knowledge-able people feel is needed is a realistic handicap rule. This rule should attempt to assess more fairly the speed of the boats and encourage whole-some, practical types, in my opinion. No handicapping system is perfect, of course, but perhaps some consideration should be given to a non-IOR type of rule, and one that measures or approximates the main forms of resistance. The principal resistance at average sailing speeds, for instance, is the wetted surface area, but this is not measured by the IOR or major ocean racing rules. However, it can be assessed in a simple way, as it has been in the Storm Trysail Club and Delta Cruising rules used in the United States, and this might help discourage overly abbreviated lateral planes and extremely short fin keels. Almost any sailor will agree that multihulls and monohulls cannot be rated equitably to compete against each other, and so they should be raced in separate classes. It seems to me that everything possible should be done to minimize comparisons in the elapsed time of these entirely different types of craft, because it is as pointless as comparing the speeds of a porpoise and a race horse. They are just different animals.

In regard to federal regulations that could possibly have a retarding effect on offshore singlehanding, I have in mind the U.S. Coast Guard's recent authority to designate a boat "manifestly unsafe" for a specific voyage. Such power could be good or bad, depending on how it will be used. Certainly it should be used to stop crackpot stunts and to prevent costly searches and rescues, but the line between a stunt and feat of seamanship is sometimes very thin, and one might wonder about the qualifications of a particular Coast Guard officer who is authorized to forbid or terminate a voyage. Had such a regulation always been in existence, would the voyages of Johnson, Andrews, Lawlor, Blackburn, Slocum, Pidgeon, Manry, Casper, and others have been terminated, and *should* they have been stopped? These are questions that cannot be answered easily, nor should they be considered lightly. Undoubtedly some of those voyages were manifestly unsafe, but it can be dangerous to give government officials the power to regulate and suppress the sense of adventure and the exploring instincts of people.

A strong case for preserving man's right to exercise these instincts is made by J. R. L. Anderson in his fine book, *The Ulysses Factor.* Anderson feels that such adventurous escapades as singlehanded voyaging not only fulfill deep needs within the performer, but also have an important influence on the public, largely by giving inspiration to low-level adventure. In fact, Anderson considers the exploring instinct, which he calls the Ulysses factor, to be a major hope for the future of mankind. Although not everyone will agree with him, perhaps, it is plain to see that the quashing of a carefully planned voyage is a responsibility that should not be taken lightly, and the judgment should be made by the most highly qualified inspectors, people who are intimately familiar with the problems involved. Not only should the boat be judged, but also the voyage plan and especially the man, for a lubber can be lost in a well-found vessel, while an outstanding seaman can survive in a flimsy cockleshell.

Organizers of long-distance singlehanded races should be extremely careful and conscientious about inspecting competing boats for the protection of the participants, obviously, and to avoid search and rescue operations, which can be very costly, risk lives, and cause great damage to the sport through bad publicity. A case in point is the break-up of the trimaran, *Yaksha,* and the rescue of her skipper, Joan de Kat, during the 1968 transatlantic race. The *Yaksha* was home-designed and hurriedly built for the race, and she all but fell to pieces in the Atlantic. Her skipper was rescued from an inflatable dinghy after a long and costly air search. It would be well for race committees to be extra thorough when inspecting every home-built multihull, for they have a bad safety record. A step in the right direction is the fairly recent insistence on a singlehander completing a trial passage before allowing him to enter a long-distance race, but on the other hand, we must remember that the well-known trimaran designer, Arthur Piver, was lost during his trial for the 1968 race. Very careful inspections would seem to be in order even if a trial is completed successfully.

Whether racing or not, a singlehander wants (or should want) maximum safety, convenience, and comfort. A great deal of progress has been made in these directions with the research and development of Waller, Hammond, Marin-Marie, Hasler, King, McLeod, and many others, including the naval architects involved, but the singlehander still has important unfilled needs.

It has often been said that the possibility of collision with ships is the offshore or coastal singlehander's greatest risk. This may be especially true today with ships becoming increasingly automated and visual watches apparently becoming more lax. An improved fully-automatic omnidirectional, radar alarm of considerable volume would be of great value. Perhaps it could be similar to the type devised by Noel Bevan (see Chapter 5). Radar reflectors and echo enhancers need further development or improvement. Also, it might be well to legalize the use of masthead strobe lights for singlehanders, when they are offshore away from an area where these lights could possibly be confused with aids to navigation. Of course, strobe lights are permitted as flare-ups under the Rules of the Road, but they are not strictly legal for continual use (see Chapter 7). Another need is a really effective emergency noise-maker, perhaps a loud siren, or explosives, such as those used by Chay Blyth, to warn ships of a small boat's presence.

In my opinion, it would be a good idea to devise a special signal for singlehanders, perhaps a large flag flown in a conspicuous spot to notify other boats in the area that the solo vessel may be somewhat limited in its maneuvering ability for lack of a full crew. Of course, two black balls (or two red lights at night) can be displayed to indicate the vessel is not under command according to the International Rules of the Road, but these signals are often impractical, not clear to many boatmen, and not strictly correct when the singlehander is on deck. One suggestion would be a white flag with one large red or black hand on it. If this flag were publicized (in chart books, cruising guides, and elsewhere), it should be easily recognizable as the singlehander's signal.

Research is needed in the control of damage resulting from collisions not only with vessels, but also with flotsam and marine life. Improvement could be made in plugging and sealing compounds, in materials that will harden instantly under water, collision mats, methods for repair from within the hull, ways of securing other materials to fiberglass, and so forth.

A great deal of work has been done on self-steering systems, but there is still room for improvement. Vane gears might be made stronger, simpler, and easier to reduce in area and remove completely when not needed. Their performance could be improved in light airs, when running in following seas, and on fast multihulls. Electrical systems could be made more reliable, and there is definitely a need for a dependable battery charger that can use natural power, such as the wind, sun, water moving past the boat, or wave action.

Sail-changing and reefing systems could also be improved. One of the greatest chores the singlehander faces is shortening down and changing headsails. Many roller systems need to be made stronger, more dependable, more efficient, and more versatile for the combination of jib changing, variable reduction, and balancing for self-steering. Roller furling for mainsails is being developed (Chapter 5), and some forms show promise, but it needs further development in my opinion. All gear for singlehanders needs the best possible reliability, because a person alone cannot afford to cope with constant breakages.

A somewhat neglected area in research and development is anchoring systems at sea. An effective drogue to mitigate drift can be of great value to a singlehander, especially during a coastal passage. The amount of drag needed will vary with the type of boat, weather conditions, and character of the seas, so it would be helpful if an efficient, variable drogue could be invented. Important design considerations would be resistance to drift, strength, ease of management, elasticity for shock absorption, and stowability.

Hasler and a few others have put much thought into comfort below deck. Their ideas should be made available to all shorthanded offshore sailors. The concept of a gimballed chair, for instance, was used very successfully by Chichester and King. In its perfected form, such a chair would be completely padded and would support all parts of the body. It would be completely adjustable, gimballed in all directions, and useable for most purposes, such as navigating, eating, cooking, reading, writing, and even sleeping. Further research might be done on controlling deck operations from below and improving visibility from the cabin without resorting to large windows (a periscope?). There also seems to be room for improvement in the galley. For instance, there could be more gimballing, greater security, better compartmentation for stowage, better stove fuel that is both safe and convenient, and so forth.

There is much room for the development of sophisticated gear, especially in reliability, low power drainage, and economy. Cheaper facsimile weather equipment, low-power drainage auto-steering controlled by a compass, and inexpensive satellite navigation are the kinds of systems that would be useful. Basic time-tested systems, however, such as celestial navigation, sail trimming for self-steering, and the "cocked weather eye" should never be forgotten or neglected. It is also well to keep firmly in mind that, where singlehanding is concerned, at least, the simplest way of performing an operation is usually the best way.

In summary, I think the future of singlehanding seems bright. Interest and participation are on the increase, and there is great potential for making suitable gear and boats more available for the average sailor. Even those who have no desire to sail entirely alone can benefit from development in solo equipment and a study of singlehanding techniques, for, sooner or later, every sailor, willingly or not, will find himself sailing shorthanded.

The rewards of singlehanding are many: the feeling of independence, sense of accomplishment, self-confidence gained from success, and gratification of the sense of adventure. Francis B. Cooke once wrote that the singlehander "is not only captain of his little ship but also captain of his soul, enjoying a freedom of action unobtainable in any other way."

BOOKS RELATING TO
SINGLEHANDED SAILING

Allcard, Edward C. **Single-Handed Passage.** Putnam, London, 1950. **Temptress Returns.** Norton, New York. 1953. **Voyage Alone.** Dodd-Mead, New York. 1964.

Solo voyages by a famous circumnavigator. Allcard is a strong individualist with definite opinions, but his advice should be heeded, for he has the background of a naval architect and surveyor and has had a lifetime of oceanic singlehanded experience. His cruising grounds have included such formidable waters as those near Cape Horn.

Anderson, J.R.L. **The Ulysses Factor.** Harcourt-Brace-Jovanovich, New York. 1970.

A profound and provocative book about the exploring instinct in man. It deals in detail with the motives of singlehanders (also of flyers and mountain climbers).

Andrews, William A. **A Daring Voyage** and **Columbus Outdone,** logs of two early transatlantic passages in the small boats *Nautilus* and *Sapolio* under the title **Dangerous Voyages of Capt. William Andrews.** Abercrombie & Fitch, New York. 1966. Compilation, editing, and brief biography by Richard Henderson.

Anthony, Irvin. **Voyagers Unafraid.** Macrae Smith Co., Philadelphia. 1930.

Stories about early transatlantic voyagers written in what has been described as a "shiver-my-timbers" style, but highly entertaining.

Bardiaux, Marcel. **4 Winds of Adventure.** John de Graff, New York. 1961.

First half of an eight year solo circumnavigation in a home-built racing-cruiser including a "wrong-way" rounding of Cape Horn near the beginning of winter.

Barton, Humphrey. **Atlantic Adventurers.** Adlard Coles, Ltd., Southhampton. 1953.

Records of small-craft passages across the North Atlantic by a designer-surveyor and highly experienced offshore sailor. Interesting critical comments and asides.

Bernicot, Louis. **The Voyage of the Anahita.** Hart-Davis, London. 1953.

Understated account of the sixth solo circumnavigation by a masterful seaman.

Blagden, David. **Very Willing Griffin.** W. W. Norton, N.Y., 1974.

Preparations and Atlantic crossing in 1972 of the smallest OSTAR entry.

Blyth, Chay. **The Impossible Voyage.** G. P. Putnam's Sons, New York. 1972.

Account of the "uphill" (against prevailing winds) circumnavigation in 1970-1971 in the *British Steel* by a former paratrooper and transatlantic oarsman.

Bombard, Alain. (**The Bombard Story.** Readers Union, London, 1955.) The **Voyage of the Heretique.** Simon and Schuster, New York. 1954.

Transatlantic passage in an inflatable boat without supplies by a French doctor to prove that castaways can survive for lengthy periods without food and water.

Borden, Charles. **Sea Quest.** Macrae Smith Co., Philadelphia. 1967.

One of the most complete collections of abbreviated cruising accounts by an experienced offshore sailor. Not exclusively about singlehanders, but most of the solo voyages up to about the mid-Sixties are included.

Brenton, Francis. **Voyage of the Sierra Sagrada.** Regnery Co., Chicago. 1968.

Voyage from the Caribbean to Chicago and thence transatlantic with minimal equipment in a dugout canoe by a true contemporary adventurer. He was eventually lost at sea according to reliable reports.

Bruce, Erroll. **Challenge to Poseidon.** Van Nostrand, New York. 1956.

Tales of blue water adventures in small craft, including some singlehanders, by a very experienced ocean racer. Not up to the high standards of the author's **Deep Sea Sailing.**

Caldwell, John. **Desperate Voyage.** Ballantine Books, New York. 1949.

The Pacific crossing of a double-ended cutter after World War II for the purpose of reuniting the skipper with his sweetheart in Australia. According to an acquaintance of Caldwell, the book was heavily ghost written, much to the chagrin of the author, because it is so full of nautical blunders.

Chichester, Francis. **Alone Across the Atlantic.** Doubleday, New York, 1961. **The Lonely Sea and the Sky.** Coward-McCann, New York, 1964. **Along the Clipper Way.** Hodder & Stoughton, London, 1966. **Gipsy Moth Circles the World.** Coward-McCann, New York, 1968. **The Romantic Challenge.** Coward-McCann & Geoghegan, Inc., New York, 1971.

The first book listed describes Chichester's transatlantic passage in the 1960 OSTAR, when he won the race in the *Gipsy Moth III.* The second book is his autobiography through his voyage in 1962. **Along the Clipper Way** is an anthology of literature relating to the Australian clipper ship routes, including commentary and some extracts from the writings of singlehanders. **Gipsy Moth Circles the World** deals with Chichester's one-stop circumnavigation in the *Gipsy Moth IV*; while **The Romantic Challenge** tells of his attempt to set a solo speed record by sailing 4,000 miles in 20 days aboard the *Gipsy Moth V.* These books are well worth reading not only for the vicarious adventure they afford, but also for their technical information; the famous seaman pulls no punches in his criticism of boats and gear.

Clarke, D. H. **The Lure of the Sea.** Adlard Coles, Ltd., London, 1970. **Trimaran Development.** Adlard Coles, Ltd., London, 1972.

The author, an English trimaran enthusiast and small-boat-voyage researcher, deals with certain aspects of voyage preparation, and **Trimaran Development** includes appendixes of records (mono as well as multihull) set by singlehanders. "Nobby" Clarke wrote me that there are certain inaccuracies about small boat voyages in **The Lure** (and there are some important omissions in **Trimaran Development**), but he assures me that very complete and accurate records will be included in his forthcoming book, to be called **An Evolution of Singlehanders.**

Cole, Guy. **Ocean Cruising.** Adlard Coles, Ltd., Southhampton, 1959.

A very slim book, only partly touching on solo sailors, with some tips on voyage planning.

Cooke, Francis B. **Single-Handed Cruising.** Edward Arnold & Co., London, 1924.

A "how-to" book by a late English "dean" of boating writers. Many of the techniques are old-fashioned but often not outdated, for there is merit in certain methods that have been time-tested and proven.

Davison, Ann. **My Ship Is So Small.** Sloan, New York, 1956.

Well-written account of the first solo transatlantic passage by a woman.

Devine, Eric. **Midget Magellans.** Harrison Smith & Hass, New York, 1935.

Early, well-known voyages in small boats, including some singlehanders.

Dumas, Vito. **Alone Through the Roaring Forties.** John de Gaff, Inc., New York, 1960.

The remarkable solo circumnavigation in the southern westerlies by the *Lehg II* which earned the first Slocum Award for her Argentinian skipper. Tantalizingly inexplicit on some points of seamanship.

Eddy, Alan. **So You Want to Sail Around the World.** Allied Boat Co., New York (no date).

Promotional publication for Allied describing Alan Eddy's circumnavigation, mostly solo, in the Seawind ketch *Apogee.*

Fenger, Frederic A. **Alone in the Caribbean.** Reprinted by Wellington Books, Mass., 1958.

Fenger, a naval architect and experimenter with self-steering rigs, writes of a six-month cruise through the Lesser Antilles in the 17-foot sailing canoe *Yakaboo.*

Garland, Joseph E. **Lone Voyager.** Little, Brown & Co., Boston, 1963.

A well-researched, fascinating biography of Howard Blackburn, the fingerless singlehander who made two transatlantic passages in small sloops and an attempted Atlantic crossing in a dory.

Garrett, Alasdair (editor). **Roving Commissions.** R.C.C. Publications, London, Annual.

Logs of Royal Cruising Club members published each year, mostly about cruises in European waters.

Gerbault, Alain. **The Fight of the Firecrest.** Hart-Davis, London, 1955. **In Quest of the Sun.** Doubleday, New York, 1955.

The first book describes the French circumnavigator's slow and trouble-fraught transatlantic passage — for which he earned the first Cruising Club of America Blue Water Medal. The second book is an account of his adventures while completing the circumnavigation. Gerbault's later books became involved with sociology and philosophy at the expense of seamanship.

Gilboy, Bernard. **A Voyage of Pleasure.** Edited and annotated by John Barr Tompkins, Cornell Maritime Press, Cambridge, Md., 1956.

The log of Gilboy's half-year, nonstop transpacific passage in the 19-foot boat, *Pacific,* in 1882-1883.

Graham, Robert D. **Rough Passage.** Houghton-Mifflin Co., Boston, 1937.

A fast, solo cruise from England to Newfoundland in the 30-foot cutter *Emanuel* in 1933.

Graham, Robin Lee. **Dove.** Harper & Row, New York, 1972.

Popular book describing the voyage of the youngest solo circumnavigator in the 24-foot *Dove* and 33-foot *Return of the Dove.* Ghost writing and commercializing the account so that it is directed to a general readership detracts from the value of the book for the experienced sailor.

Groser, John. **Atlantic Venture.** Ward Lock & Co., Ltd., London, 1968.

Good account of the singlehander's transatlantic race of 1968 by the sports editor of the London *Observer*.

Guzzwell, John. **Trekka Round the World.** Adlard Coles Ltd., London, 1963.

A splendid book about a seamanly solo circumnavigation in a tiny, home-built yawl. Informative and entertaining.

Hayter, Adrian. **Sheila In The Wind.** Hodder & Stoughton, London, 1959.

An interesting solo voyage to New Zealand from England in a 32-foot canoe yawl.

Heaton, Peter. **The Sea Gets Bluer.** Black, London, 1965.

A collection of extracts from the writings of well-known voyagers. Some single-handers included.

Hiscock, Eric. **Voyaging Under Sail.** Oxford University Press, London, 1959.

This is only one of many fine books by the circumnavigator who has cruised all over the world with his wife, Susan, in a number of boats called *Wanderer*. Of all the Hiscock books, **Voyaging Under Sail** probably includes the most information relating to solo sailing, and it has a valuable chapter on voyage planning.

Horie, Kenichi. **Koduku.** Charles E. Tuttle Co., Rutland, Vt., 1964.

A singlehanded, transpacific passage from Japan to California in 1962 in the 19-foot sloop, *Mermaid,* by a recent solo circumnavigator.

Holm, Donald. **The Circumnavigators.** Prentice-Hall, Inc., Englewood Cliffs, N.J., 1974.

This book and Charles Borden's **Sea Quest** probably are the most comprehensive collections of abbreviated accounts of small boat voyages. Many, but by no means all, were made singlehanded.

Howells, Valentine. **Sailing Into Solitude.** Dodd, Mead, New York, 1966.

Account of the author's race across the Atlantic in the folkboat *Eira* in the 1960 OSTAR.

King, William Leslie. **Capsize.** Nautical Publishing Co., Lymington, England, 1969.

The story of King's participation in the "Golden Globe", round-the-world race for singlehanders in 1968 and the roll-over of his Chinese lug-rigged *Galway Blazer II.* The singlehander was forced to withdraw from the race but subsequently completed his circumnavigation.

Klein, David, and M. L. King. **Great Adventures in Small Boats** (originally called **They Took to the Sea**), Collier Books, New York, 1963.

Excerpts and commentary about famous small boat voyages. Some of the early, better-known singlehanders are included. The book is somewhat unusual in that it is organized topically rather than chronologically.

Knox-Johnston, Robin. **A World of My Own.** Cassell, London, 1969.

The winner of the "Golden Globe" race, who is credited with the first non-stop solo circumnavigation, tells how he did it in the double-ended ketch *Suhaili.*

Letcher, John. **Self-Steering for Sailing Craft.** International Marine Publishing Co., Camden, Maine, 1974.

Mostly expository and technical writing about an important subject for single-handers. A few accounts of Letcher's own singlehanding experiences are included.

Le Toumelin, J. Y. **Kurun Around the World.** E. P. Dutton & Co., New York, 1955. **Kurun in the Caribbean.** Rupert Hart-Davis, London, 1963.

Singlehanded voyages including a solo circumnavigation in a Norwegian double-ender by a respected Breton seaman.

Lewis, Dr. David. **The Ship Would Not Sail Due West.** St. Martin's. New York, 1961. **Ice Bird.** W. W. Norton, 1976.

The adventurous doctor, who rounded the world with his family on a catamaran and attempted to circumnavigate Antarctica alone, has written books related to voyaging or navigation. The first book listed deals with singlehanding in the 1960 OSTAR, and it includes a valuable appendix on health and medical supplies. **Ice Bird** deals with the doctor's Antarctic cruise.

Lindemann, Dr. Hannes. **Alone at Sea.** Random House, New York, 1958.

Descriptions of two amazing transatlantic passages, one in a narrow dugout canoe without outriggers and the other in a rubber-canvas foldboat. The skipper of these unseaworthy craft was a German doctor interested in survival techniques.

MacGregor, John. **The Voyage Alone in the Yawl Rob Roy.** Rupert Hart-Davis, London, 1954. (First published 1867).

A mini-voyage across the English Channel in a tiny canoe yawl by an early promoter of singlehanded sailing and distance canoeing. MacGregor was very popular in the late eighteen hundreds and inspired much emulation.

Manry, Robert. **Tinkerbelle.** Harper & Row, New York, 1966.

Although this book is about a feat that must be considered a stunt, crossing the Atlantic in a 13-1/2 foot boat, it is surprisingly good; well-written, informative, and thoughtful. Some useful details are given about gear and stores.

Marin-Marie. **Wind Aloft, Wind Alow.** Charles Scribner's Sons, New York 1947.

Two solo transatlantic passages, one under sail in the double-ender, *Winnibelle,* and the other under power in the motorboat, *Arielle,* by a French marine artist and masterful seaman. Marin-Marie was a pioneer in self-steering arrangements.

McMullen, R. T. **Down Channel.** Horace Cox, London, 1893.

A classic book describing cruises based in England between 1850 and 1891 by a no-nonsense sailor of the old school. His singlehanding of the 20-ton yawl, *Orion,* is described in some detail.

Mermod, Michel. **The Voyage of the Geneve.** John Murray, England, 1973.

An "almost" circumnavigation alone by a Swiss sociologist and long-distance canoeist in a 25-foot double-ended, converted lifeboat.

Merrien, Jean. **Lonely Voyagers.** G. P. Putnam's Sons, New York, 1954.

A compendium of accounts of many transoceanic and round-the-world small boat voyages, most of them singlehanded. Includes a list of 120 long voyages by one or two people in small boats from 1849 to 1953.

Middleton, E. E. **The Cruise of the Kate.** Longmans, Green & Co., London, 1870.

A singlehanded voyage around England in a 21-foot canoe yawl by an emulator of MacGregor.

Milnes-Walker, Nicolette. **When I Put Out To Sea.** Collins, England.

Transatlantic crossing under sail by the third woman to do it alone. The author is a psychologist who was primarily interested in her own reactions to the voyage. Her book is an interesting, non-technical account, and it offers some good tips on the daily routine and provisions.

Moitessier, Bernard. **The First Voyage of the Joshua.** William Morrow, New York, 1973. **The Long Way,** Doubleday & Co., Garden City, N.Y., 1975.

Two voyages by the innovative French singlehander. The first, made with his wife, describes in detail the high-speed scudding technique he developed for heavy weather in the South Pacific. **The Long Way** is the account of his non-stop solo sail one and a half times around the world during and after his participation in the "Golden Globe" race. Entertaining and instructive.

Nicolson, Ian. **Sea Saint.** Peter Davies, London, 1957.

A solo Atlantic crossing from Nova Scotia to England by a British naval architect and surveyor in the 32-foot sloop, *St. Elizabeth,* in 1954.

Page, Frank. **Sailing Solo to America.** Quadrangle Books, Inc., New York, 1972.

Story of the *Observer* singlehander's transatlantic races with the main emphasis on the 1972 race by a yachting correspondent of the London *Observer.*

Pakenham, Stephen. **Separate Horizons.** Nautical Publishing Co., Lymington, England, 1970.

A well-done survey and analysis of the 1968 singlehander's transatlantic race.

Parkinson, John Jr. (editor). **Nowhere Is Too Far.** Cruising Club of America, New York, 1960.

A history of cruises by members of the Cruising Club of America prior to 1960. Some singlehanding.

Pidgeon, Harry. **Around the World Single-Handed.** Appleton and Co., New York, 1933.

First circumnavigation of the second man to sail around the world alone, in the home-built, 34-foot Sea Bird yawl, the *Islander.* The book is not as exciting as some because of Pidgeon's fine seamanship.

Rebell, Fred. **Escape to the Sea.** Murray, London, 1951.

An amazing west-to-east solo crossing of the Pacific in the 18-foot open boat, *Elaine,* by a do-it-yourself greenhorn who made his own navigation instruments and used home-made charts traced from an ancient Atlas.

Ridler, Donald. **Erik the Red.** William Kimber, London, 1972.

The story of the author's cruise from England across the Atlantic to the West Indies and back in a boat he built himself, a 26-foot transom-stern dory with a plank keel and a Chinese lug rig.

Rogers, Stanley. **Tales of the Fore-an-Aft.** George G.Harrap & Co., London, 1935.

A collection of voyages including those of some singlehanders presented in a somewhat dramatic style.

Rose, Alec. **My Lively Lady.** David McKay Co., New York, 1968.

A fast circumnavigation in the southern westerlies by a "grand old man" of solo voyaging. Some interesting technical information in the appendixes.

Slack, Kenneth E. **In the Wake of the Spray.** Rutgers University Press, New Brunswick, N.J., 1966.

The lovingly-done, painstaking research and analysis of Slocum's *Spray* and her replicas. A fascinating book, but one with the possible danger that it could lead a novice into acquiring a less-than-ideal boat for offshore work.

Slocum, Joshua. **Sailing Alone Around the World.** Blue Ribbon Books, New York, 1899.

The classic on singlehanded cruising by the retired clippership captain who became the first solo circumnavigator. The book is inspirational, charming, and probably will be read forever, but it has a glaring deficiency for sailor readers: lack of technical details.

Slocum, Victor. **Captain Joshua Slocum.** Sheridan House, New York, 1950.

A very interesting biography of Joshua by his oldest son. Details of his various commands and many voyages, including the one in the *Liberdade*, a home-built, 35-foot dory-sampan.

Tabarly, Eric. **Lonely Victory.** Souvenir Press, London, 1964. **Ocean Racing.** W. W. Norton & Co., New York, 1970.

Refreshingly understated books by the famous French singlehander, who is one of the most dedicated ocean racers. **Lonely Victory** gives details of his OSTAR victory in 1964, while **Ocean Racing** is a summary of his ocean racing experiences, mostly solo, with interesting details of his various craft named *Pen Duick*.

Tangvald, Peter. **Sea Gypsy.** E. P. Dutton & Co., New York, 1966.

A voyage around the world, singlehanded at times, in the 32-foot cutter *Dorothea* by a well-known ocean sailor. Tangvald is highly opinionated but a competent and resourceful seaman.

Tazelaar, James, and Jean Bussiere. **To Challenge a Distant Sea.** Contemporary Books, Chicago, 1977. The story of Jean Gau, who made two singlehanded circumnavigations and 11 singlehanded transatlantic crossings in his Tahiti ketch, the *Atom*. Includes excerpts from his logs.

Teller, Walter M. **The Search for Captain Slocum.** Charles Scribner's Sons, New York, 1956.

A well-researched biography of Slocum; most interesting but a bit depressing, as it brings out an unattractive side of our hero.

Tetley, Nigel. **Trimaran Solo.** Nautical Publishing Co., Lymington, England, 1970.

The account of Tetley's record-breaking solo circumnavigation and subsequent loss of his trimaran, the *Victress*, during the "Golden Globe" race.

Tomalin, Nicholas, and Ron Hall. **The Strange Last Voyage of Donald Crowhurst.** Stein & Day, New York, 1970.

The fascinating story of the demise of Crowhurst, a competitor in the "Golden Globe" race, who faked a voyage around the world and died from an apparent suicidal leap into the sea. Source material for the book is taken from detailed logs, photographs, and tapes found on his derelict trimaran.

Voss, John C. **The Venturesome Voyages of Captain Voss.** C. E. Lauriat Co., New York, 1926.

A classic book about Voss' voyages, including his near-circumnavigation in the dugout canoe, *Tilikum*. He rarely sailed alone, but once made a long passage singlehanded when his crew was lost over the side. Much good advice on how to handle a small boat in heavy weather, but one should not be misled into thinking a modern yacht will behave as did the *Tilikum* when lying to a sea anchor.

Vihlen, Hugo S. **April Fool.** Dolphin Book Club, Camp Hill, Pa., 1974.

Account of crossing the Atlantic in a 6-foot boat; obviously a stunt but one that was carefully planned and a fascinating challenge.

Violet, Charles. **Solitary Journey.** Rupert Hart-Davis, London, 1954.

An interesting solo cruise from England to Malta and return in the 20-foot yawl *Nova Espero*, a boat that had previously crossed the Atlantic.

Willis, William. **The Gods Were Kind.** Dutton, New York, 1955. **An Angel on Each Shoulder.** Meredith, New York, 1967.

Books by an eccentric and possibly a masochistic seaman, who claimed he could communicate with his wife long distance by mental telepathy. His usual mode of travel was solo on a sailing raft, but he was eventually lost at sea in a cockleshell boat.

INDEX